W9-CDA-004

The Blood and Iron Chancellor

Among many other publications by the author are the following books in print.

THE MAKING OF MODERN MAN: From the Renaissance to the Present; THE WEIMAR REPUBLIC: A History of Germany from Ebert to Hitler; THE WORLD IN THE TWENTIETH CENTURY; THE DYNAMICS OF NATIONALISM; THE IMPERIALISM READER; THE IDEA OF RACIALISM; WAR: A Concise History, 1939–1945; HISTORIC DOCUMENTS OF WORLD WAR I; DOCUMENTS OF GERMAN HISTORY; BASIC HISTORY OF MODERN GERMANY; FIFTY MAJOR DOCUMENTS OF THE TWENTIETH CENTURY; FIFTY MAJOR DOCUMENTS OF THE NINETEENTH CENTURY; THE AGE OF REASON; MASTERPIECES OF WAR REPORTING; TREASURY OF GREAT REPORTING (with Richard B. Morris).

The Blood and Iro

A Documentary-Biography of **Ott**

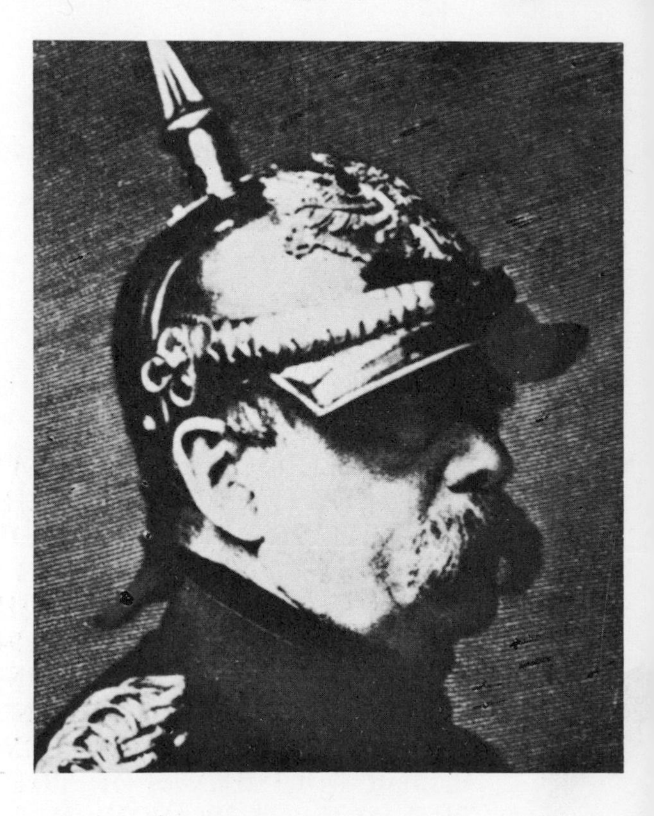

Chancellor

on Bismarck

by *LOUIS L. SNYDER*

VAN NOSTRAND COMPANY, INC. *Princeton, New Jersey* *Toronto* *London*

WINGATE COLLEGE LIBRARY
WINGATE, N. C.

VAN NOSTRAND REGIONAL OFFICES: *New York, Chicago, San Francisco*

D. VAN NOSTRAND COMPANY, LTD., *London*

D. VAN NOSTRAND COMPANY (Canada), LTD., *Toronto*

Copyright © 1967, by LOUIS L. SNYDER

Published simultaneously in Canada by
D. VAN NOSTRAND COMPANY (Canada), LTD.

No reproduction in any form of this book, in whole or in part (except for brief quotation in critical articles or reviews), may be made without written authorization from the publisher.

Library of Congress Catalog Card No. 67-18058

For permission to quote from copyright material, thanks are due:
to Macdonald & Co. Ltd. and Putnam's and Coward-McCann for passages from Werner Richter's *Bismarck*, translated by Brian Battershaw (London, 1964); copyright 1964 by Macdonald & Co., *page 116.*
to George Allen & Unwin Ltd. for passages from Erich Eyck's *Bismarck and the German Empire* (London, 1950), *pages 209, 234.*
to Harper & Row for passages from *The Kaiser vs. Bismarck,* translated by Bernard Miall; copyright 1920, 1948 by Harper & Brothers; reprinted by permission of Harper & Row, Publishers, *page 383.*

Grateful acknowledgment is made to the following publishers for material used on the pages cited below.

The American News Company, *242*; Appleton, Century, Crofts, Inc., *132;* Cassel and Company, Ltd., *49, 391;* The Century Company, *258;* Chapman and Hall, Ltd., *80, 155, 159, 199, 231, 333;* J. G. Cotta'sche Buchhandlung Nachfolger, *20;* Dean and Son, Ltd., *22, 32, 40, 45, 47, 53, 54, 86;* Deutsche Verlagsgesellschaft m.b.h., *41;* The German Publication Society, *225, 272, 368, 375;* H. Grevel and Company, *46, 157, 248, 291;* Harper and Brothers, *60, 64, 70, 77, 95, 103, 107, 108, 117, 200, 254, 256, 330, 346, 379;* William Heinemann, *100, 128, 195, 289, 307;* James Hogg and Son, *26, 44, 179;* John Camden Hotten, *143, 145, 152, 188;* The International Society, *80, 104, 110, 312;* James Maclehose and Sons, *58, 75, 124, 323;* Macmillan and Company, Ltd., *364;* John Macqueen, *144;* The McClure Company, *168;* John Murray, *91, 217, 342, 396;* C. Arthur Pearson, Ltd., *403;* G. P. Putnam's Sons, *12, 68, 86, 334;* George Routledge and Sons, *190, 316;* Charles Scribner's Sons, *51, 84, 114, 192, 207, 213, 251, 262, 266, 270, 281;* Frederick A. Stokes, *137;* Vandenhoeck and Ruprecht, Göttingen, *88.*

Title page illustration: Otto von Bismarck. (Court photographer, Loescher and Petsch, Berlin)

PRINTED IN THE UNITED STATES OF AMERICA

For Ida Mae

43296

Preface

Otto Eduard Leopold von Bismarck, man of blood and iron, was born on April 1, 1815, just a month after Napoleon's escape from Elba. The nineteenth century bore the imprint of his personality. He was the man who visualized and implemented the foundation of the Second German Reich, who elevated the Hohenzollern king of Prussia to the rank of German emperor at the Hall of Mirrors in Versailles in 1871. After a lifetime of service, he was forced to resign under ignominious conditions in 1890. He died in 1898, at the age of eighty-three, honored and glorified as the greatest German of his time.

Here is one of history's unique personalities, huge, portentous, like some vast monolith hewn from the living rock of the earth. There was little pedestrian or stilted or dry as dust about him. His was the most powerful brain of his day. He was a nineteenth-century version of Richelieu, with that same capacity for work, that same passion for enduring accomplishment, and that same tendency to melancholy that distinguished the great Frenchman. Bismarck possessed the literary ability of a Disraeli, the gusto of a Falstaff, the split personality of a Hamlet. For good reason the Germans venerate Bismarck in much the same way that Englishmen regard Winston Churchill, as an extension of the nation's personality.

There is a mountain of information about Bismarck. In 1895, on his eightieth birthday, there were already 650 books about his life. By 1908 the number had swollen to 3,500 titles. Since 1912 they have no longer been counted. Every phase of Bismarck's life has been investigated, and this documentary-biography has been fashioned from an almost bewildering wealth of material. Extracts and excerpts are presented from reminiscences, biographies, reports, conversations, interviews, letters, and newspapers. Original source materials, such as Bismarck's memoirs and letters, are interspersed with secondary material. In each case the selection has been made with a view to adding something of interest and of drama to the over-all pattern. Bismarck is presented with all his faults and blemishes as well as his positive qualities. The treatment is chronological. Each selection has been placed in its historical context.

The reader should judge for himself whether or not Bismarck's great gifts were used in the service of German and European progress. There are conflicting judgments. To many Germans he is the great statesman, the unifier of the nation, the noble Siegfried, Bismarck the Good. To others he is the shifty politician, Evil personified. He misused his enormous power, they say, to create a nation of sheeplike automatons. He had the chance, they say, to train his people in the ways of liberalism and democracy, but instead he left them a heritage of discipline, obedience, and worship of authority which led them to the verge of destruction.

In any collection of documents or readings the editor is always careful to reproduce the grammar and punctuation of the original. The problem is a bit different here. To maintain consistency of style and to prevent the annoying mixture of different styles of punctuation and spelling, all the excerpts presented here have been edited carefully. Thus, such words as emperor, king, prince, chancellor, minister for foreign affairs, etc. have been placed in lower case even where an official document used capital letters. However, no liberties have been taken with content.

In the compilation, writing, and editing of this material the work of Ida Mae Snyder has been much more than that of a collaborator or assistant. At every stage of its production her research and editorial pen have been vital and decisive. I can only thank her in these short lines for her contribution beyond the call of normal helpfulness.

New York City
October, 1966

LOUIS L. SNYDER

Table of Contents

Bismarck: A Self-Portrait in Aphorisms and Epigrams

British

—"The British are water rats, we are land rats—the two don't mix."

Colonies

—"The greed of our colonial jingoes is much greater than our need and our capacity for digestion."

—"My map of Africa lies in Europe."

Democracy

—"Faust complains of having two souls in his breast. I have a whole squabbling crowd. It goes on as in a republic."

Dogs

—"I have a great respect for my dog's knowledge of human character. He is quicker and more thoroughgoing than I."

Eastern Question

—"The direct interest of Germany in the Eastern Question is so slight as not to be worth the bones of a Pomeranian musketeer."

France and the French

—[Jules Favre complained bitterly in early 1871 about the burning of St. Cloud, whereupon Bismarck gave him the following hard answer:]

—"Have you ever visited our Germany? Have you never seen the ruins of our castles? Your armies, without pity, burned them down and destroyed them."

—"Peace between us and the French is difficult because of our common border."

—"In order to have the French leave us alone, we have to see to it that they don't get any treaty partners."

—"France is a nation of nobodies, a herd; Frenchmen have money and elegance, but no individuals, no individual feelings—only in the mass."

—"As soon as the French believe that they can win a war against us, they will begin it. That is my firm conviction." [1887]

—"The time is now past when the French can believe that a war against Germany is a kind of holiday jaunt to Berlin. In France they know how much power we have." [1893]

Germans

—"People are like other beings in nature: some are masculine and some are feminine. The Germans are masculine."

—"We Germans are kindhearted. The French don't have that virtue—they know only hate and envy."

—"It is much easier to rule Frenchmen than Germans."

—"Germans have a strong tendency toward dissatisfaction."

—"We Germans fear God but nothing else in the world."

God

—"Without wishing to be blasphemous, I should very much like to know whether our God may not perhaps have at his side some being who supplements him as a woman supplements a man."

Hate

—"Hate is just as great an incentive as love. My life is preserved and made pleasant by two things—my wife and Windhorst. One exists for love, the other for hate."

—"The best words in the Bible are: 'Oh Lord, Thou hast broken the teeth of the wicked.'"

—"If I have an enemy in my power I must destroy him."

—"Never repent! Never forgive! Long since, I have found that principle most useful in practical life."

—"When I am lying awake at night, I often turn over in my mind the unatoned wrongs that were done me thirty years back. I grow hot as I think of them, and, half asleep, I dream of retaliation."

—"'Pfui!' is an expression of disgust and contempt. Don't imagine these feelings are very far from me either."

History and Historians

—"One cannot possibly make history, although one can always learn from it how one should lead the political life of a great people in accordance with their development and their historical destiny."

—"Historians always see through their own spectacles. Why I prize Carlyle so highly is that he understands how to get inside another's soul."

Jews

—"I am no enemy of the Jews, and should they be foes of mine, I forgive them. I even like them—under certain circumstances, I would also accord to them every imaginable right, except that of holding authoritative office in a Christian realm."

—"I allow that I am full of prejudices. I have sucked them in with my mother's milk. If I think of a Jew face to face with me as representative of the king's sacred Majesty, and I have to obey him, I must confess that I should feel myself deeply broken and depressed."

—"Jews also have their virtues: respect for parents, faithfulness in marriage, and a sense of charity."

—"Jews don't really have a proper home. There is something generally European, cosmopolitan about them. They are nomads. Their Fatherland is Zion, Jerusalem."

—"Rather than have Jewish men marrying into Junker families, it might be best if one brought together *a conjunction of* a Christian stallion of German breed with a Jewish mare. There is no such thing as an evil race."

Junkers

—"I am a Junker and mean to profit from it."

—"I am no democrat and cannot be one, I was born and raised an aristocrat."

Kulturkampf

—"You need not be so anxious. We are not going to Canossa, either bodily or spiritually."

Marriage

—"The man who is not married offers one target the less for the shafts of fortune."

Monroe Doctrine

—"The Monroe Doctrine is an incomparable piece of impudence [*unvergleichliche unverschämtheit*]!"

Patriotism

—"Let us put Germany in the saddle. She will know how to ride."

Personal Philosophy

—"For my part I want to play music such as I regard as good—or else not play at all."

—"I never ask myself if a thing is popular, only if it is reasonable and justifiable."

—"I am thankful for even the sharpest criticism, so long as it is factual."

—"I've lived in Berlin and its environs for some forty years and I just don't like it. The city has grown but my terrain gets smaller. Eventually I shall probably be limited only to riding in the Tiergarten. I'm like the Indian whose hunting ground has been appropriated by the white man."

—"No glove has ever been thrown at me without a challenge."

—"There is no life without struggle. Watch plants, insects, birds. If we want to progress, we must fight."

—"The life of a hunter is a natural one for man. A day in the forest is sufficient to renew my spirits."

—"To be happy in my home is worth more to me than all the favors of potentates."

—"I just don't like the stink of civilization in the big cities."

—"Mountains separate peoples and nations, but rivers give them communication."

—"It would be wonderful if—just once—I could go into a restaurant or a theater without being recognized."

—"I've given up listening to music: the melodies stay in my head, they bring tears to my eyes, they exhaust me."

—"It's a plain libel to accuse me of being ambitious: I have only been anxious to serve."

—"I have never been able to put up with superiors."

—"Everything melts away. One day everything falls apart!"

—"Nothing exists upon this earth,
But sleight of hand and trickster's arts;
And wisdom counts it little worth
To reckon man's outward parts."

—"That which is imposing here on earth is always akin to the fallen angel, who is beautiful but lacks peace, is great in his plans and efforts but never succeeds, is proud and melancholy."

—"The stupid and the wise, when they become skeletons, look very much alike."

—"People and individuals, wisdom and folly, war and peace—they come and go like waves of the sea while the sea remains."

—"Blood is a very peculiar fluid, and our nerves are even more peculiar vital threads, at the end of which we poor creatures kick about."

—"I attach little value to human life because I believe in another world."

—"I love trees. They are ancestors. If I did not love trees as much as I do, I do not know how I could go on living."

—"I feel best in greased boots far in the forest."

—"The duty to speak seems pointed at me like a pistol."

—"My unhappy disposition is such that every situation in which I could possibly find myself seems a desirable one, only to become boring and wearisome once I have attained it."

—"I am all nerves, so much so that self-control has always been the greatest task of my life."

—"Caution is based on fear, courage on recklessness."

—"The longer one lives, the more enemies one makes."

—"I have met some thirty thousand people in my life, and while I naturally do not remember all their names, I have been able to identify them by their personality."

—"One of the advantages of getting old is that one gets used to hate, insults, and slander, but the sensitiveness for love and kindness becomes greater."

—"Sunshine and wine are the two most valuable things for an old man."

—"How many have I made unhappy! But for me, three great wars would not have been fought; eighty thousand men would not have perished; parents, brothers, sisters, and widows would not be bereaved and plunged into mourning. . . . I have little or no joy from my achievements—nothing but vexation, care, and trouble."

Poles

—"Hit the Poles in such a way that they will despair of their lives. The wolf, too, is not responsible for being what God has made it, but we kill it, nevertheless, if we can."

Politics

—"Politics is not a science, as the professors are apt to suppose. It is an art."

—"I have always found the word 'Europe' on the lips of those statesmen who want something from a foreign power."

—"Beware of sentimental alliances where the consciousness of good deeds is the only compensation for noble sacrifice."

—"I don't like women who mix themselves in politics."

—"It is never possible to be mathematical in the field of politics."

—"In foreign policy there are moments which never come again."

—"Treaties are expressions of common interests and goals."

—"Liberated people are not thankful, only more demanding."

—"Concessions and gifts are foods which arouse the appetite without satisfying it."

—"I have always been distrustful of politicians in long clothes, whether women or priests."

Power

—"It is the destiny of the weak to be devoured by the strong."

—"It is not by speeches and majority resolutions that the great questions of the day are settled. That was the great mistake of 1848 and 1849. It is by iron and blood [*'Eisen und Blut'*]."

Press

—"Whatever is in the newspaper is soon finished."

Prophecy

"Years ago I worked it out by cabalistic reckoning that I would die in 1886 at the age of seventy-one. Here it is 1887 and that has not happened. I shall, therefore, die in my eighty-third or eighty-fourth year." [Bismarck died in 1898 during his eighty-fourth year.]

—"Twenty years after the death of Frederick the Great the battle of Jena had been fought and lost. Twenty years after my death the great crash will come if things go on as they are going." (1897) [Bismarck died in July 1898; the Second Reich crashed in ruins in November 1918.]

—"There will be only one more happy day in my life, and that will be the day on which I shall not awaken again from my sleep." [1895]

Religion

—"I think I am entitled to count myself among the adherents of the Christian religion. Though in many doctrines I am far removed from their standpoint, yet a sort of treaty has been silently established between us."

Royalty

—"I am first and foremost a royalist."

—"It is easy to cling to the monarchical principle in fair weather; it is harder in foul."

—"Titles and orders have no charm for me. I firmly believe in a life after death. That is why I am a royalist."

—"I have seen three kings naked and often enough the behavior of these exalted gentlemen was by no means kingly."

—"The German's love of the Fatherland has need of a prince on whom he can concentrate his attachment."

—"For me, the words, 'by the grace of God,' which Christian rulers add to their name, are no empty phrase; I see in them a confession that the princes desire to wield the scepter which God has given them according to the will of God on earth."

—"My old master, Emperor William I, had no understanding of German national sentiment. Only gradually and slowly could he be shown the way to that position he achieved at the time of his death."

—"Kings have a peculiar sense of what is to their advantage."

—"Why, except under divine command, should I subjugate myself to these Hohenzollerns? They come of a Swabian family which is no better than my own."

War

—"Conquest in a just war is both a just and moral title of possession."

—"In our century only a war will put right the clock of Germany's development."

—"The dice have been thrown: we look forward confidently to the future; but we must never forget that God Almighty is capricious!" [1864]

—"If one has ever seen the eyes of a dying warrior on the battlefield he will think twice before he begins a war." [1867]

—"Take no more prisoners of war, because corpses need no shelter or food." [1871]

—"Every war, including a victorious war, is always a misfortune for the country that wages it."

—"A war is often less damaging to the general welfare than an insecure peace."

—"We Germans shall never wage aggressive war, ambitious war, a war of conquest. We shall never spill the blood of our children in order to conquer."

The Bettman Archive

PART I

The First Twenty Years: Education of a Pomeranian Junker, 1815-1835

1 Quick-Tempered Ferdinand von Bismarck Announces the Birth of a Son, April 1, 1815

". . . I excuse them from offering congratulations."

Otto Eduard Leopold von Bismarck was born on April 1, 1815 at the manor house of Schönhausen in the Mark of Brandenburg. One month earlier Napoleon Bonaparte had escaped from Elba and returned to the mainland to raise yet another army. As the infant Bismarck lay in his cradle, the peasants of Schönhausen, who only a few months earlier had come back from battle against France, were again called to arms.

The day after Otto's birth, Ferdinand von Bismarck sent the following strange notice to the Vossische Zeitung.[1]

> I have the honor to announce to my friends, that yesterday my wife was safely delivered of a son, and I excuse them from offering congratulations.
>
> FERDINAND VON BISMARCK
>
> SCHÖNHAUSEN
> *2nd April,* 1815

2 The Junker Lineage: Knights and Ladies, Barons and Villeins, Castles and Mansions, War and Peace

". . . far removed from the bustle and turmoil of civilization."

Throughout his life, from his early days as a chubby-faced country lad with large round head and snub nose to the years when he was a giant diplomat playing chess with the map of Europe, Otto von Bismarck would never forget his Junker heritage. The background made the man. The story of his lineage and his earliest years was told by James Wycliffe Headlam.[2]

1. *Vossische Zeitung,* April 2, 1815.
2. James Wycliffe Headlam, *Bismarck and the Foundations of the German Empire* (New York and London, 1899), pp. 1–13.

The name and family of Bismarck were among the oldest in the land. Many of the great Prussian statesmen have come from other countries: Stein was from Nassau, and Hardenberg was a subject of the Elector of Hanover; even Blücher and Schwerin were Mecklenburgers, and the Moltkes belong to Holstein. The Bismarcks are pure Brandenburgers; they belong to the old Mark, the district ruled over by the first margraves who were sent by the emperor to keep order on the northern frontier; they were there two hundred years before the first Hohenzollern came to the north.

The first of the name of whom we hear was Herbort von Bismarck, who, in 1270, was Master of the Guild of the Clothiers in the city of Stendal. The town had been founded about one hundred years before by Albert the Bear, and men had come in from the country around to enjoy the privileges and security of city life. Doubtless Herbort or his father had come from Bismarck, a village about twenty miles to the west, which takes its name either from the little stream, the Biese, which runs near it, or from the bishop in whose domain it lay. He was probably the first to bear the name, which would have no meaning so long as he remained in his native place, for the *von* was still a mark of origin and had not yet become the sign of nobility. Other emigrants from Bismarck seem also to have assumed it; in the neighboring town of Prenzlau the name occurs, and it is still found among the peasants of the Mark; as the Wends were driven back and the German invasion spread, more adventurous colonists migrated beyond the Oder and founded a new Bismarck in Pomerania.

Of the lineage of Herbort we know nothing; his ancestors must have been among the colonists who had been planted by the emperors on the northern frontier to occupy the land conquered from the heathen. He seems himself to have been a man of substance and position; he already used the arms, the double trefoil, which are still borne by all the branches of his family. His descendants are often mentioned in the records of the Guild; his son or grandson, Rudolph or Rule, represented the town in a conflict with the neighboring dukes of Brunswick. It was his son Nicolas, or Claus as he is generally called, who founded the fortunes of the family; he attached himself closely to the cause of the margrave, whom he supported in his troubles with the duke of Brunswick, and whose interests he represented in the Town Council. He was amply rewarded for his fidelity. After a quarrel between the city and the prince, Bismarck left his native home and permanently entered the service of the margrave. Though probably hitherto only a simple citizen, he was enfiefed with the castle of Burgstall, an important

WINGATE COLLEGE LIBRARY
WINGATE, N. C.

post, for it was situated on the borders of the Mark and the bishopric of Magdeburg; he was thereby admitted into the privileged class of the *Schlossgesessenen,* under the margrave, the highest order in the feudal hierarchy. From that day the Bismarcks have held their own among the nobility of Brandenburg. Claus eventually became Hofmeister of Brandenburg, the chief officer at the court; he had his quarrels with the church, or rather with the spiritual lords, the bishops of Havelburg and Magdeburg, and was once excommunicated, as his father had been before him, and as two of his sons were after him.

Claus died about the year 1385. For two hundred years the Bismarcks continued to live at Burgstall, to which they added many other estates. When Conrad of Hohenzollern was appointed margrave and elector, he found sturdy supporters in the lords of Burgstall; he and his successors often came there to hunt the deer and wild boars, perhaps also the wolves and bears, with which the forests around the castle abounded; for the Hohenzollerns were keen sportsmen then as now, as their vassals found to their cost. In 1555, Hans George, son of the reigning elector, Albert Achilles, bought the neighboring estate of Letzlingen from the Alvenslebens; there he built a house which is still the chief hunting-lodge of the kings of Prussia. Soon he cast envious eyes on the great woods and preserves which belong to Burgstall, and intimated that he wished to possess them. The Bismarcks resisted long. First they were compelled to surrender their hunting rights; this was not sufficient; the appetite of the prince grew; in his own words he wished "to be rid of the Bismarcks from the moor and the Tanger altogether." He offered in exchange some of the monasteries which had lately been suppressed; the Bismarcks (the family was represented by two pairs of brothers, who all lived together in the great castle) long refused; they represented that their ancestors had been faithful vassals; they had served the electors with blood and treasure; they wished "to remain in the pleasant place to which they had been assigned by God Almighty." It was all of no use; the prince insisted, and his wrath was dangerous. The Bismarcks gave in; they surrendered Burgstall and received in exchange Schönhausen and Crevisse, a confiscated nunnery, on condition that as long as the ejected nuns lived the new lords should support them; for which purpose the Bismarcks had annually to supply a certain quantity of food and eighteen barrels of beer.

Of the four co-proprietors, all died without issue, except Friedrich, called the Permutator, in whose hands the whole of the family property was again collected; he went to live at Schönhausen, which since then has been the home of the family. No remains of the old castle exist, but the church, built in the thirteenth century, is one of the oldest and most beautiful in the land between the Havel and the Elbe. House and church stand side by side on a small rising overlooking the Elbe. Here they took up their abode; the family to some extent had come down in the world. The change had been a disadvantageous one; they had lost in wealth and importance. For two hundred years they played no very prominent part; they married with the neighboring country gentry and fought in all the wars. Rudolph, Friedrich's son, fought in France in behalf of the Huguenots, and then under the emperor against the Turks. His grandson, August, enlisted under Bernhard of Saxe-Weimar; afterwards he fought in the religious wars in France and Germany, always on the Protestant side; lastly, he took service under the elector of Brandenburg.

It was in his lifetime that a great change began to take place which was to alter the whole life of his descendants. In 1640, Frederick William, known as the Great Elector, succeeded his father. He it was who laid the foundations for that system of government by which a small German principality has grown to be the most powerful military monarchy in modern Europe. He held his own against the emporer; he fought with the Poles and compelled their king to grant him East Prussia; he drove the Swedes out of the land. More than this, he enforced order in his own dominions; he laid the foundation for the prosperity of Berlin; he organized the administration and got together a small but efficient military force. The growing power of the elector was gained to a great extent at the expense of the nobles; he took from them many of the privileges they had before enjoyed. The work he began was continued by his son, who took the title of king; and by his grandson, who invented the Prussian system of administration, and created the army with which Frederick the Great fought his battles.

The result of the growth of the strong, organized monarchy was indeed completely to alter the position of the nobles. The German barons in the south had succeeded in throwing off the control of their territorial lords; they owned no authority but the vague control of the distant emperor, and ruled their little estates with an almost royal independence; they had their own laws, their own coinage, their own army. In the north, the nobles of Mecklenburg, Holstein, and Hanover formed a dominant class, and the whole government of the state was in their hands; but those barons whose homes fell within the dominion of the kings of Prussia found themselves face to face with a will and a power stronger than their own; they lost in independence, but they gained far more than they lost. They were the basis on which the state was built up; they no longer wasted their military prowess in purposeless feuds or in mercenary service; in the Prussian army and administration they found full scope for their ambition, and when the victories of Frederick the Great had raised Prussia to the rank of a European power, the nobles of Brandenburg were the most loyal of his subjects. They formed an exclusive caste; they seldom left their homes; they were little known in the south of Germany or in foreign countries; they seldom married outside their own ranks. Their chief amusement was the chase, and their chief occupation was war. And no king has ever had under his orders so fine a race of soldiers; they commanded the armies of Frederick and won his battles. Dearly did they pay for the greatness of Prussia; of one family alone, the Kleists, sixty-four fell on the field of battle during the Seven Years' War.

They might well consider that the state which they had helped to make, and which they had saved by their blood, belonged to them. But if they had become Prussians, they did not cease to be Brandenburgers; their loyalty to their king never swerved, for they knew that he belonged to them as he did to no other of his subjects. He might go to distant Königsberg to assume the crown, but his home was amongst them; other provinces might be gained or lost with the chances of war, but while a single Hohenzollern lived he could not desert his subjects of the Mark. They had the intense local patriotism so characteristic of the German nation, which is the surest foundation for political greatness; but while in other parts the Particularists, as the Germans called them, aimed only at independence, the Brandenburger who had become a Prussian desired domination.

Among them the Bismarcks lived. The family again divided into two branches: one, which became extinct about 1780, dwelling at Crevisse, gave several high officials to the Prussian civil service; the other branch, which continued at Schönhausen, generally chose a military career. August's son, who had the same name as his father, rebuilt the house, which had been entirely destroyed by the Swedes during the Thirty Years' War; he held the position of *Landrat,* that is, he was the head of the administration of the district in which he lived. He married a Fräulein von Katte, of a well-known family whose estates adjoined those of the Bismarcks. Frau von Bismarck was the aunt of the unfortunate young man who was put to death for helping Frederick the Great in his attempt to escape. His tomb is still to be seen at Wust, which lies across the river a few miles from Schönhausen; and at the new house, which arose at Schönhausen and still stands, the arms of the Kattes are joined to the Bismarck trefoil. The successor to the estates, August

Friedrich, was a thorough soldier; he married a Fräulein von Diebwitz and acquired fresh estates in Pomerania, where he generally lived.

He rose to the rank of colonel, and fell fighting against the Austrians at Chotusitz in 1742. *"Ein ganzer Kerl"* (a fine fellow), said the king, as he stood by the dying officer. His son, Carl Alexander, succeeded to Schönhausen; the next generation kept up the military traditions of the family; of four brothers, all but one became professional officers and fought against France in the wars of liberation. One fell at Möckern in 1813; another rose to the rank of lieutenant-general; the third also fought in the war; his son, the later Count Bismarck-Bohlen, was wounded at Grossbehren, and the father at once came to take his place during his convalescence, in order that the Prussian army might not have fewer Bismarcks. When the young Otto was born two years later, he would often hear of the adventures of his three uncles and his cousin in the great war. The latter, Bismarck-Bohlen, rose to very high honors and was to die when over eighty years of age, after he had witnessed the next great war with France. It is a curious instance of the divisions of Germany in those days that there were Bismarcks fighting on the French side throughout the war. One branch of the family had settled in South Germany; the head of it, Friedrich Wilhelm, had taken service in the Württemberg army; he had become a celebrated leader of cavalry and was passionately devoted to Napoleon. He served with distinction in the Russian campaign and was eventually taken prisoner by the Germans in the battle of Leipzig.

The youngest of the four brothers, Karl Wilhelm Friedrich v. Bismarck, had retired from the army at an early age: he was a quiet, kindly man of domestic tastes; on the division of the estates, Schönhausen fell to his lot, and he settled down there to a quiet country life. He took a step which must have caused much discussion among all his friends and relations, for he chose as wife not one of his own rank, not a Kleist, or a Katte, or a Bredow, or an Arnim, or an Alvensleben, or any other of the neighboring nobility; he married a simple Fräulein Mencken. She was, however, of no undistinguished origin. Her father, the son of a professor at the University of Leipzig, had entered the Prussian civil service; there he had risen to the highest rank and had been cabinet secretary to both Frederick William II and Frederick III. He was a man of high character and of considerable ability; as was not uncommon among the officials of those days, he was strongly affected by the liberal and even revolutionary doctrines of France.

Fräulein Mencken, who was married at the age of sixteen, was a clever and ambitious woman. From her, her son inherited his intellect; from his father he derived what the Germans call *Gemüt,* geniality, kindliness, humor. By his two parents he was thus connected with the double foundation on which Prussia had been built: on his father's side he had sprung from the fighting nobles; on his mother's, from the scholars and officials. In later life we shall find that while his prejudices and affections are all enlisted on the side of the noble, the keen and critical intellect he had inherited from his mother enabled him to overcome the prejudices of his order.

The early life of the young pair was not altogether fortunate. Several children died at a very early age; the defeat of Prussia brought foreign occupation; Schönhausen was seized by French troopers; the marks of their swords are still to be seen in a beam over one of the doors, and Rittmeister v. Bismarck had to take his wife away into the woods in order to escape their violence.

Of all the children of the marriage only three lived: Bernhard, who was born in 1810, Otto, and one sister, Malwine, born in 1827.

Otto did not live at Schönhausen long; when he was only a year old, his father moved to Pomerania and settled on the estates Kniephof and Kulz, which had come into the family on his grandfather's marriage. Pomerania was at that time a favorite residence among the Prussian nobility; the country was better wooded than the Mark, and game more plentiful; the rich meadows, the wide heaths and forests were more attractive than the heavy corn-lands and the sandy wastes of the older province. Here, in the deep seclusion of country life, the boy passed his first years; it was far removed from the bustle and turmoil of civilization. Naugard, the nearest town, was five miles distant; communication was bad, for it was not till after 1815 that the Prussian government began to construct highroads. In this distant province, life went on as in the olden days, little altered by the changes which had transformed the state. The greater portion of the land belonged to large proprietors; the noble as in old days was still all-powerful on his own estate; in his hands was the administration of the law, and it was at his manorial court that men had to seek for justice, a court where justice was dealt not in the name of the king but of the lord of the manor. He lived among his people and generally he farmed his own lands. There was little of the luxury of an English country-house or the refinement of the French noblesse; he would be up at daybreak to superintend the work in the fields, his wife and daughters that of the household, talking to the peasants the pleasant *Platt Deutsch* of the countryside. Then there would be long rides or drives to the neighbors' houses; shooting, for there was plenty of deer and hares; and occasionally in the winter a visit to Berlin; farther away, few of them went. Most of the country gentlemen had been to Paris, but only as conquerors at the end of the great war.

They were little disturbed by modern political theories, but were contented, as in old days, to be governed by the king. It was a religious society; among the peasants and the nobles, if not among the clergy, there still lingered something of the simple but profound faith of German Protestantism; they were scarcely touched by the rationalism of the eighteenth or by the liberalism of the nineteenth century; there was little pomp and ceremony of worship in the village church, but the natural periods of human life—birth, marriage, death—called for the blessing of the church, and once or twice a year came the solemn confession and the sacrament. Religious belief and political faith were closely joined, for the church was but a department of the state; the king was chief bishop, as he was general of the army, and the sanctity of the church was transferred to the crown; to the nobles and peasants, criticism of, or opposition to, the king had in it something of sacrilege; the words "by the Grace of God" added to the royal title were more than an empty phrase. Society was still organized on the old patriarchal basis: at the bottom was the peasant; above him was the *gnädiger Herr;* above him, *Unser allergnädigste Herr,* the king, who lived in Berlin; and above him, the *Herr Gott* in Heaven.

To the inhabitants of South Germany, and the men of the towns, these nobles of Father Pomerania, the *Junker* as they were called, with their feudal life, their medieval beliefs, their simple monarchism, were the incarnation of political folly; to them liberalism seemed another form of atheism, but in this solitude and fresh air of the great plain was reared a race of men who would always be ready, as their fathers had been, to draw their sword and go out to conquer new provinces for their king to govern.

3 In Which an Ambitious Mother Subjects Her Sensitive Son to a Coarse-grained Discipline "to Break His Aristocratic Pride": The Spartan Education at Plamann's Boarding School, 1822–1827

"He is too vigorous and easily distracted."

Instead of hiring a tutor, Bismarck's mother sent him at the age of seven to the rigorous Plamann's boarding school in Berlin, where he remained until the age of twelve. Here he was subjected to a discipline derived from the hard ideology of Turnvater Friedrich Ludwig Jahn, an educator famous for his system of fostering a spirit of national self-consciousness among Prussian youth. The young lad, overcome with homesickness, hated the place: he never stopped complaining about the harshness of his early education, about the stale bread, the inadequate clothing, the hard discipline. He said later: "I never had enough to eat. The meat was always tough. We had to get up at half-past five in the morning, and were writing away from six to seven. We were treated worse than recruits are treated by non-commissioned officers."

Bismarck told about these years in the opening sentences of his memoirs:

> *I brought away with me "German-National" impressions from Plamann's preparatory school, conducted on Jahn's drill system. These impressions remained in the stage of theoretical reflections, and were not strong enough to extirpate my innate Prussian monarchical sentiments. My historical sympathies remained on the side of authority. To my childish ideas of justice, Harmodius and Aristogiton, as well as Brutus, were criminals, and Tell a rebel and murderer.*

Little is known about Otto's stay at Plamann's boarding school. Here is Erich Marcks' version.[3]

The director of the Plamann school was a theologian and pedagogue who opened the institute in 1805. The school had a high rating during the War of Liberation, but in the 1820's it had begun to degenerate. Plamann's ideals were just not realized, and he himself became older, sickly, and ill-tempered. The curriculum was dedicated to the all-round development of the personality, understanding, and positive knowledge. It took complete charge of the pupil's education to his high-school years.

Thirty boarding pupils attended the school at Wilhelmstrasse 1939, which Plamann had bought in 1820. The life of every pupil was regulated every hour from half-past five in the morning until nine-thirty at night. The day began with prayers. Then lessons, gymnastics, meals, study hours. In the afternoons the boys worked in the open air. Evenings belonged to the gardens, in which each pupil had a piece of land of his own to plant. Then general play, spiritual conversation, fencing. The meals were harsh: dry bread played an important role. On Sundays the boys could go out if

3. Translated and adapted by the editor from Erich Marcks' uncompleted biography, *Bismarcks Jugend, 1815–1848* (Stuttgart, 1909), I, 53–59.

they received an invitation, while others would hike in the countryside with Plamann. On holidays those who wanted to could take a one- or two-week trip with Plamann or the teachers.

Young Otto took a dim view of all this. He complained of the Spartan life, the lack of sufficient food, the exaggerated attention to gymnastics, and the teachers' contempt for the nobility. He suffered bitterly from homesickness. As an old man he told how, when looking out of the window at Plamann's, he sometimes saw a team of oxen plowing, the tears would come to his eyes because he was so homesick for Kniephof. He would literally count the hours to his holiday. Moreover, when he later visited the gardens, he recalled the breathless running of the boys through the rooms "which have grown so small today," the gardens with cress and Indian corn, and the blue mist on the hills in the distance.

One of Bismarck's school comrades, Ernst Krigar, a book dealer, spoke to the chancellor in 1867 about their common wonderful childhood, of dreams of war and victory, of battles in which Bismarck was "the most distinguished hero of our Trojan wars." All this Krigar put into a little book which he published in 1873: how the young Bismarck aroused attention by his opposition to mistreatment of new youngsters by the older boys, how at swimming he sprang boldly into the water and nobody dared to duck him, how he made regular battles out of games and was always the leader, how he commanded the storming of the garden terrace in the winter snow, how he was the best swimmer of all—in short, a hero and victor from the beginning. How much of this description was due to afterthought and fantasy is difficult to say. One reads about it with some doubt.

Bismarck, in all probability, did take part in such Trojan wars. Later he said that he was a youngster like all youngsters: he did not want to make his school years any more heroic than they were.

We have little documentary evidence of these early days. It begins in Easter 1822 with his first school report, which notes enthusiasm for learning, childlike joy in knowledge, and excellent memory. "Everyone likes him because of his easygoing disposition and his youthful exuberance." The teachers did not notice too much melancholy or rebelliousness.

A first letter to his mother (April 27, 1822):

> Dear Mother! I came here quite safely. The report has been filled out, and I hope it will please you. We have just gotten some new jumping boards, which will enable us to do good tricks by foot or by horse. Greetings to all and stay as well as when we left you. I am, your loving son,
>
> OTTO

Then in later exchanges of letters came news of children's diseases, good report cards, happy promotions, warning of good manners at table. Soon there are French and geometry to be studied, and Otto must write if they cause him trouble. In between there are trips—unfortunately not home, but with Plamann and often with Uncle Fritz, the lieutenant-general, to his small property near Potsdam.

Of Otto's remaining letters during these years at Plamann's we have only one (Easter 1825), a very superficial one in which he speaks about his progress, about the hard learning and similar things, as well as a request for a plant pot. We do have his school report for the winter of 1825–1826 with that thoroughness that distinguished all such Plamann records: the performance (with the exception of history) was good, but Otto hurries too much in his work and thinking and even in gymnastics; he is somewhat careless in handwork because he is too vigorous and easily distracted. "He should watch himself to see that his enthusiasm does not run away with him, and that he give proper place to seriousness in his work and exhilaration in social life."

It was a normal schooling, but it showed the young man what he would have to withstand as a person of his class. He defended himself instinctively against opponents. He was not able to divest himself of all that he learned at Plamann's: the hatred for the French, which ruled there, encompassed him, too. He later told about how as a pupil he had greeted with loud cries of sarcasm a stage show that tried to glorify Napoleon. At Plamann's he acquired a sense of independence. He learned how to handle himself among other people.

4 The High School Teen-Ager, Censurable for His Pretentious Arrogance, a Disaster with His Teachers: Otto's Gymnasium Years [4]

"That is a bright boy, I'll have a special eye to him."

From the age of thirteen to seventeen young Otto attended high school in Berlin, where his family lived. It was a period of trial for the teen-ager. "I was not properly brought up. My mother was fond of society and troubled herself very little about us. Usually

4. *Bismarck and All About Him, by a Fellow Student,* ed. by Henry Hayward (London, 1898), pp. 205–211.

two generations take it in turns, a whipped and an unwhipped; at any rate, it was so in my family. I belonged to the whipped generation." The young man had no one to whom he could bring his love and problems. Little wonder that he became cynical at an early age.

"A Bright Boy"

After a stay of five years in the Plamann Institute, Bismarck was transferred, at the beginning of his thirteenth year to the *Friedrich Wilhelm Gymnasium* in Berlin. Here he won the esteem of a master who exercised a powerful influence over him in his later school days. It was Professor Bonnell, afterwards director of the Gray Cloisters. On the very first day the worthy professor was struck with the manner and bearing of the youth, and was greatly prepossessed in his favor. To use Professor Bonnell's own words:—*"The new scholars sat in the schoolroom on benches placed behind each other, so that during the inauguration proceedings they should be directly under the eyes of the tutors. I was struck with the earnest attention depicted on the features of Otto von Bismarck—his bright eyes and fresh and cheerful countenance; and I said to myself: 'That is a bright boy, I'll have a special eye to him.'"* He did not belie his master's estimate of him, for he proved one of the smartest scholars in the establishment.

Trine Neumann and her Omelettes

While attending the *Gymnasium* Otto lodged with his elder brother Bernhard at the Berlin family mansion, and in the summer when the parents went into the country the young man's bodily necessities were administered to by an old housekeeper named Trine Neumann, who was thus described later on by the roguish Otto in the following terms:—"Trine Neumann came from my father's estate of Schönhausen in the Altmark. She was very fond of us youngsters, and anticipated our smallest wants. Almost every evening she prepared us our favorite dish: omelettes. If we went out before the meal was ready, Trine would be sure to say to us: 'Don't bide out too long now, till the omelettes are overdone.' And just as regularly, on our return, she would say: 'Late again! Ah, when will young men learn reason? The omelettes are all spoilt again!' But her anger would soon dissipate when she saw with what gusto we devoured her overdone omelettes."

Confirmation

The years slipped away, and the confirmation day arrived. This was in the year 1830. What a deep impression the ceremony made upon his devout mind is clear from the fact that all through the changes and chances of his life the impression was never effaced from his memory. He was prepared for the occasion by the celebrated Berlin preacher, Schleiermacher; and in after years, long after he had reached manhood, in writing to his sister, Frau von Arnim Kröchlendorff, he recalled Schleiermacher's parting words to him:—"Whatever you do, do it for God, and not for men." "I still remember, as plainly as possible," he wrote, "the place where I sat among the other young people in the church, and how my heart beat when I was called up to take my place before the altar."

In the Gray Cloisters

When Bernhard went into the army, Trine Neumann's task was done, and Otto was put into Professor Prévost's boarding establishment; and at the same time he was removed from the *Gymnasium* to another educational establishment. This was called the Gray Cloisters, and here he came again under the influence of his old admirer, Professor Bonnell, who in the meantime had been placed at the head of this establishment. Very soon after this, too, he went into the Gray Cloisters as a boarder. Respecting the stay of Otto with the Bonnell family, the good Professor wrote in his diary:—"At Easter, 1830, Otto von Bismarck came to my house as a boarder, where he gave the least trouble and made himself as pleasant and agreeable and familiar as possible. He was thoroughly amiable in every relation in life. He very seldom went out of an evening; and when, as it sometimes happened, I was not at home, he would spend the time chatting pleasantly with my wife, and showed a strong inclination for domestic life."

His Friendship for his Old Tutor

The following extract from the memoirs which Professor Bonnell left behind him will serve to show the degree of respect and friendship which Bismarck entertained for his faithful old tutor, even after he had become a mature and celebrated man:—"The 17th April, 1871, was the day on which the city of Berlin entertained for the first time the assembled members of the German Reichstag in the great banqueting-hall of the new *Rathaus*. I was among the invited guests. In the busy throng of members and notabilities of all kinds Bismarck was of course the center of attraction. Suddenly the great man stood before me and offered both his hands in the old friendly manner. The heat of the place had made my face red, and he expressed his pleasure at seeing me so well. 'I can return your Highness the compliment,' I said, 'although you have taken so great a part of late years in the world's history.' 'Well,' he replied, 'I certainly have woven a few of its threads.' And then there was a little friendly chat, inquiries after my wife, etc., etc." Next day the papers were full of the impression made on the eye-witnesses of this scene in the banqueting-hall, and one of the reports concluded thus:—"Who is this little old man with whom Bismarck chatted so long and in terms of such familiarity? It is Dr. Bonnell, formerly the prince's tutor. It does one good to see with what respect the noble pupil now treats his old schoolmaster." . . .

Pistol Practice

As he neared his eighteenth year, young Bismarck began to feel the power that was in him, and which impelled him to all manner of rash though boyish actions. One day he determined to pay his elder brother a visit. The latter was now a *Landwehr* officer in Berlin, and lived in the family mansion in that city. His brother was out when he arrived there, so he decided to await his return. On the wall near the bookcase in the room where he was waiting hung his brother's long cavalry pistols, and as soon as Otto clapped his eyes upon them he at once saw how nicely he could while away the time with such playthings. He reached them down, cocked and uncocked them, and presently loaded them, and after hanging a target in front of the open bookcase he began firing away at it, to the great dismay of the neighbors and the people in the house, until his brother returned and put a stop to the mad practice.

A Shot at Hercules

It was a much more harmless freak which the young marksman played one day at Schönhausen. On the margin of a sedgy pool in the park stands a stone figure, representing Hercules with his club, and one hand resting on the small of his back. As young Otto was coming through the park one day with his gun on his shoulder, and cast his eyes upon the Greek demi-god disrespectfully turning his back towards him, his fingers suddenly itched to fire a shot at Hercules' hind-quarters, and the gun went to his shoulder, and the bullet went flying before he could count six. A moment later Hercules' back got a bullet-mark which it bears to this day. A few days after, Herr von Bismarck was walking through the park with his son, and he noticed the humiliating treatment to which the statue had been subjected. He put on a serious look, and asked: "Did you do that, Otto?" The youth answered, in a merry and natural voice, "Yes, father, it was I; but I did not think it would hurt him so. He put his hand to the place directly it was done, and he has kept it there ever since."

5 Otto Demonstrates the Wrong Way to Take a Holiday: Epidemic in Berlin

"Bismarck . . . never believed in the infectious nature of cholera."

Young Bismarck looked forward with the greatest eagerness to every vacation that came along. In the summer of 1831, at the hottest time of the year, the specter of cholera rose in Eastern Europe and filled the people with horror. How the young man faced this situation was described in the following report.[5]

In 1832 the time came for Bismarck to take his final examinations, a prospect that filled him with alarm. But he passed with honors. His knowledge of history won him great praise. The verdict on his Latin was: Oratio est lucida ac Latina, sed parum castigata, *meaning that his language was clear and Latin-like but not very refined.*

When the cholera broke out in Berlin in 1831, in the general cholera mania, Bismarck was desired by his father to return home so soon as the first case had declared itself in that city. Like a true schoolboy, it was utterly impossible for him to receive the news too soon. He hired a horse, and several times rode to the "Frederick's field," from which district the cholera was expected. He, however, fell with the horse by the new Guard House, and was carried into his dwelling with a sprained leg. To his greatest annoyance he was now obliged to remain for a considerable time in bed, and endure the approach of the cholera to Berlin, before he could leave. But he never lost his gaiety and good humor on this account. Bonnell, as might be expected, was greatly alarmed, when, on returning home, he learned that Bismarck had tumbled from the horse and had been carried to his room; but he was soon com-

5. John-George Louis Hesekiel, *The Life of Bismarck,* trans. and ed. by Kenneth R. H. MacKenzie (London, 1870), pp. 92–94.

forted by the good temper with which the patient recounted the particulars of the accident.

Bismarck awaited his convalescence with patient resignation, and when he was finally able to enter upon his journey to Kniephof, an event took place owing to the strange cholera measures caused by the cholera mania. Travelers by stage, for instance, might not alight at such places as Bernau or Werneuchen on any account but the coaches drove side by side until their doors touched, and then the exchanges were effected, while the local guard paraded with spears in a manner almost Falstaffian. In another place, Bismarck was allowed to alight, but he could enter no house; there was a table spread in the open street, where tea and bread and butter were provided for travelers, and the latter breakfasted, while the inhabitants retired to look upon them in abject terror. When Bismarck called to a waitress to pay her, she fled shrieking, and he was obliged to leave the price of his breakfast on the table. The saddest case was that of a lady traveler, who was proceeding as governess to Count Borck's mansion, in Stargard. This poor girl dreaded traveling, and got into the condition which so outwardly resembles an attack of cholera. The doctors of Stargard were in an uproar, so the poor governess was put into quarantine in the town jail. Bismarck himself went into quarantine, and was first locked up in the police office at Naugard, and afterwards at his native place. His mother, it should be mentioned, had taken every precaution then in fashion, and had engaged a retired military surgeon, named Geppert, who had seen much of the cholera during his residence in Russia, as a cholera doctor, for her immediate service. With this doctor Bismarck was used to hold arguments, for though his conversation was rude and desultory, he could tell the story of his voyages in a practical and animated manner. Madame von Bismarck would have been very angry had she had an idea of the carelessness with which her son observed the severe quarantine rules. However, despite all the pains which the wise lady took, cholera showed itself on her estate, while all the neighbors were free from it. At Jarchelin Mill two boys had bathed against the regulations; they had eaten fruit and drank water—they were sacrificed to the disease. It can be easily understood what a nuisance the quarantine, even in its mildest form, must have been for Bismarck, who never believed in the infectious nature of cholera. In later times, when the two brothers farmed the estates, there was a case of cholera in Külz; no one dared to enter the house; the two Bismarcks went in, and declared that they themselves would not quit it until they were properly relieved. This shamed every one, and proper medical aid was obtained.

6 The Little University Town of Göttingen Is Plagued by a Sensational Student—a Bizarre, Boorish, and Brilliant Prince of Roisterers [6]

"I request you to apologize to Fritz."

Young noblemen of Otto von Bismarck's breed invariably chose to study at a Prussian university. But Bismarck's mother was adamant—he would go to Göttingen because of its splendid reputation and the supposed lack of beer-drinking among its students. Otto registered for a course in the study of law, with the aim of a diplomatic career. But, without serious purpose, he was indifferent to the scholarly offerings of the university. Instead, he turned to the heady pleasures of wine and song, and expended his youthful energies in reckless waste.

The sleepy little university town of Göttingen, in the province of Hanover, was pleasantly situated in the broad, fertile valley of the Leine. A canal wound lazily through the town, which was surrounded by ramparts planted with lime trees to form a promenade. The streets, relics of the Middle Ages, were narrow and winding. In lacking precision of line the old buildings with their gabled roofs seemed to fall over one another.

In the center of Germany, Göttingen was one of a group of sixty villages and hamlets clustered together in the Hanover district. In the surrounding Harz region, the El Dorado of superstition, goblins and ghosts were supposed to perform fantastic feats for the benefit of wide-eyed peasants and frightened children.

The Georgia Augusta University, founded by George II in 1734, was opened in 1737. It rapidly achieved status in the German academic world until by 1823, nine years before Bismarck matriculated there, the student body numbered 1,547. By 1832 Göttingen was recognized as one of the best seats of learning in all Germany. Its faculty numbered several fine historians, distinguished natural scientists, the brothers Jakob and Wilhelm Grimm (learned literary

6. Adapted from Louis L. Snyder, "That Prince of Roisterers, Bismarck," *The New York Times Magazine,* July 20, 1930, p. 11; Louis L. Snyder, "The Iron Chancellor as a Student," *The Baltimore Sunday Sun Magazine Section,* January 11, 1931, p. 7; and Louis L. Snyder, "Morton's Hope, or the Memoirs of a Provincial," *Hochschule und Ausland,* IV (April, 1931), 10–22.

historians and collectors of the famed fairy tales), Saalfeld, Hugo, Herren, Dahlmann, and others of equal standing.

As soon as he arrived at Göttingen, Bismarck began to assert his personality. He drew attention by wearing outlandish costumes and acting in a deliberately outrageous manner. Two months after his matriculation he accepted a bid from the *Hanovera,* a student corps. In his first semester he was appointed to the post of *Fuchs-Major,* and in the second he was promoted to *Konsenior.*

The student Bismarck was attracted to the *Mensur,* or student-duel. Theoretically, such dueling was prohibited by law, but generations of Göttingen police winked an eye as students journeyed to a favorite inn, the *Kaiser,* just outside the town.

The duels took place between members of various *Landsmannschaften* (fraternities). In 1832 the leading clubs were the *Lünenburger,* the *Bremensen,* the *Hanoverian* and the *Westphalian.* The students fought with a *Schläger,* a sword blunt at the end but very sharp-edged, with a basket-hilt. A suit of stuffed leather protected vital parts of the body, only the face and breast being exposed. A visitor to the Göttingen of 1832 would have been astonished by the number of students who boasted of at least one or two large scars. Often the face was barbarously mangled. From the viewpoint of the German student, these disfiguring scars were but evidence of Spartan courage, a chance to prove the existence of Teutonic fearlessness.

The duels were arranged by an elaborate code of insults, by which the degree of satisfaction was determined. The most usual insult was *"dumme Junge"* (stupid fellow). Any student pledged to a fraternity as a *Fuchs* (fox, or freshman) was expected to fight a certain number of duels against an opposing fraternity man before he was entitled to full membership. The *Fuchs* was distinguished by a rounded cap, which he wore during the months of his provisional membership. If he showed himself courageous in his duels, he was promptly elected and allowed to wear the regular visored *Mütze* (cap).

"Der Bismarck kommt!"

The business of dusting furniture and making beds was hastily abandoned along the Weenderstrasse as housewives rushed to the windows and strained their necks to get a good view. Children came running from every direction to witness the next antics of an eccentric student about whom table talk had already created an air of legendry. The Göttingen of 1832, inured by decades of tradition to the peculiarities of a variety of students, both nitwits and geniuses, had never seen anyone quite like this young Pomeranian.

He came strutting down the street, followed by a score of shrieking children. Anyone not a citizen of Göttingen would have taken him for an escaped lunatic. He wore the usual beer-cap in flaming crimson and gold, a chaotic dressing-gown—without collar or buttons, enormously wide trousers, and boots with iron spurs and heels. His shirt collar was doubled over his shoulders, and his hair, worn long in the Göttingen fashion of the time, fell loosely about his ears and neck. Strapped about his waist was a leather girdle, in which two huge horse-pistols were thrust, as well as a long basket-hilted sword, the dueling *Schläger* of the university student. A pair of red Turkish slippers graced his feet, while his legs were bare from the ankles to the knees.

The attempt of this slim youth to raise a mustache was not convincing. His blond, scraggly hair topped a face covered with freckles, a face distinguished by a pair of piercing eyes. From the tip of his nose to the edge of his right ear extended an impressive scar, grotesque relic of a recent duel. To complete the effect he had shaved off one of his eyebrows. On his right forefinger he wore an enormous seal ring and in one hand he brandished an oaken cudgel. In the other he held a small memorandum book.

Wobbling along ahead of his master, a small Dachshund carried himself in a nonchalant manner, as if conscious of the attention his owner excited. He tiptoed along as gracefully as a pig. A wreath of artificial flowers was around his neck, and red and green ribbons were tied to his tail.

The dog and his owner paid no attention to the laughter of the housewives and the shrieks of the children.

Four students marching along the sidewalk saw the Junker and began to laugh loudly. Bismarck approached them and asked for an explanation as to why they were laughing. One said, "At the dog" and the other three, "At his master." Bismarck noted the names and addresses of the last three, writing them carefully in his notebook, and challenged them by calling them *"dumme Jungen."*

"As for you, sir," he continued, turning to the first student, "our quarrel is not so easily settled. I care not for insult to myself, because I can defend myself, but an insult to my dog, to little Fritz, is cowardly; for Fritz cannot resent the injury. Fritz, sir, as you perceive, bears the name of the immortal hero of Prussia, 'Frederick *the only,*' a monarch for whom I have the most profound reverence. I request you to apologize to Fritz."

The student laughed in his face.

"Your name?"

"Weissbier," said the student.

"Well, Mr. Weissbier, I request you to repair instantly with me to my apartment. Choose either of your three friends for your second. We will settle Fritz's quarrel with these instruments, at three paces, and no barrier," he concluded, touching his pistols.

The now thoroughly frightened student, seeing that Bismarck would not fight with sabers or swords, and realizing that he would be ousted from his fraternity if he refused the challenge, asked how he could apologize to the dog. Bismarck answered that Fritz would not understand words, that Weissbier must keep him company by indulging with the dog in its favorite sport—jumping over a stick. Weissbier, thinking that he had really gotten hold of the devil, did as he was ordered. Bismarck then said "Good-morning" to the other three astonished students and reminded them that they would hear from him that same afternoon. He turned about and repaired to his lodgings.

Bismarck's skill in dueling was respected by the other corps students, most of whom were careful about challenging him. In letters to his father, mother, and brother, he described some of his exciting battles, and spoke of a wound he had received as a trifling matter. Any slighting reference to Prussia upon the part of a student was sufficient to draw a challenge from him.

Besides his unquestioned skill with the sword, young Bismarck was distinguished by an ability to consume large quantities of beer in the *Kneipen* (drinking bouts). He often spoke about "my friend, the flask." He was always busy at cards, playing pranks upon unsuspecting students, and falling violently in love. The university officials prohibited smoking in the streets of Göttingen, which Bismarck considered a violation of personal liberty. On one occasion he was brought before the *Universitätsvorstand* and fined a *Taler* for breaking this traditional law.

Once after imbibing more wine than was good for his equilibrium, the young Junker proceeded to the canal and took a nocturnal swim. Upon two occasions he was sentenced to solitary confinement, once because he acted as referee in a pistol duel, and once when he accepted the blame for an infraction of the university rules by his fraternity. Fellow students gave him a variety of nicknames including "Child," "Baby-Head," "Achilles the Unwoundable," and *"Kassube."* They were fascinated by his contradictory personality, by his strange mixture of cynicism and sentimentality, his eccentricity and logic.

Politics interested Bismarck but little at this time. He attended lectures only when he had nothing better to do. When he asked famed professor of law, the old Dr. Hugo, for a recommendation after the course had ended, the teacher wrote: "I have never seen this student at any of my lectures." Like other German students, Bismarck visited lecture halls assiduously for the first few weeks of the term, then as the business of fighting duels and drinking beer became more and more important, his interest in dry-as-dust lectures waned. He had no use for the new *Burschenschaften,* student political clubs which extolled kaiser and Reich, especially because they were opposed to duels and beer-drinking. In his opinion they were composed of the scum of the university.

7 The Student Bismarck Is Invited by the Rector to Explain Behavior Not Considered to Be in the Best Interests of the University

"The bottle probably flew out of the window of itself."

Capable of consuming enormous quantities of beer, young Bismarck proved to be a champion at the Saturday night drinking sessions (Kneipen). *He decided on one occasion to give a party for a group of Mecklenburgers with whom he had traveled in the Harz mountains. What happened then brought him before the rector for a notable interview.*[7]

One day there was a great dinner given at the "Golden Crown," and the formidable number of empty bottles lying about showed to what extent they were all enjoying themselves. In fact their enjoyment was so great that at a given moment an empty bottle flew through the window without its being apparent from whose hand it came. A policeman happened to be passing in the street at the time, and, without apprising the jolly dogs of what he was going to do, went and reported the circumstance.

Next morning, Herr von Bismarck was quietly smoking his pipe at the window—perhaps dreaming of his future fame, but certainly not thinking in the least of the bottle the day before sent flying through the window—when some one tapped at the door.

"Come in!"

It was the university beadle, holding in his hand a bit of paper so well known to German students—"*Dominus de Bismarck citatus est.*" It must be mentioned that Bismarck was in his dressing-gown and slippers.

"All right!" he said to the beadle; "I'll follow you." And he

7. *Bismarck and All About Him . . .* , ed. Hayward, pp. 21–23.

actually went after the man dressed just as he was, and with his dog at his heels, the latter never leaving his master for a moment.

The rector was awaiting the culprit in his study. What was his astonishment at seing an enormous dog bound into the room, with an air which inspired but little confidence! His first care was to ensconce himself behind a barricade of chairs, after which, trying to assume a demeanor suited to the occasion, he asked Bismarck what he wanted.

"Me! I want nothing," was the reply. "It is you, it appears, who have something to say to me, seeing that you have sent me this *'Dominus de Bismarck citatus est.'* "

The rector, whose bearing had been anything but dignified since the entry of the mastiff, now began to recover his self-possession.

"Sir," he said, "in the first place I condemn you to pay a fine of five *Talers* for having brought that animal here; and secondly, will you be good enough to explain how it was that a bottle came to be thrown through the window of the Golden Crown Hotel last evening, of which I have the pieces here?"

"*Mein Gott,* sir! The bottle probably flew out of the window of itself."

"You know very well that a bottle cannot fly of itself, and that some one must have thrown it."

"Perhaps so, sir."

"There is no perhaps about it. Please to be more explicit."

"Well, then; it probably happened somewhat in this way." And seizing a bulky inkstand standing on the desk, Bismarck made as if he would hurl it at the poor rector's head.

The latter, however, fearing to see the projectile fly from the young man's hand, hastened to dismiss him, and the fine, it would appear, was never paid.

8 An American at Göttingen, John Lothrop Motley, Later to Become an Eminent Historian, Describes His Close Friend in the Guise of a Fictionalized Otto von Rabenmark[8]

"I shall not die until I am nineteen years and nine months old."

8. Adapted from Louis L. Snyder, "Bismarck und Motley, eine Studentenfreundschaft," *Hochschule und Ausland,* III (March, 1930), 11–16; and Snyder, "Morton's Hope, or the Memoirs of a Provincial."

At Göttingen the tempestuous Bismarck sought the comradeship of foreigners and noblemen, as befitting his own social position. The noblemen included a Freiherr von Kanitz and three brothers—Graf Hermann, Graf Alexander and Graf Heinrich Keyserling. He struck up a friendship immediately with three Americans, Amory Coffin, Mitchell C. King and John Lothrop Motley. The first two were Southerners, from South Carolina. King was accepted as a member of a German fraternity, an almost unparalleled feat for a foreigner. Motley, who remained throughout his life a close friend of Bismarck, was a New Englander, who later became a famous historian and diplomat. Motley, a young American from Boston, had come to Göttingen on the advice of George Bancroft, the historian, who had been his teacher at the Round Hill School. Motley was but eighteen, Bismarck a year younger, and the friendship between the American republican and the Prussian royalist continued until Motley's death in 1877. Motley and Bismarck were inseparable at Göttingen.

A few years after leaving Göttingen, Motley wrote his first novel, Morton's Hope, or the Memoirs of a Provincial. *In the figure of Otto von Rabenmark he drew a remarkable picture of his friend Bismarck. Thirty years later, in 1869, Motley was named ambassador to England. When he arrived in London, an enterprising publisher conceived the idea of issuing a new edition of this initial work of the "Minister of the United States." Motley, who had forgotten all about the book, suspected that publication now might be harmful to his position as ambassador. He searched in vain for a copy, until at last he was told that the only remaining one in Europe was in the British Museum. His attempt to get it was unsuccessful, as it had been withdrawn temporarily by a member of the publishing firm, who was engaged in copying the book in the reading room. Motley obtained permission to read his own work in the library on a Sunday afternoon, when the reading room was closed to the general public. A few days later the publisher was surprised by a visit from the American diplomat, who gave him a considerable sum of money to withdraw the book. To this day the only copy of* Morton's Hope *in Europe lies buried in the British Museum.*

Even though the picture of Otto von Rabenmark is exaggerated, one learns much from Motley about his own relations with Bismarck and recognizes the character of the future chancellor—his burning ambition and his positive personality.

A few minutes' walk brought us to Rabenmark's lodgings. We ascended two flights of stairs and entered his apartment. The sitting room was tolerably large, and, in its furniture and arrangements, a perfect specimen of a regular *Kneipe.* The floor was without carpet, and sanded; and the household furniture consisted of a table, a sofa, and half a dozen chairs of the most unpretending kind. The great expense had been, however, evidently made in providing the pipes, pictures, and other student luxuries. A large and well-executed engraving of a celebrated duel, which, from the notoriety of the combatants, and its tragical issue, had become historical, hung on the right side as you entered. On the left, the wall was covered with a large collection of silhouettes. These are a peculiar and invariable characteristic of a German student's room; they are well-executed profiles, in black paper on a white ground, of the occupant's intimate friends, and are usually four or five inches square, and surrounded with a narrow frame of black wood.

Rabenmark's friends seemed to be numerous, for there were at least a hundred silhouettes, arranged in regular rows, gradually decreasing by one from the bottom, till the pyramid was terminated by a single one, which was the profile of the senior of the Pomeranian Club. Most of the worthies represented possessed (as it is not uncommon with profile portaits) a singular similarity with each other. All had variegated club-caps, mustachios, and bows of ribbons in their button-holes, and looked as if they might have been furnished by an upholsterer in "lots to suit purchasers." A scarf of scarlet and gold was suspended in graceful festoons from two nails, so as to form a sort of triumphal wreath for the whole.

The third side of the room was decorated with a pair of *Schlägers,* or dueling swords, which were fastened crosswise against the wall. . . . The hilts were of blue, scarlet and gold. . . .

On the fourth side of the room were a collection of pipes, which were the pride of his hearth. There were about twenty, arranged also in a systematic row. The bowls were of porcelain, exquisitely painted; some with portraits of pretty women, some with copies from a van Ostade and a Gerard Dou, and some with the arms of his intimate friends. The stems were about three feet in length, and of a fragrant polished cherry. The tassels were large and rich, and of every combination of *Landsmannschaft* color. Besides these, there were half a dozen meerschaums of various kinds. . . .

Besides these articles, there were some half-dozen engravings in frames, a fowling piece, a saber, and two or three different species of caps hanging in different parts of the room.

"There," said Rabenmark, entering the room, unbuckling his belt, and throwing his pistols and *Schläger* on the floor. "I can leave my buffoonery for a while and be reasonable; it's rather tiresome work, this boasting."

"Have the kindness to tell me," said I, "what particular reason you have for arraying yourself and your dog in such particularly elegant costumes, and for making such an exquisite exhibition of yourself during your promenade?"

Rabenmark replied that he was interested in getting into the best *Landsmannschaft* in the quickest possible time. Instead of making friends with the magnates of the club, he insulted them publicly and in the grossest manner. "After I had cut off the senior's nose, sliced off the con-senior's upper lip, mustachios and all, besides bestowing less severe marks of affection on the others, the whole club, in admiration of my prowess, and desiring to secure the services of so valorous a combatant, voted me in by acclamation."

"Do you find any particular satisfaction," said I, "in your club, and the university life?"

"Oh, it is boy's play," said he, "but then I am a boy, in years at least. I have certain quantity of time on my hands. I wish to take the university as a school for action. I intend to lead my companions here as I intend to lead them in after life. You see I am a very rational sort of person now, and you would hardly take me for the same crazy mountebank you met in the street half an hour ago. But then, I see that this is the way to gain superiority. I determined at once, on arriving at the university, that, to obtain mastery over my competitors, who were all extravagant, savage, eccentric, I must be ten times as extravagant as any one else."

"Suppose, however, that Mr. Weissbier had happened to be a less tractable person than he proved to be?"

"Why, I should have been obliged to shoot him."

"You forget the less agreeable alternative. He might have done you the same favor."

"Oh no,—impossible. I shall not die until I am nineteen years and nine months old. If I pass that period I shall live some twelve or thirteen years longer; I forget the exact number; but I have it written down in my commonplace notebook somewhere."

This I found afterwards to be a settled conviction. Nothing could induce Rabenmark to admit the possibility of his death until that age. . . . His age was, at the time of which I am writing, exactly eighteen and a half. . . .

"In five minutes you can see a student's whole life," continued Rabenmark. "A young man usually spends three years at the university. As most of the German universities are in coalition, whatever time he spends at one is counted for him at the next, and he consequently usually passes a whole year at one, the next term at another, and so on. The first two years of the three, a student generally employs in fighting duels and getting drunk. After he has fought his fifty or a hundred duels, and drunk as much beer as he is capable of, he usually, at the end of his second year, leaves his club, and spends his third and last year in diligent study. His examination—and a very strict one it is—succeeds; and if he can pass it, he receives his doctor's degree, whether of theology, philosophy, law or medicine, and retires into private life."

"But, I suppose, he remains a long time a troublesome and ferocious individual?"

"On the contrary. Nobody ever hears of him. It is a singular anomaly,—the whole German student existence. The German students are no more Germans than they are Sandwich Islanders. They have, in fact, less similarity with Germans than with any other nation. You see in them a distinct and strongly characterized nation, moving in a definite, though irregular orbit of its own, and totally independent of the laws which regulate the rest of the social system of Germany. It presents the singular phenomenon of a rude, though regularly organized republic, existing in the heart of a despotism. In fact, every one of the main points of the German character is directly the opposite of those of the German student. The German is phlegmatic—the student fiery. The German is orderly and obedient to the authorities—the student ferocious and intractable. The German is peaceable, the student forever brawling and fighting. The German is eminently conservative in his politics—the student always a revolutionist. The government of all the states is despotic,—the student's whole existence is republican. The German is particularly deferential to rank and title. In the student's republic, and there alone, the omnipotent 'von' sinks before the dexterous *Schläger,* or the capacious *Bier-Bummel.* Lastly, the German is habitually sober, and the student is invariably drunk."

"But how, in God's name, is it that this community of desperadoes does not at last overwhelm the whole of Germany? How is it that they do not set the whole empire in a blaze?"

"Why, the process of evaporation seems, after all, to be very simple. A certain number leave the university every year; and besides that they have already been subjected to a preparatory cooling period of about a year, during which they have been preparing themselves for their examination. It usually appears that the number is so insignificant in comparison with the vast population in which they are merged, that the mischief which might have been apprehended, seems impossible. They are at once extinguished in the ocean of mankind."

"Then it seems that this last year's study acts as a sort of safety valve, and diminishes the danger?"

"Annihilates it entirely. Besides this, a great effect is produced by the sobriety of the citizen; nay, of the student himself, after his metempsychosis. A man, when he is tipsy, looks at all subjects and particularly political subjects, with much more enthusiasm than when he is sober. When the fumes of beer and *Schnapps* have been dispersed, and he is once settled in private life, he finds it much better to pocket his wages as referendary, auditor, etc., paid out to him by the despot's treasurer, and wait quietly until he receives his ultimate promotion, than to be quarreling with the government, and losing his money and his head for his pains."

[Upon another occasion, Morton met his German friend at a party. The crazy Junker appeared altogether transformed.]

I never saw such a transformation in a human being, and for an instant I would not believe my eyes. It was, indeed, Fox Rabenmark, but instead of the savage, uncouth student, I saw an elegantly dressed young nobleman, of peculiarly graceful manners, and distinguished address. His hair was curled and arranged in a becoming manner, and his graceful and very handsome figure was displayed to the greatest advantage in a rich and well-fashioned suit. He wore lace ruffles, and a magnificent solitaire; a *chapeau,* in the prevailing mode, was under his arm, and a small court-sword was by his side. [Approaching the American, he discusses his own future.] "In two and a half years I shall have completed my diplomatic studies and shall have gone through with my examination; after which, through the influence of my uncle, Count Pappenheim, I hope very soon to be provided with a diplomatic situation at some of the foreign courts. I shall by that time, also, have completed my twenty-first year, and have come into possession of a landed estate, worth at least five thousand rix-dollars a year. . . .

[Motley was a good observer. He evidently attended many of the duels which Bismarck fought, two of which he described minutely.]

For an instant they remained motionless, and eyed each other warily, but undauntedly. Suddenly Rabenmark raised his weapons, and making a feint at the head of his antagonist, directed a violent blow at his breast. It was skillfully parried by the opposite party, who retorted with a savage "quart," which, if successful, would have severed him nearly in two. The fox caught it on his sword, with a skill which I hardly believed him capable of, and then becoming animated, rained a succession of violent and rapid blows, now "quart" and now "tierce," upon his adversary. They were all parried with wonderful precision and coolness. . . .

I perceived that the dexterity of my friend was nearly exhausted, and expected every instant to see him stretched upon the floor. At last, Kopp aimed a prodigious blow at Rabenmark's head. It came within a quarter of an inch of the frontlet of the cap before Rabenmark succeeded in beating it off with a desperate and successful backhand stroke. The fox, now throwing himself entirely off his guard, rushed wildly upon his adversary. He beat down his sword before he had time to recover his posture of defense, and with one last, violent and tremendous effort, he struck at his adversary's head. It was unexpected, and too late to parry; the blow alighted full upon the cheek of the enemy. Its force was prodigious; the Westphalian, stunned and blinded, staggered a few paces forward, and then his feet slipped, and he fell upon the floor. . . .

I went up and took a look at him. The *Pauk-Doktor* was busily sponging away the blood, and an assistant was applying restoratives to awaken him from his swoon. The side of the cap had been cut through by the violence of the blow, and a deep and ghastly wound extended from the top of the head across the temple and the cheek. The whole side of the face was laid open.

"He has enough for the next six weeks," said Rabenmark, coolly turning towards the dressing room.

"*Verfluchter Fuchs* [cursed fox]!" murmured the wounded man, reviving at the sound of his adversary's voice for an instant, and then relapsing into his swoon.

Immediately afterwards Rabenmark fought Fizzleberg, who was said to be con-senior of the Westphalians and a good *Schläger*. Rabenmark toyed with him after he perceived that he was really fighting a beginner. A cut stopped the duel.

A ridiculous little scratch presented itself, from which the blood had hardly begun to flow. The second took the silver rule, and gravely adjusted it to the wound. It was discovered to be exactly one inch and one-tenth in length; and as the *Comment* only required one and one-twentieth, its size was declared sufficient. . . .

From that day Fox Rabenmark was the most renowned *Schläger* in Göttingen.

From this point on, Motley finished his novel in a fantastically romantic manner. To defend the honor of his sweetheart, Rabenmark fights a duel and kills his adversary. He escapes from Göttingen with Morton and their friends. An unbelievable series of events follows, during which the author disposes of his hero in true Shakespearean fashion. Rabenmark had previously married Berta Wallenstein, a blonde, blue-eyed, fair-haired maiden—a perfect incarnation of Germany—, "one of the handsomest women in the world." The pistol duel for her favor leaves Rabenmark an escaped murderer. Berta, delirious and driven nearly insane by her father's objections to Rabenmark, throws herself from a window and is killed. Rabenmark slays her brother, who had been as implacable as her father. Caught, the hero is placed in a dungeon, where he takes a sad farewell from his beloved friend, Morton. Brought to court, he is sentenced to death, but takes vengeance by slaying his sweeheart's father in the courtroom. He then swallows poison concealed in his huge signet ring. None of these final romantic figments of Motley's imagination concerned the real Bismarck.

9 Summoned before the Academic Tribunal, Göttingen's Peripatetic Hell-Raiser Gives some Ingenious but Unconvincing Evidence [9]

"Consider the length of my legs, . . . gentlemen."

During his second semester at Göttingen, Bismarck was summoned to appear before the Academic Tribunal on the accusation of having compromised himself in a duel with pistols. His evidence, reproduced here, did not meet with much success. The university archives reveal that the student Bismarck was condemned to three days' confinement in the black hole.

I entered, quite by accident, into the Gurkenkrug Brewery, and I found there some fellow students who were in a bit of a quandary. A duel with pistols had been arranged, and the person chosen for umpire had not arrived. My comrades urged me to take his place, and I consented. I did all I could to induce the young men to make it up, but in vain; so I insisted on the condition that the two adversaries should fire at ten paces, and not over a handkerchief as had at first been agreed upon. My proposal having been accepted, I measured the distance, counting twelve paces. And when you consider the length of my legs, you will see, gentlemen, that my intention was to render the duel less dangerous. But this was not all: I stipulated that only just enough powder should be put into the

9. *Bismarck and All About Him . . .*, ed. Hayward, pp. 23–24.

pistols to force out the bullets. I think, then, I have some reason to believe that all the merits of the harmless issue of this duel belong to me.

10

Candidate Bismarck Requests Transfer of a Term of Imprisonment from Göttingen to Berlin, November 16, 1833

"My weak health will not permit me to undertake so long a journey."

After spending a little more than a year at Göttingen, Bismarck left in September 1833. He decided to enter the University of Berlin the following May, but there was a problem. He still owed the authorities at Göttingen a term of imprisonment for violating university rules. On November 16, 1833, he sent the following letter to the pro-rector of the University of Göttingen, a communication which revealed the shrewdness of the future diplomat.[10] *There is no record of Bismarck serving this penalty in Berlin.*

Your Excellency was good enough to postpone my term of imprisonment until my return after the Christmas holidays. Now there has been a recurrence of my illness, and I see no end to it. I shall have to remain here and continue my studies, because my weak health will not permit me to undertake so long a journey. On this ground I request Your Excellency to give me permission to serve my penalty of imprisonment here instead of in Göttingen.

Your Excellency's obedient servant,
OTTO V. BISMARCK, Student of Law

10. Quoted in *Bismarck: Die gesammelte Werke,* ed. by Wolfgang Windelband and Werner Frauendienst (Berlin, 1933), XIV–I, 3.

Lithograph by Mittag-Scherl, Ber

PART II

Overture: Apprentice Years in the Service of Prussia, 1835-1851

II

Unable to Accept the Discipline of a Military Life, Twenty-Year-Old Otto von Bismarck Begins His Career as a Legal Examiner in Berlin, 1835

"Herr Auskultator, the kicking out is* my *business."

With his formal education completed, Bismarck, as the younger son of a noble Junker family, had the choice of two professions: he could enter military service or build a career as a diplomat. The military life, with its accent on discipline, had no attraction for him. Prussian administration seemed more suitable. After obtaining his law degree, he became an unpaid Auskultator *(Examiner) in the judicial and administrative service in Berlin.*[1] *Thus began a lifetime of service to the Prussian state.*

When Bismarck became sworn, after his examination about Easter, 1835, in the capacity of *Auskultator* (Examiner) he again occupied apartments in the Behrenstrasse, jointly with his brother Bernhard, who, about that time, after having served four years in the Dragoon Regiment of Guards, exchanged the sword for the pen, passed his examination in the following year, and became referendary in the government at Potsdam. During Bismarck's service as clerk in the city police, he exhibited his sense of humor by many pranks, of which we could give an account were we able to vouch for their authenticity—these are, however, so numerous, that we are sure many are ascribed to Bismarck, properly the acts of others. The following anecdote we know to be genuine. The *Auskultator* was taking the protocol of a true Berliner, who finally so tried the patience of Bismarck by his impudence, that he jumped up, and exclaimed, "Sir, behave better, or I'll have you kicked out!" The magistrate present patted the zealous official in a friendly way upon the shoulder, and said quietly, "*Herr Auskultator,* the kicking out is *my* business." They proceeded in taking evidence, but very soon Bismarck again sprang to his feet, thundering out, "Sir, behave yourself better, or the magistrate shall kick you out!" The face of the Court may be imagined.

Bismarck had a great deal to do in divorce cases, which were then treated in a manner in Prussia—with a thoughtlessness still

1. John-George Louis Hesekiel, *The Life of Bismarck,* trans. and ed. by Kenneth R. H. MacKenzie (London, 1870), pp. 104–105.

sadly remembered, although long since receiving a more solemn and worthier attention. The young jurist was deeply impressed by a lady with whom he had to arrange a divorce, when she decisively refused to attest it. She had determined otherwise. Bismarck, who had never met with such a refusal, was disconcerted, and at last went and consulted with the senior jurist, and requested his aid. Arrogantly shrugging his shoulders at the inexperience of his young colleague, he entered into the matter, and endeavored with all his wisdom and authority to induce the poor woman to consent to the divorce. She, however, continued her refusal; the matter ended without any result. Bismarck never forgot this circumstance.

12 The Future Conductor of Prussia-Germany's Foreign Policy Demonstrates One Way to Get Action

"Are Herr von Bismarck's boots done?"

During the winter of 1835–1836 the young legal examiner moved in the pleasant and amiable circle of the nobility in Berlin and was also introduced to court festivities. The story of how young Bismarck taught punctuality to a bootmaker in the Kronenstrasse was told in this anecdote, a favorite one among German schoolchildren.[2]

Being invited to a *soirée* in high-class society, Bismarck ordered a pair of patent-leather boots for the occasion from a bootmaker in Berlin. He was not quite satisfied as to the punctuality of this son of Crispin and, besides, he was teased by his companions, who, having heard of the order, chaffed him continually, saying,—

"You won't get your boots!"

Bismarck's answer was: "You will see that I *will* get them."

The day previous to the one fixed for the *soirée* he called upon the bootmaker.

"Are my boots ready?"

"Alas! no, sir."

"Very well! I give you notice that if they are not ready by the stipulated time tomorrow my dog shall devour you."

2. *Bismarck and All About Him, by a Fellow Student,* ed. by Henry Hayward (London, 1898), pp. 18–19.

And he walked out majestically from the shop, followed by his huge mastiff.

Next day, commencing as early as six o'clock in the morning, the poor cobbler was visited every quarter of an hour by a commissionaire, who asked him each time in a warning voice,—

"Are Herr von Bismarck's boots done?"

This was kept up the whole day through, until the bootmaker, almost driven out of his wits, managed to finish the boots in time. On getting them Herr von Bismarck danced about like a maniac.

From that day forward this impatient customer had not the slightest complaint to make on the score of his bootmaker's punctuality. His boots were always delivered before the appointed time.

13

Leopold Eduard Otto von Bismarck Passes the Oral Examination for the Rank of Government-Referendary by Displaying "a Very Good Standard," Aix-la-Chapelle, June 30, 1836

"Altogether, the candidate showed an excellent power of judgment."

To the fledging barrister, Berlin, with its bustling lawyers and glimpses of court life, was interesting enough, but he was not overly impressed. After a year as Auskultator *there, he moved to Aachen (Aix-la-Chapelle), where he became a candidate for the office of referendary, or unsalaried apprentice to the administrative chief of the district. Before attaining that promotion, he had to pass a strict oral examination. The testimonial was good, considering the fact that it was concerned with a young man who had infected all Göttingen with his special brand of laziness.*[3] *Note that the examiners spelled Bismarck's name without the "c" (Bismark), an idiosyncrasy which was to follow him throughout his life.*

DONE AT AIX-LA-CHAPELLE,
This 30*th June,* 1836

In accordance with official instructions there was held here this morning, from 10 A.M. to 1 P.M., the oral examination of the *Kammergerichts-Auskultator—Leopold Eduard Otto von Bismark* —a candidate for the rank of government-referendary. This examination first of all applied to the candidate's general knowledge—

3. *Bismarck's Table Talk,* ed. by Charles Lowe (London, 1895), pp. 24–25.

especially in Greek and Latin, history and philosophy, then to public law in general and several branches of political economy and finance, in particular the present system of taxation in Prussia, and finally jurisprudence, the common law of Prussia, the French civil law, as well as common German feudal law—including a number of concrete cases.

In respect of general school knowledge, the candidate displayed a very good standard (*recht gute Schulstudien*), and evinced his familiarity with the ancient tongues by translating and explaining several passages from Xenophon's *Cyropædia* as well as Cicero's *De Officiis*. Of the economic sciences the candidate showed a very good knowledge, and, above all things, his answers to the questions that were put to him in public law and administration proved that he had been reflecting on what he had learned [and that he is already on the way to independent views].

Not less good was the candidate's examination in jurisprudence. His answers showed that he had mastered the general principles of the Roman as well as of the Prussian law, and his judgments on the concrete cases that were put to him proved that he knows how to apply those principles. [His knowledge of French law was but slight.] Of French law he seemed, at least, to have acquired some knowledge. Altogether, the candidate showed an excellent power of judgment, quickness of comprehension in the questions put to him, and skill in oral expression.

Accordingly, and in consideration of the fact that the written work of the candidate has been very favorably reported on, this Examination Commission is unanimously of opinion that the *Kammergerichts-Auskultator* von Bismark appears to be very well qualified for promotion to the rank of government-referendary

14 With a Special Talent for Attracting Trouble, the New Referendary Finds Himself Embroiled in a Street Fight in the Midst of a Church Festival [4]

"Down with the heretic!"

Aix-la-Chapelle (Aachen) was a spa to which visitors streamed from all the world. Unlike provincial Berlin, Aix was elegant, cosmopolitan, fashionable. The youthful Junker plunged into a life of

4. *Bismarck and All About Him . . .*, ed. Hayward, pp. 220–221.

eating, drinking, and gaming, strolling in the Kurpark, or losing all his money at the gaming tables. He made the acquaintance of some rich English visitors. But as soon as he arrived he gravitated toward trouble.

Soon after his arrival at Aachen he found himself in conflict with the populace in the open street, on the occasion of a Catholic festival, when a procession with streaming banners was passing through the town, amid the roar of mortar-firing and church-bell ringing. This ecclesiastical pomp and ceremony was a new thing for Bismarck, and he stood at the corner of the street to see the procession go by. He did not notice that when the "host" went past everybody fell upon their knees, and presently he was standing erect alone in the multitude, and in his tall hat seemed to loom up like a giant among them. In a moment a heavy blow was dealt upon his hat from behind, and then a broad-shouldered fellow in a blue blouse stood before him with his fist raised in a threatening manner, and cries rose around him, "Take off your hat!" "Down with the heretic!" "Prussian Junker!" But Bismarck was not in the least disposed to be dictated to in this style; he slashed the broad-shouldered fellow across the face with his Spanish cane, and sprang into the midst of the soldiers bringing up the rear of the procession. No one dared to follow him; and after walking with the troops for a short distance he regained his dwelling without further molestation.

15

Alcibiades of the Marshes: Resigning from State Service and Returning Home, Bismarck Takes up the Life of a Pomeranian Squire, and Quickly Attains a Reputation in the District as "The Mad Junker"

"His wild ways, his dancing, his demon-like rides, and his drinking bouts. . . ."

After the death of his mother on New Year's Day 1839, Bismarck resigned from the state service. The world to which he returned was East Elbia, where for eight years he lived as a country squire. At Easter 1839 he and his brother Bernhard took over the paternal estates of Kniephof, Külz, and Jarchelin, and his father retained Schönhausen. In Pomerania he caroused, studied the Bible, acted as head deputy and magistrate, and made occasional excursions into the great world. Here lived the impoverished Junker aristocracy, loyal to the idea of patriarchal domination, a ruthless, arrogant, ignorant nobility. These Junkers—the name is derived from junc-herre *(young lord)—were landed nobles who understood the art of war and efficient estate administration. They knew well how to handle a rifle as well as modern bookkeeping. From their ranks came the generals, statesmen, and businessmen later to play an important role in German history. During the long winter months the young Bismarck found time for reflection amid all his cares of "night-frosts, sick oxen, . . . dead lambs, half-starved sheep, want of straw, fodder, money, potatoes, and manure."* [5]

On the 7th of June, 1840, died King Frederick William III and his son Frederick William IV reigned in his stead. What his successor had often promised, yet never given, the people now fairly expected from their new sovereign; but, instead of granting them a constitution, he merely flung them an amnesty. In October of the same year there was a high state ceremony in Berlin, and old Captain von Bismarck with his two sons went up to see it. Conspicuous on a canopied platform, before the royal castle, did the new king solemnly vow to the various representatives of the nation who had crowded thither to swear allegiance to him, that "he would rule in the fear of God and in the love of men, with open eyes when it concerned the wants of his people, but with closed ones in matters of justice." And then, with fervor in his voice, he asked them whether "with heart and soul, and word and deed, in the sacred faith of Germans, and the still more sacred love of Christians, they would help and assist him to maintain Prussia *as it was,* and as it must always remain if it were not to perish"; to which all the gazing (but surely not listening) multitude acclaimed with a loud, enthusiastic *"Ja!"* Before the lapse of seven short years that much-too-sentimental multitude was to repent them bitterly of the verbal contract which their thoughless patriotism had wrung from them, and cancel it, too, in blood.

Returned to Pomerania, Herr von Bismarck threw himself heart and soul into the task that was before him, and he seems to have had as little notion that a country life was not his true vocation, as Oliver Cromwell at one time never doubted that he was born to be a grazier. In fact, not to speak of later resemblances in their career, the early life of the Pomeranian squire had much in common with

5. *Prince Bismarck, An Historical Biography,* ed. by Charles Lowe, 2 vols. (London, 1885), I, 26–27.

that of the Huntingdonshire farmer, albeit the passion for prayer-meetings and communion with the saints might not have been equally strong in both. Bismarck now attended fairs, sold wool, inspected timber, handled grain, drove hard bargains, gathered rents, and sat as deputy in the local diet. It was surely a poor enough beginning for the man on whose diplomatic utterances all Europe afterwards came to hang, that his first speech in the rural assembly treated of "the excessive consumption of tallow in the workhouse." Humble in his debut an an orator, he has recorded that his first attempt at journalism proved a total failure. But with all his manifold sorrows he had a splendid appetite and "slept like a badger," despite such interruptions as the "melancholy howling of the sheep-dog, locked up for immoderate love of hunting."

> "I have been writing and walking in the sun," he wrote to his sister, "and yesterday looked on at the dancing in Plathe, and drank a good deal of Montebello champagne." And again, "ever almost since the wool-market I have been representing our roving *Landrat* [his brother Bernhard]; have held with much energy many a court in the hottest of weathers, and driven so constantly through the sandy pines that I and my horses have already had more than enough of this business. And now, after barely a week's quiet, I have again to begin to serve my country as a soldier. . . .

If his life, however, in the Mark was dull, he took care to give it a very different complexion in Pomerania, where he soon came to be the talk and the terror of the neighborhood. His wild ways, his dancing, his demon-like rides, and his drinking bouts, soon procured him an uncanny name, and he was known in the district as "mad Bismarck." "Esthetic teas" were not at all to his taste, but he would willingly gallop twenty or thirty miles after a hard day's work to a county ball. His wine-cellar was his first care, and we find him bewailing the loss of one of his carts, with its load of "three casks of spirits," which had been carried away by a flood. A worthy successor at Kniephof to that ancestor of his whose toasts were accompanied by volleys of musketry, Bismarck often relieved his rural solitude by entertaining the boldest spirits from the surrounding garrisons, and he easily bore away the bell among a set of boon companions by whom the strongest headed three-bottle men of a past era would very speedily have been put under the table. He quaffed huge cups of mixed champagne and porter, he awoke his guests in the morning by firing off pistols close to their ears, and he terrified his lady-cousins by turning foxes into the drawing room. With a character of this kind, therefore, it was surely no wonder that, having once plunged into an election contest, he "emerged with the certainty that four voters were inclined to go in for me for life or death, and two more with a certain amount of lukewarmness, . . . so that I thought on the whole I had better retire."

Another picture of Junker Otto at Kniephof was given by Moritz Busch in the following passages.[6]

Bismarck played many practical jokes some forty odd years ago when he had turned his back upon the state service and was farming at Kniephof. His guests now and then underwent strange and startling surprises. One day, while he was chatting to his fair cousins, the door of the drawing room suddenly opened and four young foxes rushed in, jumping upon the sofas and chairs and tearing their coverings to tatters. Male visitors had need of steady nerves; for it not infrequently happened that when they had fallen asleep, soothed by a comfortable nightcap lined with porter and champagne, they were suddenly aroused from their slumbers by pistol shots, and the bullets, striking the ceiling above their heads, brought down showers of plaster upon them.

A lively specimen of his peculiar humor at that period was related to me by the chancellor himself. Once he had a young lieutenant of hussars staying with him at Kniephof, who was called upon to pay a visit to a worthy old uncle in the neighborhood—a venerable gentleman extremely tenacious with respect to etiquette and elegant manners, who had invited a party of relatives and friends of his own kidney to a grand birthday feast. On the eve of this occasion Bismarck persuaded the youthful warrior to drink a great deal more than was good for him; and next morning conveyed him in a springless cart to his uncle's castle. The roads were not good at any time; but heavy rains had transformed them into mud lakes, so that the two gentlemen arrived desperately besplashed. The lieutenant's moral and physical condition was a dismal one, for the consequences of his debauch overnight had been seriously aggravated by the shaking and jolting of the cart, and expressed themselves in somewhat alarming symptoms. The company that greeted them on their arrival, consisting of about forty persons—the ladies *en grande toilette,* the gentlemen in tail coats and white ties—contemplated them with mingled amazement and horror. The hussar soon became invisible; but Junker Otto,

6. Moritz Busch, *Bismarck: Sketches for a Historical Picture,* trans. by William Beatty-Kingston (New York, 1891), II, 266–299.

despite the loathing with which the highly proper, stiff and respectable people regarded him, sat down to dinner with them as coolly and cheerfully as though nothing out of the way had taken place. Everybody said how astonishing, how extremely astonishing it was that he had no notion, not the shadow of a notion, what an unpleasant person he was.

I relate the following anecdote, although I doubt its authenticity, as an illustration of the view taken by the people round Kniephof of "Junker Otto's" fancies and freaks. One day, so says the story, he went out snipe-shooting with a friend. They had to traverse a verdant morass, into which Bismarck's companion, a short, stout, ponderous gentleman, suddenly sank up to his armpits. After struggling for some time to extricate himself and reach firm ground, he called aloud for help; and, seeing his friend picking his way slowly towards him, looking about all the while to see whether a stray snipe would get up, he fervently implored him to let the confounded snipe alone and drag him out of the vile bog-hole, the muck of which was fast rising to his mouth and nose. "My beloved friend," answered Bismarck with the utmost calm, "you will certainly never be able to scramble out of that hole; and it is quite impossible to save you. It would pain me extremely to watch your futile struggles, or to see you slowly stifle in that disgusting filth. I'll tell you what, my boy; I'll spare you a protracted death-agony through suffocation by lodging a charge of shot in your head. Thus shall you die with promptitude and dignity." "Are you beside yourself?" shouted the other, making frantic efforts to wriggle out of the swamp; "I don't want either to suffocate or to be shot; so help me out, in the name of three devils!" Raising his gun to his shoulder and taking careful aim, Bismarck replied in mournful accents, "Keep still for one second. It will soon be over. Farewell, dear friend; I will tell your poor wife all about your last moments." Stimulated to superhuman exertions by the danger threatening him so imminently, the unlucky sportsman contrived somehow to wrench himself out of the mud, and crawled on all-fours to *terra firma.* As soon as he felt himself safe he burst out into a torrent of vehement reproaches. Bismarck, smiling, listened to him a while; then, simply remarking, "You see I was right; every one for himself," turned his back upon his infuriated companion, and strolled off leisurely to look for more snipe.

16

A Bored Lieutenant, Stationed with the Fourth Regiment of Pomeranian Uhlans in Garrison at Treptow in 1842, Tries to Smoke out the Bürgermeister and Later Wins His First Decoration

"I forbid you to walk in the streets with a lighted cigar."

Every young Prussian, including Bismarck, was required to fulfill a military obligation. In 1837 Bismarck began a year as a private in the Jaeger *or Rifles in the* Garde Corps *stationed at Potsdam. A few weeks later he was transferred to the* Jaeger *in Stettin. In 1841, at the age of twenty-six, he was made a lieutenant in the* Landwehr, *a kind of National Guard. That he had not given up the habits learned at Göttingen was revealed by the following incident.*[7]

Just after Bismarck had joined the cavalry, and at the time of his appointment as officer in the *Landwehr,* he was staying for a few months with the Fourth Regiment of Pomeranian Uhlans, in garrison at Treptow.

The colonel of the regiment, who was a strict disciplinarian, was very particular that the officers' conduct and deportment should be irreproachable. This, naturally, did not very well suit the tastes of the younger officers, who, always and in all countries, are very apt to break through the bonds of strict discipline.

At this date smoking in the streets was prohibited, both for officers and men, and this prohibition went very much against the grain of the smokers. Most of them, therefore, broke the rule whenever it was possible to do so without running too great a risk of being discovered.

One day the *Bürgermeister* of Treptow, thinking to ingratiate himself with the colonel, went and informed him that a great many of his officers set this regulation boldly at defiance, and that they were not averse to smoking in the public thoroughfares like common laborers. The colonel boiled over with rage on hearing this, and called his officers together to remind them of the regulation prohibiting smoking. He wound up his harangue with the following words: "I forbid you to walk in the streets with a lighted

7. *Bismarck and All About Him . . . ,* ed. Hayward, pp. 27–28.

cigar," and while he was saying the words he fixed his eyes in a significant way upon Lieutenant von Bismarck, whom he knew to be an inveterate smoker.

Next day this young lieutenant, accompanied by several other officers who were in the plot, went and seated themselves on a wooden bench placed just underneath the *Bürgermeister*'s windows. As soon as they had taken up their position there, they all lighted up enormous cigars, the smoke from which was carried through the windows into the apartments of their denouncer; and thus they passed the greater part of the afternoon. On several succeeding days this conduct was repeated, until the *Bürgermeister,* nearly smoked out, went again with his complaint to the colonel.

It may be easily guessed what was the defense of the culprits when they were again summoned to the bar to answer for their fresh infraction of the rule. The colonel laughed at the joke; but from that day forward it was forbidden to the officers not only to walk, but also to *seat themselves* in the street and smoke.

Throughout his youth and during his adult years Bismarck was an excellent swimmer. In letters to his wife he wrote about his bouts of swimming in the Rhine, Danube, and Thiess rivers. His strength and skill as a swimmer were shown in the following incident when he was on military maneuvers with the Pomeranian Uhlans. The people of the little town of Lippehne, where the incident took place, were greatly excited by Bismarck's gallant deed. Local clergymen called upon him in full canonicals to congratulate him on the divine mercy vouchsafed to him. Later the king conferred on him a medal for life-saving—Bismarck's first decoration.[8]

In the afternoon of the 24th of June (1842), Lieutenant von Bismarck rode with Lieutenant von Klitzing and two servants to the Wendel Lake. On arriving there the officers dismounted and stood upon the bridge, while Hildebrandt, his servant, and an Uhlan named Kuhl, rode the horses into the water. Hildebrandt was first in the lake with his horse, but instead of going straight out from the shore the horse persisted in turning round and round. On his rider tugging at the reins to lead him in the proper direction the horse plunged so furiously that Hildebrandt was thrown in deep water. The Uhlan, Kuhl, observing the accident, rode his horse into the lake to his comrade's assistance, but at the spot where he left

8. *Ibid.,* pp. 223–224.

the land the water was deep close up to the shore, and both he and his horse pitched in headlong. In an instant Lieutenant von Bismarck stripped off his tunic, leapt off the bridge, which stood several feet above the water, and after having helped the sinking Uhlan ashore, swam out to the assistance of his own servant, who by this time was quite exhausted. He managed to bring Hildebrandt safely back to land, and then he went into the water again and got the horses ashore, thus saving at one stroke, and at the risk of his own life, the lives of two men and two horses.

17 Weary and Indifferent, Otto Falls into a Tragic Love Affair with Marie von Thadden, a Christian Pietist

"With him I always feel that I am skating on thin ice."

There is a legend that in 1835 the nineteen-year-old Ann Rutledge, sweetheart of the twenty-six-year-old Abraham Lincoln, suddenly died at New Salem, Illinois. For the rest of his days Lincoln was said to have suffered from this tragic loss: he would alternately change from a state of melancholy to boisterous mirth. The twenty-eight-year-old Bismarck was to endure a similar sorrow, although he recovered from the unfortunate affair more easily than the sentimental Lincoln.[9] *It was a turning point in Bismarck's life.*

In 1843, in the midst of his wildest years, Bismarck met Marie von Thadden-Trieglaff, at that time the betrothed of his close friend, Moritz von Blanckenburg. Marie belonged to a circle of Pomeranian nobility with strong religious beliefs. As Pietists they held every word of the Bible to be inspired. Marie was an attractive young lady, tall, powerful, rather buxom, enthusiastically and fervently pious. A religious spirit had shaped her upbringing.

Among the pious gentry of the neighborhood, Bismarck had acquired a reputation as a hard-drinking, hard-riding bachelor with a tendency toward impropriety. He was the "crazy Junker," the "mad Bismarck," who thought "every sin is permissible." Frustrated in his career, he had come to the conclusion that life was "shallow and fruitless." He was a freethinker who looked to Spinoza for guidance. His bizarre behavior was due in large part to his discontent and purposeless existence. In a blind appetite for pleasure he squandered his youth, his mind, and his future.

9. Account contributed by the editor.

"Thus do I drift on the stream of life with nothing to steer by except the inclination of the moment, and I am fairly indifferent as to where the waters may cast me up on the shore."

It was in this skeptical mood that Bismarck underwent the disturbing experiences of a tragic love affair and a religious conversion. A neighbor of the von Thaddens, he met Marie through Moritz von Blanckenburg. Although he regarded the Pomeranian Pietists with contempt, he looked on Moritz as a trusted friend, and Marie attracted him by her wit and charm. Soon he was meeting and debating religious questions with both of them.

Marie was immediately drawn to the tall Junker with close-cropped blond hair, trimmed beard, and gentle voice. The fact that other young women were also dazzled by the cold elegance of Bismarck probably added to his attractiveness for Marie. "His fine carriage, his brilliance, both internal and external, attract me more and more. But when I am with him I always feel that I am skating on thin ice and might go through at any moment." Bismarck may have been a devilish character, but the young lady of impeccable family was fascinated.

It must have been a strange spectacle. The beautiful young girl began to work on the arrogant Junker of the Marshes. She would act like a sister to him and subtly, by degrees, she would conquer his skepticism and agnosticism and bring him to God. It would be a triumph for the Pietist revival. Granted that his views were "unhappy," she had confidence in her ability to convert him to the path of religion.

At first Bismarck pretended indifference. He told Marie frankly that it was impossible for him to endure religion. "How can I believe, seeing that I have no faith? God must either take possession of me Himself, or must instill faith in me without my contributing thereto, and without wish on my part!" He was deeply moved. On one occasion, his face became flushed with excitement, but he could not make up his mind. The complicating factor was that he had fallen in love with Marie. She, too, was in love with him: the "sister" attitude did not suffice. It was a dilemma—engaged to Moritz and in love with Otto. In a garden she solved the problem for the moment in strictly feminine fashion by pinning a blue flower on the coat of her betrothed, blue for the color of faithfulness, and at the same time giving Otto a dark red rose, "the flaming color of love."

Marie and Moritz were married in October 1844. During the festivities there was an evil omen—the rockets that were set off in celebration set fire to the village, and the guests, including Bismarck, had to put out the flames. After the marriage Bismarck continued to visit the young couple, both of whom persisted in their efforts to convert him to the true faith. It was Marie who introduced Bismarck to Johanna von Puttkamer, who was to become his wife. Both women worked energetically to cure Bismarck of his skepticism.

In the autumn of 1846 a strange epidemic swept through East Elbia. Apparently nothing could be done once the disease struck. Marie died on November 11 from inflammation of the brain. For Bismarck it was a shattering personal tragedy. Grieved and tortured, he visited her bedside, where he looked in amazement at her serene countenance. The dying woman and her husband were certain that the separation was only temporary and that they would meet again in the next world. For the first time in fifteen years Bismarck prayed. "This is the first heart that I lose of which I know that it truly beat warmly for me." He never forgot Marie.

From that day on Bismarck accepted prayer and devotion as a part of his life. He would soon write to the father of his intended wife to describe his religious conversion. Marie von Thadden had convinced him that self-control came not through reflection but more positively through faith. He found justification for his own ambitions in the belief in God. In 1851 he was to say: "I do not understand how a man who thinks about himself only, and does not want to know anything about God, can bear a life of contempt and boredom." In 1870 he declared: "If I did not believe in the divine order that this German nation is destined for something good and great, then I would never have taken up the profession of a diplomat."

8

Sibling Loyalty: Otto's Adored Sister, Malwine, Marries Oskar von Arnim-Kröchlensdorff, and Kniephof Becomes Very Lonely after Her Departure

"So, now I live here with father, reading, smoking, and walking."

Malwine Bismarck, called Malle for short, was born in 1827, just twelve years later than Otto. Brother and sister both had fair skin and reddish blonde hair as well as similar likes and dislikes. Between them there developed a close relationship which lasted for the rest of Malwine's life. In 1843, after her confirmation, the sixteen-year-old girl returned to the country to live with her big brother. Left to themselves, with an ill father, brother and sister together ran the house. For Malwine the comfort of her adored brother was of supreme importance: she watched over him as if she were a zealous bride. In his long correspondence with his sister, Bismarck addressed her in such intimate, almost lover's terms as Liebe Kleine, Theure Kleine, Liebe Maldewine, Theureste Kreusa, Madame, *and* Soeur. *Brother and sister were both skeptical eccentrics who loved to mock everyone and everything. There was an intense, secret communion between them.*

In 1844, at the age of seventeen, Otto's beloved Malwine was married to his friend, the gruff, bearded Oskar von Arnim-Kröchlensdorff. Otto's deep regard and tender affection for his only sister are apparent in this letter, in which he complains humorously of an inconsiderate sister who deserted her bachelor brother.[10]

I naturally found the house very lonely after your departure. I sat myself down before the stove, smoked and reflected how unnatural and selfish it is that girls who have brothers, and these besides bachelors, get married without a thought about them, and act as if they were in the world only to carry out their own monstrous whims—a selfishness from which I know our sex, including myself, is happily free.

After realizing the fruitlessness of these reflections, I got up from the green leather chair in which you, Miss—and Oskar used to kiss and whisper, and threw myself headlong into the election turmoil, from which I returned convinced that five votes for a certainty, and two with some lukewarmness, were willing to support me, while four were for Krug, sixteen to eighteen for Arnim, and twelve to fifteen for Alvensleben, so that I preferred to withdraw. So now I live here with father, reading, smoking, and walking. I help him to eat lampreys, and sometimes play a little comedy with him, which he chooses to call fox-hunting: thus we go out in heavy rain or, as now, in six degrees of frost, with Ihle, Bellin, and Carl, and with every sportsmanlike precaution, noiselessly, and, watching carefully the direction of the wind, surround a pine coppice in which we all, and perhaps also father, are absolutely convinced that there is no living thing except some old woman gathering sticks. Then Ihle, Carl, and two dogs go through the

10. Quoted in William Jacks, *The Life of Prince Bismarck* (Glasgow, 1899), pp. 17–21.

coppice, emitting, especially Ihle, the most singular and terrible cries; the father like a statue stands attentive and ready with his gun, exactly as if he expected to see some animal, until Ihle shouts "Bu, la, la, he, he, seize, hah, hah!" in the most extraordinary gutturals close to him. Then the father asks me quite gravely whether I have not seen anything, and I reply, in a tone of the most naturally feigned astonishment, "No, absolutely nothing." Then we go on, abusing the weather, to another coppice in which Ihle, with a most naturally acted certainty, as usual proclaims a probable abundance of game, and plays *dal segno;* so it goes on for three or four hours, without father, Ihle, or Fingal seeming for a moment to allow their passion to cool. Besides, we visit the orange house twice daily, the sheepfold once, and the four barometers in the room hourly. We set the indicator of the weather glass, and since the weather has been bright we have got the clocks into such exact accord with the sun that only the one on the bookcase gives one stroke behind when the others have struck *a tempo*. Charles the Fifth was a stupid fellow.*

You can understand that with such manifold occupations I have only little time for visiting the clergymen, and as they have no votes in the county council election, I have not been to see them at all; it was impossible.

Bellin for the last three days is full of a journey which he made to Stendal, and of the stage coach which he missed.

Ice is in the Elbe; the wind is east-south-east; the newest thermometer from Berlin shows 8 degrees, the barometer 28·8 with a rising tendency.

I tell you all this to give you an example how you might write more in your letters to father of the little details of your life. These give him the greatest possible entertainment: who has been to visit you and the Curts, whom you visit, what you have eaten, how the horses are doing, how your servants are behaving, whether the doors creak, and the windows fit well, in short, facts, *facta.*

Further, he cannot bear being called *papa;* he does not like the term; *avis au lecteur*. Antonie wrote him a really fine letter on his birthday, and gave him a green purse, at which he was very much touched, and replied in two sheets' length. The Rohrs lately drove

* This refers to a passage in the life of Charles V.—"He was particularly curious with regard to the construction of clocks and watches, and having found, after repeated trials, that he could not bring any two of them exactly alike, he reflected, it is said, with a mixture of surprise and regret on his own folly in having bestowed so much time and labor on the more vain attempt to bring mankind to a precise uniformity of sentiment regarding the intricate and mysterious doctrines of religion."—*History of Charles V*, by Wm. Robertson, D.D., Book XII.

through here without letting us know anything about it, after feeding for two hours in the ale house at Hohen-Göhren, and sitting in the bar with wife and children, with ten peasants who were smoking. Bellin asserts that they are annoyed with us. That would be hard, as it would interfere with my dearest intercourse. Father sends his kindest regards, and follows me soon to Pomerania. He thinks about Christmas; there is a *cafe dansant* at Genthin the day after to-morrow, which *en passant* I will visit in order to have a shot at least at the old county councillor, and to take leave of this district for four months at all events. I have made the acquaintance of ——. There are moments when she is really beautiful, but she will soon lose the tint and become red. I was in love with her for four and twenty hours. Hearty regards to Oskar, and farewell, my angel; don't hang the bride's dog by the tail, and commend me to the Curts. If you are not in A—— on the 8th, then may—*à tantôt.*

For ever your devoted, BISMARCK

19

The "Monster" of Kniephof, Seeking Parental Approval for His Marriage to Johanna von Puttkamer, Sends a Masterly Letter, Classic in its Diplomacy, to Her Pious Father

"The only security I offer for the welfare of your daughter lies in my prayer for God's blessing."

Johanna von Puttkamer was not a radiant beauty: she was short, dark, and slight and Italian in type. Bismarck, now thirty and aware that the days of his adventurous youth were over, decided that Johanna was to be his wife. But it was not easy to win the girl whose parental home in Reinfeld, Further Pomerania, was governed by deep piety. Bismarck's reputation as a kind of monster was such that this family scarcely could accept so bizarre a character. But this did not deter the persistent Junker. He made his declaration and was immediately accepted, but Johanna's consent was qualified by the need for the approval of her parents.

Bismarck's letter to Johanna's father, Heinrich von Puttkamer, reveals the shrewd art of the born diplomat.[11] *It was carefully calculated to suit the piety of the recipient.*

11. *The Love Letters of Bismarck,* ed. and trans. by C. T. Lewis (New York and London, 1901), pp. 3–8.

P. A. TRUCHOT.
Hôtel de Prusse, Stettin.
(Not dated: written about the end of December, 1846.)

To Herr von Puttkamer:

MOST HONORED SIR,—I begin this communication by indicating its content in the first sentence—it is a request for the highest thing you can dispose of in this world, the hand of your daughter. I do not conceal from myself the fact that I appear presumptuous when I, whom you have come to know only recently and through a few meetings, claim the strongest proof of confidence which you can give to any man. I know, however, that even irrespective of all obstacles in space and time which can increase your difficulty in forming an opinion of me, through my own efforts I can never be in a position to give you such guarantees for the future that they would, from your point of view, justify intrusting me with an object so precious, unless you supplement by trust in God that which trust in human beings cannot supply. All that I can do is to give you information about myself with absolute candor, so far as I have come to understand myself. It will be easy for you to get reports from others in regard to my public conduct; I content myself, therefore, with an account of what underlay that—my inner life, and especially my relations to Christianity. To do that I must take a start far back.

In earliest childhood I was estranged from my parents' house, and at no time became entirely at home there again and my education from the beginning was conducted on the assumption that everything is subordinate to the cultivation of the intelligence and the early acquisition of positive sciences. After a course of religious teaching irregularly attended and not comprehended, I had at the time of my confirmation by Schleiermacher, on my sixteenth birthday, no belief other than a bare deism, which was not long free from pantheistic elements. It was at about this time that I, not through indifference, but after mature consideration, ceased to pray every evening, as I had been in the habit of doing since childhood; because prayer seemed inconsistent with my view of God's nature; saying to myself, either God Himself, being omnipresent, is the cause of everything—even of every thought and volition of mine—and so in a sense offers prayers to Himself through me, or, if my will is independent of God's will, it implies arrogance and a doubt as to the inflexibility as well as the perfection of the divine determination to believe that it can be influenced by human appeals. When not quite seventeen years old I went to Göttingen University. During the next eight years I seldom saw the home of my parents; my father indulgently refrained from interference; my mother censured me from far away when I neglected my studies and professional work, probably in the conviction that she must leave the rest to guidance from above: with this exception I was literally cut off from the counsel and instruction of others. In this period, when studies which ambition at times led me to prosecute zealously—or emptiness and satiety, the inevitable companions of my way of living—brought me nearer to the real meaning of life and eternity, it was in old-world philosophies, uncomprehended writings of Hegel, and particularly in Spinoza's seeming mathematical clearness, that I sought for peace of mind: in that which the human understanding cannot comprehend. But it was loneliness that first led me to reflect on these things persistently, when I went to Kniephof, after my mother's death, five or six years ago. Though at first my views did not materially change at Kniephof, yet conscience began to be more audible in the solitude, and to represent that many a thing was wrong which I had before regarded as permissible. Yet my struggle for insight was still confined to the circle of the understanding, and led me, while reading such writings as those of Strauss, Feuerbach, and Bruno Bauer, only deeper into the blind alley of doubt.

I was firmly convinced that God has denied to man the possibility of true knowledge; that it is presumption to claim to understand the will and plans of the Lord of the World; that the individual must await in submission the judgment that his Creator will pass upon him in death, and that the will of God becomes known to us on earth solely through conscience, which He has given us as a special organ for feeling our way through the gloom of the world. That I found no peace in these views I need not say. Many an hour have I spent in disconsolate depression, thinking that my existence and that of others is purposeless and unprofitable—perchance only a casual product of creation, coming and going like dust from rolling wheels.

About four years ago I came into close companionship, for the first time since my school-days, with Moritz Blanckenburg, and found in him, what I had never had till then in my life, a friend; but the warm zeal of his love strove in vain to give me by persuasion and discussion what I lacked—faith. But through Moritz I made acquaintance with the Trieglaff family and the social circle around it, and found in it people who made me ashamed that, with the scanty light of my understanding, I had undertaken to investigate things which such superior intellects accepted as true and holy with childlike trust. I saw that the members of this circle were, in their outward life, almost perfect models of what I wished to be. That confidence and peace dwelt in them did not surprise me, for

I had never doubted that these were companions of belief; but belief cannot be had for the asking, and I thought I must wait submissively to see whether it would come to me. I soon felt at home in that circle, and was conscious of a satisfaction that I had not before experienced—a family life that included me, almost a home.

I was meanwhile brought into contact with certain events in which I was not an active participant, and which, as other people's secrets, I cannot communicate to you, but which stirred me deeply. Their practical result was that the consciousness of the shallowness and worthlessness of my aim in life became more vivid than ever. Through the advice of others, and through my own impulse, I was brought to the point of reading the Scriptures more consecutively and with resolute restraint, sometimes, of my own judgment. That which stirred within me came to life when the news of the fatal illness of our late friend in Cardemin tore the first ardent prayer from my heart, without subtle questionings as to its reasonableness. God did not grant my prayer on that occasion; neither did He utterly reject it, for I have never again lost the capacity to bring my requests to Him, and I feel within me, if not peace, at least confidence and courage such as I never knew before.

I do not know what value you will attach to this emotion, which my heart has felt for only two months; I only hope that it may not be lost, whatever your decision in regard to me may be—a hope of which I could give you no better assurance than by undeviating frankness and loyalty in that which I have now disclosed to you, and to no one else hitherto, with the conviction that God favors the sincere.

I refrain from any assurance of my feelings and purposes with reference to your daughter, for the step I am taking speaks of them louder and more eloquently than words can. So, too, no promises for the future would be of service to you, since you know the untrustworthiness of the human heart better than I, and the only security I offer for the welfare of your daughter lies in my prayer for God's blessing. As a matter of history I would only observe that, after I had seen Fräulein Johanna repeatedly in Cardemin, after the trip we made together this summer, I have only been in doubt as to whether the attainment of my desires would be reconciliable with the happiness and peace of your daughter, and whether my self-confidence was not greater than my ability when I believed that she could find in me what she would have a right to look for in her husband. Very recently, however, together with my reliance on God's grace, the resolution which I now carry out has also become fixed in me, and I kept silent when I saw you in Zimmerhausen only because I had more to say than I could express in conversation. In view of the importance of the matter and the great sacrifice which it will involve for you and your wife in separation from your daughter, I can scarcely hope that you will give a favorable decision at once, and only beg that you will not refuse me an opportunity for explanation upon any considerations which might dispose you to reject my suit, before you utter a positive refusal.

There is doubtless a great deal that I have not said, or not said fully enough, in this letter, and I am, of course, ready to give you exact and faithful information as to everything you may desire to know; I think I have told what is most important.

I beg you to convey to your wife my respectful compliments, and to accept kindly the assurance of my love and esteem.

BISMARCK

Address: Schönhausen, near Fischbek-on-the-Elbe

20 The "Vassal" of Schönhausen Expresses His Love for His Lady Fair

"How little you know the world, my heart!"

After Johanna's father gave his somewhat reluctant consent, Bismarck and Johanna became formally engaged. There followed an exchange of love letters between the happy couple, in which the squire of Schönhausen, not yet thirty-two, revealed a new maturity of mind and purpose.[12] *He was intrigued by the quiet and loyal Johanna, who seemd to neutralize his volcanic temperament. Delighted that he had won the hand of a beloved partner, he lectured her gently as if she were a young child. The days of his tempestuous youth were over. The marriage was celebrated on June 28, 1847.*

SCHÖNHAUSEN, *February* 21, 1847

JOHANNA, MY OR OUR BETTER HALF!—I received your letter of the 18th today, and first I express my deep-felt thanks for the cordial love in it that touches me. Love knows no thanks and expects none, someone says. Thanks is a cold word. Never mind, I feel gratitude towards you, and yet love you. This afternoon I received your letter, and could not immediately sit down to reply to you, because I had to comply with a tiresome invitation, and had postponed my departure until five in order to get the mail first. I have just come back, cold, wet, and irritated by the stupid people, but I must still write a few lines today.

12. *Ibid.*, pp. 46–50.

I answer your letter point by point. To be dyke-captain is certainly very unfortunate this year, when one has a *fiancée* seventy miles away. Since last Sunday we have had thawing weather, and for several days we have expected the river to break up, but it is quiet yet. A few hours ago I received a message by courier saying that the ice at Dresden and in Bohemia has been moving for two days—a dangerous thing, when it breaks up above earlier than here, which may cause us much trouble. Tomorrow, or Tuesday at latest, the ice-drive must extend to this point. A fortnight is the shortest period in which the performance can be finished; sometimes it lasts six, usually three to four weeks. My sentimental tirades in relation to poor people and expenses of the journey will apparently remain empty phrases, and my virtue will not be put to the test, since the service will probably not leave me free much before the middle of March, without regard to possible postponements. At any rate, I will endeavor to have the meeting of the equestrian order, which was set for the 20th, held before that time.

Tell me, my angel—you write so earnestly about postage-scruples—am I or are you the Pomeranian who does not understand a joke? Do you really believe it concerns me how much postage a letter costs?—that I should write one less if it were ten times as much? This idea makes me uncommonly merry, if you meant it seriously, as by the tone I almost believe you did; and if I could draw caricatures I would depict my profile on the margin more sarcastic-sardonic-ironic-satiric than you have ever seen it. You remember, perhaps, that in Zimmerhausen I wondered at your courage in accepting me, a half-stranger, in the character I still sustain; but that you know me so little that you regard me, a born spendthrift, as avaricious, shows that you have surrendered yourself in blind trust, in trust that can alone be inspired by a love for which I kiss your hands and feet. How little you know the world, my heart!

Why do you so lament your last letter? I found nothing in it that was not dear to me, or could have been dearer. And, were it otherwise, where should you in future find a breast on which to disburden your own of that which oppresses it, if not with me? Who is more bound and entitled to share suffering and anxiety with you, bear your sicknesses, your faults, than I who have obeyed my impulse to do this, voluntarily, without being compelled to it by the obligation of relationship or other duty? You had a woman friend with whom you could take refuge at all times, by whom you were never repulsed. Do you miss her in this way in an exigency? My dear, dear Johanna, must I tell you once more that I love you; *sans phrase,* that we ought to share with each other joy and suffering—I your suffering and you mine; that we are not united for the sake of showing and sharing with each other only that which gives pleasure; but that you may pour out your heart at all times to me and I to you, whatever it may contain; that I must and will bear your sorrows, your thoughts, your naughtinesses, if you have any, and love you as you are—not as you ought to be or might be? Make me serviceable, use me for what purpose you will, ill-treat me without and within, if you have the wish to do so. I am there for that purpose, at your disposal; but never be embarrassed in any way with me. Trust me unreservedly, in the conviction that I accept everything that comes from you with profound love, whether it be glad or patient. Do not keep your gloomy thoughts for yourself while you look on me with cheerful brow and merry eyes, but share with me in word and look what you have in your heart, whether it be blessing or sorrow. Never be faint-hearted with me, and if anything in yourself appears to you indiscreet, sinful, depressing, reflect that everything of that kind is present in me a thousand times more, and that I am saturated with it far too thoroughly and deeply to look on such things with contempt when seen in others, or to become aware of them in you otherwise than with love, even if not always with patience. Look upon us as mutual father-confessors; as more than that, since we, according to the Scripture, are to be "one flesh."

The 22d, morning

I have just been abruptly torn from sweetest dreams to be told that the ice is beginning to move—in itself a very favorable bit of news. The water is rising an inch every hour, and will probably continue at that rate and somewhat slower, if no ice-pack ensues, until it stands ten or twelve feet higher than at present. How long it will then remain at such a height—on that it depends when I shall see you. For I must see you at last as soon as the Elbe allows me to go, in spite of the Diet of the Circle and everything: otherwise your image will grow fainter and fainter until it will be invisible. For the meeting of the equestrian order, however, I must be here. I can only write a few lines while the horses are saddled, and that makes me heartily sorry, since I was so full of instruction last evening that today I should have liked to give you a good stroking until you purred comfortably; but who knows when I can write again in the next few days? And so I will not keep this letter, though it is short. Do not take pains to become a stiff, smooth hedge from the outset; it can be strong and green only on condition that it grows up unrestrained and is trimmed down to the quick by the gardener—and that I shall certainly not prevail on my heart to do. Rather have the free growth of the wild rose: the hateful moss and the too-sharp thorns we shall both endeavor to remove without pain, or at least carefully. Farewell; the cakes of ice are playing the "Pappenheim March" as a summons to me, and the chorus of mounted peasants is singing "Lively, Comrades!" Why do the ice blocks not really do it? How beautiful that would be, and how poetical! It is to me like a breath of fresh life that this tiresome waiting is past, and the affair begins to move. To-night "I stand in the dark midnight," and you "To the Lord devoutly pray for your dearest far away." *Je t'embrasse.* Your vassal.

B.

SCHÖNHAUSEN, *February* 23, 1847

MY ANGEL!—I shall not send this letter on its way tomorrow, it's true, but I do want to make use of the few unoccupied minutes left to me to satisfy the need I am conscious of every hour, to communicate with you, and forthwith to compose a "Sunday letter" to you once more. Today I have been "on the move" all day long. "The Moorish king rode up and down," unfortunately not "through Granada's royal town," but between Havelberg and Jerichow, on foot, in a carriage, and on horseback, and got mighty cold doing so—because, after the warm weather of the last few days, I had not made the slightest preparation to encounter five degrees below freezing, with a cutting north wind, and was too much in haste or too lazy to mount the stairs again when I noticed the fresh air. During the night it had been quite endurable and superb moonlight. A beautiful spectacle it was, too, when the great fields of ice first set themselves massively in motion, with explosions like cannon-shots, shattering themselves against one another; they rear, shoving over and under each other; they pile up house-high, and sometimes build dams obliquely across the Elbe, in front of which the pent stream rises until it breaks through them with rage. Now are they all broken to pieces in the battle—the giants—and the water very thickly covered with ice-cakes, the largest of which measures several square rods, which it bears out to the free sea like shattered chains, with grumbling, clashing noises. This will go on so for about three days more, until the ice that comes from Bohemia, which passed the bridge at Dresden several days ago, has gone by. (The danger is that the ice-cakes by jamming together may make a dam, and the stream rise in front of this—often ten to fifteen feet in a few hours.) Then comes the freshet from the mountains which floods the bed of the Elbe, often a mile in width, and is dangerous in itself, owing to its volume. How long that is to last we cannot tell beforehand. The prevailing cold weather, combined with the contrary sea wind, will certainly retard it. It may easily last so long that it will not be worth while to go to Reinfeld before the 20th. If only eight days should be left me, would you have me undertake it, nevertheless?—or will you wait to have me without interruption after the 20th, or perhaps 18th? . . .

B.

21

Start of a Political Career: Bismarck Comes to the Prussian States General as a Delegate in 1847 and Straightway Reveals His Conservatism by Defending the Christian Monarchy

"I allow I am full of prejudices, which . . . I have sucked in with my mother's milk."

In 1840 the old King Frederick William III died and was succeeded by his son, Frederick William IV. Although a man of great learning and noble character, Frederick William IV had little understanding of the political currents of his day. The beginning of the railway system in Prussia made it necessary for him to call the States General in early 1847 to give its approval to a new loan. Bismarck came to this assembly as a substitute for a member who had become ill. The young Pomeranian Junker soon gave evidence of a deeply engrained conservative sentiment. He expressed his indignation at the idea that the Prussian people had earned constitutional government. He saw no parallel with England's experience: "We possess a crown whose rights are actually unlimited, a crown held by the grace not of the people but of God." His longest speech, in defense of the Christian monarchy, was part of a discussion to increase the privileges of the Jews.[13]

I am no enemy of the Jews; if they become my enemies I will forgive them. Under certain circumstances I love them; I am ready to grant them all rights but that of holding the magisterial office in a Christian state. This they now claim; they demand to become *Landrat,* general, minister, yes even, under circumstances, minister of religion and education. I allow that I am full of prejudices, which, as I have said, I have sucked in with my mother's milk; I

13. Quoted in James Wycliffe Headlam, *Bismarck and the Foundations of the German Empire* (New York and London, 1899), pp. 41–42.

cannot argue them away; for if I think of a Jew face to face with me as a representative of the king's sacred Majesty, and I have to obey him, I must confess that I should feel myself deeply broken and depressed; the sincere self-respect with which I now attempt to fulfill my duties towards the state would leave me. I share these feelings with the mass of the lower strata of the people, and I am not ashamed of their society. . . .

It is as old as every European state; it is the ground in which they have taken root; no state has a secure existence unless it has a religious foundation. For me, the words, "by the Grace of God," which Christian rulers add to their name, are no empty phrase; I see in them a confession that the princes desire to wield the scepter which God has given them according to the will of God on earth. As the will of God I can only recognize that which has been revealed in the Christian Gospel—I believe that the realization of Christian teaching is the end of the state; I do not believe that we shall more nearly approach this end by the help of the Jews. . . . If we withdraw this foundation, we retain in a state nothing but an accidental aggregate of rights, a kind of bulwark against the war of all against all, which ancient philosophy has assumed. Therefore, gentlemen, do not let us spoil the people of their Christianity; do not let us take from them the belief that our legislation is drawn from the well of Christianity, and that the state aims at the realization of Christianity even if it does not attain its end.

22 The Revolution of 1848: Arming His Peasants with Pitchforks and Knives, an Aroused Country Squire Marches on Berlin to Rescue His King from the Villains on the Barricades

"Deeply grieved, I returned to Schönhausen."

When, on March 18, 1848, Bismarck received news of the outbreak of revolution, his first reaction was of uncontrolled fury. He rallied his peasants and hurried off to Berlin. Here he found virtually everyone, including the Prussian guards bivouacked in the streets, unimpressed by his plans. He was barred from entering the castle.

The next day he was off to Potsdam to study the situation. William, brother of the king and heir to the throne, was in hiding. Bismarck, therefore, approached the Princess Augusta and urged her to seize the regency in the name of her son, Frederick William, who was still a minor. Augusta had her own ideas on the subject: she wanted no help from Bismarck and rebuffed him. Thus began the deadly hatred between the two that ended only with death. Here is Bismarck's picture of the stormy days of 1848.[14]

I received the first intelligence of the events of March 18 and 19, 1848, while staying with my neighbor, Count Wartensleben, at Karow, whither ladies from Berlin had fled for refuge. At the first moment I was not so much alive to the political range of what was going on as filled with bitterness at the massacre of our soldiers in the streets. Politically, I thought the king would soon be master of the situation if only he were free; I saw that the first thing to be done was to liberate him, as he was said to be in the power of the insurgents.

On the 20th I was told by the peasants at Schönhausen that a deputation had arrived from Tangermünde with a demand that the black, red, and gold flag should be hoisted on the tower, as had already been done in the above-named town; threatening, in case of refusal, to visit us again with reinforcements. I asked the peasants if they were willing to defend themselves. They replied with a unanimous and brisk "Yes," and I advised them to drive the townspeople out of the village; which was attended to, the women zealously cooperating. I then had a white banner with a black cross in the shape of the Iron Cross, which happened to be in the church, hoisted on the tower, and ascertained what supply of weapons and ammunition was available in the village, when about fifty peasants' fowling-pieces came to light. Including ancient specimens, I myself possessed some twenty more, and had powder fetched by mounted messengers from Jerichow and Rathenow. Next, accompanied by my wife, I went the round of the villages and found the peasants already eager to march to the help of the king in Berlin. Especially enthusiastic was an old dyke-surveyor named Krause of Neuermark, who had been a sergeant in my father's regiment of carabineers. Only my next-door neighbor sympathized with the Berlin movement, accused me of hurling a firebrand into the country, and declared that if the peasants really prepared to march off, he would come forward and dissuade them. I replied, "You know that I am a quiet man, but if you do that I shall shoot you." "I am sure you won't," said he. "I give you my word of honor that I will," I replied, "and you know that I keep my word: so drop that."

14. *Bismarck: The Man and the Statesman (Reflections and Reminiscences)*, trans. by A. J. Butler (New York and London, 1897), I, 22–29.

I immediately went quite alone to Potsdam, where, in the railway station, I saw Herr von Bodelschwingh, who up to the 19th had been Minister of the Interior. It was plain that he had no desire to be seen in conversation with me, the reactionary. He returned my greeting in French, with the words, "Do not speak to me." "The peasants are rising in our part," I replied. "For the king?" "Yes." "That rope-dancer!" said he, pressing his hands to his eyes while the tears stood in them. In town itself I found a bivouac of the footguard among the trees adjoining the garrison church. I spoke to these men and found them enraged at the order to retire, and eager for more fighting. All the way back along the canal I was followed by civilians with the look of spies, who had attempted to parley with the troops, and used threatening language towards me. I had four rounds of ammunition in my pocket, but had no need to use them. I dismounted at the residence of my friend Roon, who, as governor to Prince Frederick Charles, occupied some rooms in the castle; and visited in the *"Deutsches Haus"* General von Möllendorf, whom I found still stiff from the treatment he had suffered when negotiating with the insurgents, and General von Prittwitz, who had been in command in Berlin. I described to them the present temper of the country people; they in return gave me some particulars as to what had happened up to the morning of the 19th. What they had to relate, and the later information which came from Berlin, could only strengthen my belief that the king was not free.

Prittwitz, who was older than I, and judged more calmly, said: "Send us none of your peasants, we don't want them. We have quite enough soldiers. Rather send us potatoes and corn, perhaps money too, for I do not know whether the maintenance and pay of the troops will be sufficiently provided for. If auxiliaries came up I should receive, and should have to carry out, an order from Berlin to drive them back." "Then fetch the king away," I said. He replied: "There will be no great difficulty about that; I am strong enough to take Berlin, but that means more fighting. What can we do after the king has commanded us to play the part of the vanquished? I cannot attack without orders."

In this condition of affairs I hit upon the idea of obtaining from another quarter a command to act, which could not be expected from the king, who was not free, and tried to get at the prince of Prussia. Referred to the princess, whose consent thereto was necessary, I called upon her in order to discover the whereabouts of her consort, who, as I subsequently discovered, was on the Pfaueninsel. She received me in a servant's room on the *entresol,* sitting on a wooden chair. She refused the information I asked for, and declared, in a state of violent excitement, that it was her duty to guard the rights of her son. What she said rested on the supposition that the king and her husband could not maintain their position, and naturally led to the conclusion that she meant to be regent during the minority of her son. In order to obtain the cooperation of the Right in the Chambers to this end, formal overtures had been made to me by George von Vincke. As I could not get at the prince of Prussia, I tried my luck with Prince Frederick Charles, representing to him how necessary it was that the royal house should remain in touch with the army, and, if his Majesty were not free, should act in the cause without the king's command. He replied, in a state of lively agitation, that however much my idea might appeal to him, he nevertheless felt himself too young to carry it out, and could not follow the example of those students who meddled with politics, for all he was no older than they. I then determined to attempt to get at the king.

Prince Charles gave me at the palace at Potsdam, by way of passport and credentials, the following open letter: "The bearer, with whom I am well acquainted, has the commission from me to inquire *personally* as to the health of his Majesty, my most gracious brother, and to bring me back word for what reason I have had *no* answer for thirty hours to the repeated inquiries I have written in my own hand, whether I ought not to come to Berlin."

CHARLES, Prince of Prussia

Potsdam: March 21, 1848, 1 P.M.

I hastened to Berlin. Being known, since the days of the United Diet, to many people by sight, I considered it advisable to shave my beard and to put on a broad-brimmed hat with a colored cockade. As I hoped for an audience I was in dress clothes. At the exit of the railway station a collecting box was set up, inviting contributions on behalf of those fighting on the barricades, and beside it stood a lanky civic champion with a musket on his shoulder. A cousin of mine, whom I had encountered on leaving the train, took out his purse. "You surely are not going to give anything for those murderers?" said I; adding, in reply to the warning look he gave me, "Surely you are not afraid of that lout?" I had already recognized the sentinel for Meier, of the Supreme Court of Justice, a friend of mine, who, on hearing the word "lout," turned round furiously and then exclaimed, "Gad's my life, Bismarck! What a sight you look! Here's a pretty dirty job!"

The civic guard at the palace asked me what I wanted there. On my replying that I had to deliver a letter to the king from Prince

Charles, the sentinel looked suspiciously at me and said that could not be so, as the prince was with the king at that minute. He must therefore have set off from Potsdam before me. The guard asked to see the letter which I had; I showed it, as it was open and the contents harmless, and I was allowed to go, but not into the palace. At a window on the ground-floor of the Hotel Meinhard sat a doctor whom I knew, so I joined him. There I wrote to the king what I wanted to say to him. I went with the letter to Prince Boguslaw-Radziwill, who had the entrée to the court and could hand it to the king. In this letter I said, among other things, that the revolution was confined to the great cities, and that the king would be master in the country as soon as ever he left Berlin. The king gave me no reply, but told me later that this letter, badly written on bad paper, had been carefully preserved by him as the first token of sympathy which he received at that time.

As I went about the streets to observe the traces of the contest, some unknown person whispered in my ear: "Are you aware that you are being followed?" In Unter den Linden another unknown whispered to me: "Come along with me." I followed him into the Kleine Mauerstrasse, where he said: "Be off, or you will be arrested." "Do you know me?" I asked. "Yes," he replied, "you are Herr von Bismarck." I have never discovered from what quarter danger threatened me, or from whom the warning came. The unknown quitted me at once. A street boy bawled out after me, "Look, there goes another Frenchy!" an expression of which I have been sundry times reminded by later investigators. My long "goatee," which alone had escaped the razor, my slouch hat and dress suit, had made the youngsters take me for an exotic product. The streets were empty, no carriage was visible, and the only pedestrians were some groups of men wearing blouses and carrying banners, one of which, in the Friedrichstrasse, was escorting a laurel-crowned hero of the barricades to some ovation or other.

The same day I returned to Potsdam—not because of the warning, but because in Berlin I found no ground on which to operate—and consulted once more with Generals Möllendorf and Prittwitz as to the possibility of independent action. "How shall we set about it?" said Prittwitz. I was sitting by the open piano, and began to strum the infantry charging-march. Möllendorf, who was stiff with his wounds, fell upon my neck with tears in his eyes, and exclaimed, "If you could only manage that for us!" "I cannot," I replied, "but if you do it without orders, what can happen to you? The country will thank you, and ultimately the king too." "Then," said Prittwitz, "can you get me any certainty that Wrangel and Hedemann will go along with us? We cannot allow dissension as well as insubordination to enter the army." I promised to manage that; I promised to go to Magdeburg myself, and to send a confidential man to Stettin, in order to sound both the commanding generals. From Stettin came this message from General von Wrangel: "Whatever Prittwitz does I will do also." I myself was less fortunate at Magdeburg. First of all, I got access to General von Hedemann's aide-de-camp, a young major to whom I explained my errand and who expressed his sympathy. In a short time, however, he came to me at the inn, and begged me to depart immediately in order to save myself unpleasantness, and to prevent the old general from making a fool of himself, as it was his intention to have me arrested for high treason.

Herr von Bonin, who was then chief president, and the highest authority in the province, had issued a proclamation to the following effect: "A revolution has broken out in Berlin. I will take up a position above parties." This "pillar of the monarchy" was subsequently a minister, and filled high and influential positions. General Hedemann belonged to the Humboldt clique.

On my return to Schönhausen I tried to make the peasants understand that an armed expedition to Berlin was not feasible, and thereby incurred the suspicion of having been infected by the revolutionary mania in Berlin. I therefore made a proposal to them, which was accepted, that a deputation from Schönhausen and the other villages should set off with me to Potsdam to see for themselves, and to speak to General von Prittwitz, and perhaps to the prince of Prussia also. On the 25th, when we reached the Potsdam station, the king had just arrived there, and been favorably received by a great mob of people. I said to my rustic companions: "There is the king. I will present you; speak to him." They, however, nervously declined the proposition, and speedily retired to the back of the crowd. I greeted the king respectfully; he acknowledged the salute without recognizing me, and drove to the palace. I followed him, and there heard the address which he delivered to the officers of the guard in the Marble Saloon. At the words "I have never been freer or more secure than when under the protection of my citizens," there arose a murmuring and the clash of sabers in their sheaths, such as no king of Prussia in the midst of his officers had ever heard before, and, I hope, will ever hear again.

Deeply grieved, I returned to Schönhausen.

23

Attacked as the "People's Enemy," Bismarck Stands for Election in a Tumultuous Campaign and Wins a Seat in the Prussian Second Chamber, August 7, 1849 [15]

"Herr von Bismarck, don't venture out, they will assault you."

After Frederick William refused the imperial crown, reaction in Prussia and the whole of Germany was soon in full swing. Universal suffrage was abolished in Prussia, to be replaced by a three-class ballot (Drei-Klassen-Wahlrecht), *in which the voters were classified in three groups according to the amount of taxes they paid. Under such circumstances Bismarck was elected to a seat in the new Chamber, but the election was not without incident.*

The attitude which Bismarck took up at this time was severely criticized, as if he were opposed to German unity; and he was accused of looking at things from an "antediluvian standpoint," of being a "feudal Junker," guided by medieval prejudices, and out of touch with the moving spirit of the times. It is easy to understand how those who, fighting for the cause of popular freedom and people's sovereignty, and listening to his vigorous defense of the "divine right of the sovereign," and of the duty of submitting to authority, should regard him in this light; but a thoughtful perusal of his utterances clearly shows that even then he was not opposed to unity, indeed the reverse, but that he had determined to have a powerful Prussia as the heart of that union to fill the arteries of the German national body, a policy which he gradually made clear and unmistakable, and which he carried to such a triumphant issue in the Palace of Versailles on the memorable 18th January, 1871.

Meantime, the elections were ordered under a new electoral law, by which the electors were divided into three classes, according to the taxes paid, and the voting was open. Bismarck again offered himself as a candidate, and although he was elected, his attitude had sorely displeased many of the Rathenow electors, and he had a very stormy experience.

After addressing a large public meeting, when he explained the motives which guided his votes, and defended the measures of the government, which he contended were for the well-being of

15. Jacks, *op. cit.*, pp. 91–92.

Prussia, many of the leading citizens expressed their thanks and acknowledgments, but a large and threatening crowd surrounded the door, while cries of "reactionary Junker" and "People's enemy" rent the air.

"Boldly attacked, they will soon withdraw," said Bismarck, and took hold of the door handle to go out, when Master-Chimney-sweep Wolf, not black today, but white as a ghost, rushed in from the street and whispered to Bismarck, "Herr von Bismarck, don't venture out, they will assault you." "Oh, don't mind the blusterers," said Bismarck, and stepped unconcernedly into the street into the midst of the excited multitude. Master Wolf and the town clerk Noak, courageously walked one on each side of him through the masses of shouting and raging people to the *Deutsches Haus* Inn, where he had taken up his quarters. When, however, shortly afterwards, he came out of the inn and took his place in the carriage of Squire von Steckow, to drive with him to his country house, the noise and tumult had greatly increased. Several stones flew over Bismarck's head, but a heavy one was sent into the carriage and wounded him in the left arm. Smarting with pain, and burning with indignation, he seized the stone, and springing to his full height, sent it thundering back amongst the mob, who quickly sprang to right and left, pretty well cowed.

However, Bismarck was elected in spite of these outbursts, and took his seat in the Second Chamber, which met on the 7th August, 1849, and which proceeded to consider the Prussian constitution as projected on the 5th December of the previous year, and was also occupied with the German as distinguished from the Prussian question.

24 The Bismarcks Build a Family: An Impatient Husband Pines in Berlin for His Bride, Proudly Announces the Birth of His First Male Child, and Complains of the Perils of Fatherhood

"I must have you here, my angel. What are we married for?"

In the summer of 1849 Johanna joined her parents at their home in Reinfeld. Bismarck, alone in Berlin, rented a furnished room, where he complained of his landlady's four screaming children in the house and too many bedbugs in his room. Johanna urged him to take up permanent quarters with her in Reinfeld, but he was opposed to that. While in Berlin he wrote her tender letters of solicitude and love.[16] *Pregnant with her second child (Marie von Bismarck, the first child, was born in 1848), Johanna came to Berlin to share a ground-floor flat in the Behrenstrasse.*

BERLIN, Sunday
(Postmarked *September* 10, 1849)

DEAREST NANNIE,—I have just found your charming letter, much to my delight, for already the time was beginning to hang heavily on my hands, and I was getting jealous of Hans, who meanwhile had a letter from mother in which she is again hard on me; but that is no matter—she will come back to Schönhausen, anyway. I am physically well, and probably God will not allow my spirits to fail. Day before yesterday I wrote you two letters, Nos. 2 and 3; since then I have nothing new to tell you, only the old news that I love you very much, and that, therefore, I cannot let you remain at Reinfeld, much as it grieves me for your dear parents' sake. *Le vin est tiré, il faut le boire*—he who gives another man his daughter in marriage must accustom himself, withal, to the fact that she is married; to have your confinement at Reinfeld would be a semi-divorce; I neither can, nor will, be so long without my Nan; we are separated often enough as it is. About the end of this month I shall take you away either from Reinfeld or from Zimmerhausen, that is certain, if God wills. . . . Early this morning Malle and I heard Büchsel; he preached about the ten lepers, of whom only one showed gratitude. Very pretty, if he would only prepare himself somewhat; he always talks out of his sleeve; but his sermon made me deeply realize once more how ungrateful we are towards God. However, I am never satisfied with the singing of the Protestant congregations; I like much better to pray silently, while *good* church music is played by people who are proficient in it, and, withal, I prefer a church whose interior is like that of the Tein church, and Morlach masses, with white-robed priests, smoke of tapers and incense; that is more solemn, is it not, *angela*? There Büchsel had a boy choir, who sang without the organ, a hymn inserted in the service; somewhat out of tune, and in truly democratic Berlin dialect; this innovation also disturbed me. . . . Only let me thank you once again most heartily for your very dear letter, and do write soon, my darling; it is always for me the "sweet familiar note in the terrible confusion" whenever I read anything

16. *The Love Letters of Bismarck,* ed. Lewis, pp. 46–49.

from you, and then, to Hans's terror, I have an inclination to get out of politics, resign my mandate, and live quietly with you at Schönhausen; for it is all very much like my good old father at Kniephof, getting men and hounds to search the little bushes, and on every such occasion waiting with earnest and anxious watchfulness for the fox to appear, though he surely knew quite as well as I that there was no fox there. . . . God protect you, my angel.

Your most faithful

v. B.

Berlin, *September* 11, 1849
(Postmarked *September* 10)

I wrote yesterday, my Nannie, but as it costs me nothing, not even for paper, for this is the Chamber's, I do want to improve a wearisome moment, during which I must listen to the reading of a confused report on normal prices, to send you another little greeting; but again without the ribbon, for I am going to buy that later on. This morning I attended the cavalry maneuvers, on a very pleasant horse of Fritz's; rode sharply, swallowed much dust, but, nevertheless, had a good time; it is really pretty, these brilliant, rapidly moving masses, interspersed with the clanking of iron and the bugle signals. The queen, my old flame, greeted me so cordially. Having driven past without noticing me, she rose and turned backward over the bar of the carriage, to nod to me thrice; that lady appreciates a Prussian heart. Tomorrow I shall take a look at the grand parade, in which the infantry also participates. I believe I have written you that the king and Leopold Gerlach visited the emperor of Austria at Teplitz, where there was also a Russian plenipotentiary. The proletariats of the Chamber are now gradually coming to see that on that occasion something may have been concocted which will cast mildew on their German hot-house flowers, and the fact that his Majesty has conversed with the ruler of all the Croatians frightens them somewhat. *Qui vivra verra.* Those Frankfort cabbage-heads are incorrigible; they and their phrases are like the old liars who in the end honestly believe their own stories; and the impression produced on our Chamber by such ridiculous things as they say, without any regard for the matter in hand, or for common-sense, will be sure at last to convince people generally that peasants and provincials are not fit to make laws and conduct European politics. Now I must listen. Farewell, my much-beloved heart. Love to my daughter and your parents.

Your most faithful

v. B.

BERLIN, Wednesday
(Postmarked *September* 12, 1849)

. . . Yesterday I was much pleased to receive mammy's little letter; it is gratifying to me to know that many hearts outside of the Chamber are in accord with me, particularly that of my beloved; in the Chamber I am like the owl among the crows. . . . Just now, as I was writing this and not paying attention, I voted on the wrong side, very stupidly, because I let myself be guided by my neighbor, Dewitz-Wussoff, who is usually right, instead of sticking to the much safer plan of always voting in opposition to Auerswald. I will close, so as not to let it happen again. Farewell, my beloved heart. Don't forget that you must leave in about two weeks, and keep well for my sake, my angel. . . . Farewell, my darling. Hearty love to the old folks.

Your most faithful

v. B.

(Postmarked BERLIN, *September* 14, 1849)

Just now, my Nannie, Friday noon, in the usual tiresome Auerswald Committee, I received yours of Monday, and your letter and your love truly strengthen my heart in this ocean of boredom. What Hans told Adelaide about cholera symptoms was simply a lie to make himself interesting; he is even suffering from the reverse malady, the gray little wight, and I feel like a fish in water, but not like a trout in the Kamenz, rather like a carp in its moldy hole, bored and dull in spirit. I must have you here, my angel. What are we married for? And the middle of October is quite out of the question, even if you are not ill; by that time, too, it would be too cold for the child to remain so long *en route,* and if you don't come soon I shall take to gaming and drinking. I will not hear of your awaiting your confinement there; that could be only provided we were first definitely dissolved or adjourned, and provided I could remain during that time in Reinfeld; for otherwise we are half divorced, since it will then be impossible to return home before May.

Your most faithful

v. B.

In Berlin on December 28, 1849 Bismarck was delighted by the birth of his first son, Herbert. In the following letter the proud father summoned the clergyman, Gossner, to christen his son. Herbert later became his father's confidential assistant, and the father hoped to be succeeded as chancellor by his son. Father and son adored one another. When the elder Bismarck resigned his post in 1890, Herbert, too, ended his political career.[17]

BERLIN, *11th February,* 1850

REVEREND SIR,

Although I have not the honor of being known to you personally, still, as we have many mutual friends, I cherish the hope that you will not decline to christen my first-born son, and I therefore permit myself respectfully to inquire whether your leisure will allow you to perform this holy ceremony the day after tomorrow, Wednesday, the 13th, at half-past eleven in the morning, at my residence, Dorotheen Street, No. 37, first floor; and whether, to the above intent, you will then do me the honor of visiting me?

In the event of your consent, may I ask you at the same time to fix an hour tomorrow afternoon or evening when I can arrange more particular details with yourself personally at your house?

With the greatest respect,
Your Reverence's
Most obedient
v. BISMARCK-SCHÖNHAUSEN

In a combination of annoyance and good humor, Bismarck wrote to his sister, Malwine, about the difficulties of traveling with his infant children. Marie von Bismarck was two years old and Herbert was just one year old. The thirty-five-year-old father found it an ordeal, but not altogether obnoxious.[18]

SCHÖNHAUSEN, *August 7th,* 1850

The fact is, this journey, and I see it more clearly the nearer it approaches, gives me a right of reversion on the new lunatic asylum, or at least a seat for life in the Second Chamber. I can already see myself on the platform of the Genthiner station; then both of us packed in the carriage, surrounded with all sorts of child's necessaries—an embarrassing company; Johanna ashamed to suckle the baby, which accordingly roars itself blue; then the passports, the inn; then at Stettin railway station with both bellowing monkeys; then waiting an hour at Angermünde for the horses; and how are we to get from Kröchlendorf to Külz? It would be per-

17. *Prince Bismarck's Letters to His Wife, His Sister, and Others from 1844 to 1870,* trans. by Fitz. Maxse (London, 1878), pp. 24–25.

18. *Letter to Frau von Arnim,* quoted in Charles Dudley Warren, ed., *Library of the World's Great Literature* (New York, 1896), V, 1934–1935.

fectly awful if we had to remain for the night at Stettin. I did that last year with Marie and her squallings. I was in such a state of despair yesterday over all these visions that I was positively determined to give the whole thing up, and at last went to bed with the resolve at least to go straight through, without stopping anywhere; but what will one not commit for the sake of domestic peace? The young cousins, male and female, must become acquainted, and who knows when Johanna will see you again? She pounced upon me last night with the boy in her arms, and with all those wiles which formerly lost us Paradise; of course she succeeded in wringing my consent that everything should remain as before. I feel, however, that I am as one to whom fearful injustice is done, and I am certain that I shall have to travel next year with three cradles, wet-nurses, long-clothes, and counterpanes. I am now awake by six o'clock, and already in a gentle simmer of anger; I cannot get to sleep, owing to all the visions of traveling which my imagination paints in the darkest colors, even up to the "picnics" on the sandhills of Stolpmünde. And then if one were only paid for it! But to travel away the last remnants of a once handsome fortune with sucking babies! —I am very unhappy!

Well—Wednesday, then, in Gerswalde—I should have done probably better by driving over Passow, and you would not have had so far to Prenzlau as to G——. However, it is now a *fait accompli,* and the pain of selection is succeeded by the quiet of resignation. Johanna is somewhat nervous about her dresses, supposing you Boitzenburgers have company.

The Bettman Archive

PART III

The Leaps to Power, 1851-1862

25

Making of a Statesman: Bismarck Begins Service as Prussian Ambassador to the German Confederation in Frankfort-on-Main by Besting Austria in "The Battle of the Smoke"

"I began to feel bored . . . as he did not offer me a cigar."

When Bismarck arrived in Frankfort-on-Main on May 11, 1851 as Prussian envoy to the German Confederation (Bund), *he brought with him the germs of its destruction. The* Bund *had been dissolved during the Revolution of 1848; its revival had been sparked by Austria. Austria retained the permanent presidency of the* Bund. *Bismarck had been sent to Frankfort because he was considered to be as reactionary and anti-revolutionary as the Austrians, and it was expected that he would work well with them. The opposite happened—he became the most zealous opponent of Austrian leadership. Always in his mind was that day when Prussia would reverse the terrible disgrace of Olmütz—November 29, 1850—when Prussia surrendered every object of dispute between herself and Austria. This had been one of the most complete humiliations to which any European state had ever been subjected. One of the few to defend the agreement at the time was Bismarck. Although new to the political scene, he recognized that Prussia was not yet strong enough to challenge Austrian hegemony. He preferred to wait. At Frankfort he studied his powerful opponent.*

How Bismarck made known his antipathy to Austria was revealed in the "Battle of the Smoke," a story familiar to every German schoolchild. As a matter of protocol he had to call on Count Thun, the Austrian president of the Bund, *who had snubbed him on a previous occasion when he was still only a secretary of legation. Seated, smoking, and in his shirt sleeves, Thun received the new envoy. It was considered to be bad manners to smoke in a superior's presence unless specifically asked to do so. Bismarck astonished Thun by lighting a cigar and blowing smoke in Thun's general direction. He was careful to let all the world know this the next day. Bismarck's account of this incident plus another cigar story was recounted by Moritz Busch.*[1]

1. Moritz Busch, *Bismarck: Sketches for a Historical Picture,* trans. by William Beatty-Kingston (New York, 1891), II, 258–259.

"The Frankfort people slumbered with their eyes open. It was, indeed, a sleepy dull lot, until I flavored it with my own pepper." I asked about the famous cigar incident. "Which one do you mean?" "That in which your Excellency, finding Rechberg smoking, lit up a cigar too." "You mean Thun. Yes, that was a simple matter enough. He asked me to wait a minute. I did wait some time; when I began to feel bored, however, as he did not offer me a cigar, I took one out of my pocket and asked him for a light, which he gave me with astonishment depicted upon his countenance. But there is another story of the same sort. At the sittings of the military committee, when Rochow represented Prussia at the Federal Diet, Austria alone smoked. Rochow, who was an inveterate smoker, would have gladly done the same, but did not dare to. When I arrived, seeing no reason to the contrary, I asked the presiding power to oblige me with a light. This request was apparently regarded by the chairman and the other gentlemen with amazement and displeasure. Obviously it was an event. As matters then stood, only Austria and Prussia smoked. But the others considered it a question of such importance that they reported upon it to their respective governments. Somebody must have written to Berlin about it, too; for an enquiry reached me from his late Majesty, who was not a smoker, and probably did not find the occurrence to his taste. The incident called for serious consideration at the smaller courts, and six months elapsed, during which only the two great powers smoked. Then Schrenkh, the Bavarian, began to vindicate the dignity of his position by smoking. Nostitz, the Saxon, had doubtless a great mind to do as much, but had not received permission from his minister. When, however, at the next sitting he saw the Hanoverian, Bothmer, light up, he must have come to some arrangement with Rechberg (Nostitz was under Austrian influence, having two sons in the imperial army), for he took a cigar out of his case and puffed away vigorously. The only ones left were the Württemberger and the Darmstädter, neither of whom smoked. But the honor and importance of their states imperatively required that they *should* smoke, and so next time the Württemberger (von Reinhard) also produced a weed—I think I see it now, a long thin, pale yellow thing, the color of rye straw—and smoked it with sullen determination half through, as a burnt sacrifice for his Suabian fatherland. The only one who altogether refrained from tobacco was the representative of Hesse-Darmstadt."

As soon as he arrived in Frankfort, Bismarck found that Prussians were not popular. His method of obtaining quick service was very much a part of the Bismarck pattern.[2]

Bismarck had taken apartments in the house of a patrician of this free city, who held the Prussians in great repugnance; and when Bismarck applied to him to have a bell fixed up in his servant's room, he answered that that was not in the agreement, and that if Bismarck wanted a bell he must get it fixed himself, and at his own expense.

A few days later, the whole house was turned topsy-turvy. A loud report of firearms was heard to proceed from the delegate's room. The landlord, frightened to death, rushed up to his lodger's apartments, and bursting, all out of breath, into Bismarck's study, found him seated at his desk before a great pile of documents and calmly smoking his big pipe. There was a pistol lying on the table, still smoking at the barrel.

"For the love of heaven, what has happened?" asked the frightened landlord, more dead than alive.

"Nothing, nothing," answered Bismarck quietly. "Don't disturb yourself; I was only calling my servant. It is a very harmless signal, to which you will have to accustom yourself, for no doubt I shall want oftentimes to use it again."

The bell was fixed up next day.

That the way of the Junker in Frankfort was not easy was indicated by Bismarck in the following extracts from letters to his wife. He expressed his loneliness, thoughts on his new duties, and his opinion of Count Thun, his Austrian colleagues, and diplomats from other countries.[3]

On Saturday I drove with Rochow to Rüdesheim; there I took a boat and rowed out on the Rhine, and bathed in the moonlight—only nose and eyes above the water, and floated down to the Rat Tower at Bingen, where the wicked Bishop met his end. It is something strangely dreamlike to lie in the water in the quiet, warm

2. *Bismarck and All About Him, by a Fellow Student*, ed. by Henry Hayward (London, 1898), pp. 28–29.
3. Quoted in James Wycliffe Headlam, *Bismarck and the Foundations of the German Empire* (New York and London, 1899), pp. 88–90.

light, gently carried along by the stream; to look at the sky with the moon and stars above one, and, on either side, to see the wooded mountain tops and castle parapets in the moonlight, and to hear nothing but the gentle rippling of one's own motion. I should like a swim like this every evening. Then I drank some very good wine and sat long talking with Lynar on the balcony, with the Rhine beneath us. My little Testament and the starry heavens brought us on Christian topics, and I long shook at the Rousseau-like virtue of his soul.

Yesterday I was at Wiesbaden, and with a feeling of melancholy revisited the scenes of former folly. May it please God to fill with His clear and strong wine this vessel in which the champagne of twenty-one years foamed so uselessly. . . . I do not understand how a man who reflects on himself, and still knows, and will know, nothing of God, can endure his life for contempt and weariness. I do not know how I endured this in old days; if, as then, I were to live without God, thee, and the children, I do not know why I should not put life aside like a dirty shirt; and yet most of my acquaintances live thus. . . .

Our intercourse here is at best nothing but a mutual suspicion and espionage; if only there was anything to spy out and to hide! It is pure trifles with which they worry themselves, and I find these diplomatists with their airs of confidence and their petty fussiness much more absurd than the member of the Second Chamber in his conscious dignity. Unless some external events take place, and we clever men of the diet can neither direct nor foresee them, I know already what we shall bring about in one or two or three years, and will do it in twenty-four hours if the others will only be reasonable and truthful for a single day. I am making tremendous progress in the art of saying nothing in many words; I write reports many pages long, which are smooth and finished like leading articles, and if Manteuffel after reading them can say what they contain, he can do more than I. We all do as though we believed of each other that we are full of thoughts and plans, if only we would express them, and all the time we none of us know a hair's breadth more what will become of Germany. . . .

Thun [Austrian envoy and president of the Federal Diet] in his outward appearance has something of a hearty good fellow mixed with a touch of the Vienna *roué*. Underneath this he hides, I will not say great political power and intellectual gifts, but an uncommon cleverness and cunning, which with great presence of mind appears from underneath the mask of harmless good-humor as soon as politics are concerned. I consider him as an opponent who is dangerous to anyone who honestly trusts him, instead of paying back in his own coin. . . .

One must never expect that [the Austrian diplomats] will make what is right the foundation of their policy for the simple reason that it is the right. Cautious dishonesty is the characteristic of their association with us. They have nothing which awakens confidence. They intrigue under the mask of good-fellowship. . . . Their mouths are full of the necessity for common action, but when it is a question of furthering our wishes, then officially it is, "We will not oppose," and a secret pleasure in preparing obstacles. . . .

[The envoys of other countries] are caricatures of diplomatists who put on their official physiognomy if I ask them for a light, and select gestures and words with a truly Regensburg caution, if they ask for the key of the water-closet.

26

Duel with Vincke: In a Letter Tinged with Humility Written to His Mother-in-Law, Ambassador Bismarck Describes His Encounter with a Political Rival over an Acrimonious Conversation [4]

"God forgive me for my awful sin in not recognizing His grace."

Since March 1848 Bismarck had nurtured a hatred for George von Vincke, leader of the moderate Liberal party in the Prussian Chamber and Bismarck's political rival. At the time of Bismarck's interview with Augusta, Vincke was her confidant, and he was aware of Bismarck's mission to change the country's leadership in the counterrevolution. At the tribune of the Chamber, Vincke described Bismarck as a diplomat whose whole performance in history had been determined by Count Thun, the Austrian envoy at Frankfort, and his cigar. Bismarck attacked Vincke as ill-bred. Vincke replied by challenging him to a duel.

On March 24, 1852, the night before the duel, Bismarck asked his pastor whether or not it would be correct for him to take careful aim as well as to fire his pistol. It was a strange question, but it revealed much about Bismarck's personality. As a man of iron it was permissible to shoot, but to take aim against a human being

4. Translated and condensed by the editor from *Bismarck Briefe*, ed. by Hans Rothfels (Göttingen, 1955), pp. 165–167.

was un-Christian and immoral. Bismarck told the story in a letter to his mother-in-law in which he clothed his hatred of Vincke with a veneer of humility.

Bismarck was wholly serious in his account, but other observers described the proceedings as something of a farce. It was rumored that before the order to fire was given, Bismarck removed his hat in order to pray. Vincke, taking this as a gesture of salute, also removed his hat. Then each fired a shot which went wild. Immediately there was a general shaking of hands.

FRANKFORT, 4 *April* 1852

DEAR MOTHER:

I wanted to write to you in detail today, but I don't know how much I can do, since I have spent so much time enjoying a Sunday walk in the forest, and scarcely have time to make the post. Because of her condition, Johanna is somewhat tired. I would have had her with me in the woods, and we would still have been there. Heartiest thanks for you and Father for your expressions of love with good wishes and gifts.

In the Vincke matter I feel the same way you do: I cannot praise God's grace enough that there was no disaster on either side. Being so close to death had a salutary effect on my inner being. I know you will not share my comprehension of the matter, but really I have never felt my complete trust in God and His will as in that moment of truth. Some day we can talk about it in detail; now I shall tell you what happened.

I have been very much annoyed repeatedly by Vincke's rudeness against the government and against me, and I was ready to strike back against him at the next opportunity. He accused me of lacking diplomatic discretion, and said that until now I have accomplished nothing other than that "burning cigar." With it he meant to allude to a very insignificant but funny incident which happened in the Federal Palace about which I told him confidentially on his special request. I then said from the tribune that his remarks not only went beyond the bounds of diplomacy but also of that ordinary discretion which one might expect from any man of breeding.

The next day he sent Herr von Saucken-Julienfelde to me as his second to challenge me to a duel of two bullets each. I accepted it after Oskar Arnim's proposition that it be fought with sabers was declined by Saucken. Vincke wanted the matter finished within forty-eight hours, to which I agreed.

At 8 A.M. on the 25th we rode to Tegel, a beautiful spot in the woods on the shore of a lake. It was lovely weather, and the birds were singing sweetly in the sunshine, so that all my gloomy thoughts vanished as soon as we entered the woods. To avoid any sense of weakness I forced myself not to think of Johanna. With me were Arnim and Eberhard Stolberg as witnesses and my brother as a very depressed observer. With Vincke were Saucken and Major Vincke of the First Chamber, in addition to a Bodelschwingh [cousin of the minister and of Vincke] as disinterested witnesses. The latter declared before the beginning of the duel that the challenge seemed to him under the circumstances a bit too hard, and proposed that the number of shots be reduced to one each. Saucken was ready to agree to this in Vincke's name, and then said to me that the whole thing would be dropped if I were willing to express regret for my words. Since it was a simple matter of having told the truth, I could not do this.

So we took our posts. On command of Bodelschwingh we both shot, and we both missed. God forgive me for my awful sin in not recognizing His grace. I cannot deny that when I could see through the smoke, and realized that my adversary was still standing, I was by no means inclined to join the general jubilation. Bodelschwingh wept. I was annoyed that the number of shots we were to exchange had been reduced, and I should have been glad to go on with the combat. But dueling etiquette did not allow me, being the challenged, to demand another round. It was all over and we shook hands.

We went home, and I ate alone at my sister's house. Everyone seems to have been dissatisfied about the way things went. Well, God knows what use He expects to make of Vincke. Now that my blood is calm, I am thankful that things turned out this way. A contributory factor was that a pair of very good pistols that originally were supposed to be used were badly loaded, so that for the moment they could not be used, and we had to take substitute weapons which were not easy to handle.

I must close now because of official business. Only I want to add that I spoke about the duel beforehand with the elder Stolberg, General Gerlach, Minister Uhden, and Hans, and all were of the opinion that it had to take place. Büchsel also saw no way of avoiding it, although he did admonish me to give in. With him and Stolberg on the evening previous to the duel I held an hour of prayer. I never for a moment doubted that I had to appear for the duel, but I was not sure if I would fire on Vincke. I fired, without feeling any anger, and missed. Now be well, my very beloved Mother, and greet Father and the others warmly from your true son,

v. B.

27 John Lothrop Motley, Friend of His Student Days, Comes to Visit Bismarck at Frankfort in the Summer of 1855 and Is Received with Almost Hysterical Joy

"It is one of those houses where everyone does what one likes."

Twenty years had flown by since Bismarck and Motley were fellow students at Göttingen and Berlin. In the summer of 1855 Bismarck was Prussian envoy to the German Confederation at Frankfort, and Motley was in Europe completing his book, The Rise of the Dutch Republic, *which was to bring him fame as a historian. Motley came to visit his old university friend, a joyful event described in three letters sent by Motley to his wife.*[5] *The Keyserling mentioned in the first letter was Count Hermann Keyserling, the third of the trio of student friends.*

FRANKFORT,
July 27th, 1855

MY DEAREST MARY,—The waiters have brought me a tremendously large sheet of paper, but I am afraid that I shall hardly be able to fill it up in a very interesting manner. . . . The journey to Basel only occupied ten hours, the last hour on the railway, so that you get to the hotel soon after five. . . . The next morning I started from the railway terminus (the railroad is finished to Basel) at 7:30, and reached Frankfort at 4:30. As soon as I was dressed I started for Bismarck's house, having previously learned that Keyserling, to my great regret, had not arrived.

When I called, Bismarck was at dinner, so I left my card, and said I would come back in half an hour. As soon as my card had been carried to him (as I learned afterwards) he sent a servant after me to the hotel, but I had gone another way. When I came back I was received with open arms. I can't express to you how cordially he received me. If I had been his brother, instead of an old friend, he could not have shown more warmth and affectionate delight in seeing me. I find I like him even better than I thought I did, and you know how high an opinion I always expressed of his talents and disposition. He is a man of very noble character, and of very

5. *The Correspondence of John Lothrop Motley,* ed. by George William Curtis (London, 1889), I, 173–178.

great powers of mind. The prominent place which he now occupies as a statesman sought *him*. He did not seek it, or any other office. The stand which he took in the Assembly from conviction, on the occasion of the outbreak of 1848, marked him at once to all parties as one of the leading characters of Prussia. Of course I don't now go into the rights and wrongs of the matter, but I listened with great interest, as you may suppose, to his detailed history of the revolutionary events of that year, and his share in them, which he narrated to me in a long conversation which we had last night. He wanted me to stay entirely in his house, but as he has his wife's father and mother with him, and as I saw that it was necessary to put up a bed in a room where there was none, I decidedly begged off. I breakfasted there this morning, and am to dine there, with a party, today. Tomorrow, I suppose, I shall dine there *en famille*. I am only afraid that the landlord here will turn me into the streets for being such a poor *consommateur* for him, and all I can do is to order vast quantities of seltzer water.

The principal change in Bismarck is that he has grown stouter, but, being over six feet, this is an improvement. His voice and manner are singularly unchanged. His wife I like very much indeed —very friendly, intelligent, and perfectly unaffected, and treats me like an old friend. In short, I can't better describe the couple than by saying that they are as unlike M. and Madame de —— as it is possible to be.

In the summer of 1851, he told me that the minister, Manteuffel, asked him one day abruptly, if he would accept the post of ambassador at Frankfort, to which (although the proposition was as unexpected a one to him as if I should hear by the next mail that I had been chosen governor of Massachusetts) he answered, after a moment's deliberation, yes, without another word. The king, the same day, sent for him, and asked him if he would accept the place, to which he made the same brief answer, *"Ja."* His Majesty expressed a little surprise that he made no inquiries or conditions, when Bismarck replied that anything which the king felt strong enough to propose to him, he felt strong enough to accept. I only write these details that you may have an idea of the man. Strict integrity and courage of character, a high sense of honor, a firm religious belief, united with remarkable talents, make up necessarily a combination which cannot be found any day in any court; and I have no doubt that he is destined to be prime minister, unless his obstinate truthfulness, which is apt to be a stumbling block for politicians, stands in his way. . . .

Well, he accepted the post and wrote to his wife next day, who was preparing for a summer's residence in a small house they had taken on the sea coast, that he could not come because he was already established in Frankfort as minister. The result, he said, was three days of tears on her part. He had previously been leading the life of a plain country squire with a moderate income, had never held any position in the government or in diplomacy, and had hardly ever been to court. He went into the office with a holy horror of the mysterious nothings of diplomacy, but soon found how little there was in the whole *"galimatias."* Of course my politics are very different from his, although not so antipodal as you might suppose, but I can talk with him as frankly as I could with you, and I am glad of an opportunity of hearing the other side put by a man whose talents and character I esteem, and who so well knows *le dessous des cartes.* M. de Veh is here, but goes back to Vevey, I believe, tomorrow. Bismarck has invited him to dinner today. He is as surprised as I not to find Keyserling, and can't account for his absence. Good-bye, my dearest Mary, I have got to the end of the sheet without saying a word about you and my darlings. . . .

FRANKFORT,
Saturday, July 28th, 1855

I have just consented to wait here until Wednesday morning. . . . I send the dispatch from Bismarck's house, and I have just come back to write you this hurried line, as I must go back to dine with him at four. Madame de Bismarck begs me to convey the kindest messages on her part to you, and to say that she depends upon the pleasure of making your acquaintance here this autumn or the end of the summer, and I have promised that we will stop a day or two in Frankfort on our way to Paris. I am perfectly sure that you will like her—you could not help it. She is so amiable, gentle and agreeable in every way, that I feel as if we had been ten years acquainted. She and her mother have both assured me over and over again that Bismarck was nearly out of his wits with delight when he saw my card. *I should certainly not say such a thing to anybody but you,* but you and I are not so overburdened with self-esteem but that we may afford to tell each other the truth in such matters, and it really gives me pleasure to know that a man of whom I think so highly has such a warm and sincere friendship for me. I am sure that you will like him, and I only regret that we can see so little or nothing of each other for the rest of our lives. There are three children—a little girl named Marie, as sweet as Susie, to whom I gave this morning a little locket in Susie's name, and told her that Susie would give her a lock of red hair to put in it when she saw her. She put her arms around my neck and kissed me, and trotted off in the greatest glee to show it to her grandpapa and grandmama.

I feel as much at home already as at Mr. Cabot's, and I should have almost as little fear of wearing out my welcome here as there. At the dinner yesterday were some strangers—Prussians—Count Roedern, brother of the Prussian minister in Dresden, and his wife and sister. M. de Veh was there, and as friendly and agreeable as ever. He is off this morning to Schwalbach, and tomorrow returns to Vevey. After dinner, Bismarck and his wife, myself, and a youthful *attaché* with the terrific name of Baron Schreckenstein, took a long ride on horseback in a beautiful forest on the other side of the Main, and on our return found M. de Veh and the father-in-law still deeply absorbed at the chess table where we had left them. At eleven o'clock we tried very hard to eat supper, but nobody succeeded very well, and at twelve I came home.

FRANKFORT,
Monday, July 30th, 1855

. . . . The Bismarcks are as kind as ever—nothing can be more frank and cordial than her manners. I am there all day long. It is one of those houses where everyone does what one likes. The show apartments where they receive formal company are on the front of the house. Their living rooms, however, are a *salon* and dining room at the back, opening upon the garden. Here there are young and old, grandparents and children and dogs all at once, eating, drinking, smoking, piano-playing, and pistol-firing (in the garden), all going on at the same time. It is one of those establishments where every earthly thing that can be eaten or drunk is offered you, porter, soda water, small beer, champagne, burgundy or claret are about all the time, and everybody is smoking the best Havana cigars every minute. Last night we went to the theatre to see the first part of *Henry IV*. The Falstaff was tolerable, the others very indifferent. By the way I was glad to find that both Bismarck and his wife agree with me that Emil Devrient was a very second-rate actor. I must go out directly and buy a brooch for my dear little Mary. Little Bill, as the Bismarcks call their youngest boy of two years, was born on the same day, and I am going to buy him a trumpet. A thousand kisses to Lily, Mary and Susie, and accept for yourself the fondest and deepest affection of

Your own
J. L. M.

28 The Rising Diplomat Journeys to Paris Where He Meets Napoleon III, with Whom He Was Later to Have a Confrontation of Enormous Importance

"He is not so clever as the world esteems him."

In 1855, while envoy to the Bundestag *in Frankfort, Bismarck made his first visit to Paris. Here, surrounded by the glitter of the World's Fair, he could judge the splendor of the new French empire. More important, he met Napoleon III. A bond of sympathy was immediately established between the two, and Bismarck formed a lasting impression of the man who was to become his opponent. Bismarck saw that the latter-day Napoleon was a mixture of crusading idealism and realistic self-interest. The dreaded first Napoleon had been crude, bold, and calculating: the nephew was subtle, sly, and limited. Bismarck sensed that Prussia need not fear a resurgence of French imperialism on a grand scale. In his memoirs Bismarck tells of his first impressions.*[6]

In the summer of 1855 Count Hatzfeldt, our ambassador in Paris, invited me to visit the Industrial Exhibition; he still shared the belief then existent in diplomatic circles that I was very soon to be Manteuffel's successor at the Foreign Office. Although the king had entertained such an idea on and off, it was already then known in the innermost court circles that a change had taken place. Count William Roedern, whom I met in Paris, told me that the ambassadors continued to believe I was destined to be made a minister and that he himself had also believed this; but that the king had changed his mind—of further details he was ignorant. Doubtless since Rügen.

August 15, Napoleon's day, was celebrated among other ways by a procession of Russian prisoners through the streets. On the 19th the queen of England made her entry, and on August 25 a state ball was given in her honor at Versailles at which I was presented to her and to Prince Albert.

The prince, handsome and cool in his black uniform, conversed with me courteously, but in his manner there was a kind of malevo-

6. *Bismarck: The Man and the Statesman (Reflections and Reminiscences)*, trans. by A. J. Butler (New York and London, 1897), I, 163–170.

lent curiosity from which I concluded that my anti-occidental influence upon the king was not unknown to him. In accordance with the mode of thought peculiar to him, he sought for the motives of my conduct not where they really lay, that is, in the anxiety to keep my country independent of foreign influences—influences which found a fertile soil in our narrow-minded reverence for England and fear of France—and in the desire to hold ourselves aloof from a war which we should not have carried on in our own interests but in dependence upon Austrian and English policy.

In the eyes of the prince—though I of course did not gather this from the momentary impression made during my presentation, but from ulterior acquaintance with facts and documents—I was a reactionary party man who took up sides for Russia in order to further an absolutist and "Junker" policy. It was not to be wondered at that this view of the prince's and of the then partisans of the duke of Coburg had descended to the prince's daughter, who shortly after became our crown princess.

Even soon after her arrival in Germany, in February 1858, I became convinced, through members of the royal house and from my own observations, that the princess was prejudiced against me personally. The fact itself did not surprise me so much as the form in which her prejudice against me had been expressed in the narrow family circle—"she did not trust me." I was prepared for antipathy on account of my alleged anti-English feelings and by reason of my refusal to obey English influences; but from a conversation which I had with the princess after the war of 1866 while sitting next to her at table I was obliged to conclude that she had subsequently allowed herself to be influenced in her judgment of my character by further-reaching calumnies. I was ambitious, she said, in a half-jesting tone, to be a king or at least president of a republic. I replied in the same semi-jocular tone that I was personally spoiled for a republican; that I had grown up in the royalist traditions of the family and had need of a monarchical institution for my earthly well-being: I thanked God, however, I was not destined to live like a king, constantly on show, but to be until death the king's faithful subject. I added that no guarantee could, however, be given that this conviction of mine would be universally inherited, and this not because royalists would give out, but because perhaps kings might. *Pour faire un civet, il faut un lièvre, et pour faire une monarchie il faut un roi.* I could not answer for it that for want of such the next generation might not be republican. I further remarked that in thus expressing myself I was not free from anxiety at the idea of a change in the occupancy of the throne without a transference of the monarchical traditions to the successor. But the princess avoided every serious turn and kept up the jocular tone as amiable and entertaining as ever; she rather gave me the impression that she wished to tease a political opponent.

During the first years of my ministry I frequently remarked in the course of similar conversation that the princess took pleasure in provoking my patriotic susceptibility by playful criticism of persons and matters.

At that ball at Versailles, Queen Victoria spoke to me in German. She gave me the impression of beholding in me a noteworthy but unsympathetic personality, but still her tone of voice was without that touch of ironical superiority that I thought I detected in Prince Albert's. She continued to be amiable and courteous like one unwilling to treat an eccentric fellow in an unfriendly way.

In comparison with Berlin it seemed a curious arrangement to me that at supper the company ate in three classes, with gradations in the menu, and that such guests as were to sup at all were assured of this by having a ticket bearing a number handed to them as they entered. The tickets of the first class also bore the name of the lady presiding at the table to which they referred. These tables were arranged to accommodate fifteen or twenty. On entering I received one of these tickets for Countess Walewska's table and later on in the ballroom two more from two other lady patronesses of diplomacy and of the court. No exact plan for placing the guests had therefore been made out. I chose the table of Countess Walewska, to whose department I belonged as a foreign diplomatist. On the way to the room in question I came across a Prussian officer in the uniform of an infantry regiment of the guard, accompanied by a French lady; he was engaged in an animated dispute with one of the imperial household stewards who would not allow either of them to pass, not being provided with tickets. After the officer, in answer to my inquiries, had explained the matter and indicated the lady as a duchess bearing an Italian title of the First Empire, I told the court official that I had the gentleman's ticket, and gave him one of mine. Now, however, the official would not allow the lady to pass and I therefore gave the officer my second ticket for his duchess. The official then said significantly to me: *"Mais vous ne passerez pas sans carte."* On my showing him the third, he made a face of astonishment and allowed all three of us to pass. I recommended my two *protégés* not to sit down at the tables indicated on the tickets, but to try and find seats elsewhere; nor did any complaints concerning my distribution of tickets ever come to my ears. The want of organization was so great that our table was not fully occupied, a fact due to the absence of any understanding among the *dames patronesses.* Old Prince Pückler had either received no ticket or had been unable to find his table; after he had turned to me, whom he knew by sight, he was invited by Countess Walewska to take one of the seats that had remained empty. The supper, in spite of the triple division, was neither materially nor as regards its preparation upon a level with what is done in Berlin at similar crowded festivities; the waiting only was efficient and prompt.

What struck me most was the difference in the regulations for the free circulation of the throng. In this respect the palace of Versailles offers much greater facilities than that of Berlin on account of the larger number and, if we except the White Hall, the greater spaciousness of the apartments. Here those who had supped in class 1 were ordered to make their exit by the same way as the hungry ones of class 2 entered, their impetuous charge betraying certainly less acquaintance with the customs of court society. Personal collisions occurred among the belaced and beribboned gentlemen and superelegant ladies, giving rise to scuffles and abusive language, such as would be impossible in our palace. I retired with the satisfactory impression that in spite of all the splendor of the imperial court, the court service, the breeding and manners of court society were on a higher level with us, as well as in St. Petersburg and Vienna, than in Paris, and that the times were past when one could go to France and to the court of Paris to receive a schooling in courtesy and good manners. Even the etiquette of small German courts, antiquated as it was, especially in comparison with St. Petersburg, was more dignified than the practice of the imperial court. It is true that I had already received this impression in Louis Philippe's time, during whose reign it became quite the fashion in France to distinguish oneself in the direction of excessively free and easy manners, and of abstention from courtesy, especially towards ladies. Although it had become better in this respect during the Second Empire, the tone in official and court society and the demeanor of the court itself still remained below the standard of the three great eastern courts. Only in the Legitimist circles aloof from the official world were things different both in the time of Louis Philippe and in that of Louis Napoleon; there the tone was faultless, courteous, and hospitable, with occasional exceptions of the younger gentlemen spoiled by their contact with Paris, who borrowed their habits not from the family but from the club.

The emperor, whom I saw for the first time during this visit to Paris, gave me to understand in several interviews, but at that time only in general phrases, his desire and intentions respecting a Franco-Prussian alliance. His words were to the effect that these two neighboring states, which by reason of their culture and their institutions stood at the head of civilization, were naturally thrown upon each other's assistance. Any inclination to express before me such grievance as might arise from our refusal to join the Western Powers was kept out of the foreground. I had the feeling that the pressure which England and Austria exercised in Berlin and Frankfort to compel us to render assistance in the western camp was much stronger, one might say more passionate and rude, than the desires and promises expressed to me in an amicable form, with which the emperor supported his plea for our understanding with France in particular. He was much more indulgent than England and Austria respecting our sins against occidental policy. He never spoke German to me, either then or later.

That my visit to Paris had caused displeasure at the court at home, and had intensified, especially in the case of Queen Elizabeth, the ill-feelings already entertained towards me, I was able to perceive at the end of September of the same year. While the king was proceeding down the Rhine to Cologne to attend the cathedral building festival, I reported myself at Coblentz and was, with my wife, invited by his Majesty to perform the journey to Cologne on the steamer; my wife, however, was ignored by the queen on board and at Remagen. The prince of Prussia, who had observed this, gave my wife his arm and led her to table. At the conclusion of the meal I begged for permission to return to Frankfort, which was granted me.

It was not until the following winter, during which the king had again approached me, that he asked me once at dinner, straight across the table, my opinion concerning Louis Napoleon; his tone was ironical. I replied: "It is my impression that the Emperor Napoleon is a discreet and amiable man, but that he is not so clever as the world esteems him. The world places to his account everything that happens, and if it rains in eastern Asia at an unseasonable moment chooses to attribute it to some malevolent machination of the emperor. Here especially we have become accustomed to regard him as a kind of *génie du mal* who is forever only meditating how to do mischief in the world. I believe he is happy when he is able to enjoy anything good at his ease; his understanding is overrated at the expense of his heart; he is at bottom good-natured, and has an unusual measure of gratitude for every service rendered him."

The king laughed at this in a manner that vexed me and led me to ask whether I might be permitted to guess his Majesty's present thoughts. The king consented, and I said: "General von Canitz used to lecture to the young officers in the military school on the campaigns of Napoleon. An assiduous listener asked him how Napoleon could have omitted to make this or that movement. Canitz replied: 'Well, you see just what this Napoleon was—a real good-hearted fellow, but so stupid!' which naturally excited great mirth among the military scholars. I fear that your Majesty is thinking of me much as General von Canitz thought of his pupils."

The king laughed and said: "You may be right; but I am not sufficiently acquainted with the present Napoleon to be able to impugn your impression that his heart is better than his head." That the queen was dissatisfied with my view I was enabled to gather from the external trifles by which impressions are made known at court.

The displeasure felt at my intercourse with Napoleon sprang from the idea of "legitimacy," or, more strictly speaking, from the word itself, which was stamped with its modern sense by Talleyrand, and used in 1814 and 1815 with great success and to the advantage of the Bourbons as a deluding spell.

29 Motley Writes to Bismarck from Rome, February 16, 1859

"May you prosper and succeed—as you deserve to succeed."

The strange friendship between the boisterous Junker and his staid New England friend was a lasting one. In early February 1859 Motley was in Rome seeking to obtain entrance into the papal archives. Bismarck was on the verge of being sent to St. Petersburg as ambassador. The American wrote the following letter to Bismarck from Rome on February 16, 1859.[7]

ROME, *February* 16, 1859

MY DEAR BISMARCK,

Are you really going to St. Petersburg? I have seen rumors to that effect from time to time, in the newspapers, but I always took it for granted that they were only rumors. But now, it seems to be stated so formally that it must be a settled thing. I wish you could find time,—(I know you have very little to spare) to write me a

7. Quoted in *The Correspondence of William I and Bismarck, with Other Letters to and from Bismarck,* trans. by J. A. Ford (2 vols., London, 1903), II, 62–64.

single line, just to say if the fact is really so. I can't tell you how much disappointed I am. I really don't know whether it is a political advancement for you or not—but it seems to me that you and Mme. de Bismarck are so happy and contented in Frankfort, and that you have so much less of the "pomp and circumstance" of courts—which I know is a bore to both of you—to make me doubt whether you will be at first much gratified by plunging into the arctic circle whither you seem to be bound.

But I confess that my emotions on the subject are very selfish. I always thought that I had you safe in Frankfort—and that I was sure to see you very often—as long as I remained in Europe, which—off and on—is likely to be for the greater part of my life —but now that you are going to Petersburg, it seems to me as though you were about migrating to the planet Jupiter.

Russia is so much farther off, in every respect, than America. Does your wife like the idea of removing from Frankfort? Pray give her my kindest regards and good wishes, and say to her how deeply disappointed I am to lose the opportunity of seeing you all again—I wished so much to introduce my wife and children to you and yours, and we even have talked of spending a year or two in Frankfort, as I don't think that Rome agrees much with any of us.

Do write me a word or two, if you can spare a few moments' time, and tell me what your plans are, why you are going to Russia and when, how your wife likes it, and all the other ifs and ands—I haven't written to you before, because I knew that you didn't care much for correspondence, and would be glad perhaps not to be obliged to write.—Now you must write, for I don't like to think that I have lost my hold upon you for ever.

I have seen Canitz here this winter. He seems desirous of getting appointed to this place, but I infer from what he says that he is likely to remain at Naples. There is a young English lady here to whom it is said that he is engaged to be married—but it is not officially announced. She is a Miss W——, very young, pretty, and with a handsome fortune. The family occupy apartments in the same *palazzo* with us, and we have exchanged calls and cards—but we have not yet seen very much of them. I am sure I wish Canitz every happiness, for he is certainly one of the best hearted, most excellent fellows in the world. We had the pleasure of seeing him very often during his brief visit here—rather the oftener, you will infer, from the propinquity of lodgings, to which I have alluded—and my wife likes him as much as I do.

Pray tell me if you have heard of Keyserling—and if you know his address. He owes me a letter since May, having let our correspondence drop in the most flagitious manner. I don't know his address now, or I would write to him again—but I am quite ignorant whether he has returned to Courland or has remained in Paris. Who is to be your Prussian minister here? You were kind enough to give me a letter of introduction to Mr. von Thiele, but he had already left his post before we arrived, and, as I understand, is not to return. If the new minister—whoever he may be—happens to be an acquaintance of yours, perhaps you would not object to send me a line of introduction to him.

Thus far, I have not been able to get into the papal archives, and doubt very much whether I shall succeed. Our minister here is very obliging, and is doing all that he can, but I suspect that there is no key which will unlock those secrets to a Protestant. Meantime I am working hard at the materials which I brought with me from other archives—particularly those of Belgium, Holland, Spain and England, and have got enough work on my hands to last me for years. Nevertheless, I shall have finished two or three volumes, I suspect, before you will have read the first work.* Pray tell Madame de B. that I hope one of these days she will read the work for "old acquaintance sake." If she objects to reading English, there is a German translation—published in Dresden—and two French translations, one published in Brussels, the other in Paris. Pray forgive this egotism—for it is the egotism of friendship, not of vanity. I can't help wishing that you would both sometimes recall me to your memory, and I know no better way than by asking her to sometimes read a chapter or two of my writings. I am sure I shall never forget her and you—our early friendship, and the to me delightful days we have passed together since it has been renewed. I always feel when I am with you, as if twenty years had rolled off my back in one lump, like a knapsack, as if my shoes were not covered with the dust of the long life's turnpike along which we have been trailing since the early days.

God bless you and yours, my dear Bismarck. May you prosper and succeed—as you deserve to succeed—*domi militiæque*. Write me half a dozen lines, as soon as you conveniently can, and with best regards to your wife and children, believe me,

Most sincerely your friend
J. L. Motley

Address
aux soins de Tarlonia & Cie.
Rome

* *The Rise of the Dutch Republic.* Motley was then writing his *History of the United Netherlands.*

Technical Promotion: Bismarck Accepts with Ill Grace His Recall from Frankfort and Transfer to a Key Diplomatic Post at St. Petersburg

"Russians very amiable. . . ."

In the autumn of 1857 it became obvious that Frederick William IV's personality suffered from more than "peculiarities" and that, in fact, he had become insane. The next November he surrendered his royal powers to his brother William, who became prince-regent. Unimpressed by Bismarck's work at Frankfort, William ordered his recall but did not dismiss him. Instead, he gave him another and more important post, the ambassadorship to the Russian court. Bismarck was not pleased by the change, but he accepted. Leaving his family behind for the moment, he went to St. Petersburg. On the way he wrote to Johanna.[8]

KOWNO, *March* 25, 1859

MY LOVE,—Snow storms all the way from Königsberg here, six inches deep; everything white; 36° to 47°; ice. Rode one hundred and forty-nine miles in twenty-eight hours, with post horses, in Prussia and Russia equally bad; crossed the Niemen at night in beautiful clear winter weather; old city, river banks mountainous, prettily lighted by stars and snow and window lights; black, rushing water, broad as the Elbe. Russians very amiable, but post horses bad, and often none. We shall sleep here four hours, then on to Düna. Good-night, with love.

Your most true

v. B.

PSKOV, *March* 28, 1859

MY DEAR HEART,—Russia has stretched out under our wheels; the versts increased in number at every station, but at last we are in the haven of the railway. Drove ninety-six hours from Königsberg without stopping, only in Kowno we slept four hours, and three in Egypt (a station near Dünaburg)—I think it was day before yesterday. I feel very well now, only my skin burns, for I sat

8. *The Love Letters of Bismarck*, ed. and trans. by C. T. Lewis (New York and London, 1901), pp. 316–317.

outside almost all the way, and the temperature was from two to twenty-four degrees below freezing point. In the wagon there was not room for Klüber and me, so I changed places with Engel. We had snow so deep that, with six and eight horses, we literally got stuck, and had to get out. Still worse were the slippery mountains, especially going down; for twenty paces we took an hour, because the horses fell four times and eight times interfered with one another; added to that night and wind, a real winter journey, without modification. The wagon was too heavy. Klüber had about four hundred pounds of things. . . .

Bismarck was careful to inform his wife of every detail of his work. Following are letters he sent Johanna from Moscow and St. Petersburg before she joined him there with the children.[9]

Moscow, *June 6th*, 1859

I will send you at least a sign of life from here, while I am waiting for the samovar; and a young Russian in a red shirt is exerting himself behind me with vain attempts to light a fire—he puffs and blows, but it will not burn. After having complained so much about the scorching heat lately, I woke today between Twer and here, and thought I was dreaming when I saw the country and its fresh verdure covered far and wide with snow. I shall wonder at nothing again, and having convinced myself of the fact beyond all doubt, I turned quickly on the other side to sleep and roll on farther, although the play of colors—from green to white—in the red dawn of day was not without its charm. I do not know if the snow still lies at Twer; here it has thawed away, and a cool gray rain is rattling on the green tin of the roofs. Green has every reason to be the Russian favorite color. Of the five hundred miles I have passed in traveling here, I have slept away about two hundred, but each hand-breadth of the remainder was green in every shade. Towns and villages, and more particularly houses, with the exception of the railway stations, I did not observe. Bushy forests with birch-trees cover swamp and hill, a fine growth of grass beneath, long tracts of meadow land between; so it goes on for fifty, one hundred, two hundred miles. Ploughed land I do not remember to have remarked, nor heather, nor sand. Solitary grazing cows or horses awoke one at times to the presumption that there might be human

9. Letters to Frau von Bismarck, quoted in Charles Dudley Warren, ed., *Library of the World's Great Literature* (New York, 1896), V, 1936–1939.

beings in the neighborhood. Moscow, seen from above, looks like a field of young wheat: the soldiers are green, the cupolas green, and I do not doubt that the eggs on the table before me were laid by green hens.

You will want to know how I come to be here. I also have already asked myself this question, and the answer I received was that change is the soul of life. The truth of this profound saying becomes especially obvious after having lived for ten weeks in a sunny room of a hotel, with the lookout on pavements. The charms of moving become rather blunted if they occur repeatedly within a short period; I therefore determined to forego them, handed over all paper to ——, gave Engel my keys, declared that I would put up in a week at Stenbock's house, and drove to the Moscow station. This was yesterday at noon, and this morning, at eight o'clock, I alighted here at the Hôtel de France. First of all I shall pay a visit to a charming acquaintance of former times, who lives in the country, about twenty versts from here; tomorrow evening I shall be here again; Wednesday and Thursday shall visit the Kremlin and so forth; and Friday or Saturday sleep in the beds which Engel will meantime buy. Slow harnessing and fast driving lie in the character of this people. I ordered the carriage two hours ago: to every call which I have been uttering for each successive ten minutes of an hour and a half, the answer is, "Immediately," given with imperturbably friendly composure; but there the matter rests. You know my exemplary patience in waiting, but everything has its limits; afterwards there will be wild galloping, so that on these bad roads horse and carriage break down, and at last we reach the place on foot. I have meanwhile drunk three glasses of tea and annihilated several eggs; the efforts at getting warm have also so perfectly succeeded that I feel the need of fresh air. I should, out of sheer impatience, commence shaving if I had a glass. This city is very straggling, and very foreign-looking, with its green-roofed churches and innumerable cupolas; quite different from Amsterdam, but both the most original cities I know. No German guard has a conception of the luggage people drag with them into the railway carriage; not a Russian goes without two real pillows in white pillowcases, children in baskets, and masses of eatables of every kind. Out of politeness they bowed me into a sleeping car, where I was worse off than in my seat. Altogether, it is astonishing to me to see the fuss made here about a journey.

Moscow, *June 8th*

This city is really, as a *city,* the handsomest and most original existing: the environs are cheerful, not pretty, not ugly; but the view from the top of the Kremlin on this panorama of green-roofed houses, gardens, churches, spires of the strangest possible form and color, mostly green, or red or bright blue, generally crowned at the top with a gigantic golden onion, and mostly five or more on one church,—there are certainly a thousand steeples!—anything more strangely beautiful than all this lit up by the slanting rays of the setting sun it is impossible to see. The weather has cleared up again, and I should stay here a few days longer if there were not rumors of a great battle in Italy, which may perhaps bring diplomatic work in its train, so I will be off there and get back to my post. The house in which I am writing is, curiously enough, one of the few that survived 1812; old, thick walls, like those at Schönhausen, Oriental architecture, big Moorish rooms.

June 28th, Evening

After a three hours' drive through the gardens in an open carriage, and a view of all its beauties in detail, I am drinking tea, with a prospect of the golden evening sky and green woods. At the emperor's they want to be *en famille* the last evening, as I can perfectly well understand; and I, as a convalescent, have sought retirement, and have indeed done quite enough today for my first outing. I am smoking my cigar in peace, and drinking excellent tea, and see, through the smoke of both, a sunset of really rare beauty. I send you the inclosed jasmine as a proof that it really grows and blossoms here in the open air. On the other hand, I must own that I have been shown the common chestnut in shrub form as a rare growth, which in winter is wrapped up; otherwise, there are very fine large oaks, ash trees, limes, poplars, and birches as thick as oaks.

Petersburg, *July* 26, 1859

Half an hour ago a cabinet courier woke me with war and peace. Our policy drifts more and more into the Austrian wake; and when we have once fired a shot on the Rhine, it is over with the Italian-Austrian war, and in its place a Prussian-French comes on the scene, in which Austria, after we have taken the burden from her shoulders, stands by us or fails to stand by us just so far as her own interests require. She will certainly not allow us to play a very brilliant victor's part.

As God wills! After all, everything here is only a question of time: nations and individuals, folly and wisdom, war and peace, they come and go like the waves, but the sea remains. There is nothing on this earth but hypocrisy and jugglery; and whether fever or grape-shot tear off this fleshly mask, fall it must sooner or later: and then, granted that they are equal in height, a likeness will after all turn up between a Prussian and an Austrian which will make it difficult to distinguish them. The stupid and the clever, too, look pretty much alike when their bones are well picked. With such views, a man certainly gets rid of his specific patriotism; but it would indeed be a subject for despair if our salvation depended on them.

Always the observant visitor, Bismarck studied the people he visited with the aim of ascertaining their strengths and weaknesses. Following is one impression of a Russian peculiarity, described in his own words.[10]

At the time of my first stay at St. Petersburg, in 1859, I had an example of another Russian peculiarity. During the first spring days it was then the custom for every one connected with the court to promenade in the Summer Garden between Paul's Palace and the Neva. There the emperor had noticed a sentry standing in the middle of a grass plot; in reply to the question why he was standing there, the soldier could only answer, "Those are my orders." The emperor therefore sent one of his adjutants to the guardroom to make inquiries; but no explanation was forthcoming except that a sentry had to stand there winter and summer. The source of the original order could no longer be discovered. The matter was talked of at court, and reached the ears of the servants. One of these, an old pensioner, came forward and stated that his father had once said to him as they passed the sentry in the Summer Garden: "There he is, still standing to guard the flower; on that spot the Empress Catherine once noticed a snowdrop in bloom unusually early, and gave orders that it was not to be plucked." This command had been carried out by placing a sentry on the spot, and ever since then one had stood there all the year round. Stories of this sort excite our amusement and criticism, but they are an expression of the elementary force and persistence on which the strength of the Russian nature depends in its attitude towards the rest of Europe. It reminds us of the sentinels in the flood at St. Petersburg in 1825, and in the Shipka Pass in 1877; not being relieved, the former were drowned, the latter frozen to death at their posts.

10. *Bismarck: The Man and the Statesman . . .* , trans. Butler, I, 250.

31

In Which Bismarck, Complaining of an Injury in a Hunting Accident, Falls into the Hands of a Quack Doctor and Nearly Loses a Leg by Amputation

"I anticipated my end with that calmness which is induced by unendurable pain."

In August 1857, while on a hunting expedition in Sweden, Bismarck struck his left leg on a rock and injured the shin bone. At the time he thought nothing of it. But in St. Petersburg the leg began to pain him beyond endurance. It was his misfortune to fall into the hands of a quack who called himself Dr. Walz. The doctor clumsily opened the wound and destroyed a vein in Bismarck's leg. A Russian physician, called in for consultation, urged immediate amputation. Bismarck himself told the sordid story.[11]

. . . I returned home without a fur and stopped a little on the way to watch some recruits at drill. Next day I had rheumatism in all my limbs, which gave me trouble for a long while. When the time came for setting out to fetch my wife to St. Petersburg I had quite recovered, except for a slight pain still noticeable in my left leg, which I had injured in 1857 by a fall over a rock during a hunting expedition in Sweden, and which, in consequence of careless treatment, had become *locus minoris resistentiæ*. Dr. Walz, who had been recommended to me when I set out, by the former grand duchess of Baden, offered to prescribe a remedy for me, and when I said that I thought it unnecessary since the pain was but slight, he assured me that the matter might become worse on the journey, and it was advisable to take precautions. The remedy was a simple one; he would put a plaster in the knee hollow, which would cause me no annoyance, and after a few days would fall off of its own accord and only leave a slight redness behind. Being unacquainted with the previous history of this doctor, who came from Heidelberg, I unfortunately yielded to his persuasion. Four hours after I had put on the plaster I woke up from a sound sleep in violent pain and tore off the plaster, but without being able to remove it entirely from the knee hollow, into which it had already burnt a wound. Walz came a few hours afterwards and

11. *Ibid.*, I, 258–260.

assured me that he could scrape away the black plaster mass from the wound, which was as big as a hand, with some sort of metallic blade. The pain was unbearable and the result unsatisfactory, since the corrosive action of the poison continued. I realized the ignorance and unconscientiousness of my physician, in spite of the recommendation from high quarters which had determined me in chosing him. He himself assured me, with an apologetic smile, that the ointment had been peppered rather too strongly; it was a mistake of the chemist's. I sent to the latter for the prescription, and he sent the answer that Walz had taken it back again, but, according to his own statement, the doctor no longer possessed it. I was therefore unable to discover who was the poisoner, and could only learn from the chemist that the chief ingredient of the ointment was the stuff which was used in making cantharides ointment, and as far as he could remember there was an unusually strong dose of it set down in the prescription. I have been asked since whether this poisoning might have been done on purpose; for my part, I merely ascribe it to the ignorance and audacity of this medical swindler.

Upon the recommendation of the Dowager Grand Duchess Sophie of Baden, he had been made director of all the children's hospitals in St. Petersburg; further inquiries on my part resulted in the discovery that he was the son of the university confectioner at Heidelberg, had been an idle student, and failed in his examination. His ointment had destroyed a vein and it caused me many years' suffering.

With a view to seeking help from German doctors, I set out in July for Berlin, traveling by sea to Stettin. Violent pain induced me to consult the celebrated surgeon Pirogow, who was one of the passengers. He wanted to amputate the leg, and on my asking where he would take it off, above or below the knee, he pointed to a place a long way above it. I declined, and after trying various kinds of treatment at Berlin in vain, I was so far restored by the baths of Nauheim under the treatment of Professor Benecke of Marburg, that I was able to walk and ride, and in October to accompany the prince regent to Warsaw to a meeting with the tsar. On my way back to St. Petersburg in November, when I was on a visit to Herr von Below at Hohendorf, the clot which had formed and settled in the injured vein, becoming detached, according to the medical view, entered the circulation and brought about inflammation of the lungs. The doctors expected it to be fatal, but it was cured after a month of grievous sickness. The impressions which a dying Prussian had at that time on the subject of trusteeship seem very strange to me now. My first desire, after my condemnation by the doctors, was to write down a last direction which should exclude all interference by the courts with the trustees appointed by me. Satisfied on this point I anticipated my end with that calmness which is induced by unendurable pain. At the beginning of March 1860 I was well enough to be able to travel to Berlin, where I awaited the completion of my cure, taking part in the sittings of the Upper House. Here I stayed until the beginning of May.

32 Consolation for the Arnims on the Death of a Son

"We are powerless and helpless in God's mighty hand."

The depth of Bismarck's feelings for his sister Malwine is revealed in this letter which he sent to his brother-in-law, Oskar von Arnim, on the death of their son.[12] *On occasions of this kind the great man became aware of his insignificance as a human being. All the glory of great power vanished in this moment of grief.*

REINFELD, *August 16th,* 1861

I have just received the news of the terrible misfortune which has befallen you and Malwine. My first thought was to come to you at once, but in wanting to do so I overrated my powers. My *régime* has touched me up a good deal, and the thought of suddenly breaking it off met with such decided opposition that I have resolved to let Johanna go alone. Such a blow goes beyond the reach of human consolation. And yet it is a natural desire to be near those we love in their sorrow, and to lament with them in common. It is the only thing we can do. A heavier sorrow could scarcely have befallen you. To lose such an amiable and a so-happily-thriving child in such a way, and to bury along with him all the hopes which were to be the joys of your old days,—sorrow over such a loss will not depart from you as long as you live on this earth; this I feel with you, with deep and painful sympathy. We are powerless and helpless in God's mighty hand, so far as He will not Himself help us, and can do nothing but bow down in humility under His dispensations. He can take from us all that He gave, and make us utterly desolate; and our mourning for it will be all the bitterer, the more

12. Bismarck to Oskar von Arnim, as quoted in Warren, ed., *op. cit.*, V, 1940–1941.

we allow it to run to excess in contention and rebellion against His almighty ordinance. Do not mingle your just grief with bitterness and repining, but bring home to yourself that a son and a daughter are left to you, and that with them, and even in the feeling of having possessed another beloved child for fifteen years, you must consider yourself blessed in comparison with the many who have never had children nor known a parent's joy.

I do not want to trouble you with feeble grounds for consolation, but only to tell you in these lines how I, as friend and brother, feel your suffering like my own, and am moved by it to the very core. How all small cares and vexations, which daily accompany our life, vanish at the iron appearance of real misfortune! and I feel like so many reproaches the reminiscences of all complaints and covetous wishes, over which I have so often forgotten how much blessing God gives us, and how much danger surrounds us without touching us. We are not to attach ourselves to this world, and not regard it as our home. Another twenty, or in happiest case thirty years, and we are both of us beyond the cares of this life, and our children have reached our present standpoint, and find with astonishment that the freshly begun life is already going down hill. It would not be worth while to dress and undress if it were over with that.

Do you still remember these words of a fellow traveler from Stolpmünde? The thought that death is the transition to another life will certainly do little to alleviate your grief; for you might think that your beloved son might have been a true and dear companion to you during the time you are still living in this world, and would have continued, by God's blessing, the memory of you here. The circle of those whom we love contracts itself and receives no increase till we have grandchildren. At our time of life we form no fresh bonds which are capable of replacing those that die off. Let us therefore keep the closer together in love until death separates us from one another, as it now separates your son from us. Who knows how soon? Won't you come with Malle to Stolpmünde, and stay quietly with us for a few weeks or days? At all events I shall come to you at Kröchlensdorff, or wherever else you are, in three or four weeks. I greet my dearest Malle with all my heart. May God give her, as well as you, strength to bear and patiently submit.

33

Interlude: While Ambassador to Paris and Awaiting a Call to Berlin as Foreign Minister, Bismarck Makes an Excursion to London where He Stimulates a Historic Judgment of Character

Disraeli: "Take heed of that man: he means what he says!"

Bismarck had been bitten by the bug of political power, but thus far it was only an annoying itch for ministerial office. In May 1861, after an absence of ten months, he was back at his post in St. Petersburg. Much against his will he spent the winter of 1861–1862 in Russia. He was recalled to Berlin in March 1862 because of the developing struggle with parliament. On May 23, 1862, newly decorated with the Order of the Eagle, first class, he was sent off to Paris as ambassador.

There were weeks of solitude as Bismarck awaited a call to Berlin as foreign minister. At home his case was presented by Albrecht von Roon, a "militaristocrat," who felt that Bismarck was ready for high office. Bismarck, in Paris, nervously awaited the decision. "I feel," he said, "like that animal that goes dancing on the ice when it feels too well." Recalling his brief visit to London as a young man, he decided to take a trip there. It was important, he believed, to make the acquaintance of leading British statesmen with whom he might soon be in contact. Besides, there was an International Industrial Exhibition taking place in London, and everyone was going there.

Bismarck remained in London until the beginning of July 1862. He discussed constitutional questions, his military budget, and political parties in Prussia with Lord Palmerston, the British prime minister. He described his version of the Danish problem to Lord John Russell, who led British foreign policy. But his most important conversation was with Benjamin Disraeli, at that time leader of the Opposition in the House of Commons. The meeting which took place at a dinner given by the Russian ambassador to the grand duchess of Saxe-Weimar, led to a remarkable episode.[13]

[Disraeli] expressed a desire to learn what Bismarck would do in the event that he came to political power. With his special

13. From Bismarck's interviews with Palmerston, Russell, and Disraeli in Heinrich von Poschinger, "Aus Bismarcks dunklesten Periode," *Deutsche Revue*, XXXVI, 279 ff.

kind of frankness, disconcerting to listeners, Bismarck declared: "When I come to power, my first care will be, with or without help of the Second Chamber, to reorganize the army. When the army has been brought to such a state as to command respect, then I shall take the first opportunity to declare war on Austria, burst asunder the German Confederation, bring the middle and smaller states into subjection, and give Germany national unity under the leadership of Prussia."

As Disraeli, a bit astonished and puzzled, repeated these remarks to Count Vitzthum von Eckstädt, the Saxon envoy, he added: "Take heed of that man: he means what he says!" Here Disraeli showed himself to be a much better judge of character than Napoleon III, to whom Bismarck had revealed a similar program, and who, after their farewell audience at St. Cloud on September 24, 1862, had dropped the remark: "That Bismarck is not a serious man."

34 Devoted Family Man or Straying Husband? Under Great Nervous Strain Bismarck Takes a Holiday in Biarritz and Meets the Bewitching Princess Orlow

"I am only very glad indeed that my dear husband has found this charming woman."

Before his marriage to Johanna von Puttkamer, Bismarck had trouble with his amours. He himself described it in an engaging metaphor: "My poor inflamed blood burned up like steam." Yet, his marriage turned out to be a singularly happy one—it lasted for a lifetime.

Any discussion of Bismarck's love life depends on the point of view and the inquisitiveness of the biographer. For that reason two versions are presented here. The first, by his warm journalistic supporter, Moritz Busch, paints a picture of Bismarck as an honorable husband, a man of strict principles. The second portrait of a man in love is by Werner Richter, Bismarck's most recent biographer. It is the story of how for a time Bismarck forgot his wedding day and was conquered by a Russian beauty, whom he saw half a dozen times.

In the summer of 1862 Bismarck, already marked out as the future director of Prussian policy, found his nerves under great strain. He spent several happy weeks at Biarritz, a resort close to the Spanish frontier, far from the center of political power. He wrote his wife: "I have a bad conscience for seeing so many beautiful things without you." Perhaps one of the "beautiful things" might have been the entrancing Princess Orlow, described by Werner Richter.

Prince Bismarck in Private Life[14]

It therefore rejoices us heartily to learn that the mighty statesman who has politically reconstructed our nation, took to him betimes a wife who has made him happy and has adorned his home life with many graces and charms. Born in 1824 (therefore nine years younger than her husband) and married to him in 1847, Frau von Bismarck was the daughter of the Nether-Pomeranian landowner Heinrich von Puttkamer, who died in 1872 at a good old age. Her betrothal to Bismarck was at first opposed by her parents—especially by her mother—as his irregularity of habits did not seem to promise well for the future of a daughter of a pious house. "All right," wrote the wooer to his sister, Malwine von Arnim, when he at last obtained the consent of Herr and Frau von Puttkamer; and he and his wife may well have reiterated those words when, while celebrating their Silver Wedding at Varzin (July 28, 1872), they looked back into their conjugal past. The princess was brought up in the fear of God, but is of a quick, lively disposition, endowed with a good share of mother wit, sensibility and good taste. Fond of music and an excellent pianist, she is also a careful and judicious housewife, and skilled in the use of drugs, after the manner of noble dames in the olden days. She has made her husband's home comfortable and intelligently shared his cares and hopes—even to a certain extent, those connected with politics, although she is not one of those ladies who busy themselves with affairs of state. Judging by his letters to her, the intercourse between them when business compelled him to leave her for a time has always been of a lively and affectionate character. In his correspondence he addresses her as "my heart" and "my beloved heart;" he sends her jessamine from Peterhof, heather-bells from Bordeaux and edelweiss from Gastein; on the sixteenth anniversary of their wedding day he reminds her that she "brought sunshine into his bachelor life." From Ofen he wrote to her "Good night from afar. Where did I hear the song that has been haunting me all day long —'Over the dark blue mountain, Over the white sea foam, Come, thou beloved one, Come, to thy lonely home'?" In his letters to his wife and sister we frequently encounter the expression of his long-

14. Busch, *Bismarck: Sketches for a Historical Picture,* trans. Beatty-Kingston, II, 275–278.

ing for his family and quiet home:—"I really yearn for the country, the woods and idleness, supplemented by loving wives and well-behaved, clean children. Whenever I hear one of these hopeful beings squalling in the street, my heart is filled with paternal feelings and educational axioms. How do our successors get on together; and are mine pretty orderly?" In another letter to his sister written from Tsarskoe Selo (1860) he observed:—"After knocking about ever since the commencement of 1859, the sensation of living with my own people again, anyhow and anywhere, is so comforting that I can hardly tear myself away from the house." To his wife he wrote from Biarritz:—"My conscience smites me for seeing so much that is beautiful without you. If you could be suddenly carried hither through the air, I would straightway take you off to San Sebastian." Writing from Nuernberg he said:—"I should have liked to go from Vienna to Salzburg, where the king is —our wedding tour over again." In a note from Babelsberg (1863) he assured his wife that he should be delighted "soon again to see you assuming command of the empty apartments at Berlin. Meanwhile I hope you will get over the hammering and rummaging which inevitably results from your return home, and that when I return I shall find everything in its place." From the pavilion of Stanislaus Augustus near Warsaw, he wrote:—"The wind blows recklessly over the Vistula, and works such havoc in the chestnut and lime trees surrounding me that their yellow leaves hurtle against the panes; but sitting here with double windows, tea, and thoughts of you and the children, I can smoke my cigar quite comfortably." On another occasion, while shooting in the wilds of Smaland, he expressed the wish for "a castle, peopled by my dear ones, hard by one of the quiet lakes, surrounded with coverts and heather, of this Swedish landscape."

Many other passages in his letters denote how dear his wife is to him and how often he thinks of her and his children. They also indicate that the pious lady he espoused has brought herself in time to share his energetic way of thinking and feeling. Two days after the fall of Sedan the chancellor read aloud to us an extract from one of her letters praying, in Scriptural language, that the French might be destroyed. "May I ask how the Countess is?" enquired Prince Albrecht (Oct. 29, 1870) while dining with the chancellor at Versailles. "Oh," replied the latter, "she is all right, now that her son is getting better; but she is still suffering from her grim hatred of the Gauls, whom she would like to see shot and bayoneted, every man Jack of them, even the tiny children, who really cannot help having been born of such abominable parents." A few days later he imparted to us a remark made by her conceived in a not much milder spirit than the above—"I fear that you will not find any Bibles in France, and therefore shall send you the Psalm book, so that you may read the prophecy against the French: 'I say to you the godless shall be exterminated.' "

The Princess Orlow[15]

On the 4th of August [1862], Bismarck was in Biarritz and here was joined at the Hôtel de l'Europe, where he lived, by Prince Orlow, the Russian ambassador in Brussels who arrived on the 7th and whom he knew from his St. Petersburg days.

Prince Orlow was a veteran of the Crimea who had had his right arm shattered and wore a black silk eye shield to conceal the loss of an eye. Princess Orlow—her name was Katherine, and she was by birth a Trubetzkoi—was twenty-two years old and utterly bewitching. She had been brought up in France and spoke French, English, and German, and hardly any Russian. She was a stranger to Bismarck, but there rapidly developed between them a companionship which, though our information is scanty, seems to have gone rather beyond the permitted informalities of a holiday resort.

Bismarck and the Orlows took their meals together in the Orlows' rooms. Apart from this, a small company gathered daily consisting of Bismarck, the Orlows, the princess's French lady-in-waiting, and a Russian diplomat named von Hamburger, Gortchakoff's *homme de confiance,* whom Bismarck described to his wife as "hunchbacked, intelligent, and a good fellow." The prince called Bismarck "uncle." The prince, a great gentleman of the old school, always more or less of an invalid, gave his wife, his junior by some thirteen years, the maximum of freedom and left her no opportunity of asking for it. For Bismarck the idyll was all too short, but while it lasted politics seemed to be forgotten, nervous tensions relaxed. Indeed, when von Galen, the Prussian ambassador in Madrid, and an old friend of his, called to see him, Bismarck did not find this visit altogether welcome.

To Malle [Malwine, Bismarck's sister] who, as always, was again his confidante, he declared quite openly that he had fallen slightly in love with the *"niedliche principessa."* "You know that this type of thing sometimes happens to me"; and to Johanna he wrote, with rather less candor, that the princess was "original, jolly, intelligent and friendly, pretty and young. . . . When you meet her you will forgive my being somewhat *épris.*" Johanna at that time was writ-

15. Werner Richter, *Bismarck,* trans. by Brian Battershaw (London, 1964), pp. 74, 116–117.

ing to Keudell, "If I had any disposition toward envy or jealousy, I could no doubt let these passions tyrannize over the very depths of my being . . . but there is no aptitude for that kind of thing in my soul. I am only very glad indeed that my dear husband has found this charming woman." In all this Johanna showed a very magnanimous side of her character. There can be little doubt that she did experience jealousy and suffer from it, although the knowledge of her own worth compelled her to be silent. . . .

On arrival [at Biarritz, 1865], he suffered yet another disappointment. Princess Orlow had failed to arrive. She said she feared cholera, but it is quite likely that she was now shrinking from the rather sinister monster that for so many of his contemporaries Bismarck had become.

35

Fulfillment: In a Historic Audience Held on September 22, 1862, King William Tears up His Abdication Statement and Decides to Name Bismarck Minister-President of Prussia

"I will rather perish with the king than forsake your Majesty in the contest with parliamentary government."

Albrecht von Roon, minister of war since 1859, and a man of strongly absolutistic and anti-liberal conviction, had already prepared the way. William I, who had been crowned king of Prussia on October 18, 1861, found himself embroiled in a developing struggle with parliament over the matter of army credits, Roon urged the monarch to accept Bismarck as ministerial candidate, but William was reluctant. Nevertheless, Roon prepared Bismarck for a summons to Berlin. The story of the historic conference in Berlin on September 22, 1862 was told by Bismarck himself in his own way, a fascinating tale, although not strictly accurate.[16] *Actually, William had no other recourse: he had to entrust the government to the only man who was willing and able to defy parliament and who had no scruples about constitutional means. The king, less inclined to abdication than he was several days before the meeting, was impressed by Bismarck's fearlessness and energy. When the audience was over, Bismarck was the new minister-president.*

16. *Bismarck: The Man and the Statesman . . .* , trans. Butler, I, 293–297.

In Paris I received the following telegram, the signature of which had been agreed upon:

Berlin: *le 18 Septembre*
PERICULUM IN MORA. DÉPÊCHEZ-VOUS
l'oncle de Maurice
Henning

Henning was the second name of Moritz Blanckenburg, Roon's nephew. Although the wording left it doubtful whether the invitation was given on Roon's own initiative, or was suggested by the king, I did not hesitate to set out.

I arrived at Berlin in the morning of September 20, and was summoned to the crown prince. To his question as to my view of the situation, I could only give a very cautious answer, because I had read no German papers during the last few weeks, and from a sort of *dépit* had neglected to inform myself about home affairs. The cause of my vexation was the king's having led me to believe that in six weeks at latest he would come to a decision about my future—*i.e.* whether I was to take up my residence in Berlin, Paris, or London—that a quarter of a year had already passed away, and that autumn was come before I knew where I was to spend the winter. I was not sufficiently acquainted with the particulars of the situation to be able to give the crown prince a detailed opinion; nor did I consider myself justified in expressing my views to him before I had done so to the king. The impression which the fact of my audience had made was at once discernible from Roon's statement that the king had said to him, referring to me: "He is no good either; you see he has already been to see my son." The bearing of this remark was not at once comprehensible to me, because I did not know that the king, having conceived the idea of abdication, assumed that I either knew or suspected it, and had therefore tried to place myself favorably with his successor.

As a matter of fact, however, the idea of the king's abdication was fresh to me when I was received at Babelsberg on September 22, and the situation only became clear to me when his Majesty defined it in some such words as these: "I will not reign if I cannot do it in such a fashion as I can be answerable for to God, my conscience, and my subjects. But I cannot do that if I am to rule according to the will of the present majority in parliament, and I can no longer find any ministers prepared to conduct my government without subjecting themselves and me to the parliamentary majority. I have therefore resolved to lay down my crown, and have already sketched out the proclamation of my abdication, based on the motives to which I have referred." The king showed me the document in his own handwriting lying on the table, whether already signed or not I do not know. His Majesty concluded by repeating that he could not govern without suitable ministers.

I replied that his Majesty had been acquainted ever since May with my readiness to enter the ministry; I was certain that Roon would remain with me on his side, and I did not doubt that we should succeed in completing the cabinet, supposing other members should feel themselves compelled to resign on account of my admission. After a good deal of consideration and discussion, the king asked me whether I was prepared as minister to advocate the reorganization of the army, and when I assented he asked me further whether I would do so in opposition to the majority in parliament and its resolutions. When I asserted my willingness, he finally declared, "Then it is my duty, with your help, to attempt to continue the battle, and I shall not abdicate." I do not know whether he destroyed the document which was lying on the table, or whether he preserved it *in rei memoriam.*

The king invited me to accompany him into the park. During the walk he gave me a program to read, which filled eight pages of his close writing, embraced all eventualities of the politics of the time, and went into such details as the reform of the district sub-diets. I cannot say whether this elaboration had already served as the basis of discussion with my predecessors, or whether it was to serve as a security against a policy of conservative thoroughness such as I was credited with. At the time when he was meditating my appointment, some fear of this nature had doubtless been aroused in him by his wife, of whose political understanding he had originally a very high opinion, dating from the time when his Majesty was only permitted a crown prince's privilege of criticizing his brother; without the obligation to do better himself. In criticism the princess was her husband's superior. The first doubts as to her intellectual superiority were wakened in him when he was compelled, instead of criticizing, to act himself, and to bear the official responsibility for improvements. As soon as the tasks of the two royal persons became practical, the king's sound common sense had begun gradually to emancipate itself more and more from her ready feminine volubility.

I succeeded in convincing him that, so far as he was concerned, it was not a question of Liberal or Conservative of this or that shade, but rather of monarchical rule or parliamentary government, and that the latter must be avoided at all costs, if even by a period of dictatorship. I said: "In this situation I shall, even if your Majesty command me to do things which I do not consider right, tell you my opinion quite openly; but if you finally persist in yours, I will rather perish with the king than forsake your Majesty in the contest with parliamentary government." This view was at that time strong and absolute in me, because I regarded the negations and phrases of the opposition of that day as politically disastrous in face of the national task of Prussia, and because I cherished such strong feelings of devotion and affection for William I, that the thought of perishing with him appeared to me, under the circumstances, a natural and congenial conclusion to my life.

The king tore the program to pieces, and was about to throw them down from the bridge into the dry ditch in the park, when I reminded him that these papers in his well-known writing might fall into very wrong hands. He saw that I was right, put the pieces in his pocket to commit them to the flames, and on the same day ratified my appointment as minister and interim chairman of the ministry, which was made public on the 23rd. The king kept my nomination as president in reserve, until he had completed the correspondence on the subject with Prince von Hohenzollern, who still occupied this post constitutionally.

Painting by Siemer

BISMARCK REPORTS TO WILHELM I

PART IV

The Sculptor of German Unification, 1862-1871

36

The Fortunes of the Kingdom of Prussia in the Hands of Bismarck as Minister-President and Minister for Foreign Affairs, 1862[1]

"Let us wait; by his deeds he shall be judged."

Bismarck, now at the pinnacle of political power, was greeted with a chorus of hostility. The London Spectator *called him the most outspoken Junker who had ever ruled in Prussia, a man of strong but limited understanding. Almost immediately the new minister-president came into conflict with the Chamber of Deputies.*

Bismarck seemed now to feel that it rested with him to realize the vision of a strong and powerful Prussia, the head of that united Germany, which had long floated before his imagination. Prussia, and indeed the whole of Germany, looked with eager anxiety to the formation of the ministry, and to the adoption of a policy led by a man who had proved himself so bold, resolute, and inflexible. Bismarck had only to look at the papers to see the hostility with which his appointment was regarded. Caricatures of his past life appeared in the booksellers' windows as the feudal Junker, who would sweep away the large cities as nests of revolution; and as the sometime worshipper of Napoleon. Bismarck, it is said, bought copies of them all, though some were suppressed by the police; what amusement they must have furnished the chancellor if he came across them in after years.

The party newspapers, which unfortunately, I suppose in all countries, allow their prejudices, one-sidedness, and bitterness, to make them so ridiculous in the eyes of thoughtful men, launched at him a perfect torrent of the rudest and most disparaging epithets, which, read in the light of succeeding events, should suggest to editors a principle of more prudence, thought, and justice. Thus wrote, for example, the *Berliner Allgemeine Zeitung,* "He began his career as a country nobleman with little political education. . . . His penetration and knowledge were not above what are common to ordinary people. He gained his fame in the House of Representatives, not so much by his own eloquence as by Herr von Thadden-Trieglaff, who served him as a foil, and because his party had no other speaker upon whom to rely. He reached the high-water

1. William Jacks, *The Life of Prince Bismarck* (Glasgow, 1899), pp. 144–147.

mark of his parliamentary aim in the Revision Chamber of 1849, and in the Union Parliament of 1850."

Then comparing him unfavorably with others whose names are now lost in oblivion, the article proceeded:

"He has gained in Frankfort some knowledge of diplomatic ceremonies, and learned in St. Petersburg and Paris how to extract their secrets from intriguing princesses; but to the heavy labor of daily governmental control he is a stranger. The clear insight necessary for the management of the state he has never and nowhere been able to acquire," etc.

It is hoped that the writer of this article lived to see his own insight tried. The party papers of his own side were naturally more friendly, and the *Augsburger Allgemeine Zeitung* closed an article with the prudent words, "Let us wait; by his deeds shall he be judged."

Every effort was made to excite popular hostility against the new minister, and Bismarck may be said, about this time, to have reached the zenith of that unpopularity, little short of hatred, with which he was for years regarded. He took up his duties calmly and firmly, showing both to his friends and foes by his words, but more strikingly by his deeds, how little these things moved him; that as minister of state he was above partisanship, and that he regarded neither the favor nor disfavor of any party weak or strong, but would be guided by one consideration, and one only—the true welfare of his country. Many years later, on the 24th February, 1881, he said: "For myself, one single compass, one Polar star, has given me the direction in which to steer, *Salus Publica;* I have, since the beginning of my career, perhaps often acted rashly and incautiously, but . . . I was always dominated by one question, What is the best for my Fatherland, for the dynasty?"

Certainly the state of affairs which met him on his entry into the ministry required all the ability and force of character with which he was endowed, and the singleness of purpose with which he was inspired. Never, perhaps, in the history of the world was such an entangled and dangerous web of difficulties presented for the solution of any statesman. At home he inherited the quarrel between parliament and the government on the military budget, abroad the continued and embittered struggle with Austria as to the supremacy of Germany, and their relative positions in that government demanded his closest attention, and while the relations with Russia had become strained, those with the other powers not very harmonious; France, he says, was the only power with which their relations were comparatively good.

All these difficulties he met with firmness and unflinching confidence; as he afterwards said, "I may say, although I stood alone against a world of hate and anger, I never lost sight of my purpose."

To Russia he brought better personal relations, and strengthened them by the treaty made on the Polish outbreak against Russia. He secured the friendliness of France by a generous treaty of commerce, which treaty, however, he had no desire to continue, although through it he kept that country friendly during the Danish war, and favorable during the war with Austria; he says, however, that "Napoleon reckoned that the Austrians would be victorious, and that then he might show his good feeling toward us, though not without securing an equivalent (the left bank of the Rhine). But it is my opinion that until the Battle of Sadowa led to his disillusion as to our relative military strength, he was favorably inclined to us, and to me personally he was especially friendly."

37

Blood and Iron: The New Minister-President Makes One of the Most Striking Speeches in History, Thereby Throwing All Europe into Astonishment and Setting the Tone for His Regime

". . . That was the mistake of 1848 and 1849. . . ."

September 30, 1862. Shortly after his appointment Bismarck appears before thirty members of the budget commission of the Prussian Lower House and urges them to vote for army increases. Speaking wittily and incisively, he warns his listeners not to exaggerate their powers. He declares emphatically that the constitution did not give the Lower House the sole power of arranging the budget. The Upper House and the crown had just as much to say in the matter. He ends his speech with the "iron-and-blood" challenge reprinted below.[2]

The words soon spread through the country, with the rhythm changed to "blood-and-iron." There was much criticism, but Bismarck never repudiated his words. He explained somewhat lamely that by this allusion he meant that the weapons of war had first to shed human blood before great decisions became possible. Ac-

2. *Die politische Reden des Fürsten Bismarck,* ed. by Horst Kohl (Stuttgart, 1892–1904), II, 29–30.

cording to biographer Werner Richter, Bismarck's phrase was nothing more than a slip of the tongue, but the words were to adhere like pitch to his name.

The Landtag *refused to vote for the requested credits, whereupon Bismarck, defying the constitution of 1850, and pleading that "necessity alone is authoritative," began to collect and spend funds without presenting either a budget or an accounting.*

. . . It is true that we can hardly escape complications in Germany, although we do not seek them. Germany does not look to Prussia's liberalism, but to her power. The south German states—Bavaria, Württemberg, and Baden—would like to indulge in liberalism, and because of that no one will assign Prussia's role to them! Prussia must collect her forces and hold them in reserve for an opportune moment, which has already come and gone several times. Since the Treaty of Vienna, our frontiers have not been favorably designed for a healthy body politic. Not by speeches and majorities will the great questions of the day be decided—that was the mistake of 1848 and 1849—but by iron and blood.

38 Bismarckian Reaction versus a Royal Version of Liberalism: Minister-President and Crown Prince Clash over a Governmental Press Decree

"Youth is always ready with words!"

From the beginning of his career as minister-president, Bismarck found himself at odds with Crown Prince Frederick William. The heir to the throne was troubled by Bismarck's reactionary policies. He was convinced that the British parliamentary system was best for Prussia, an attitude shared by his wife, the daughter of Queen Victoria. On his part, Bismarck was angered by the intrusion of the English way of life in the crown prince's household.

On June 1, 1863, just a little over eight months after he became minister-president, Bismarck issued a press ordinance in which he made it clear that he would suppress any periodical which attacked the government.

Distressed by what he regarded as the beginning of an anti-parliamentary dictatorship, the liberal-minded crown prince, who until this time had imposed a regimen of silence upon himself, publicly deplored the breach between government and people brought by Bismarck's decree. At the same time he informd Bismarck by letter of his feelings. The correspondence revealed a growing coolness between the two.[3] *The forty-eight-year-old minister-president looked upon the thirty-two-year-old crown prince as a kind of naughty boy. Bismarck advised the king, who was deeply hurt by the attitude of his heir, to "deal gently with the boy Absalom."*

The Crown Prince Frederick to Bismarck

STETTIN, *June* 30, 1863

I learn from your letter of the tenth instant that, by command of his Majesty the King, you have abstained from communicating officially to the ministry of state, my protest against the press-restrictions decree, which I sent you from Graudenz on the third instant.

I can quite imagine that you would not find it undesirable to treat as a purely personal matter a procedure which, as you yourself acknowledge, might acquire general importance in its consequences. It would avail nothing if I insisted on that communication being presented,(1) and, indeed, as I gather from your letter, this will already have been done *non*-officially. It is, however, of importance to me to speak my mind clearly to you in respect of the alternative you put to me: to facilitate or to render more difficult the task before the ministry. I cannot make it easier for you, as I am on principle opposed to the decree.

The principles which, in my opinion, must guide every government in its treatment of the country are: loyal administration of the laws and the constitution, esteem for and benevolence towards an easily guided, intelligent and capable people. I cannot reconcile with these principles the policy evinced in the regulation of June 1st.

You seek to prove to me that that decree is in accordance with the constitution, and to assure me that you and your colleagues are mindful of your oath. I think, however, that a government needs a firmer foundation than what are at least extremely questionable interpretations, which do not appeal to the healthy common sense of the people. You yourself refer to the fact that even your opponents esteem the honesty of your convictions. I leave this statement undiscussed,(2) but if you attach any value to the opinion of your opponents you must be impressed by the circumstance that the decided majority of the educated classes of our people denies that the contents of the regulation in question are in accord with the

3. *The Correspondence of William I and Bismarck, with Other Letters to and from Bismarck,* trans. by J. A. Ford (2 vols., London, 1903), II, 105–110.

constitution. The ministry knew beforehand that this would be the case, as it also knew that the *Landtag* would never have sanctioned the contents of that decree; therefore it did not lay the matter before the *Landtag,* but settled it itself, and a few days afterwards published the regulation by virtue of the powers granted by clause 63 of the constitution.

If the country does not recognize in this procedure a loyal administration of the constitution, I should like to ask what the ministry has done to win public opinion over to its own view. It has found no other means of coming to an understanding with public opinion than by imposing silence on it.

It is useless to waste words on the question as to how the regulation can be made compatible with the esteem and the benevolence due to a willing, loyal people, which, however, as the government will not hear its voice, is condemned to assume the role of the mute.

And what results do you anticipate from this policy? The pacification of agitated feelings, and the restoration of peace?

Do you imagine that you can pacify agitated feelings by means of fresh violations of the sense of justice?

It is true, you expect to be more successful in the new elections.(3) It appears to me to be contrary to human nature to hope for a change of opinions which are constantly being roused and irritated by the procedure of the government.

I will tell you what results of your policy I foresee: You will tamper with the constitution until it loses its value in the people's eyes, and in this way you will incite anarchist endeavors which go beyond the constitution. You will also be driven, whether you wish it or not, from one venturesome interpretation to another, until finally the naked, undisguised breach of the constitution is recommended.

I regard those who lead his Majesty the King, my most gracious father, along such ways, as the most dangerous advisers for the crown and the Fatherland.(4, 5)

FRIEDRICH WILHELM K. P.

P. S. Even before the first of this month I made a very limited use of my right to be present at the sittings of the ministry of state.

After the convictions I have expressed above, you will not be surprised that I shall ask his Majesty the King to permit me to abstain altogether in future from taking part in the sittings during the continuance of the present ministry.

To be constantly giving public and personal expression to my opposition to the ministry would accord neither with my position nor with my inclination. I shall, however, impose no constraint on myself in respect of expressing my opinion in all other relations, and the ministry may reckon on the fact that it depends entirely on itself and on its further action whether, notwithstanding my great reluctance to do so, I shall feel compelled not to shrink from taking other public steps, should duty seem to demand this.

F. W. K. P.*

July 2, 1863

Marginal notes by Bismarck:

(1) No.

(2) Not very polite.

(3) No.

(4) I not. (5) Youth is always ready with words!

Bismarck to the Crown Prince Frederick
(Draft)

CARLSBAD, *July* 10, 1863

YOUR ROYAL HIGHNESS,

I beg to announce that I have had the honor to receive the letter of June 30, July 2.

Your Royal Highness says in it that a constant personal expression of your opposition to the ministry would accord neither with your position nor your inclination. I believe, therefore, that I shall be complying with your Royal Highness's wishes if I respectfully refrain from replying to the judgment which your Royal Highness passes on the procedure of his Majesty's government.

As regards the position which your Royal Highness wishes to take in future towards the government of his Majesty the King, this is a matter of such great bearing on the welfare and the future of the state, that, in my most humble opinion, it cannot be brought up for discussion before the conclusion of the present "cure" without prejudicing the good effects looked for from the same on the king.

v. BISMARCK

The Crown Prince Frederick to Bismarck

July 14, 1863

While thanking you for your letter of July 10th, I hasten, with reference to the concluding sentence, to request you most decidedly not to mention my intention to his Majesty the King until you hear from his Majesty, or from me, that his Majesty is already acquainted with it. When I wrote to you that I would ask his Majesty

* The postscript was added at Putbus.

to relieve me from attendance at the sittings of the ministry of state, it was by no means my intention that his Majesty should learn of my decision through you. I know quite well that his Majesty must be spared all mental effort, both now and after the "cure," and will myself discuss my views and plans with his Majesty at a time which seems to me suitable.

I expect, therefore, that you will not speak to the king on this subject until you hear that his Majesty is acquainted with my purposes.

FRIEDRICH WILHELM K. P.

Bismarck to the Crown Prince Frederick
(Draft)

BERLIN, *July* 16, 1863

I have just had the honor of receiving your Royal Highness's letter of the 14th, and hasten most respectfully to inform your Royal Highness that I have not mentioned your Royal Highness's letter of the 2nd instant to his Majesty the King, and in accordance with your Royal Highness's command will abstain from taking the initiative in the matter. Some reports, respecting the contents of your Royal Highness's correspondence with the king, which have been circulated by the newspapers since the 2nd instant, unexpectedly came to the notice of his Majesty the day before yesterday. In consequence of this his Majesty summoned me again just before my departure and commanded me to make investigations, with the object of discovering how these communications found their way into the *Weser Zeitung*.

I beg most respectfully to report to your Royal Highness that I leave Berlin again on Saturday, to join his Majesty's suite at Regensburg, en route for Gastein, as the king has commanded me to be present at the approaching meeting with the emperor of Austria.

V. BISMARCK

39 The Hard-Bitten Politician Seeks Relief from His Everyday Battles by Writing to Motley, May 23, 1864

"Jack, my dear, where . . . are you . . . ?"

Bismarck and John Lothrop Motley, who had become a distinguished historian, kept in touch with one another. Motley always addressed his letters: "My dear Bismarck," while the latter preferred to write "My dear Jack," or "Jack, my dear." When writing in German, both used the familiar form Du, *thus remaining true to their* Schmollis *(friendship pledge over wine) at Göttingen. Motley's letters were filled with expressions of admiration for the success of Bismarck's career.*

Bismarck's letters to Motley reveal good control of English: the chancellor learned English through what he called the "ear-method," without attention to grammatical rules. His lines bubble with the enthusiasm of his youth. Once again he was the carefree student avoiding serious thought and seeking always for a laugh. He never forgot the Yankee expressions he had learned from Motley. He liked to repeat the phrases taught him by his American friends, such as "pig-doggery" and "sleep—the sweet restorer." "In Good Old Colony Times" was a favorite song:

> *In good old colony times,*
> *When we lived under a king,*
> *Three roguish chaps*
> *Fell into mishaps*
> *Because they could not sing!*

Bismarck's sentiments during the American Civil War were revealed in this letter to Motley, dated May 23, 1864.[4]

Jack, my dear, where the devil are you, and what do you do that you never write a line to me? I am working from morn to night . . . and you have nothing to do at all; you might as well tip me a line as well as looking on your feet tilted against the wall of God knows what a dreary color. I can not entertain a regular correspondence; it happens to me that during five days I do not find a quarter of an hour for a walk; but you, lazy old chap, what keeps you from thinking of your old friends? When just going to bed in this moment, my eye met with yours on your portrait, and I curtailed the sweet restorer, sleep, in order to remind you of "Auld Lang Syne"; why do you never come to Berlin? It is not a quarter of an American's holiday journey from Vienna, and my wife and me should be so happy to see you once more in this sullen life. When can you come, and when will you? I swear that I will make out the time to look with you on old Logier's quarters, and drink a bottle with you at Gerolt's, where they once would not allow you to put your slender legs upon a chair. Let politics be hanged, and come

4. Quoted in *Bismarck's Speeches and Letters,* ed. by Hermann Schoenfeld (New York, 1905), pp. 250–251.

and see me. I promise that the Union Jack (*sic!*) shall wave over our house, and conversation and the best old hock shall pour damnation upon the rebels. Do not forget old friends, neither their wives, as mine wishes nearly as ardently as myself to see you, or at least to see as quickly as possible a word of your handwriting.

Sei gut und komm oder schreibe.

Dein

v. BISMARCK

Haunted by the song, "In good old Colony times."

40 Stage Number One—German Unification: In an Incredibly Dexterous Performance by a Diplomatic Genius, Prussia Goes to War against Tiny Denmark, 1864

"The second was a German professor, who became mad."

How Bismarck utilized a quarrel with Denmark to test his Prussian army is a story of diplomacy at its shrewdest.[5] *In bewildering twists and turns he isolated Denmark from help, brought Austria into war with him against Denmark, and set the first stage for German unity. It was a calculated step: he would settle matters with his partner later.*

Schleswig-Holstein was a complicated problem. Lord Palmerston described it: "Only three men have understood it. One was Prince Albert, who is dead. The second was a German professor, who became mad. I am the third, and I have forgotten all about it."

Denmark in 1815 extended down to the German city of Hamburg. Denmark proper was a kingdom consisting of islands in the North Sea and the northern part of the Jutland peninsula. The population in 1864 was largely Danish. On the neck of the peninsula were the two duchies of Schleswig and Holstein, both about the same size, between the North and Baltic seas. The Duchy of Holstein was closer to Prussia, and its people spoke German. The Duchy of Schleswig, between Denmark proper and Holstein, contained both Danish- and German-speaking people.

The three distinct parts—Denmark, Schleswig, and Holstein—were ruled by the King of Denmark. They were united in what was

5. Account contributed by the editor.

called a "personal union." Holstein, the southern duchy, was also part of the German Confederation (*Bund*), which included Austria. Schleswig was not in the *Bund* and was not subject to its authority.

The two duchies, on the strength of a royal decree that dated from the fifteenth century, considered themselves to be "for all times united" (*up ewig ungedeelt*). But there were quarrels between Germans and Danes. In May 1852 the Great Powers, tired of having their commerce disturbed by unrest in the duchies, enforced a compromise (Treaty and Protocol of London). This confirmed Danish control of the duchies, but ordered Denmark to respect German rights. Nobody was satisfied by this arrangement.

King Frederick VII of Denmark died on November 15, 1863. Frederick had no children. Who would become his successor in the kingdom of Denmark and in the duchies? The Germans in the duchies hoped that they would now be separated from Denmark.

The situation became more and more confused. On the death of the king, Christian of the House of Gluckburg ascended the throne as Christian IX of Denmark and as duke of Schleswig and Holstein. This was in accordance with the Treaty of London and by a law which was valid in Denmark and Schleswig, but not in Holstein.

Then a new claimant appeared to dispute the title to the duchies. The day after the death of the king, Frederick, eldest son of the duke of Augustenburg and the lawful heir of Holstein, announced his succession as Frederick VIII of Holstein. The German people received this news joyfully. They wanted to see Frederick VIII of Holstein become head of both duchies.

At this stage Bismarck decided that he would allow neither of the two pretenders to take the duchies. He would simply take them for Prussia. He set to work with his customary shrewdness. One after another he broke down the barriers standing in his way.

First, it was certain that Denmark would not agree to Bismarck's design on the two duchies. Bismarck decided that he would have to use force to subjugate the small country, even if he had to goad it into fighting.

Second, he knew that the *Bund,* the German Confederation under Austrian control, would protest against his designs. But the *Bund* was weak, and Bismarck would simply disregard it.

Third, what to do about the German people? Bismarck was a little worried about the reaction of the Germans to his plans, but he would appeal to their sense of nationalism and bring them to his side. He guessed correctly that they would become wildly excited by his war.

Fourth, what about Great Britain? It was certain that London looked upon the integrity of Denmark as vital for the European balance of power. Perhaps Britain would fight. But Palmerston, the British prime minister, was eighty years old, and no match for the wily Prussian minister-president.

Fifth, Bismarck knew that Great Britain and France might work together and frustrate his plans. He carefully separated the two powers. He hinted to Napoleon III that in exchange for France's neutrality, Prussia might just possibly give France the left bank of the Rhine. To Napoleon III this was bait he could not afford to ignore.

Sixth, Austria was the greatest obstacle of all. Austria was the formidable barrier to Prussia's expansion. Bismarck was aware that Austria would never permit him to appropriate the duchies. Bismarck solved this in a simple way—he made Austria his partner in an attack on both duchies.

Thus, one by one, Bismarck surmounted the obstacles. It was a remarkable performance.

On February 1, 1864, Prussian and Austrian troops crossed the border and moved into Schleswig. Saxon and Hanoverian troops, sent by the *Bund* as a defensive measure, were quickly pushed aside. The Danes fought heroically for two months, but it was an unequal struggle. The Prussian army, outfitted with artillery and needle guns, moved ahead. Prussian troops stormed the last Danish stronghold on April 18, 1864. The little country capitulated.

The peace treaty was signed at Vienna on October 30, 1864. Denmark renounced all her rights to the two duchies in favor of Prussia and Austria. Schleswig and Holstein were combined in a "condominium" under the joint control of Prussia and Austria.

Bismarck had won a major victory. The Austrians had helped him, but he would know how to pick a quarrel with them later. He had achieved his goal without permitting the Great Powers to intervene. He had obtained the support of his own king, and he had pleased Napoleon III. He had won the hearts of the German people in what they regarded as a master stroke. He had boldly engineered the most important territorial *coup* since the days of Frederick the Great. He now began to taste the heady wine of popularity.

All Europe marveled at this diplomatic genius whose fearlessness and recklessness had brought Prussia new territory and new glory. Lord Robert Cecil, later to become British prime minister, described it as "one of the most unblushing spoliations which history records." Spoliation or not, Bismarck had achieved his aim.

41 In a Classic Case of Adult Pettiness, the Fifty-Year-Old Bismarck Reverts to His Swashbuckling Youth and Challenges Dr. Virchow to a Duel

Virchow: "I decline. . . ."

Dr. Rudolf Virchow was forty-four years old in 1865 and already the outstanding physician of his generation. An intensely active man, small and frail in physique, he was called to Berlin in 1856 to a new chair of pathological anatomy to direct the Pathological Institute especially built for him. His Cellularpathologie *(1858), one of the great books on medicine, had caused a revolution in medical thinking.*

In 1862 Virchow was elected a member of the Prussian Chamber of Deputies. A founder and leader of the Progressive party, he was later the originator of the expression "Kulturkampf." *A vigorous antagonist, he lost few opportunities to criticize Bismarck from the tribune. The exchanges were sarcastic and bitter:*

> VIRCHOW: *I wish the minister-president were likely to win among the diplomats of Europe a position so highly esteemed as my own among the specialists of my profession. His policy is undefinable. We might even say that he has no policy.*

> BISMARCK: *I fully recognize the honorable member's high position in his own specialty, and I admit that in this respect he has the advantage of me. But when the honorable member forsakes his own province, and, uninstructed, trespasses, upon my field, I must tell him that in political matters his opinion weighs very little with me. I really think, gentlemen, I do not exaggerate in saying that I understand these things better.* [*Loud laughter.*] *The honorable member charges me with a lack of understanding of national politics. I can throw back the charge while suppressing the adjective. To me it seems that the honorable member has no understanding of politics of any kind.*

At the sitting of the Chamber of Deputies on June 2, 1865, Virchow reproached Bismarck by expressing his doubts as to the latter's truthfulness. The fifty-year-old Bismarck promptly reverted to the days of his youth: he sent a challenge to the famed doctor. When his friends prevailed upon him not to be silly and fall into Bismarck's trap, Virchow sent a refusal. Bismarck expressed satisfaction when Dr. Virchow made an apology in the Chamber on June 17, 1865. The whole story is told in these letters.[6]

Adolf v. Kleist, President of the Court of Appeal, to Bismarck

BERLIN, *June* 7, 1865

MOST ESTEEMED FRIEND,

I dare not interfere unrequested in this extremely delicate matter, and least of all draw your wife into it; when, therefore, she referred to it yesterday evening I did not enter into it. I feel bound, however, to bring to your notice a letter which I have *just* received from Gerlach, and to remark that I quite agree with it and do not consider the insult *in itself* is of a nature to demand such an issue; all men of honor with whom I have discussed the affair are of the same opinion and also are of opinion that a very serious precedent would be established for all the ministers of his Majesty and King if such affairs had to have such an issue.

With the old esteem,

Your faithfully devoted,

v. KLEIST

Kindly return Gerlach's letter *without any answer;* my services in *any* capacity are, of course, at your disposal.

v. Natzmer to Bismarck

BERLIN, *June* 7, 1865

ESTEEMED BISMARCK,

You will pardon me, and attribute it to the great esteem in which I hold you, if I meddle in your affairs without being asked to do so. My object is to ask permission to step into your place if an insidious bullet should prevent you from continuing the fight. The caprices of fate are inscrutable, and my excitement over your affair is so great that I cannot express it to you.

Once more I beg you to forgive my obtrusiveness, not to misconstrue my intention, and to permit me the assurance of my devotion in any eventuality.

With expressions of the highest regards,

Your

C. E. NATZMER

6. *The Correspondence of William I and Bismarck,* trans. Ford, I, 120–127.

Bismarck to Prof. Virchow

BERLIN, *June* 8, 1865

During the sitting on the 2nd instant you personally insulted me by casting doubt upon my veracity. On the following day I requested you, through Herr v. Puttkamer,* to grant me the satisfaction to which I consider myself entitled. Your reply led me to hope that you would settle the matter with an apology, but the negotiations which have been interrupted by your absence have not produced this result.

I am, therefore, compelled to repeat my demand for satisfaction made on the 3rd instant, and to ask you to state if you are ready to comply with my demand made to you through Herr v. Puttkamer. In this case I beg you to name one of your friends to make further arrangements respecting place and time with the minister for war, who will be kind enough to act as my witness.

Awaiting your kind reply, I am,

Your obedient servant

v. BISMARCK-SCHÖNHAUSEN

War Minister v. Roon to Bismarck

BERLIN, *June* 8, 1865

DEAR B.,

I have just been to Virchow's and found that he had gone out at 7 o'clock. I am now going to the Chamber, where, if possible, I will execute my commission. All things considered, it seems to me that you can hardly settle the business in question in time to leave for Stralsund this evening. I will do my best, however.

Your

v. ROON

War Minister v. Roon to Virchow

BERLIN, *June* 8, 1865

As I have endeavored in vain yesterday evening and this morning to find you at your home, in order to execute a commission I have undertaken, I beg you to grant me a moment in the ministers' room. I leave you to choose the most convenient moment.

Faithfully yours,

v. ROON

* Bernhard v. Puttkamer, Captain in the second Guard regiment.

War Minister v. Roon to Bismarck

BERLIN, *June* 8, 1865

The president [of the House of Deputies] has declared, on the motion of Forckenbeck, that Virchow may not fight, and that it is for the House alone to decide whether a minister is insulted. I replied: "A man is the guardian of his own honor."

The discussion on the subject has been going on for three-quarters of an hour. At the present moment the lion of the tribe of Judah is roaring. The shorthand report shall be sent to you as soon as possible.

v. ROON

My letter to Virchow cannot be delivered, as he has not returned home. I enclose it herewith.

Minister F. zu Eulenburg to Bismarck
(Telegraphic despatch)

PRENZLAU, *June* 8, 1865

Send news to Stralsund immediately.

EULENBURG

Bismarck to Minister F. zu Eulenburg
(Telegraphic despatch)

BERLIN, *June* 8, 1865

Several hours' debate this morning on Forckenbeck's motion declaring duels inadmissible for deputies. No statement yet obtained from Virchow as to acceptance or refusal.

BISMARCK

v. Hennig to v. Keudell

BERLIN, *June* 8, 1865

I have received no further intelligence as to whether you consider that there is no longer a prospect of the difference between Herr v. Bismarck and Prof. Virchow being adjusted.

Prof. Virchow wishes to end the matter and has charged me to inform you that he considers that he has done everything possible on his part toward a settlement in expressing his readiness to make the statement desired by Bismarck on one condition, at which no offense can be taken. As no reply has as yet been received to this I am further charged to inform you that Prof. Virchow decidedly declines to fight a duel, the more so as the affair has been made public through no fault of his, and has even been discussed today in the Chamber of Deputies. His political friends, and also the president of the House, have imposed on him as a duty the non-acceptance of the duel.

Kindly acquaint Herr von Bismarck with this, and at the same time inform him that Prof. Virchow is ready to make the promised statement in the House, with the condition formulated by me; I would add explicitly that only the sense and not the wording of the latter is of moment to him.

Respectfully yours,
HENNIG

v. Keudell to War Minister v. Roon

BERLIN, *June* 8, 1865

YOUR EXCELLENCY,

I have the honor to submit the enclosed for your information, and most obediently to state that I have replied to Herr von Hennig that I am no longer empowered to receive statements from Prof. Virchow.

v. KEUDELL

War Minister v. Roon to Bismarck *

BERLIN, *June* 8, 1865

Herr Virchow replied by my messenger who took the letter of which you are acquainted, that he would come to me this evening between 7 and 8 o'clock. Until now, 9 o'clock, he has not appeared. In these circumstances I consider the affair, in view of today's proceedings in the Chamber of Deputies, as essentially settled.

v. ROON

Prof. Virchow to Gen. von Roon, Minister for War

(Undated—Postmark, *July* 8, 1865, 9 A.M.)

YOUR EXCELLENCY,

I beg to reply to your favor of today's date that Herr v. Hennig has today informed Herr v. Keudell in my name:

1, that I decline the duel.

2, that I am ready to make the statement in the House desired by the minister-president as soon as I receive the minister-presi-

* Affixed to v. Keudell's letter.

dent's assurance that there was no personal insult intended to the members of the committee in his remarks on Hannibal Fischer.

As I have gone to the utmost bounds of possibility in making this concession, I should be glad if any further negotiations respecting the wording of the statement might be conducted, as heretofore, through the medium of Herr v. Hennig.

Accept the assurance of my highest esteem, with which I subscribe myself

Your Excellency's most respectful
R. VIRCHOW
Member of the House of Deputies

War Minister v. Roon to Bismarck *

It is sufficient in my opinion that Herr Virchow *declines the duel* . . . Further negotiations—for which I am, of course, always at your disposal—*will lead to nothing.* There is no doubt of that, especially as Herr Virchow refuses personal negotiation with me, and interposes Hennig, who is responsible for today's parliamentary comedy.

v. R.

Regierungsrat Zitelmann to Bismarck

June 8, 1865

Virchow was in the Charité Hospital until about twelve o'clock; the red Becker † called for him there, bringing with him a letter from Hennig, and the two drove off to the House of Deputies. It is evident from this that Virchow was privy to the scene in the Chamber.

ZITELMANN

Regierungsrat Zitelmann to Bismarck

June 8, 1865

Virchow told Faddel ‡ at two o'clock that he declines the duel, and that Herr v. Hennig will write to Herr v. Puttkamer on the subject today.

ZITELMANN

* Marginal note to Virchow's letter.
† Hermann Becker, member of the Progressist party, afterwards *Bürgermeister* of Cologne.
‡ Member of the Progressist party in the Chamber of Deputies.

Count Arnim-Boytzenburg to Bismarck

BERLIN, *June* 8, 1865

YOUR EXCELLENCY,

I have just heard of the Virchow affair, on my return from the country. As many of your Excellency's intimate acquaintances are away, I beg of you to dispose of me if I can be in any way useful; otherwise do not take up your time with replying to me.

May God be with you!

Your
COUNT ARNIM-BOYTZENBURG

General Count Nostitz to Bismarck

BERLIN, *June* 9, 1865

YOUR EXCELLENCY,

The sincere sympathy I feel towards you keeps me also in a state of apprehension concerning the result of the step you have taken against Herr Virchow, and excuses my indiscretion in asking you for a few confidential lines on this affair. I hope you will not refuse me this.

With true respect and esteem,

COUNT V. NOSTITZ

Minister F. zu Eulenburg to Bismarck

STRALSUND, *June* 9, 1865

Many thanks for your telegram, my dear friend. You cannot think how anxious we were during the whole of yesterday; I was unable to swallow any food until a reassuring telegram came from Roon, and finally your own late in the evening. Do telegraph or write to me again telling me how the affair is definitely settled. I shall be at Putbus today and tomorrow. Everything went off well here yesterday, only the thought of you disquieted your friends.

Most cordially yours,

EULENBURG

42 Scandal or Harmless Incident at Bad Gastein? The Otherwise Shrewd Manipulator of Public Opinion Allows Himself to Be Photographed with the Celebrated Prima Donna, Pauline Lucca

"Life is earnest, Art is gay."

While Bismarck was at Bad Gastein in 1865 negotiating the Convention which was to decide the question of the Duchies of Schleswig-Holstein, his picture was taken with the celebrated prima donna, Pauline Lucca, the Countess Rahden. The photograph caused something of a scandal. Johanna never forgave her husband for what she regarded as a shocking lapse in taste. An aura of mystery surrounds this episode; little is known about it. Bismarck himself claimed that it was a harmless incident. Following are two versions by Bismarck biographers.

George Bulten's Account[7]

At another ball Bismarck met the celebrated Pauline Lucca, and addressed her without any previous introduction. She not knowing him, thought this a bit of presumption, and turned away from him. When she afterwards learned from the gentleman with whom she was conversing at the time, that it was Bismarck himself that she had treated so slightingly, she entreated her companion to give her an opportunity of making an apology. This was done at a later period of the evening, when Bismarck observed, as he held out his hand to her, "It is for me, madam, to apologize for my intrusiveness"; adding laughingly, "Let there be peace between us; it would be sad if the two greatest persons in Prussia should be at enmity with each other"—alluding to the stature of each, he being so tall and she *petite*. They afterwards met at Ischl, when the great singer wishing to befriend a poor photographer, proposed that Bismarck and herself should be portrayed on the same *carte-de-visite,* which was no sooner said than done, much to the photographer's delight and pecuniary advantage.

7. George Bulten, *The Story of Count Bismarck's Life* (London, n.d.), pp. 126–127.

Version by Jules Hoche [8]

One day, when the president was taking a walk in the Gastein Park, he met the celebrated prima donna, Pauline Lucca (Countess Rahden).

"You look very miserable," said the lady.

"You cannot always be cheerful," was the reply; "and for my part, I have no reason to be so now."

"Well, come with me and have your photograph taken," suggested the actress. "That will cheer you up for a moment."

Bismarck accepted the invitation, and this is the origin of a photograph on which Bismarck has inscribed these words: "Life is earnest, Art is gay," and which exists at Friedrichsruh. The application of the words (if there be any) we fail to grasp.

This photograph, as one can easily imagine, much scandalized the people of Germany.

To his friend André de Roman, who reproached him with his unseemly conduct, Bismarck replied in a long and extremely ironical homily, from which the following passage is quoted:

"Countess Rahden is a lady to whom objectionable conduct has never been imputed any more than it has to me. But, notwithstanding that, had I, in a calm moment, reflected on the annoyance which this frolic was likely to give my faithful friends, I should have stepped back from the range of the lens that was directed at us. . . .

"But from your friendship and your own Christian principles, I expect that on future occasions you will recommend to my censors the practice of prudence and charity. We all have need of them. Though among the full number of those sinners who come short of the glory of God, I hope that His mercy will not take away even from me, among the doubts and dangers of my career, the staff of humble belief by which I endeavor to find my way."

43 Blueprint for Conflict: Bismarck Tells a French Journalist that He Will Rescue Germany from Austrian Oppression, 1866

"To attain this object I would brave everything: exile and even the scaffold."

How Bismarck utilized the foreign press to circulate his ideas is

8. Jules Hoche, *Bismarck at Home,* trans. from the French by Therese Batbedat (London, 1899), pp. 68–69.

illustrated in an interview in which he sketched his own life portrait. Just before the final rupture with Austria and the beginning of hostilities, M. Vilbort, a correspondent for the Siècle, *sought an interview with the Prussian minister-president. It was granted. Bismarck rose to receive him, shook hands, led him to a chair, and then offered him a cigar. The conversation that took place is slightly abridged here.*[9]

"*Monsieur le Ministre,*" I said to him, "I have undertaken to inform the French public, as well as I can, concerning everything that takes place in Germany. Allow me then to address you with perfect frankness. It is easy to perceive that in her foreign policy, Prussia appears at the present day to tend towards objects with which the French nation eminently sympathizes, for instance, the complete emancipation of Italy from the Austrians, and Germany constituted on the basis of universal suffrage. You proclaim a national parliament as the only source from which Germany can issue regenerated—as the sole supreme power which is capable of accomplishing her new destinies; and at the same time you treat the Second Chamber at Berlin after the fashion of Louis XIV, when he entered the parliament of Paris whip in hand. In France we cannot admit the possibility of an alliance between absolutism and democracy. And to speak the entire truth, public opinion at Paris does not believe in your project of a national parliament; it is regarded only as a war machine of excellent invention, which you will break after it has served your purpose, or whenever it shall become inconvenient or useless."

"*A la bonne heure!*" replied Bismarck. "You go to the bottom of things. In France, I know that I have the same unpopularity as in Germany. Everywhere I am held solely responsible for a situation which I have not made, but which has been imposed upon me as upon all. I am the scapegoat of public opinion, but I do not trouble myself about it. I pursue, with a perfectly tranquil conscience, an object which I believe to be of the utmost utility to my own country and Germany; as for the means, I have availed myself of such as offered themselves to me, for want of any others. With respect to the internal condition of Prussia there would be much to say. To judge of it impartially would require study and a profound acquaintance with the character of the people. While France and Italy form each at the present time a vast social body animated by one spirit and one sentiment, in Germany, on the contrary, it is individualism that rules. Each one here lives apart in his own little

9. Quoted in Bulten, *op. cit.*, pp. 127–132.

corner, holding his own opinion in the circle of his wife and children, always mistrustful of the government as well as of his neighbor; judging everything from his personal point of view, and never from that of society at large. The sentiment of individualism and the need of contradiction are developed in a German to an inconceivable degree; show him an open door, and rather than pass through it, he will obstinately seek to make a hole in the wall by the side of it. Consequently, whatever may take place, no government will ever be popular in Prussia. . . . Our revolutionists are not very terrible. Their hostility exhausts itself in epithets against the minister, but they respect the king. It is I alone who have done them any harm, and I am the only object of their vengeance. With a little more impartiality they would perhaps see that I could not have acted otherwise. In the actual position of Prussia in Germany, and in face of Austria, an army was our prime necessity. In Prussia it is the only force that is *disciplinable*. I am not sure whether the word is French."

"Certainly, *Monsieur le Ministre,* it might be used in France."

"Should a Prussian break one of his arms at a barricade," continued M. de Bismarck, "he would go home to his lodging quite sheepish; but in the army he is an admirable soldier, and fights like a lion for the honor of his country. This necessity for a great armed force, imposed by circumstances, has not been recognized by our carping politicians, however clearly seen. For myself I could not hesitate; by birth, by education, I am a king's man before anything else. Now the king held to the new military organization as firmly as he did to his crown, because he also in his soul and conscience judged it to be indispensable. On this point no one could make him yield or compromise. At his age, now seventy, and with his traditions, it is natural that he should be obstinate in his opinion, especially when he believes it to be right. For the rest, so far as concerns the army, I entirely share his views.

"Sixteen years ago I was living as a country gentleman, when, by the choice of my sovereign, I was appointed the envoy of Prussia at the Frankfort Diet. I had been brought up in admiration, I might almost say in the worship, of the Austrian policy. It was not long before I lost the illusions of my youth with respect to Austria and became her declared adversary.

"The humiliation of my country, Germany sacrificed to foreign interests, a crafty and perfidious policy—all this was not of a nature to please me. I never anticipated the part I should have to fill in the future, but from that moment I conceived the idea, which I am now seeking to realize; namely, the rescue of Germany from

Austrian oppression; at all events of that part of Germany which is united by its genius, religion, manners, and interests to the destinies of Prussia—the Germany of the North. In the projects which I have put forth there is no question of overturning thrones, of taking a duchy from this one, or a petty domain from that. Even were it my wish to do so, the king would not give his consent. Then there are family relations, cousinships, a crowd of hostile influences against which I have had continually to fight.

"All this, added to the opposition which I have met with Prussia, has not prevented me from devoting myself soul and body to this idea—the establishment of Northern Germany in its logical and natural form under the aegis of Prussia. To attain this object I would brave everything: exile and even the scaffold. I have said to the prince royal, who by his education and tendencies is in favor of parliamentary government, 'What matter if they hang me, provided only that the cord shall securely bind your throne to this new Germany?' "

"May I also ask you, *Monsieur le Ministre,*" I said, "how you can reconcile the liberal mission of a national parliament with the rigorous treatment which the Berlin Chamber has experienced? How, above all things, have you been able to persuade the king, the representative of divine right, to accept universal suffrage, which is the democratic principle *par excellence*?"

Bismarck replied with animation: "It is a victory gained after four years of struggle. When the king sent for me four years ago, the situation was full of difficulties. His Majesty placed before me a long list of liberal concessions, not one of them, however, concerning the military question. I said to the king: 'I accept, and the more liberal the government shows itself, the greater will be its strength.' The Chamber was obstinate on one side and the crown on the other. In this conflict I sided with the king. My veneration for him, all my antecedents, all the traditions of my family, made this my duty. But that I am, either by nature or system, an adversary of national representation, a born enemy of parliamentary government, is an entirely gratuitous supposition."

44

Attentat: A Deranged Student, Believing that He Must Save Liberty by Killing Its Most Dangerous Opponent, Tries to Assassinate the Minister-President, May 7, 1866 [10]

"Don't be frightened, my love, but I have been shot at."

On May 7, 1866, came the first attempt to assassinate Bismarck. The incident revealed how deep was the hostility of certain people to the minister-president. Startled by shots, Bismarck quickly recovered his presence of mind, closed with the would-be murderer, and held him in a tight grip. The incident was complicated by passers-by, who at first took Bismarck for the aggressor. On reaching home Bismarck wrote a brief account of the event for the king, and then, entering the drawing room, greeted the guests as if nothing had happened. The family doctor declared that the minister had been saved only by a miracle.

The would-be assassin was a student of agriculture who, inspired by revolutionary agitation, took it upon himself to save Europe from the threatening catastrophe of war. He would rescue German freedom by killing its most dangerous enemy. The young man, Ferdinand Cohen, was a stepson of Karl Blind, a democratic fugitive from Baden living in London. Cohen committed suicide in his cell on the night of his arrest.

So unpopular was Bismarck that the sympathy of the German people seemed to be with the assailant. Professor Dubois-Reymond, famous physiologist at Berlin University, hurried into a bookseller's shop on Unter den Linden and exclaimed indignantly: "How bad revolvers are in this country!"

In a table talk with friends that night Bismarck gave his version of what happened, as reported in the first selection below by Robert von Keudell, Bismarck's co-worker in the foreign ministry. A little over a year later, on August 29, 1867, Bismarck gave additional details to Gustav von Wilmowski, his family attorney and overseer of the Varzin estate. In 1874 Bismarck added further details at a gathering of parliamentary leaders in Berlin.

10. Robert von Keudell, *Fürst und Fürstin Bismarck* (Berlin and Stuttgart, 1901), pp. 259 ff.; Gustav von Wilmowski, *Meine Erinnerungen an Bismarck* (Berlin, 1900), pp. 58 ff.; Lucius von Ballhausen, *Bismarck-Erinnerungen* (Stuttgart, 1920), pp. 60 ff. Translations by the editor.

Keudell's Report on Bismarck's Version of the Attempted Assassination

While in the cabinet room the issue of war and peace was being debated endlessly, in the living room of the large residence there remained the peaceful and cheerful mood of the earlier years. The circle of the guests present had not become appreciably larger.

When, late in the evening, Bismarck opened the door of his workroom and entered through the small hall into the living room, he seemed to be in good humor. Ordinarily he always led the conservation, but he never spoke of the day's business. The princess naturally knew the nature of his work, but he invariably tried to spare her knoweldge of the daily, often unhappy, events. To him it was refreshing to be in his family circle without hearing a word of politics, relaxing by talking about harmless things.

On May 7, after 5 o'clock, he returned home as usual from the royal palace, but stayed a bit longer in his office to write a short report to his Majesty. When he finally arrived home, after excusing himself for being late, he entered the salon. Before the company sat down to dinner, he turned to his wife, kissed her on the forehead, and said: "Don't be frightened, my love, but I have been shot at. Through the grace of God I have not been hurt."

That was told me shortly afterward by one of the guests. The king came personally to offer his congratulations. He was followed by other distinguished personages who expressed their joy and relief at the wonderful news that Bismarck had escaped injury. Bismarck described the incident to a small circle of friends in roughly these words:

"I was walking on the footpath between the trees of Unter den Linden from the palace to my home. As I came to the vicinity of the Russian embassy, I heard two pistol shots right behind me. Without thinking that it might concern me, I automatically turned around and saw, just about two steps away, a small man who was aiming a revolver at me. I grasped the wrist of his right hand just as he fired the third shot and at the same time I clutched at his throat with my other hand. He quickly transferred the revolver to his left hand, pressed it against my overcoat, and fired two more times. An unknown civilian helped me hold him. Several policemen hurried to the scene, together with a company of Guards who chanced to be marching down the Linden, and he was led away.

"As a hunter myself, the thought ran through my mind: 'If those last two bullets had reached their mark, I would have been a dead man.' One of my ribs hurt a bit, but to my amazement I could get home quite easily. Once home I examined myself. I found holes in my overcoat, jacket, vest, and shirt, but the bullet had slid off the silk underjacket without breaking the skin. The rib hurt as if someone had punched it, but the pain soon stopped. Sometimes it happens with red deer that a rib bends like an elastic when a bullet strikes. One can see afterward where the bullet glanced off, because several hairs are missing at the spot. Similarly, the same thing may have happened to my ribs. Or perhaps the power of the shot was not fully developed because the mouth of the revolver had been pressed directly against my coat."

All those present were in a joyful mood, as if there had been a miracle. Bismarck, however, calmly regarded the incident as if it were of no consequence whatever. On the next day it became known that the criminal, whose name was Cohen-Blind, and who had come from London to shoot Bismarck, had committed suicide in his cell by opening a vein. That evening, when the same circle of house friends met again, a servant reported that there was a huge throng in front of the house. The gathering went into the Chinese room, and the window facing the street was opened. Little had been known previously about the temper of the Berliners, but now there came a seemingly endless call: "Three cheers for Bismarck!" From the window Bismarck spoke the following words in a high-pitched voice:

"Gentlemen and fellow countrymen. My warmest thanks for this demonstration of your concern. I hold it to be the highest good fortune to give one's life for our king and for the Fatherland, whether on the field of battle or on the sidewalk, and I implore God that such a death be granted to me. But this time He wanted it to be otherwise: God willed that I lived to do my duty. You share that patriotic sentiment with me and you will be glad to say with me: 'Long live his Majesty, our King and Sovereign Lord!' "

An outcome of the attempted assassination was Bismarck's sense of elation. Often I had the impression that he now felt himself to be God's "chosen vessel" to bring blessings to his Fatherland. But he never expressed that feeling.

Conversation with *Justizrat* von Wilmowski on August 29, 1867 in Varzin

"There were four bullets, two from behind, and then, as I turned around, one bullet grazed my breast and penetrated the clothing without touching the body. The fourth struck me from in front, after I had turned around. As shown afterward, this bullet went through my clothes right down to a silk undershirt, whose weave was squeezed but not separated. That was the 'armor' about which some newspapers spoke. As I took this last bullet I felt that I was mortally wounded. It took only an instant, but in that moment, just as people say about one's last hours, my whole life passed with lightning speed before me, including thoughts of my wife and children. I noted," he added in a joking manner, "that I was holding on to life in a manner which seldom had occurred to me in the past.

"Immediately after that I regained my strength. Since the bullet had left no wound, I thought about my hunting experiences, when one could see a stag break down yet immediately continue its flight. I can only explain the thing in this way: the bullet somehow struck a bony rib and immediately bounced off.

"Meanwhile, I held Blind in a vise. The military, which was just then marching by (belonging to the 1st Battalion of the Second Guard Regiment), surrounded both of us. A bookbinder, who took a bullet in the shoulder, turned out to be the one who saved my life. But before I could get away from the shots and until I recovered from the shock, no one sprang to free me from Blind. The thing took place too quickly. As I came to, I saw a soldier with a rifle trained on me, and then an officer grabbed him. The soldier apparently thought I was the aggressor, because I had Blind by the throat and the right hand, and he undoubtedly thought that he would have to use his rifle butt to free the poor man from this discreditable treatment."

Report by Lucius von Ballhausen on a Conversation in a Parliamentary Gathering in Varzin, December 5, 1874

Practically all the members of the Reichstag's exclusive Center appeared, and there was an interesting scene at Bismarck's working table. Together with several women I saw the Blind assassination weapon on the table. Bismarck came into the room and demonstrated what happened during the attempted assassination. At that time, in May 1866, as he walked through the street, small toy torpedoes were being thrown and exploded. He noticed two people on the corner of the Chancellery, a large fellow, and a small man whom he later found to be Blind, who were looking intently at him. He thought at the time that they certainly did not have friendly faces.

The first two shots came from behind about hip deep and went through his coat, but he did not know it. He had turned around quickly and five paces from him, even through the cloud of smoke, he saw the smiling face of the young man, who was aiming at him again and firing two more shots. By this time he could reach his assailant and was holding him in an iron grip. One bullet struck a rib and glanced off, although Bismarck thought he had been shot through. Blind fired the last shot while being held by Bismarck. The bullet scorched his coat. All this while Blind was laughing sardonically, apparently in the belief that he had inflicted mortal wounds on his quarry. Bismarck himself thought that he would become unconscious. Around them was a thick crowd of people, and he anticipated the thrust of a knife any moment, especially when a rifle butt appeared over his shoulder. The weapon was pushed aside by the white glove of an officer. He was with a detachment of the Guard Regiment on foot, which just at that moment happened to be marching by, and arrested the would-be assassin. Bismarck had always believed that at its best life was short enough, but he did feel relieved when he saw that he had escaped death.

The group standing around the writing table, the elegant women and the large number of Reichstag delegates, formed an interesting picture. All of them looked at the hero with an air of great suspense and enthusiasm.

45

Journalists Present Pen Portraits of the Great Man in His Early Fifties, 1866 [11]

"... eyes ... which become terrible when lighted up by the fire of anger."

By 1866 Bismarck's reputation had spread throughout the world. There was intense interest everywhere in the Prussian who was impressing his ideas and way of life upon the German people. Journalists began to write about his personal appearance and manners, and many began to seek interviews with him.

Bismarck's personal appearance and manners have been often described. M. Vilbort, the Paris journalist, who saw him in 1866, speaks of him thus: "Count Bismarck is a man of lofty stature; he has an anxious countenance; a high forehead, large and full, in which you see benevolence combined with obstinacy. He has large eyes, deep-set and soft, but which become terrible when lighted up by the fire of anger. He has light hair scattered thinly over the top of his head. He wears a military moustache, which veils the irony of his smile. In his language, always full of imagery, the

11. Bulten, *op. cit.*, pp. 123–126.

bluntness of the soldier is joined to the circumspectness of the diplomatist. He is at the same time the great lord, and the courtier armed with all the seductions of a refined politeness."

A writer in the *Daheim,* Arnold Wellmer, who met Bismarck at the house of Prince Putbus, in the island of Rügen, soon after the war of 1866, thus describes him:—

"He is a tall, stately man, slenderly but yet powerfully built. His bearing has something of a military stiffness, but yet full of youthful elegance, notwithstanding his fifty-three years. His movements are dignified and bold, and at the same time light and unconstrained. And upon this knightly figure, sits a head not very big, nor even beautiful, one which it is difficult to describe, which you are never weary of looking at, and which you will never forget to your dying day.

"The thoughtful arched forehead is shaded by scanty darkish-blond hair, already sprinkled with gray. A thick moustache gives to the otherwise smoothly-shaven face a military character. The eye, which is rather too prominent, is clear and lively, frequently permeated with a light that makes it difficult to recognize its true color. The complexion is dull and of a peculiar paleness, fixed there by bodily suffering, hard work, sleepless nights, and days full of anxious thought and mental exertion.

"Around the thin lips plays an intellectual (*geistreich*) smile; for the moment, an amiable, harmless, cheerful smile; but one that it is easy to see requires only a slight twist to convert it into one of withering irony.

"Bismarck cannot be said to dress with taste. He had on a buckskin coat, waistcoat of the same, and gray trousers. But these seemed to tally so well with his general appearance; indeed, gave the figure such a youthful, almost *burschen* air, that I fancy the light dress coat would annoy the eye more than the substantial buckskin."

Max Schlesinger, by no means a partial critic, writing in 1866, says: * "He is well fitted to be amiable in society, for he has elegant manners, likes animated conversation, is talkative to excess, communicative often to indiscretion, full of wit and original thought, not too impatient of contradiction, and when in good temper, quite open to argument. Whatever prejudices he may have, he knows how artfully to conceal them, and even to laugh at them; but as the boundary between prejudice and conviction, fancy and belief, is hard to define, he only too often ridicules what is looked upon by the mass of mankind as most noble and sacred. In such moments

* *Fortnightly Review,* July, 1866.

his wit becomes frivolous, his cleverness commonplace, and his whole demeanor repelling.

"He may be hard, but he is certainly not spiteful, not even to Austria. It is true that he wishes to drive her out of Germany, and break her power forever; but if it had been possible, he would have used far gentler instruments for that purpose than Krupp's steel cannon and the needle gun, and would have preferred to drive her to suicide by mere diplomatic means—bare promises and threats. He has just as little hatred in his heart for the kings of Saxony and Hanover, although it has always been his favorite idea to mediatize them, together with a few others."

A friend of our own, writing from Berlin, says:—"The personal appearance of the count is that of a grave thinker, but at the same time that of a very kind man, placing himself on an equal footing with everyone with whom he comes in contact. About two years ago I met him at a public ball, to which I accompanied an English family then in Berlin, including a very pretty young lady, who, when the count's entrance made some stir in the room, said rather loudly, how happy she would be if she could have a full look at him. He had come very near to where we stood in a great crowd, and when he heard his name uttered with a female English accent, he turned around, and I seized the opportunity of introducing the young lady to him. To her great delight he immediately entered into conversation with her in English, which he speaks fluently."

46 Stage Number Two—German Unification: The Austro-Prussian War as Seen through the Eyes of Bismarck

"The battlefield was . . . full of touching sights."

Bismarck, always intent upon removing Austria as an obstacle to German unification, shrewdly isolated the Hapsburgs from foreign help. On April 8, 1866, he concluded an alliance with Italy, promising Venetia to the Italians in the event of a Prusso-Austrian war. This alliance was in defiance of the constitution of the German Confederation, which forbade any member to make a treaty with a foreign power against any other member. Living in dreams of Napoleonic splendor, Louis Napoleon was unable to adopt any hard and fast policy to thwart the designs of the scheming Prussian. Bismarck, on the other hand, was certain of his policy—he must goad Austria into aggression.

The issue again revolved around Schleswig-Holstein. On June 1, 1866, Austria challenged Prussia by submitting the question to the Federal Diet at Frankfort. On June 12 the Austrian ambassador at Berlin and the Prussian envoy at Vienna asked for their passports. When the Federal Diet passed an Austrian motion to mobilize the non-Prussian armies, Prussia declared the German Confederation ended and invited the German states to join a union under Prussian leadership. Bismarck now had his war with Austria. "If we are beaten," he said, "I shall not return. I can die only once, and it befits the vanquished to die."

In the hot summer of 1866 Bismarck went off to war against the Austrians. He was clad as a major of the Landwehr *cavalry, with a steel helmet and a long gray coat. He had no part in the management of the army (that was the assignment of King William as commander-in-chief). Bismarck's authority as the political leader of the state ceased as soon as military and technical matters arose. But he was careful to stay close to the king, lest anyone else reach the monarch's ear on political matters. Bismarck thoroughly enjoyed the campaign, despite its bloody aspects, as indicated by these excited reports to his wife.*[12]

SICHROW, 1 *July*, 1866

We left Reichenberg today; just arrived here; still uncertain whether we remain here or in Turnau. The whole journey has been a dangerous one. The Austrians, if they had sent cavalry from Leitmeritz yesterday, might have taken the king and all of us. I am sorry to say that the coachman Carl has just had a severe fall with the chestnut mare, which ran away with him. At first he was thought to be dead. He is lying in the hospital here, near Sichrow, in the next village. Kurt is to come in his place. We meet prisoners everywhere, according to the reports that have come in, there must already be over 15,000. Jitschin was taken by us yesterday at the point of the bayonet; Frankfort division; General Tümpling severely wounded in the hip, not mortal. Heat fearful. Bringing up of supplies difficult; our troops suffer from exhaustion and hunger.

In the country, as far as this place, not many traces of war, beyond trodden-down cornfields. The people not at all afraid of our soldiers, stand with wife and child in Sunday attire before their doors and look astonished. In Trautenau, the inhabitants have murdered twenty unarmed musicians of ours who remained there behind the front after their regiments had passed. The perpetrators

12. *Prince Bismarck's Letters to His Wife, His Sister, and Others from 1844 to 1870*, trans. by Fitz. Maxse (London, 1878), pp. 246–249.

at Glogau, before court-martial. At Münchengrätz, a master brewer enticed twenty-six of our soldiers into his spirit cellar, made them drunk, set it alight. The distillery belonged to a convent. With the exception of such things, we hear less here than in Berlin; this castle, a very handsome one by-the-way, belongs to Prince Rohan, whom I used to see every year at Gastein.

JITSCHIN, *not Gitschin,* 2 *July,* 1866

Just arrived here from Sichrow; all along the battlefield up to here was still covered with corpses, horses, and weapons. Our victories are much greater than we supposed; it seems that we have already more than 15,000 prisoners, and the loss of the Austrians in dead and wounded is given as still more—20,000 men. Two of their corps are completely broken up, some of their regiments annihilated to the last man. Hitherto I have seen more Austrian prisoners than Prussian soldiers. Send me by the courier more cigars, 1000 every time, if you can, price three pounds, for the hospitals. All the wounded ask me for them. Then either through the associations, or at our own expense, take an *abonnement* for a few dozen copies of the *Kreutz Zeitung* for the hospitals; for instance, for the Reichenberg hospital; try to get at the names of the other places at the War Office. How is Clermont-Tonnerre? Is he not coming? I have no letter as yet. Send me, please, a revolver of large caliber, holster pistol. Carl the coachman is better; he will probably have no permanent injury, but be unable to work for some time yet. Carl B. deserves all praise, that active spirit of our traveling *ménage*. Best love. Send me a novel to read, but only one at a time.

God shield you!

Just received your letter with the Homburg enclosure. A thousand thanks. I can so fully understand the dead stillness after the departure. Here in this turmoil it is impossible to realize the situation, notably at night in bed.

On July 3, 1866, the Prussians defeated the Austrians at Königgrätz, or Sadowa, as the battle is named in Western Europe. When the crown prince arrived at precisely the right moment, the tide of battle swung in Prussia's favor. A general remarked to Bismarck: "Excellency, you are now a great man. But if the crown prince had come too late you would now be the greatest villain." This was true, and Bismarck was aware of it. The victory made an extraordinary impression throughout Europe and elevated Bismarck to new heights as a national hero.

Bismarck himself gave an account of his experiences at Königgrätz when he afterwards went with his family to the island of Rügen, in the Baltic, to recover from the fatigue of the campaign. At a dinner given him by Prince Putbus, magnate of the place, Bismarck told about his part in the battle.[13]

As the king himself went through everything, so the soldier bore all privations and hardships easily. At the battle of Königgrätz, I was in the king's suite, and often enough we were in the midst of the turmoil of the fight. At midday there was a momentary lull in the roar of battle; the crown prince was expected on the field—eagerly expected. During this anxious pause, the king asked his suite if any one had anything to eat—he was hungry. The groom had a little wine, an officer drew, rather shamefacedly, a diminutive piece of sausage from his haversack, and, with a beaming face, a soldier stepped up with a piece of *commisbrod* in his open hand. "My son, have you had your own dinner, then?" asked the king. "No, your Majesty!" "Then we will divide fairly." And the king broke the piece of bread into two pieces, returned one-half to the soldier saying, "Take it, my son; your sovereign thanks you." Not long after, the crown prince came up with his army, just at the nick of time, and hence our Platt-Deutsch soldiers ever afterwards called him *"Prinz taur rechten Teit,"* "Prince Nick-of-Time."

After that the battle began to rage afresh. The attention of the king was wholly fixed on the progress of the battle, and he paid not the slightest heed to the shells that were whizzing thickly around him. To my repeated request that his Majesty might not so carelessly expose himself to so murderous a fire, he only answered, "The commander-in-chief must be where he ought to be." Later on, at the village of Lipa, when the king in person had ordered the cavalry to advance, and the shells were again falling round him, I ventured to renew my request, saying, "If your Majesty will take no care of your own person, have pity at least on your poor minister-president, from whom your faithful Prussian people will again demand their king; and in the name of that people I entreat you to leave this dangerous spot." Then the king gave me his hand, with a "Well, then, Bismarck, let us ride on a little." So saying, his Majesty wheeled his black mare and put her into as easy a canter as if he had been riding down the Linden to the Tiergarten.

13. *Bismarck's Table Talk*, ed. by Charles Lowe (London, 1895), pp. 94–97.

But for all that I felt very uneasy about him, . . . and so, edging up with my dark chestnut to Sadowa (the name given to the king's mare *after* the battle), I gave her a good (sly) kick from behind with the point of my boot; she made a bound forward, and the king looked round in astonishment. I think he saw what I had done, but he said nothing." . . .

I only once regretted not having [a revolver]. It was soon after the battle of Königgrätz. I was riding alone over the dead-strewn field. It was a sight to freeze the blood in the veins—horrible, bloody, never to be forgotten. In one place I came upon a poor horse, a beautiful animal, both of whose hind feet had been torn away by a shell. While trying to support himself upon his forefeet, quivering and neighing piteously, he looked up at me with his great moist eyes, as if beseeching my help—and then I longed for a revolver to send a bullet into his heart, and so relieve him from his sufferings.

But the battlefield was otherwise full of touching sights. For example, during the heat of the conflict, I saw a youthful officer, pale and fair, as if sleeping, leaning against a garden hedge. He was dead. Inside the garden the roses were in full bloom. A trooper was just plucking a handful. He then got over the hedge and placed the roses on the breast of the young hero, where a small round hole showed itself in his uniform.

"Do you know that young officer?" said I.

"No, Major," he replied; "but I saw him fighting like a lion, and now fallen like a lamb; I thought that I would save him at least from the horses' hoofs, and so I carried him to the hedge. We laid roses on my own dear mother when we placed her in the earth." So saying, he flung himself upon his horse, this brave trooper, and rushed madly into the heat of the battle.

In spite of the seriousness of the situation, I never saw anything more comic than the caperings of the big regimental goat of the Berlin Guard Artillery, as it went careering about at the bugler's side, in the thickest of the bullet rain, and making for the enemy with its grotesque leaps and bounds. The Austrians, too, are really said to have believed that the form of this goat had merely been assumed by Satan, with whom the wicked Bismarck had entered into a compact against their invincible Iron Brigade.

Königgrätz meant victory for the Prussians. A joyful Bismarck continued the story in further letters to his wife.[14]

HOHENMAUTH, *Monday,* 9 *July,* 1866

Do you still remember, my heart, how, nineteen years ago we passed through here on the way from Prague to Vienna? No mirror showed the future, neither when, in 1852, I went along this line with the good Lynar. Matters are going well with us; if we are not immoderate in our demands, and do not imagine that we have conquered the world, we shall acquire a peace, which will be worth the trouble. But we are just as quickly intoxicated as discouraged, and I have the ungrateful task of pouring water in the foaming wine, and to make them see that we are not living alone in Europe, but with three neighbors still. The Austrians are in Moravia, and we are already so bold that their positions today are fixed for our headquarters tomorrow. Prisoners are still coming in, and guns, since the 3rd up to today, 180. If they call up their southern army, with God's good help, we shall beat them again; confidence is universal. I could hug our fellows, each facing death so gallantly, so quiet, obedient, well-behaved, with empty stomachs, wet clothes, wet camp, little sleep, the soles of their boots falling off, obliging to everybody, no looting, no incendiarism, paying where they can, and eating moldy bread. There must after all abide in our man of the soil a rich store of the fear of God, or all that would be impossible. News of acquaintances is difficult to obtain; people are miles apart from one another; no one knows where the other is, and nobody to send; men enough, but no horses. I have had Philip * searched for for four days; he is *slightly* wounded in the head by a lance as G. wrote to me, but I cannot find out where he is, and now we are already forty miles farther on. The king exposed himself very much indeed on the 3rd, and it was a very good thing that I was with him, for all warnings on the part of others were of no avail, and no one would have ventured to speak as I allowed myself to do the last time, and with success, after a heap of ten men and fifteen horses of the Sixth Regiment of Cuirassiers were wallowing in their blood near us, and the shells whizzed round the sovereign in the most unpleasant proximity. The worst luckily did not burst. But after all I like it better than if he should err

14. *Prince Bismarck's Letters . . .* , trans. Maxse, pp. 250–255.
* His nephew.

on the other side. He was enchanted with his troops, and rightly, so that he did not seem to remark all the whistling and bursting about him; as quiet and comfortable as on the Kreuzberg, and kept constantly finding battalions that he wanted to thank and say good evening to, until there we were again under fire. But he has had to hear so much about it, that he will leave it alone for the future, and you can be at ease; besides, I hardly believe in another real battle.

If you have *no* news of a person, you can all implicitly believe that he lives and is well, as all casualties occurring to one's acquaintances are known in twenty-four hours at the longest. We have not come at all into communication with Herwarth and Steinmetz, I have therefore neither seen Sch. . . . , but know that they are both well. G. quietly leads his squadron with his arm in a sling. Good-bye, I must go on duty.

Your most true,
v. B.

ZWITTAU, IN MORAVIA, 11 *July,* 1866

I am in want of an inkstand, as all are in use, else there is nothing the matter with me, as I have slept very well on my camp bed and air mattress, and was awoke at eight by a letter from you. I had gone to bed at eleven. At Königgrätz I rode the large chestnut; thirteen hours in the saddle without a feed. He held out very well, was not startled either by the firing or by corpses; ate corn ears and plum-tree leaves with gusto at the most serious moments, and went on swimmingly to the end, when I seemed more tired than the horse. My first bed for the night was on the pavement of Horic, without straw, and with the aid of a carriage cushion. Everywhere crowds of wounded; the grand duke of Mecklenburg discovered me, and then shared his room with me, R., and two aides-de-camp, which was very welcome to me on account of the rain. With regard to the king and shells, I have already written to you. The generals all had the superstition that they, as soldiers, ought not to speak to the king of danger, and sent me, who am also a major, each time to him. In cocking the revolver, the hammer hid the line of sight, and the notch on the top of the hammer was not in an exact line with sight and bead. Tell that to T. Good-bye, my dear heart; I must to S.

Your most true,
v. B.

PRAGUE, 3 *August,* 1866

I have stolen away from the station before everybody, am waiting now here alone, and without luggage, until the king comes, and, after him, my belongings. I employ the moment of enforced inactivity in greeting you from here, and telling you that I am well, and hope to be tomorrow in Berlin. The king is in excellent health. The masses of people along the road hither from the station were so dense that I am afraid it won't end without somebody's being driven over, or the like.

Evening

The king came sooner than I thought, and since then business of all kinds, then dinner. I have this moment come back from a drive with his Majesty over Hradschin, Belvedere, and have seen all the beauties of the landscape around Prague. In a few days it will be nineteen years since we viewed all this together. What strange things were to happen to lead me today in this manner to the same spot, without B. *"Hei cerstwa!"* I had still remembered, to the delight of my coachman. Tomorrow we expect to be in Berlin. Great contention about the speech from the throne. The good people have not enough to do, and see nothing but their own nose, and exercise their swimming powers on the stormy waves of phrase. Our enemies we can manage, but our friends! They almost all of them wear blinkers, and see only one spot of the world.

v. B.

To the dismay of William I and the Prussian Junkers, Bismarck insisted upon moderate peace terms. The Treaty of Prague (1866) required Austria to recognize the end of the German Confederation, the incorporation of Schleswig-Holstein with Prussia, and the annexation of Venetia by Italy. Austria was to pay a small indemnity of twenty million talers, but she lost no territory. Bismarck, desiring Austrian neutrality in the event of a war with France, regarded these magnanimous terms as necessary insurance. "We shall need Austria's strength in the future for ourselves."

47 Flushed with Victory, Bismarck Hastens to Assure the British Public, the French People, and the Entire World that He Is a Man of Peace, 1867

"We shall never begin a war."

Bismarck was surrounded with militaristocrats who wanted to settle issues with France as soon as possible, but he was not yet ready for this great confrontation. For the moment he decided to isolate Napoleon III from possible help. One of his main tasks was to allay British fears. When a British journalist, W. Beatty-Kingston, interviewed Bismarck on September 22, 1867, he came away with a story of peace. There was method in this serious interview: Bismarck wanted no trouble with Britain if and when the Franco-Prussian quarrels became critical. This is a good example of Bismarck's technique in nurturing his public image.[15]

I have had a four hours' palaver with The Man, but, as I expected, shall be able to make very little of it public, for he commenced our talk by saying, "I have experience of your discretion; I shall therefore have no concealment from you, but I reckon confidently upon your using all the personal part of what I may tell you with all necessary reserve; and you will understand that the more unreservedly I speak to you, the greater proof I give you of my conviction that you will not compromise me with the people who are looking out for every word I say, by letting them know what I really think." Now, as the personal or anecdotical part of his conversation is the most interesting and startling of all, being put "upon honor" with regard to it necessarily lessens the importance of the published results of an interview such as I have this evening enjoyed; but I will do my best to tell you in this private letter all that is comprised in his prohibition. What I write in the public letter you may print without hesitation.

He believes in peace, and for many reasons—but I had better, as nearly as possible, reproduce, his own words: "I do not believe for a moment that France will fight us alone, for, reckoning that every Prussian is at least as good as every Frenchman, we are numerically stronger than she is. The attack must come from her; we shall never begin a war, if war there ever be, for we have nothing to gain. Suppose France entirely conquered, and a Prussian garrison in Paris; what are we to do with our victory? We could not even decently take Alsace, for the Alsatians are become Frenchmen, and wish to remain so. Belgium we do not want; besides, England guarantees her integrity. Therefore, should this possibility—which is always being dinned into my ears as a probability—ever come to pass, France will undoubtedly attack us, in which case, if she stand alone, she is lost, for our system is such that the farther she may advance (supposing she be at first victorious) into our country, the more armies will spring up against her, like Cadmus' teeth. You will say, 'Old men, *à la fin,*' but a

15. Reprinted in the *Daily Telegraph* (London), August 4, 1898.

Prussian is not so senile at forty-five as some people think. And every German is with us now, despite creeds and bias; we have not sought, we have waited—they run after us, like the roast sucking pig in the Chinaman's dream, crying, 'Come, eat me!' You remember, a hundred years ago, at the battle of—[I did not catch the name.—K.]—when a Prussian dragoon was fighting a French Cuirassier hand to hand, a German horseman, one of France's mercenaries, rode up to strike in on the part of his comrade. The Prussian called out to him, 'Hold, brother! let me finish this Frenchman; he belongs to me!' and the German reined up, saluted, and rode off in another direction. That was a century ago. Since then what have not the Germans learned to comprehend of the brotherhood that naturally binds them together against the Frenchman or anybody else or all the world besides! If the French fight us alone they are lost; therefore, as they know this, they seek for allies. Will they find them? I will tell you why I think not.

"France, the victor, would be a danger to everybody—Prussia to nobody. That is our strong point. England wished to see a power in Europe strong enough to counterbalance France. That is the reason she supported and sympathized with Austria as long as Austria seemed to be strong; that is the reason why I told the king, when he wished to carry out the 'execution' in Denmark alone, 'We must have Austria with us, or England will join her against us'—and that is the reason why England is now turning towards us—because she sees in us the continental *contrepoids* to France, which you English, in spite of your loudly protested alliance with Napoleon, are too sensible not to understand the necessity of. Your alliance has already cost you dearly enough in loss of continental influence, and I should not wonder if the proud English people were to get tired some day of playing a bad second fiddle to the old foe they have so often conquered. You will never take up arms against us in the cause of France.

"I have no little fear of Austria. Austria is like a house built of bad bricks, which, however, are kept together by an excellent mortar—how do you call it? cement—that cement is her German population. Whatever good has been done in her barbarous provinces, has been done by the Germanizing of her institutions. Everywhere in Austria, German is spoken; the inhabitants of the different Slav, Magyar, and Latin provinces must use German to understand one another. An alliance, therefore, with France, having for its purpose the arrest of German unity in its majestic progress, and the devastation of German territory, would be fatal to Austria, whichever way the tide of victory might set. She would surely be ruined through such an alliance, and she knows it. I am not the least apprehensive of an Austro-French alliance, I give you my word of honor.

"Russia will never join France against us, of that be assured—it is impossible." (Bismarck said this with great emphasis, leaning on both his arms half across the table towards me, and looking into my eyes with the greatest earnestness.) "It is true that there has been some talk of an understanding upon the Oriental question—of a common plan of action in the East. Gortschakoff is a funny fellow—he has been taken in six or seven times by French humbug and protestations of an *entente cordiale* which always lasts from three to five weeks; then he invariably finds out that he is the victim of French cunning and ignorance mixed, and begins to curse and swear by all the devils and saints in the Russian calendar *qu'on ne le prendra plus*. And then he drops into the next trap with inimitable *naïveté*. Poor Gortschakoff! he gained his prestige in the Polish business, and thinks the only way to keep it up is to lend himself to the Oriental proclivities of Russia. Popularity is his one ambition. Russia is in a horrid state, and a big war is out of the question for her till she has set her house in order. If I were the emperor's prime minister—as he very much wished me to be six years ago—I should begin by cutting the army down to exactly half its present numbers, and knocking the privileges of the Tchinovnik on the head. That foul and useless Tchin causes half Russia's misfortunes. Just now public feeling in Russia is as bad as can be against France; but, 'whatever happens,' make your mind up that we are quite safe from Russia.

"I do not think I need tell you why a French-Italian offensive alliance against us is out of the question—*cela saute aux yeux*. But I will tell you something that I am told by our agents at both courts, who are not often mistaken, and that is, that Napoleon is going to add another to the list of horrible mistakes he has made within the last five years. He is going to let the Italian troops occupy the Pontifical States, with the mere exception of Rome itself—by which he will bring down the whole of the Catholic, Legitimist, and Orleanist parties upon him, and make his position infinitely worse than it is—and it is bad enough, God knows! But to return to our peace or war prospects. There remains to France, therefore, in Europe (putting Denmark and the other Scandinavians out of the question—they are not worth counting) only Spain as an ally." Here Bismarck looked at me comically, and we both laughed.

"What do I think might bring about war? Of course, an excuse would not be wanting if the French really needed one, but I think the greatest danger of all proceeds from Napoleon's vacillating state of mind. He is become old, but he is also become young—that is to say, he indulges in vagaries, gives way to impulses, and allows his fair wife to exercise a good deal too much influence over him. The Mexico business was her doing, as I suppose you know. He is not the man he used to be, and Europe will never be safe while his present state of intellect continues. Another source of danger is the intense ignorance and mendacity of the men who represent France everywhere. Look around Europe for one capable or honest French agent! Yours, Latour, is the only man of integrity among them all —the only gentleman. All the others are knaves, or so crassly ignorant and prejudiced that an intelligent schoolboy is worth all of them put together. Gramont, for instance, is half a fool and a notorious liar—I beg your pardon, I should have said a lover of hoaxes. Benedetti is more clever than the run of French statesmen, though quite as dishonest; but why is he more clever? Because he is an Italian. He is also more amiable—also because he is an Italian. These fellows will neither learn anything, nor will they keep quiet. The consequence is, that Napoleon is worse informed upon European affairs than any other sovereign. They made him go to Salzburg. You were quite right about that meeting; it was an utter fiasco; but I knew it would be from the first, and my people warned Napoleon of it, and advised him not to go. I was much amused afterward to hear how he had been maneuvering for three days, and the Austrians counter-maneuvering all the time. He went to shear, and came away shorn. Why did he go to look for wool—he had the Golden Fleece already? But these shallow, trumpery French clerks—I cannot call them ministers or ambassadors—may bring their master and their countrymen into trouble.

"When I was in Paris with the king, I told Rouher before his colleagues and Gortschakoff, who happened to be present, 'Unless you want war with us, don't put yourself to the trouble of looking out for another Luxemburg—this is the last; I am *collé au mur,* and I will not give way an inch to any new demand. I owe my compatriots a war. I have cheated them out of one, in which they had a good chance of success, and it required all my popularity to enable me to do so. If you give me any opportunity, I shall certainly pay my debt.' Gortschakoff tried to turn the conversation, as everybody looked dreadfully uncomfortable at my *boutade*. But Moustier had something on his stomach, and managed to bring it up with many grimaces. They thought of urging that Luxemburg should leave the *Zollverein*—should I offer any objection to that? I broke out, 'Don't talk to me of Luxemburg. I won't hear of Luxemburg. The duke of Luxemburg has got to stay in the *Zollverein* till 1873, and then he can leave if he likes; but till then he shall not go out of it, and if you urge him to make a question of it, I shall say to the king, *"Flamberge au vent, sire!"* and I don't think his Majesty will say me nay.' They did not mention Luxemburg any more to me the whole time I was in Paris." Here Bismarck indulged in another cigar, beer, and went on.

"You would like to know something about our plans, our aggregation projects, and our ambitions, would you not? I will tell you exactly what they are, and only two or three besides the king and myself know. First of all, there is Austria. Now, the German provinces of Austria, except the Tyrol and Salzkammergut, both of which are blindly Catholic and Hapsburg, may experience a strong gravitation towards us. I do not deny it for a moment; but, I assure you, were I offered Upper and Lower Austria tomorrow I should refuse them. They are too far off; there are Bohemia, Austrian Silesia, Moravia, with three-fifths Slav populations, between us. If those provinces of German Austria were where Bohemia, etc., are, if Prague and Vienna could change places, I do not say no. Then we might think of it; as it is we do not. I assure you it is our earnest desire to see Austria strengthen herself around her German nucleus and stand firmly alone. Of course, we do not suffer any new oppression of Hungary any more than we would of the Austro-Germans, but we shall gladly enter into a fast and sincere alliance with a constitutional king of Hungary, who, as emperor of Austria, allows the German element full play in his other provinces. There is Bohemia, Silesia, etc., again. They would prove a second Poland to us. We should have to learn how to manage the Czechs, whereas Austria has some experience in that task, although I admit it has been very bad experience. We don't want Bohemia, Silesia, Moravia, or any other part of Austria; let her get strong and be our ally—*voilà tout.*

"All the nonsense you have heard about part of Russian Poland, Courland, or the Baltic provinces is as stupid as it is untrue. It is true there is some dissatisfaction amongst those Northerns, half German, half Scandinavian, on account of the Russian language being imposed upon them, but we shall not interfere. What should we do with provinces we could not defend? Besides, depend upon it, we shall not meddle with Russian territory or affairs any more than they will with ours.

"Beust is *trop fin.* Some time ago, about the vexed question of Bavaria and Württemberg, I let him know that although we were prepared to maintain openly the Treaty of Nikolsburg, we would give our best attention to any proposals he might like to make, and, if we could not accept them, would faithfully keep his secret. He wanted to be too clever, and answered to my confidential communication that he thought the propositions ought to come from our side—that it was our turn to hold out a hand. I did not agree with him, and so the matter dropped. But we have since been very careful about South Germany, and have remained quite passive. We can stop as we are for ten years or more, only insisting upon the terms of the treaty, but the Southerners will not let us, and if they come to offer us an accession of power, we shall certainly not kick them downstairs. But we wish it clearly understood that if Austria must disintegrate, we don't want any of the pieces. There is nothing in our attitude to annoy or alarm France. I think, barring the accidents at which I have hinted, there is nothing to prevent the maintenance of peace for ten or fifteen years, by which time the French will have got accustomed to German unity, and will consequently have ceased to care about it.

"I told our generals this spring, when they endeavored to prove to me, by all sorts of arguments, that we must beat the French if we went to war then, 'If you can make it as clear to me as that God be'—[verbatim.—K.]—'that we can crush France, and occupy Paris, I will still do all I can to prevent war; for you must remember, gentlemen, a war between such near neighbors and old enemies as France and Prussia, however it may turn out, is only the first of at least six; and supposing we gained all six, what should we have succeeded in doing? Why, in ruining France, certainly, and most likely ourselves into the bargain. Do you think a poor, bankrupt, starving, ragged neighbor is as desirable as a wealthy, solvent, fat, well-clothed one? France buys largely of us, and sells us a great many things we want. Is it in our interest to ruin her completely?' I strove for peace then, and I will do so as long as may be; only, remember, German susceptibilities must be respected, or I cannot answer for the people—not even for the king! The French, I am quite aware, are buying horses and provisions. That does not frighten me. Their harvest is a bad one, and they are quite right to take precautions against distress. They cannot want provisions for a war with us, for in such a war they must be the aggressors; and if they invade Germany they will find food and provender enough for ten French armies. Their preparations do not disquiet me in the least. *We are always ready.*"

48

The Prussian Arch-Conservative Meets a Distinguished German-American Liberal-Democrat and the Two, from Widely Different Viewpoints, Discuss the Condition of Their Countries

"I am not a democrat, and cannot be."

Forced to leave the Germanies during the Revolution of 1848, Carl Schurz emigrated to America and began a brilliant career as military leader and statesman. In the American Civil War he fought as a general on the side of the Union. After the war he became ambassador to Madrid and in 1868 was elected United States senator. While on a trip to Europe he journeyed to Germany, where, on January 28–29, 1868, he had two interviews with Bismarck. In his Reminiscences, *Schurz gave a fascinating report on Bismarck at the height of his power.*[16]

After having spent Christmas with my family in Wiesbaden I went to Berlin. I wrote a note to Lothar Bucher, whom I had last seen sixteen years before as a fellow refugee in London, and whom I wished very much to meet again. Bucher answered promptly that he would indeed be glad to see me again, but would I not like to make the acquaintance of "the Minister" (Bismarck), who had expressed a wish to have a talk with me? I replied, of course, that I should be happy, etc., whereupon I received within an hour an invitation from Count Bismarck himself (he was then only a count) to visit him at eight o'clock that same evening at the chancellor's palace on the Wilhelmstrasse. Promptly at the appointed hour I was announced to him and he received me at the door of a room of moderate size, the table and some of the furniture of which were covered with books and papers, evidently his working cabinet. There I beheld the great man whose name was filling the world—tall, erect and broad-shouldered, and on those Atlas shoulders that massive head which everybody knows from pictures—the whole figure making the impression of something colossal—then at the age of fifty-three in the fullness of physical and mental vigor. He

16. *The Reminiscences of Carl Schurz* (New York, 1908), III, 265–280. Schurz wrote two versions of this interview. A second version, in the form of notes, was found by his daughter among his papers and published by R. Fester, ''Das Gespräch Bismarcks mit Karl Schurz, 28 Januar 1868,'' in *Süddeutsche Monatshefte,* 1913–1914, pp. 362 ff. There is no substantial difference in fact in the two versions.

was dressed in a general's undress uniform, unbuttoned. His features, which evidently could look very stern when he wished, were lighted up with a friendly smile. He stretched out his hand, which gave mine a vigorous grasp. "Glad you have come," he said in a voice which appeared rather high-keyed, issuing from so huge a form, but of pleasing timbre. "I think I must have seen you before," was his first remark while we were still standing up facing one another. "It was sometime in the early fifties on a railway train from Frankfort to Berlin. There was a young man sitting opposite to me who, from some picture of you which I had seen in a pictorial paper, I thought might be you." I replied that this could not be, as at that period I was not in Germany. "Besides," I added,—a little impudently perhaps,—"would you not have had me arrested as a malefactor?" "Oh," he exclaimed with a good-natured laugh, "you mistake me. I would not have done such a thing. You mean on account of that Kinkel affair.[17] Oh, no! I rather liked that. And if it were not highly improper for his Majesty's minister and the chancellor of the North-German Confederacy, I should like to go with you to Spandau and have you tell me the whole story on the spot. Now let us sit down." He pointed out to me an easy chair close to his own and then uncorked a bottle which stood with two glasses on a tray at his elbow. "You are a Rhinelander," he said, "and I know you will relish this." We touched glasses, and I found the wine indeed very excellent. "You smoke, of course," he continued, "and here are some good Havanas. I used to be very fond of them, but I have a sort of superstitious belief that every person is permitted to smoke only a certain number of cigars in his life, and no more. I am afraid I have exhausted my allowance, and now I take to the pipe." With a burning strip of paper, called in German *Fidibus,* he lighted the tobacco in the porcelain bowl of his long German student pipe and presently blew forth huge clouds of smoke.

This done, he comfortably leaned back in his chair and said: "Now tell me, as an American Republican and a Forty-eighter of the revolutionary kind, how the present condition of Germany strikes you. I would not ask you that question," he added, "if you were a privy-counsellor (a *Geheimrat*), for I know what he would answer. But you will tell me what you really think." I replied that I had been in the country only a few weeks and had received only superficial impressions, but I had become sensible of a general atmosphere of newly inspired national ambition and a confident

17. Professor Johann Gottfried Kinkel, Schurz's teacher and friend, who was jailed at Rastatt prison for democratic activities and who with Schurz's assistance was rescued in a sensational escape in 1849.

hope for the development of more liberal political institutions. I had found only a few old fogies in Nassau, and a banker in Frankfort, who seemed to be in a disappointed and depressed state of mind. Bismarck laughed heartily. The disgruntled Nassauers, he said, had probably been some sort of purveyors to the late ducal court, and he would wager that the Frankfort banker was either a member of one of the old patrician families, who thought they were the highest nobility in all the land, or a money-maker complaining that Frankfort was no longer, as it had been, the financial center of Southern Germany. Here Bismarck gave full rein to his sarcastic humor. He had spent years in Frankfort as the representative of the defunct *Bundestag,* and had no end of funny anecdotes about the aristocratic pretensions of the patrician burghers of that ancient free city, and about their lofty wrath at the incorporation of that commonwealth in the Prussian monarchy.

Then he began to tell me about the great difficulties he had been obliged to overcome in bringing about the decisive struggle with Austria, one of the most serious of which difficulties, as he said, consisted in the scrupulous hesitancy of old King William to consent to anything that seemed to be in any sense unconstitutional or not in harmony with the strictest notion of good faith. In our conversation Bismarck constantly called the king *der alte Herr*—"the old gentleman"—or as it might also have been translated, "the old master." One moment he would speak of the old gentleman with something like sentimental tenderness, and then again in a tone of familiar freedom which smacked of anything but reverential respect. He told me anecdotes about him which made me stare, for at the moment I could not help remembering that I was listening to the prime minister of the crown to whom I was an entire stranger and who knew nothing of my discretion and sense of responsibility. As if we had been confidential chums all our lives, he gave me, with apparently the completest abandon and exuberant vivacity, inside views of the famous "conflict" period between the crown and the Prussian parliament when, seeing the war with Austria inevitably coming, he had, without legislative authorization, spent millions upon millions of the public funds upon the army in preparation for the great crisis; how the liberal majority of the chambers and an indignant public opinion, not recognizing the great object of national unification in view, had fiercely risen up against that arbitrary stretch of power; how the king himself had recoiled from such a breach of the constitution; how the king had apprehended a new revolution which might cost each of them his head—which might have become true if they had failed in the Austrian war—how then he had "desperately used his spurs to make the noble old horse clear the ditch and take the risk," and how, the victory having been won, they were, on their return from the war, received by the people with the most jubilant acclamations instead of having their heads cut off, which had pleased the old gentleman immensely and taught him a lesson as to his reckless prime minister.

It was not the cautious and conservative spirit of the king alone that he had occasionally to overcome. Still more was he clogged and not seldom exasperated by what he called the stupid old bureaucracy which he had to get out of its accustomed ruts whenever anything new and bold was to be done. He fairly bubbled over with humorous anecdotes, evidently relishing himself his droll descriptions of the antiquated *Geheimrat* (privy-counsellor) as he stared with his bleared eyes wide open, whenever anything unusual was proposed, seeing nothing but insuperable difficulties before him and then exhausting his whole ingenuity in finding the best sort of red tape with which to strangle the project. His patience tried to the utmost, he, the minister, would then go to the king and tell him that such and such a rusty official could no longer be got along with and must necessarily give place to a more efficient person—whereupon the "old gentleman," melting with pity, would say, "Oh, he has so long been a faithful servant of the state, would it not be cruel to cast him aside like a squeezed-out orange?—no, I cannot do it." "And there," said Bismarck, "there we are." I ventured to suggest that an offer to resign on his part, if he could not have his way, might make the king less tender of his inefficient friends in high places. "Oh," said Bismarck, with a laugh, "I have tried that so often, too often, perhaps, to make it impressive. What do you think happens when I offer my resignation? My old gentleman begins to sob and cry—he actually sheds tears, and says, 'Now you want to leave me, too?' Now, when I see him shed tears—what in the world can I do then?" So he went on for a while from one funny anecdote and from one satirical description to another, while I grew more and more amazed at the apparently reckless freedom of his talk with a person unknown to him. My amazement would have been less had I then known what I afterward learned, that this style of conversation was not unusual with him and that the old king only smiled when he heard of it.

He then came back to the Austrian war and he told me much about the diplomatic fencing which led up to it. With evident gusto he told me story after story showing how his diplomatic adversaries at that critical period had been like puppets in his hands, and how he had managed the German princes as they grouped themselves on one side or the other. Then he came to speak of the battle of Königgrätz and especially of that "anxious moment" in it before the arrival of the crown prince in the rear of the Austrians, when some Prussian attacks had failed and there were signs of disorder among the repulsed troops. "It was an anxious moment," said Bismarck, "a moment on the decision of which the fate of empire depended. What would have become of us if we had lost that battle? Squadrons of cavalry, all mixed up, Hussars, Dragoons, Uhlans, were streaming by the spot where the king, Moltke, and myself stood, and although we had calculated that the crown prince might long have appeared behind the Austrian rear, no sign of the crown prince! Things began to look ominous; I confess I felt not a little nervous. I looked at Moltke, who sat quietly on his horse and did not seem to be disturbed by what was going on around us. I thought I would test whether he was really as calm as he appeared. I rode up to him and asked him whether I might offer him a cigar, as I noticed Moltke was not smoking. He replied that he would be glad if I had one to spare. I presented to him my open case in which there were only two cigars, one very good Havana, and the other of rather poor quality. Moltke looked at them, and even handled them with great attention, in order to ascertain their relative value, and then with slow deliberation chose the Havana. 'Very good,' he said composedly. This reassured me very much. I thought if Moltke can bestow so much time and attention upon the choice between two cigars, things cannot be very bad. Indeed, a few minutes later we heard the crown prince's guns, we observed unsteady and confused movements in the Austrian positions, and the battle was won."

I said that we in America who had followed the course of events with intense interest, were rather surprised at the time that the conclusion of peace followed the battle of Königgrätz so quickly and that Prussia did not take greater advantage of her victory. Bismarck replied that the speedy conclusion of peace had been a great surprise to many people, but that he thought it was the best thing he had ever done, and that he had accomplished it against the desire of the king and of the military party who were greatly elated by that splendid triumph of the Prussian arms and thought that so great and so successful an effort should have a greater reward. Sound statesmanship required that the Austrian empire, the existence of which was necessary for Europe, should not be reduced to a mere wreck; that it should be made a friend, and, as a friend, not too powerless; that what Prussia had gone to war for, was the leadership in Germany, and that this leadership in Germany would not have been fortified, but rather weakened, by the acquisition from Austria of populations which would not have fitted into the Prussian scheme. Besides, the chancellor thought that, the success of the Prussians having been so decisive, it was wise to avoid further sacrifices and risks. The cholera had made its appearance among the troops, and, that so long as the war lasted, there would have been danger of French intervention. He had successfully fought off that French intervention, he said, by all sorts of diplomatic maneuvers, some of which he narrated to me in detail. But Louis Napoleon had become very restless at the growth of Prussian power and prestige, and he would, probably, not have hesitated so much to put in his hand, had not the French army been weakened so much by his foolish Mexican adventure. But now when the main Prussian army was marching farther and farther away from the Rhine, and had suffered serious losses, and was threatened by malignant disease, he might have felt encouraged by these circumstances to do what he would have liked to do all the time.

"That would have created a new situation. But to meet that situation, I would have had a shot in my locker which, perhaps, will surprise you when I mention it."

I was indeed curious. "What would have been the effect," said Bismarck, "if under those circumstances I had appealed to the national feeling of the whole people by proclaiming the constitution of the German empire made at Frankfort in 1848 and 1849?"

"I think it would have electrified the whole country and created a German nation," I replied. "But would you really have adopted that great orphan left by the revolution of 1848?"

"Why not!" said the chancellor. "True, that constitution contained some features very objectionable to me. But after all it was not so very far from what I am aiming at now. But whether the old gentleman would have adopted it, is doubtful. Still, with Napoleon at the gates, he might have taken that jump too. But," he added, "we shall have that war with France anyhow."

I expressed my surprise at this prediction—a prediction all the more surprising to me as I again thought of the great statesman carrying on his shoulders such tremendous responsibilities, talking to an entire stranger—and his tone grew quite serious, grave, almost solemn, when he said: "Do not believe that I love war. I have seen enough of war to abhor it profoundly. The terrible scenes I have witnessed will never cease to haunt my mind. I shall never consent to a war that is avoidable, much less seek it. But this war with France will surely come. It will be forced upon us by the French emperor. I see that clearly."

Then he went on to explain how the situation of an "adventurer on a throne," such as Louis Napoleon, was different from that of a legitimate sovereign, like the king of Prussia. "I know," said he with a smile, "you do not believe in such a thing as the divine right of kings. But many people do, especially in Prussia—perhaps not as many as did before 1848, but even now more than you may think. People are attached to the dynasty by traditional loyalty. A king of Prussia may make mistakes, or suffer misfortunes, or even humiliations, but that traditional loyalty will not give way. It may be somewhat disturbed in spots, without on the whole being dangerously shaken. But the adventurer on the throne has no such traditional sentiment behind him. He has constantly to play to the galleries. His security depends upon personal prestige, and that prestige upon sensational effects which must follow one another in rather rapid succession to remain fresh and satisfactory to the ambition, or to the pride, or, if you will, to the vanity of the people—especially to such a people as the French. Now, Louis Napoleon has lost much of his prestige by two things—the Mexican adventure, which was an astounding blunder, a fantastic folly on his part—and then by permitting Prussia to become so great without his obtaining some sort of 'compensation' in the way of an acquisition of territory that might have been made to appear to the French people as a brilliant achievement of his diplomacy. It was well known that he wanted such a compensation, and tried for it, and was maneuvered out of it by me without his knowing what happened to him. He is well aware that thus he has lost much of his prestige, more than he can afford, and that such a loss, unless soon repaired, may become dangerous to his tenure as emperor. He will, therefore, as soon as he thinks that his army is in good fighting condition again, make an effort to recover that prestige which is so vital to him, by using some pretext for picking a quarrel with us. I do not think he is personally eager for war, and would rather avoid it, but the precariousness of his situation will drive him to it. My calculation is that the crisis will come in about two years. We have to be ready, of course, and we are. We shall win, and the result will be just the contrary of what Napoleon aims at—the total unification of Germany outside of Austria, and probably Napoleon's downfall."

This was said in January 1868. The war between France and Prussia and her allies broke out in July 1870, and the foundation of the German empire and the downfall of Napoleon were the results. No prediction was ever more shrewdly made and more accurately and amply fulfilled.

I have here introduced Bismarck as speaking in the first person. I did this to present the substance of what he said to me in a succinct form. But this does not pretend to portray the manner in which he said it—the bubbling vivacity of his talk, now and then interspersed with French or English phrases; the lightning flashes of his wit scintillating around the subjects of his remarks and sometimes illuminating as with a searchlight a public character, or an event, or a situation; his laugh now contagiously genial, and then grimly sarcastic; the rapid transitions from jovial, sportive humor to touching pathos; the evident pleasure taken by the narrator in his tale; the dashing, rattling rapidity with which that tale would at times rush on, and behind all that this tremendous personality—the picturesque embodiment of a power greater than any king's—a veritable Atlas carrying upon his shoulders the destinies of a great nation. There was a strange fascination in the presence of the giant who appeared so peculiarly grand, and yet so human.

While he was still speaking with unabated animation I looked at the clock opposite me and was astounded when I found that midnight was long behind us. I rose in alarm and begged the chancellor's pardon for having intruded so long upon his time. "Oh," said the chancellor, "I am used to late hours, and we have not talked yet about America. However, you have a right to be tired. But you must come again. You must dine with me. Can you do so tomorrow? I have invited a commission on the Penal Code—mostly dull old jurists, I suppose, but I may find some one among them fit to be your neighbor at the table and to entertain you." I gladly accepted the invitation and found myself the next evening in a large company of serious and learned-looking gentlemen, each one of whom was adorned with one or more decorations. I was the only person in the room who had none, and several of the guests seemed to eye me with some curiosity, when Bismarck in a loud voice presented me to the countess as "General Carl Schurz from the United States of America." Some of the gentlemen looked somewhat surprised, but I at once became a person of interest and many introductions followed. At the table I had a judge from Cologne for my neighbor who had enough of the Rhenish temperament to be cheerful company. The dinner was a very rapid affair—lasting hardly three-quarters of an hour—certainly not more. My judge from Cologne confidentially remarked to me that his appetite outlived the feast. Coffee and cigars were served in a rather plain-looking salon. The guests divided into groups among which the chancellor went to and fro amusing them with humorous remarks. But before the smokers could have got half through with their cigars, the minister of justice, who seemed to act as mentor and guide to the gentlemen of the Penal Code Commission, took leave of the host, which was taken by the whole company as a signal to depart. I followed their example, but the chancellor said: "Wait a moment. Why should you stand in that crowd struggling for your overcoat? Let us sit down and have a glass of Apollinaris." We sat down by a small round table, a bottle of Apollinaris water was brought and he began at once to ply me with questions about America.

He was greatly interested in the struggle then going on between President Johnson and the Republican majority in Congress, which was then approaching its final crisis. He said that he looked upon that struggle as a test of the strength of the conservative element in our political fabric. Would the impeachment of the president and, if he were found guilty, his deposition from office, lead to any further conflicts dangerous to the public peace and order? I replied that I was convinced it would not; the executive power would simply pass from the hands of one man to the hands of another according to the constitution and the laws of the country without any resistance on the part of anybody; and on the other hand, if President Johnson were acquitted, there would be general submission to the verdict as a matter of course, although popular excitement stirred up by the matter ran very high throughout the country.

The chancellor was too polite to tell me point blank that he had grave doubts as to all this, but he would at least not let me believe that he thought as I did. He smilingly asked me whether I was still as firmly convinced a republican as I had been before I went to America and studied republicanism from the inside; and when I assured him that I was, and that, although I had in personal experience found the republic not as lovely as my youthful enthusiasm had pictured it to my imagination, but much more practical in its general beneficence to the great masses of the people, and much more conservative in its tendencies than I had imagined, he said that he supposed our impressions or views with regard to such things were largely owing to temperament, or education, or traditional ways of thinking. "I am not a democrat," he went on, "and cannot be. I was born an aristocrat and brought up an aristocrat. To tell you the truth, there was something in me that made me instinctively sympathize with the slaveholders as the aristocratic party in your civil war. But," he added with earnest emphasis, "this vague sympathy did not in the least affect my views as to the policy to be followed by our government with regard to the United States. Prussia is and will steadily be by tradition as well as by well-understood interest, the firm friend of your republic, notwithstanding her monarchical and aristocratic sympathies. You may always count upon that."

He asked me a great many questions concerning the political and social conditions, in the United States, the questions themselves, in the order in which they were put, showing that he had thought much on those things and that he already knew much about them —in fact more than any European I had met, who had never been in this country. What new information I could give him he seemed to receive with great pleasure. But again and again he wondered how society could be kept in tolerable order where the powers of the government were so narrowly restricted and where there was so little reverence for the constituted or "ordained" authorities. With a hearty laugh in which there seemed to be a suggestion of assent, he received my remark that the American people would hardly have become the self-reliant, energetic, progressive people they were, had there been a privy-counsellor or a police captain standing at every mud puddle in America to keep people from stepping into it. And he seemed to be much struck when I brought out the apparent paradox that in a democracy with little government things might go badly in detail but well on the whole, while in a monarchy with much and omnipresent government, things might go very pleasingly in detail but poorly on the whole. He saw that with such views I was an incurable democrat; but would not, he asked, the real test of our democratic institutions come when after the disappearance of the exceptional opportunities springing from our wonderful natural resources which were in a certain sense common property, our political struggles became—which they surely would become—struggles between the poor and the rich, between the few who have, and the many who want? Here we entered upon a wide field of conjecture.

The chancellor was much interested in hearing from me whether the singular stories he had been told about the state of discipline existing in our armies during our Civil War were true. I had to admit that that state of discipline would in many respects have shocked a thoroughbred Prussian officer, and I told him some anecdotes of outbreaks of the spirit of equality which the American is apt to carry into all relations of life, and of the occasional familiarities between the soldier and the officer which would spring from that spirit. Such anecdotes amused him immensely, but I suppose his Prussian pride inwardly revolted when I expressed the opinion that in spite of all this the American soldier would not only fight well, but would, in a prolonged conflict with any European army, although at first put at a disadvantage by more thorough drill and discipline, after some experience prove superior to all of them.

The conversation then turned to international relations, and especially public opinion in America concerning Germany. Did the

Americans sympathize with German endeavors toward national unity? I thought that so far as any feeling with regard to German unity existed in America at all, it was sympathetic; among the German-Americans it was warmly so. Did Louis Napoleon, the emperor of the French, enjoy any popularity in America? He did not enjoy the respect of the people at large and was rather unpopular except with a comparatively small number of snobs who would feel themselves exalted by an introduction at his court. There would, then, in case of a war between Germany and France, be no likelihood of American sympathy running in favor of Louis Napoleon? There would not, unless Germany forced war on France for decidedly unjust cause.

Throughout our conversation Bismarck repeatedly expressed his pleasure at the friendly relations existing between him and the German Liberals, some of whom had been prominent in the revolutionary troubles of 1848. He mentioned several of my old friends, Bucher, Kapp and others, who, having returned to Germany, felt themselves quite at home under the new conditions, and had found the way open to public positions and activities of distinction and influence, in harmony with their principles. As he repeated this, or something like it, in a manner apt to command my attention, I might have taken it as a suggestion inviting me to do likewise. But I thought it best not to say anything in response. I simply dropped a casual remark in some proper connection that my activities in the United States were highly congenial to me and that, moreover, I was attached to the American Republic by a sense of gratitude for the distinctions which it had so generously bestowed upon me.

Our conversation had throughout been so animated that time had slipped by unawares, and it was again long past midnight when I left. My old friends of 1848 whom I met in Berlin were of course very curious to know what the great man of the time might have had to say to me, and I thought I could, without being indiscreet, communicate to them how highly pleased he had expressed himself with the harmonious cooperation between him and them for common ends. Some of them thought that Bismarck's conversion to liberal principles was really sincere, that he was charmed with his popularity, and that he would thenceforth endeavor to keep it by being in the true sense a constitutional minister. Others were less sanguine, believing as they did, that he was indeed sincere and earnest in his endeavor to create a united German empire under Prussian leadership; that he would carry on a gay flirtation with the Liberals so long as he thought that he could thus best further his object, but that his true autocratic nature would assert itself again and he would throw his temporarily assumed Liberalism unceremoniously overboard as soon as he felt that he did not need its support any longer, and especially as he found it to stand in the way of his will. Excepting on the occasion of a formal leave-taking call I was not to see Bismarck again until twenty years later.

49 The Bismarcks, Arbiters of Society, Give a Brilliant Party and Make Beer Fashionable in Berlin Salons

"The whole royal house is present."

The Bismarcks, social arbiters of Berlin, lived at a modest residence in that portion of the Wilhelmstrasse bounded on one side by the animated Unter den Linden and on the other by the noisy and busy Leipzigerstrasse. It was a plain one-storied house, with twelve windows in the front. Here the Bismarcks held evening parties with supper after midnight for the most scintillating guests in Prussia. The following description of a ball at the Bismarcks was given by John-George Louis Hesekiel, one of Bismarck's earliest biographers.[18] *The time was in the late 1860's, between the wars with Austria and France.*

. . . when the minister-president and the countess of Bismarck-Schönhausen send out their invitations, no house in Berlin has the courage to vie with them and open its door on the same evening. The consequence of this is, that all the guests arrive early and stop as long as ever they can. Now, as we have already said, the apartments at the ministry of foreign affairs are exceedingly small, and thus there is a crush of which it is impossible to form any idea unless one has seen it. Add to this the temperature of the dog days in the brilliantly lighted saloons, and the impossibility of sitting down; an enjoyment only appreciated to its full extent by the members of the Reichstag and deputies of the diet, who here find ample opportunity, after their long plenary and committee sittings, to stand.

The guest reaches the first saloon by the stairs, through a forest of tropical plants and orange groves, with livery servants sprinkled in, to the place where the minister-president, in his white uniform, with the star and collar of his order, aided by his wife, receives the guests, interchanging a few friendly expressions with

18. John-George Louis Hesekiel, *The Life of Bismarck,* trans. and ed. by Kenneth R. H. MacKenzie (London, 1870), pp. 434–444.

them, and then they enter. But after this the guest literally founders in the ocean of dazzling light and crowds of people; it is only after a considerable interval that a person, unless accustomed for years to these parties, recovers his self-possession. . . .

Suddenly all the heads, decked with feathers, flowers, and jewels, bow slowly and then rise again; it is as if the evening breeze passed gently over the meadow, the flowers all bending up and down, hither and thither.

King William is entering, conducted by the minister-president. The stately royal man bows with chivalrous politeness, now to this lady, now to that; he pronounces kind words, which are really more kind and fewer in number than is usually the case. Here he shakes hands with one general, there he nods to another gentleman—the path by which the king has passed is marked by proud and happy faces. Those who feel disposed to jeer, cannot in the least know how a Prussian feels when the king's hand touches his own, and the king's eye looks so grandly and mildly into his.

But to enjoy a really heart-warming sight, King William and Bismarck must be seen together. The great hero, Prince Eugene, or Eugenio von Savoye, as he wrote it in Italian, German, and French, once said of the three emperors whom he had served—"Leopold was my father, Joseph my friend, Carl is my sovereign!" In Bismarck's conduct towards the king may be seen the reverence for a father, the attachment of a friend, and the fullest respect for a sovereign. A unique spectacle, this!

Now the queen passes through the brilliant throng, dressed with royal simplicity; she speaks with several of the members of the Reichstag. When the sailing boat passes through the waves of the sea, when the swan glides over the shining mirror, a silver line marks the passage they have taken. Such a line denotes the path which the queen had followed through the throng.

The whole royal house is present.

The tall stately man yonder, with the brave handsome countenance, who looks still taller in his light blue dragoon uniform with the yellow collar, in which he is not often seen, is the crown prince. He is engaged in animated conversation with a foreign diplomatist, in a golden full dress, and is evidently in the best of tempers. Prince Albrecht, the king's younger brother, passes swiftly in a frank military manner, shaking one or the other person cordially by the hand. His elder brother, Prince Carl, the commander-in-chief, is a singular contrast to him. He stands erect and proudly in the middle of a circle, but without stiffness. A mocking smile plays over his features; there is a remarkable intermixture in his eyes of sharp observation and indifference. How he brings first this person and then that to his side, without raising his hand! This is the reproachless manner of a *grand seigneur* of days gone by; one cannot but feel that Prince Carl still retains whole and undivided the princely consciousness of former times. In his eyes every one—not of princely rank—stands on the same level. Rank, titles, honors, have no distinction in his eyes. He is as gracious to the ministers and high dignitaries, as to the author whom he has just summoned to him. He alone really exercises the *métier de prince.*

Yonder stalwart form, with the good brave countenance, in the admiral's uniform, is Prince Adalbert, a cousin of the king, he is talking with Herr von Selechow, the minister of agriculture, who at a distance looks like an officer in the cavalry. All the princes of the royal house wear the cross of the order *pour le mérite,* and therefore have all been under fire.

Prince Frederick Carl yonder is talking with Count Eulenburg, who has made his way through typhoons and Japan to the ministry of the interior. The prince, with his high forehead, firm bearded countenance, large eyes with their lonely quiet expression, and spare form, in the red jacket of the Ziethen Hussars, is the hero of Düppel and Sadowa, also a member of the North German Reichstag.

All the faces in yonder group are well known, for their portraits hang in every window; they have written their names in the book of history with the sword. At every step here one may greet a hero. Certainly, designed and undesigned mistakes sometimes happen, as, for instance, that pretty young lady cannot sufficiently wonder that the valiant old Steinmetz, the famous hero of Nachod and Skalitz, is still so young, and dresses in private clothes. They had pointed her out a Reichstag deputy from Pomerania as the famous general, and left her in the error.

Through the brilliant throng and excitement, in the dazzling illuminations and heat, children wise in their generation, and lucky dogs who know everything, have discovered the way to obtain a thorough course of refreshments, which is hidden in a dark thicket yonder, and slyly wins in semi-concealment. In noble silver vases there is cool—deliciously cool—beer. All the thirsty souls who drink at this fount sing the praises of Bismarck, for he has introduced this innovation. Bismarck first made beer fashionable in Berlin *salons.* And so readily has it been received within a short time, that even tender ladies and high princes no longer hesitate to pay their court openly to King Gambrinus.

There is lively conversation over the beer. A wit has spread a rumor that the delicious drink has come from Schwechat, and is a present from the Austrian imperial chancellor to the chancellor of the North German Confederation. Some give a friendly assent to this, others kindly add, that Bismarck has already, in return, sent some Neunaugen and Flunder from Pomerania, to his colleague in Vienna; and why should it not be believed? Formerly, at any rate, the most friendly and social relations existed between Bismarck and Beust.

An old Colonel D—— mutters something like *"timeo Danaos,"* but swallows the rest of the words, as he cannot immediately find the Latin terminations in the lumber-room of his memory, but instead, enjoys another goblet of the supposed gift. He is almost frightened when his neighbor remarks, that Beust as well as Bismarck is a descendant of an Alt Mark family; Büste, the family seat of the Beust family, is only distant a few miles from Bismarck; certainly, the family had not lived there for a long time. Colonel D—— begins to have a better opinion of the Austrian chancellor, and drinks up his beer in comfort.

Another is telling how Bismarck laughingly said, that "his colleague, the minister of finance, would today convince himself that this dwelling was much too small for the minister-president, and would think of how he could get him out of the difficulty." Thus the little circle got happily into the downward way of telling anecdotes, whence there is no return.

To a somewhat complaining deputation from the new provinces, Bismarck good-humoredly explained, that Prussia was like a woolen jacket, very unpleasant at first, but when people got accustomed to it they found it very comfortable, and at last came to think it a great benefit.

Bismarck allowed another deputation to whine for a long time about universal military service and the weight of taxation; he then said, very seriously and in a tone of the greatest astonishment, "Dear me, these gentlemen probably thought they could become Prussians for nothing!"

A well-known politician promulgated a very paradoxical statement at Bismarck's dinner table; some one present started forward to refute it. "Pray don't trouble yourself," exclaimed Bismarck, "if you will only have patience for two minutes, the learned Herr Professor will at once contradict himself in the most brilliant manner!"

In the year 1848 there was a great deal rumored about a falling away of the Rhine provinces. "Where are they going to fall to?" asked Bismarck.

"And in France they no longer say, *'travailler pour le roi de Prusse,'* to indicate a lost labor of love, but *'travailler pour le maître de M. de Bismarck!*'" whispered a fat diplomatist cautiously to his neighbor.

"How is it," King William merrily once asked the minister-president and his cousin Herr von Bismarck-Briest, "that the Bismarcks of Schönhausen are all such tall, strapping fellows, and those of Briest the contrary?" Count Bismarck replied, "Because my ancestors all served the king as soldiers in battle, while my cousins were engaged in civil affairs!" Herr von Bismarck-Briest added, with presence of mind, "That is why I have put my seven sons into the army."

It was true that six Bismarck-Briests fought in the last war under the king's standard; a pity that the seventh was not there, but as a *Landrat* he was "exempt."

"But," whispered a pale assessor, who has been guilty of innumerable verses, "Bismarck is deficient in esthetic culture; I have heard from the best authority, that once at Frankfort, when Goethe's pearl, 'Happy he who closes up his door without hatred of the world!' was performed on the piano, Bismarck burst out with, 'What a tailor's soul this Goethe had!'"

The pale assessor looked as if such barbarism froze him; some laughed, others shrugged their shoulders.

"The ideas of the moment were confused with opinions or meaning!" said a provincial government councillor, who knew how to combine his reverence for Bismarck with his esthetic aspirations; for in fact he only knew Bismarck and Goethe.

"I remember you in my boyish days very well," said Bismarck, in 1864, to the body-physician of Prince Albrecht, the Privy-Councillor Dr. von Arnim; "you then enormously struck me with your energy."

"This is completely altered now," replied Arnim, quietly, "you now strike me enormously with yours." . . .

Anecdote succeeded anecdote, one joke the other; each departing storyteller leaving another in his place, until the circle round the altar of Gambrinus was broken up by the news that their Majesties and the court, after having partaken of supper in the countess's salon, had taken their departure. This was the signal for supper for the rest of the guests.

A buffet supper is the saddest conclusion of a "rout"—it is almost somewhat humiliating to stand with one's hat under one's arm and the plate in one's hand, after having had great difficulty to procure knife, fork, and all the other utensils employed in civilized nations for the business of eating! But humanity can even support this, and with a little care and patience it is possible gradually to get a complete supper, from a cup of soup to a fruit ice.

Modest minds content themselves certainly by absorbing a gigantic portion of ham pie with a spoon—or whatever the fortune of war has favored their plates with—ask for nothing more—but "go in" for the wine which is foaming in any quantity.

In the meantime the dance music is beginning again, and with it the actual period of enjoyment for dancers, and the terrible hour for chaperonizing mothers and aunts, who sit out the last cotillion with a heroism brave unto death.

The non-dancing guests now really begin to enjoy themselves—the crowd being no longer so thick, there is more room, as the saloons reserved for the court are now open, and there are plenty of seats. Presently a smoking room suddenly opens—a smoking room with noble cigars, iced champagne, and hot coffee. Everywhere one sees the minister-president busy among his guests, conversing in the most agreeable tone, seeing that there is nothing wanting, inviting every one to drink, and himself rejoicing in the gaiety he disperses. And whoever departs at about five in the morning, with a hearty shake of the hand from Bismarck, will certainly carry away with him the impression that the first minister of Prussia is also the most delightful host in Prussia.

50

Road to War with France: Bismarck Tells how He Edited the Ems Dispatch, July 13, 1870

"It will have the effect of a red flag on the Gallic bull."

To achieve his main object of German unification, Bismarck knew that he had to goad France into action at the right moment and, at the same time, make it appear that Napoleon III was the chief disturber of the peace of Europe. The idea was to lure the French ruler into a trap from which he would declare war on Prussia. This was done by means of a fortunate (for Bismarck) and a fortuitous set of circumstances.

A conflict has arisen over the projected Hohenzollern candidacy for the throne of Spain. In 1868 Queen Isabella of Spain was dethroned by a military coup. The monarchists, undoubtedly stimulated by Bismarck, proposed a candidate in the person of Prince Leopold von Hohenzollern—Sigmarin, a member of the Swabian branch of the Hohenzollern family. The specter of a revived empire of Charles V to threaten France on both sides of her borders was one to haunt the nervous French emperor.

When King William of Prussia was taking the cure at Bad Ems in the middle of July 1870, he was approached by Count Vincent

Benedetti, the French ambassador, who requested him to abandon, once and for all time, any claims of his dynasty on Spain. Privy-Councillor Heinrich Abeken telegraphed an account of the meeting to Bismarck, who was in Berlin. The latter craftily edited the dispatch and released it to the press the next day, July 14, 1870, timed on the French national holiday. The effect was exactly what Bismarck had intended, for in its abbreviated form the telegram gave the impression of an ultimatum, "like a flourish of trumpets in answer to a challenge." France declared war at once.

Admirers of Bismarck insist that he was entitled to use any shrewd move in the international battle of wits. Others claim that Bismarck's version of the telegram was an unscrupulous trick, deliberately designed to instigate war. The first selection below gives Bismarck's own version of the incident from his memoirs. The second selection is the original Abeken text and Bismarck's edited version.

I Bismarck on the Ems Dispatch *

I invited Generals Moltke and Roon to have dinner with me on July 13th, and spoke to them concerning my views and intentions. During the dinner conversation it was reported to me that a code telegram had been received from Ems, and it was then in process of decoding. I then read it to my guests, who were so crushed that they refused to eat or drink.

All considerations, conscious or unconscious, strengthened my opinion that war could be avoided only at the cost of the honor of Prussia and of the national confidence in her.

Under this conviction I made use of the royal authority communicated to me through Abeken to publish the contents of the telegram. In the presence of my guests I reduced the telegram by deleting words, but without adding or altering a single word. . . .

The difference in the effect of the shortened text of the Ems telegram as compared with that of the original was not the result of stronger words but of the form, which made the announcement appear decisive.

After I had read the condensed version to my two guests, Moltke said:

"Now it has a quite different ring. In its original form it sounded like a parley. Now it is like a flourish of trumpets in answer to a challenger!"

I went on to explain:

"If, in execution of his Majesty's order, I immediately communi-

* Otto von Bismarck, *Gedanken und Erinnerungen* (Stuttgart and Berlin, 1898), II, 406–408.

cate this text, which contains no changes in or additions to the telegram, not only to the newspapers but also by wire to all our embassies, it will be known in Paris before midnight. Not only on account of its contents but also because of the manner of its distribution, it will have the effect of a red flag on the Gallic bull.

"We must fight if we do not want to act the part of the defeated without a battle. However, success depends essentially upon the impression which the beginning of the war makes upon us and others. It is most important that we should be the ones attacked. Gallic insolence and sensitivity will bring this about if we announce before all Europe, as far as we can without the speaking tube of the Reichstag, that we are courageously meeting the public threats of France."

This explanation drew from both generals a metamorphosis into a more joyous mood, whose liveliness surprised me. They had suddenly recovered their desire to eat and drink and began to speak in a more cheerful tone.

Roon said: "Our God of old still lives, and will not let us die in disgrace."

Moltke relinquished his passive equanimity so much that, glancing up joyously to the ceiling and abandoning his usual punctiliousness of speech, he pounded his chest with his hand and exclaimed:

"If I may but live to lead our armies in such a war, then right afterwards let the devil come and haul away the old carcass." He was then more frail than later and had his doubts as to whether he could live through the fatigue of a field campaign.

II Original and Edited Versions of the Ems Dispatch *

THE ABEKEN TEXT

Ems, July 13, 1870.

To the Federal Chancellor, Count Bismarck, No. 27, No. 61 *eod.* 3:10 P.M. (*Station Ems:* Rush!)

His Majesty the King writes to me:

"M. Benedetti intercepted me on the promenade in order to demand of me most insistently that I should authorize him to telegraph immediately to Paris

BISMARCK'S EDITED VERSION

After the reports of the renunciation by the hereditary prince of Hohenzollern had been officially transmitted by the royal government of Spain to the imperial government of France, the French ambassador presented to his Majesty the King at Ems the demand to authorize him to telegraph to Paris that his Majesty the King would obligate himself for all

* *Propyläen Weltgeschichte* (Berlin, 1930), VIII, 248. Heinrich Abeken was German Councillor of Legation at Paris.

that I shall obligate myself for all future time never again to give my approval to the candidacy of the Hohenzollerns should it be renewed. I refused to agree to this, the last time somewhat severely, informing him that one dare not and cannot assume such obligations *à tout jamais*. Naturally, I informed him that I had received no news as yet and since he had been informed earlier than I by way of Paris and Madrid, he could easily understand why my government was once again out of the matter."

Since then his Majesty has received a dispatch from the prince [Charles Anthony]. As his Majesty has informed Count Benedetti that he was expecting news from the prince, his Majesty himself, in view of the above-mentioned demand and in consonance with the advice of Count Eulenburg and myself, decided not to receive the French envoy again but to inform him through an adjutant that his Majesty had now received from the prince confirmation of the news which Benedetti had already received from Paris, and that he had nothing further to say to the ambassador. His Majesty leaves it to the judgment of your Excellency whether or not to communicate at once the new demand by Benedetti and its rejection to our ambassadors and to the press.

[*Signed*] A[beken] 13.7.70

future time never again to give his approval to the candidacy of the Hohenzollerns should it be renewed.

His Majesty the King thereupon refused to receive the French envoy again and informed him through an adjutant that his Majesty had nothing further to say to the ambassador.

51

To "Defend Its Honor and Its Injured Interests," France Declares War on Prussia, and Bismarck Recognizes "That War Imposed by France"[19]

"The whole civilized world will admit that the motives put forward by France do not exist."

On July 19, 1870, M. Le Sourd, the French chargé d'affaires *in Berlin, handed over the declaration of war made by France against Prussia. The exact text follows. That same day, Bismarck, as chancellor of the North German Confederation, addressed a circular to its diplomatic agents. Reproduced in the second excerpt below, Bismarck's circular is an excellent specimen of his trenchant style.*

French Declaration of War, July 19, 1870

The undersigned, *chargé d'affaires* of France, has the honor, in conformity with the orders he has received from his government, to bring the following communication to the knowledge of his Excellency the Minister of Foreign Affairs of his Majesty the King of Prussia. The Government of his Majesty the Emperor of the French being unable to view the project of placing a Prussian prince on the Spanish throne otherwise than as an action directed against the security of the territories of France, found itself obliged to demand of his Majesty the King of Prussia the assurance that such a combination could not be realized with his consent. His Majesty having refused to give any such guarantee, and having, on the contrary, declared to the ambassador of his Majesty the Emperor of the French that he intends to reserve to himself for that eventuality, as for any other, the right to be guided by circumstances, the imperial government has been forced to see in this declaration of the king an *arrière-pensée,* menacing in like manner to France and the European equilibrium. This declaration has been rendered worse by the communication made to the different cabinets of the king's refusal to receive the ambassador of the emperor, and to enter into further explanation with him. In consequence hereof, the French government has thought it its duty

19. Quoted in Bulten, *op. cit.,* pp. 163–167.

to take immediate steps for the defense of its honor and its injured interests, and has resolved to adopt, for this object, all measures which the situation in which it has been placed renders necessary. It considers itself from this moment in a state of war against Prussia.

The undersigned has the honor to be your Excellency's, &c. &c.,

LE SOURD

Berlin, July 19, 1870

Bismarck's Circular, July 19, 1870

The imperial government of France has sent us, through its *chargé d'affaires,* the enclosed document, which contains the declaration of war. It is the first official document we have received from the French government relative to the grave affair which has occupied the world for a fortnight. In that document the French government gives the following reasons for the war it makes against us. Firstly, the refusal by the king to pledge himself that the advent of a Prussian prince to the throne of Spain should not take place with his consent; secondly, the alleged notifications to the cabinets of the refusal by the king to receive the ambassador of France, and to continue negotiations with him. We summarily answer to those allegations that his Majesty the King, having full respect for the independence and the autonomy of the Spanish nation, and for the freedom of the resolutions of the prince of the Hohenzollern house, never thought of putting Prince Leopold on that throne.

The demands to which his Majesty has been subjected to obtain assurances for the future were both unjustifiable and arrogant. To have a suspicion that he entertained an afterthought of an intention hostile to France was but a gratuitous invention. The alleged notification to the cabinets never took place, and the king never refused to treat with the French ambassador. On the contrary, the French ambassador never expressed the wish to enter into official negotiations with the king's government. It was personally, and in private conversation with the king at Ems, that he spoke about the questions referred to at home and abroad. The German nation has recognized that the efforts of the French government had but one aim—a humiliation, which the nation cannot bear. It has recognized that war, which Prussia could never have thought of, was imposed by France. The whole civilized world will admit that the motives put forward by France do not exist; that they are merely pretexts invented for the occasion. The German Confederation and the allied governments of Southern Germany protest against an aggression which never was called for, and they will repulse it with all the means that God has given to them.

You will leave a copy of the present dispatch with the minister of foreign affairs of the government to which you are accredited.

VON BISMARCK

52 Stage Number Three—German Unification: In a Spiked Helmet and Long Boots Last Fashionable in the Seventeenth Century, Junker Bismarck Goes Off to War against France

"The face is one that can never be mistaken."

When William I left for the front, Bismarck, attired in a long-outmoded uniform, was right behind him. Again, as in 1866, he never let the king out of his sight, so that no would-be advisers could sabotage his plans. Within a few days Bismarck was interviewed by William Howard Russell, England's most famous war correspondent, who had earned the nickname of "Bull Run" Russell in the American Civil War.[20]

July 22. . . .

We . . . caught the five o'clock train at Potsdam with difficulty. Dined with Lord Augustus Loftus at six. Telegrams arriving. The outbreak of hostilities seems to be deferred but for a moment. The emperor is reported to be close to the frontier near Saarbrück, at the head of the Imperial Guards; and here am I without a horse or vehicle of any sort, and as yet without that permission to go, without which nothing can be done. The trains are all in the occupation of government, and are filled with troops. On returning to the hotel found an intimation from Count Bismarck that he desired to see me, and would receive me tomorrow. The courier had been all over Berlin, and reported that the price of vehicles was ridiculous, and that horses were not to be had at any price. . . .

July 23. . . .

At two o'clock repaired to Count Bismarck's, a large, plain-fronted house—but for the *porte-cochère* very like the residences

20. William Howard Russell, *My Diary During the Last Great War* (London, 1874), pp. 23–26.

in which the Irish nobility delighted to dwell when they honored Dublin by their presence. There was no outward state, no sentries at the door, no bustle in the passages; but a grave gentleman in black led me upstairs, along a passage, put me in a small room, and, returning in a minute, said, "His Excellency will see you," and in another moment I was face to face with the great man. He was seated at a table covered with papers when I entered, and there was an odor of tobacco in the room which showed that the great count was fond of good cigars. He rose, and advanced to meet me with outstretched hand and a most charming frankness of manner. He was dressed in a military frock coat, the lapels turned back, showing his military stock, and certainly bore more resemblance in his outward aspect to a soldier than to a statesman. The face is one that can never be mistaken. The coarsest caricatures are like, just as the finest photographs or most delicate engravings fail to convey an idea of the infinite subtlety of expression, the play of the mouth, and—need it be said—the varying expression of the eye. First, business. He said, "You shall go. I have no power to give you an order; that is the war minister's business. We put up a general defense against newspaper correspondents going with our army. But you shall be an exception, and in a short time you will receive your *Legitimation.*" Then, for more than an hour Count Bismarck found time to expound the situation, to give his views of France, Frenchmen, French statesmen and the emperor; to retrace the story of French interference in German politics, and his own policy in his interviews with the emperor, speaking of matters of the highest importance with a frankness and unreserve characteristic of the man, but embarrassing to one in my position. His English is excellent. Now and then there is a word which is strange in use, but logically correct. The time is too near for me now to permit myself to repeat what Count Bismarck said, although he took occasion to remark long afterwards that he did not intend anything he said to me to be kept as secret. Alluding to Luxembourg he made one remark which puzzled me. "At that time," said he, "if the French had not been so foolish, they might have had Luxemburg, for I am sure Germany would not have asked me to fight for it. As your Shakespeare says of Kent, '*Gens mal sana in patria sana,*' or some such words, quotation and allusion being to me equally abstruse."

How Bismarck worked at the front in the early days of the war was described by Moritz Busch, his press aide.[21]

On the 31st July, 1870, at half-past five in the afternoon, the chancellor, who had some days before partaken of the sacrament in his own room, drove from his residence in the Wilhelmstrasse to the station, accompanied by his wife and daughter, in order to start with King William for the seat of war, in the first instance for Mainz. Several councillors of the Foreign Office, a secretary of the dispatch department of the Central Bureau, two experts in secret ciphering, and three or four messengers of the chancellor's department were appointed to go with him. The rest of us followed him only with our good wishes, as, helmet on head, he walked down the stairs between the two sphinxes, through the great hall, and stepped into the carriage. I had resigned myself to taking part in the war only on maps and in newspapers. But a much better fate was in store for me. . . .

The chancellor wore uniform during the whole of the war, generally the undress of the yellow regiment of heavy *Landwehr* cavalry, with its white cap and great top-boots. When riding, after a battle, or in watching its course, he wore a black leather case, fastened by a strap around the chest and back, which held a field glass, and sometimes a revolver and a sword. During the first months he generally wore as a decoration the cross of the order of the Red Eagle; afterwards he also wore the Iron Cross. I never saw him but once, in Versailles, in a dressing gown, and then he was not well—his health was excellent through the whole campaign. During the journey he generally drove with Councillor Abeken, since dead, and once, for several days in succession, with me also. As to quarters, he was most easily satisfied, and even where better were to be had, he put up with the most modest accommodation. At Versailles, when colonels and majors had splendidly furnished suites of apartments, the chancellor, all the five months we were there, was content with two little rooms, of which one was study as well as bedchamber, and the other, on the ground floor, though neither spacious nor elegant, served as a reception room. Once, in the schoolhouse at Clermont, in Argonne, where we stayed some days, he had not even a bed, so that we had to make him up one on the floor.

21. Moritz Busch, *Bismarck in the Franco-German War, 1870–1871* (New York, n.d.), pp. 1, 8–12.

During the journey we generally drove close behind the king's carriage. We started about ten in the morning, and usually accomplished nearly forty English miles a day. On arriving at our quarters for the night we at once established a bureau, in which work was seldom wanting, especially when the field telegraph reached us; by its means the chancellor again became—what, indeed, he always was at this time, with brief interruptions—the center of the civilized world of Europe. Even where we only halted for one night, restlessly active himself, he kept all about him in constant employment till quite late. Orderlies came and went, couriers arrived with letters and telegrams, and were immediately sent off again. According to the directions of the chief, the councillors prepared notes and orders; the clerks copied and registered, ciphered and deciphered. Material streamed in from all points of the compass in the shape of reports, questions, articles in the newspapers, and such like, most of which required immediate attention.

Among the councillors the one who was fastest at work before the arrival of Bucher, was, undoubtedly, Abeken. He was in fact a very power in himself. From long years of service he was thoroughly acquainted with all the ins and outs of business, a lover of routine, furnished with a fine store of phrases, which dropped from his pen without much necessity for thought. Master of several languages, so far, at any rate, as was needed for the work required of him, he seemed made to put the thoughts of his chief into proper dress. He did it with the rapidity of a steam engine. The substance was supplied by the genius and knowledge of the minister, who occasionally improved the style in which Abeken had presented his ideas.

The almost superhuman capacity of the chancellor for work, sometimes creating, and sometimes appropriating and sifting the labors of others, his power of solving the most difficult problems, of at once seeing the right thing, and of ordering only what could be practically done, was, perhaps, never so wonderfully displayed as at this time; and this inexhaustible power of work was the more remarkable as his strength was kept up with so little sleep. The minister lived in the field much as he did at home. Unless an expected battle summoned him before daybreak to the army at the side of the king, he generally rose late, as a rule about ten o'clock. But he passed the night sleepless, and fell over only when the morning light shone through his window. Often, hardly out of bed, and not yet dressed, he began to think and work, to read and make notes on dispatches, to study the newspapers, to give instructions to the councillors and other fellow workers, to put questions or state problems of the most various kinds, even to write or dictate. Later in the day there were visits to receive, or audiences to give, or a statement to be made to the king. Then came the study of dispatches and maps, the correction of papers he had ordered to be prepared, the jotting down of ideas with the well-known big pencil, the composition of letters, the news to be telegraphed or sent to the papers for publication, and in the midst of all this the reception of unavoidable visitors, who must sometimes have been far from welcome. It was not till two or often three o'clock that the chancellor, in places where a halt of any length was made, allowed himself a little breathing-time; then he generally took a ride in the neighborhood. Afterwards he went to work again till dinner at five or six o'clock, and in an hour and a half at the latest he was back once more in his room at his writing table, midnight frequently finding him reading or putting his thoughts on paper.

The count differed from other men in the matter of sleep, and he arranged his meal times in a peculiar manner. Early in the morning he took a cup of tea, and perhaps one or two eggs; after that, generally nothing till dinner in the evening. He very seldom took a second breakfast, and then only tea, which was served between nine and ten o'clock. Thus, with very few exceptions, he ate only once during the four-and-twenty hours, but then, like Frederick the Great, he ate plentifully and with appetite. Diplomatists proverbially keep a good table, and, I am told, come next to prelates. It is part of their daily business to entertain distinguished guests, who, for some reason or other, have to be put into a good humor by the contents of a well-stocked cellar and the efforts of a skillful cook. Count von Bismarck therefore kept a good table, which, when circumstances permitted, rose to the rank of a very good table. This was the case, for instance, at Rheims, Meaux, Ferrières, and Versailles, where the genius of the artist who wore the livery of the household prepared breakfasts and dinners for us, to which persons accustomed to simple fare did justice, feeling almost as if they were sitting in Abraham's bosom, especially when, beside the other good gifts of God, champagne was not wanting in the list of drinkables. For such feasts the traveling kitchen contained pewter plates, tumblers of some silver-like metal, gilt inside, and cups of the same kind. During the last five months of the campaign presents from home added grace to our hospitable board: for home, as it was right it should, thought lovingly of its chancellor, and liberally sent him dainty gifts both solid and fluid, corned geese, game, fish, pheasants, cakes, capital beer, and fine wine, with many other excellent things.

To conclude this chapter I remark that, beside the chancellor, only the councillors at first wore uniform, von Keudell that of the

Blue Cuirassiers, Count Bismarck-Bohlen that of a regiment of dragoon guards, Counts Hatzfeldt and Abeken the undress uniform of officers in the Foreign Office. It was afterwards suggested that all persons belonging to the minister's permanent staff, not of course the two first-named gentlemen, who were also military officers, should wear this dress. The chief consented, and so Versailles saw the chancery messengers in a costume which consisted of a dark blue coat, with two rows of buttons, with black velvet collar and cuffs, a cap of the same color, and for the councillors, secretaries and cipherers, a sword with a gold *porte-épée*. In this costume old Privy-Councillor Abeken, who made his horse prance about bravely, had quite a military air, and I think he knew this and liked it. He was well pleased to look like an officer, just as he once traveled through the Holy Land in Oriental costume, without understanding either Turkish or Arabic.

53 Trapped and Defeated at Sedan, Emperor Napoleon III Asks to Speak to Bismarck, September 2, 1870

"Yesterday and the day before cost France 100,000 men and an emperor."

Defeated at Sedan, Napoleon III asked to speak to Bismarck. It was obvious that this meant the beginning of negotiations for capitulation. Bismarck immediately sent to King William a full report, which is reproduced in the first selection below. In a lighter vein Bismarck sent a letter to his wife in which he told how, unwashed and without breakfast, he rushed off to meet the French emperor. The letter destined for his wife never reached her. Together with the entire post it was captured by franctireurs *and later published by a French newspaper.*

Report to King William, September 2, 1870[22]

DONCHERY, *September* 2, 1870

After I came here yesterday evening, by your Royal Majesty's command, to take part in the negotiations on the capitulation, these were interrupted until one o'clock in the night, by time for consideration, which General Wimpffen solicited, being granted, after General von Moltke had definitely stated that no other terms

22. *The Correspondence of William I and Bismarck,* trans. Ford, II, 124–128.

will be granted than the laying down of arms, and that the bombardment would recommence at nine o'clock in the morning if the capitulation were not concluded by that time. At about six o'clock this morning General Reille was announced, who informed me that the emperor wished to see me, and was already on his way here from Sedan.

The general returned at once to report to his Majesty that I was following, and shortly afterwards I met the emperor near Fresnois, about half way between this place and Sedan. His Majesty was driving in an open carriage with three officers of high rank, and was escorted by three others on horseback. Of these officers I knew personally Generals Castelnau, Reille, Moskowa, who seemed to be wounded in the foot, and Vaubert. As soon as I reached the carriage I dismounted, walked to the emperor's side at the carriage door, and asked for his Majesty's orders. The emperor at first expressed the wish to see your Imperial Majesty, evidently in the belief that your Majesty was also at Donchery. When I replied that at present your Majesty's headquarters were at Vendresse, thirteen miles away, the emperor enquired whether your Majesty had decided where he should go, and what my opinion on the subject was. I replied that, as it was quite dark when I arrived here, I knew nothing of the district, and offered to place at his disposal at once the house in which I was staying at Donchery.

The emperor accepted this offer, and drove off at a walking pace in the direction of Donchery; about a hundred yards from the Maas bridge, which leads into the town, he stopped in front of a lonely, workman's cottage, and asked me if he could not stay there. I had the house examined by Councillor of Legation Count Bismarck-Bohlen, who in the meantime had followed me; when it was reported that the interior arrangements were very poor and inadequate, but that there were no wounded men in the house, the emperor alighted, and invited me to accompany him inside. Here, in a very small room containing a table and two chairs, I had about an hour's conversation with the emperor. His Majesty emphasized especially the wish to obtain more favorable conditions of capitulation for the army. I declined from the outset to treat this question with his Majesty, as this was a purely military question, to be settled between General von Moltke and General von Wimpffen. On the other hand, I asked if his Majesty were inclined to peace negotiations. The emperor replied that, as a prisoner, he was not now in a position to do so, and to my further inquiry by whom, in his opinion, the executive power was at present represented in France, his Majesty referred me to the government in Paris. When this point, which was indistinct in the emperor's letter to your Majesty yesterday, was cleared up, I recognized, and did not conceal the fact from the emperor, that the situation today, as yesterday, was still a purely military one, and emphasized the necessity arising from it for us to obtain by the capitulation of Sedan above all things a material pledge for the security of the military results we had attained. I had already weighed from all sides with General von Moltke yesterday evening, the question whether it would be possible, without detriment to the German interests, to offer to the military feelings of honor of an army which had fought well more favorable terms than those already laid down. After due and careful consideration we both came to the conclusion that this could not be done. When, therefore, General von Moltke, who in the meantime had arrived from the town, went to your Majesty to submit the emperor's wishes, he did not do so, as your Majesty is well aware, with the intention of advocating them.

The emperor then went out into the open air, and invited me to sit beside him just outside the door of the cottage. His Majesty asked whether it would not be practicable to allow the French army to cross into Belgium, to be disarmed and detained there. I had discussed also this eventuality with General v. Moltke on the previous evening, and adduced the motive already given for not entering into the question of this course of procedure. With respect to the political situation, I myself took no initiative, and the emperor went no further than to deplore the ill-fortune of the war, stating that he himself had not wished for war, but was driven into it by the pressure of public opinion in France. I did not regard it as my office to point out at that moment that what the emperor characterized as public opinion was only the artificial product of certain ambitious coteries of the French press, with a very narrow political horizon. I merely replied that nobody in Germany wished for the war, especially not your Majesty, and that no German government would have considered the Spanish question of so much interest as to be worth a war. I continued that your Majesty's attitude towards the Spanish succession question was finally determined by the misgiving whether it was right, for personal and dynastic considerations, to mar the endeavor of the Spanish nation to reestablish, by this selection of a king, their internal organization on a permanent basis; that your Majesty, in view of the good relations existing for so many years between the princes of the Hohenzollern house and the emperor, had never entertained any doubt but that the hereditary prince would succeed in arriving at a satisfactory understanding with his Majesty the Emperor respecting the acceptance of the Spanish election, that, however, your

Majesty had regarded this, not as a German or a Prussian, but as a Spanish affair.

In the meantime, between nine and ten o'clock, inquiries in the town, and especially *reconnaissances* on the part of the officers of the general staff had revealed the fact that the castle of Bellevue, near Fresnois, was suited for the accommodation of the emperor, and was not yet occupied by the wounded. I reported this to his Majesty by designating Fresnois as the place I should propose to your Majesty for the meeting, and therefore referred it to the emperor whether his Majesty would proceed there at once, as a longer stay in the little workman's cottage would be uncomfortable, and the emperor would perhaps need some rest. His Majesty readily assented, and I accompanied the emperor, who was preceded by an escort of honor from your Majesty's Own Cuirassier Regiment, to the castle of Bellevue, where in the meantime the rest of the emperor's suite and his carriages, whose coming had, it appears, been considered doubtful, had arrived from Sedan. General Wimpffen had also arrived, and with him, in anticipation of the return of General von Moltke, the discussion of the capitulation negotiations, which were broken off yesterday, was resumed by General v. Podbielski in the presence of Lieut. Col. von Verdy and the chief of General v. Wimpffen's staff, these two officers acting as secretaries. I took part only in the commencement of the same by setting forth the political and judicial situation in accordance with the information furnished me by the emperor himself, as it was thereupon reported to me by Major Count von Nostitz, by direction of General von Moltke, that your Majesty wished to see the emperor only after the capitulation of the army had been concluded—on the receipt of which announcement the hope cherished by the opposite party of securing other terms than those decided on was given up. I then rode off in the direction of Chehery with the intention of reporting the situation to your Majesty, met General v. Moltke on the way, bringing the text of the capitulation approved by your Majesty, and this, when we arrived with it at Fresnois, was accepted and signed without opposition.

The demeanor of General v. Wimpffen, as also that of the other French generals, during the previous night was very dignified, and this brave officer could not forbear expressing to me how deeply he was pained that he should have been called upon, forty-eight hours after his arrival from Africa, and half a day after he had assumed command, to set his name to a capitulation so fatal to the French arms, that, however, lack of provisions and ammunition, and the absolute impossibility of any further defense imposed upon him, as a general, the duty of suppressing his personal feelings, as further bloodshed could in no way alter the situation. The permission for the officers to be released on parole was received with great thankfulness, as an expression of your Majesty's intention not to hurt the feelings of an army, which had fought bravely, beyond the point demanded by the necessity of our political interests. General v. Wimpffen also subsequently gave expression to this feeling in a letter in which he thanks General v. Moltke for the consideration he showed in conducting the negotiations.

v. BISMARCK

Bismarck's Lost Letter to His Wife, September 3, 1870 [23]

VENDRESSE, *September* 3

MY DEAR HEART,—

I left my present quarters before early dawn the day before yesterday, came back today, and have in the meantime witnessed the great battle of Sedan, in which we made about 30,000 prisoners, and threw the remainder of the French army, which we have been pursuing since Bar-le-Duc, into the fortress, where they had to surrender themselves, along with the emperor, prisoners of war. Yesterday morning at five o'clock, after I had been negotiating until one o'clock A.M. with Moltke and the French generals about the capitulation to be concluded, I was awakened by General Reille, with whom I am acquainted, to tell me that Napoleon wished to speak with me. Unwashed and unbreakfasted, I rode towards Sedan, found the emperor in an open carriage, with three aides-de-camp and three in attendance on horseback, halted on the road before Sedan. I dismounted, saluted him just as politely as at the Tuileries, and asked for his commands. He wished to see the king; I told him, as the truth was, that his Majesty had his quarters fifteen miles away, at the spot where I am now writing. In answer to Napoleon's question where he should go to, I offered him, as I was not acquainted with the country, my own quarters at Donchery, a small place in the neighborhood, close by Sedan. He accepted, and drove, accompanied by his six Frenchmen, by me and by Carl (who, in the meantime had ridden after me) through the lonely morning towards our lines. Before coming to the spot, he began to hesitate on account of the possible crowd, and he asked me if he could alight in a lonely cottage by the wayside; I had it inspected by Carl, who brought word it was mean and dirty. *"N'importe,"* said N., and I ascended with him a rickety, narrow staircase. In an apartment of ten feet square, with a deal table and two rush-

23. *Prince Bismarck's Letters . . .* , trans. Maxse, pp. 256–259.

bottomed chairs, we sat for an hour, the others were below. A powerful contrast with our last meeting in the Tuileries in 1867. Our conversation was a difficult thing, if I wanted to avoid touching on topics which could not but affect painfully the man whom God's mighty hand had cast down. I had sent Carl to fetch officers from the town and to beg Moltke to come. We then sent one of the former to reconnoitre, and discovered two and one-half miles off, in Fresnois, a small château situated in a park. Thither I accompanied him with an escort of the cuirassier regiments of lifeguards, which had meantime been brought up, and there we concluded with the French general-in-chief, Wimpffen, the capitulation, by virtue of which 40 to 60,000 Frenchmen, I do not know it accurately at present, with all they possess, became our prisoners. Yesterday and the day before cost France 100,000 men and an emperor. This morning the latter, with all his suite, horses and carriages, started for Wilhelmshöhe, near Cassel.

It is an event of great weight in the world's history, a victory for which we will humbly thank the Almighty, and which decides the war, even if we have to carry it on against France shorn of her emperor.

I must conclude. With heartfelt joy I learned from yours and Maria's letters that Herbert has arrived among you. Bill I spoke to yesterday, as already telegraphed, and embraced him from horseback in his Majesty's presence, while he stood motionless in the ranks. He is very healthy and happy. I saw Hans and Fritz Carl, both Bülows in the second dragoon guards, well and cheerful.

Good-bye, my heart; love to the children.

Your

v. B.

54

Seeking to Make the Best of a Bad Situation, the Frenchman Thiers Meets Bismarck and Tries to Negotiate a Peace [24]

"Have you any news from Paris?"

Louis Adolphe Thiers, historian and statesman, was elected president of the French assembly after the debacle at Sedan. A short time later he became president of the executive government. On

24. *Conversations with Bismarck,* collected by Heinrich von Poschinger, ed. by Sidney Whitman (New York and London, 1900), pp. 37–43.

October 30, and again on November 4 and 6, 1870, he met Bismarck at Versailles and sought to negotiate a peace with him. What happened was explained by Thiers.

M. Thiers arrived at Versailles on the 30th of October, 1870, after a very fatiguing journey. Hotly contested actions were being fought around Orleans, railway communication had been interrupted, and, as no post horses could be provided, artillery horses were taken from the guns and harnessed to his carriage, and thus he arrived at Versailles, where he found Bismarck awaiting him.

The French statesman's first remark was, "I can only tell you that I have nothing to report."

Bismarck replied, "I will give you two officers to precede you, and if you should meet with an accident—every letter costs me a life; you will be safe in the hands of the Germans—these gentlemen will remain at your disposal. I think it will take you many days before you convince the leading men; but the officers commissioned to accompany you will be there, ready to escort you back when you give them the signal to fetch you."

Thiers and his companions arrived at the outpost line, but the firing was so protracted that it was not easy for the party to make themselves understood. Two small boats were found on the bank of the Seine, and Thiers crossed over the river, after saying to the officers, "Expect me daily at four o'clock, at which time I shall endeavor to get out of Paris, if I have full powers to return to the German headquarters."

At 2 P.M. on the following day Thiers returned to the appointed spot, and, having given the signal, saw the two German officers appear. The same boat served for his return to the German bank of the river, and in a short while he reached Versailles. Bismarck, on hearing of his arrival, was much astonished at his speedy and safe return, and sent an officer to congratulate him.

At the interview, which commenced at 11 A.M. on the 1st of November, Thiers demanded a month's supplies of food. Count Bismarck replied, "You make a somewhat exaggerated demand, for Paris is already on half rations, and now you ask for whole rations for a month. Nevertheless, I am ready to concede this; the king would consent, but the soldiers consider an armistice disadvantageous to us. You ask for more than you hope to get, and doubtless this is not your only request."

Thiers replied, "No; it is not my last word regarding the multitude."

"Well, then," said the Prussian minister, "put it on paper, so that we may have something definite to discuss."

Thiers drew up a memorandum, and handed it to Bismarck, who found fault only with the quantities of supplies demanded; and by this he allowed it to be noticed that an understanding on this point would be arrived at.

The negotiations were continued the following day. It can readily be understood that Thiers strove to give Bismarck the most favorable impression of his tour around the courts of London, Vienna, Petersburg, and Turin, for he particularly wished Bismarck to believe that he had received numerous proofs of sympathy from "his friend" Prince Gortschakoff, and that if Germany did not cut short her victorious progress through France, Russia might at length grow angry. Thereupon Bismarck got up and rang the bell. "Bring me the portfolio with the Russian papers." A portfolio was brought in, which he handed to M. Thiers, saying, "Read these; there you will find thirty letters, which have been sent me from St. Petersburg." M. Thiers read them, and abandoned all further representations.

At the fifth meeting, which took place on the 3rd of November, M. Thiers found Bismarck disquieted, depressed, and much excited.

"Have you any news from Paris?" asked the latter.

"None."

"Well, a revolution has taken place, and has changed everything."

Thiers was not exactly surprised at this, since he was acquainted with the condition of the capital, which he had quitted only four days ago, though he refused to believe the news.

"Such an attempt has probably been made," he replied, "but it will have been suppressed: the National Guard will not allow anarchy to triumph."

"I know nothing about it," replied Bismarck, and then read aloud a number of outpost reports, each one more confusing than the other. It struck Thiers that Bismarck himself was seriously put out by the news from Paris, for he evidently wished for peace, and did not conceal his fear that a revolution in Paris would lessen the chances of obtaining it.

Bismarck then asked Thiers whether he could ascertain exactly what had happened in Paris. M. Thiers had two capable and courageous secretaries, MM. Remusat and Cochery, one of whom he offered to send to Paris for news. Bismarck sent officers to accompany M. Cochery (the first of the two secretaries whom M. Thiers met), and their return was anxiously awaited, so that the new situation might be fully understood.

Thiers saw Bismarck several times that day, for a new fact had cropped up which greatly aggravated the situation: this was the proclamation published at Tours concerning the surrender of Metz. The violence with which the actual or supposed authors of the capitulation were condemned had excited everybody in Versailles in the highest degree.

"The king wished for peace," said Bismarck to Thiers, "and he was inclined to grant an armistice in the hope that the passions of the war party would calm down. He has resisted the war party in Prussia—for I will not conceal the fact that our soldiers are against the armistice, as they think that an armistice will only prolong your resistance, and they say that we must immediately conclude a peace or continue the attack on Paris. And now this new revolution in Paris and the language used at Tours have discouraged all those who hoped that these passions were allayed; this fresh outburst on your part has reawakened our fears. Yesterday I was full of confidence, today I have utterly lost it."

Bismarck had only spoken the truth. Thiers was acquainted with several diplomatists and princes present in Versailles, and all the news which he was able to collect showed him that many changes had taken place within the last twenty-four hours.

Cochery returned during the night, having met with great difficulties on the way. Thiers learned from him that a revolution had been attempted on the 31st—the day of his departure from Paris—and that, though it had been suppressed, the half-conquered anarchists, unwittingly supported by honorable people whose misguided patriotism had been overexcited by the events of Metz, had nevertheless obtained the complete mastery of Paris.

Once more M. Thiers had an interview with Bismarck, and communicated to him all that he had learned. Bismarck was as well posted as Thiers, but the latter was convinced that if he could but achieve the acceptance of that which Bismarck called the "First volume of peace," *i.e.* the armistice, he could not, with the best will in the world, obtain the acceptance of the second.

"If I thought," said Bismarck, "that the publisher would bring out the second volume, I would willingly assist you in publishing the first." He then informed him of the conditions of the armistice: either no food supplies to be brought in, or the surrender of a fort; but Thiers was not empowered to agree to any such conditions, and he was therefore obliged to break off the negotiations.

Thiers and Bismarck looked at one another, and asked almost simultaneously whether an immediate peace was not possible. The night was spent in arguments, and Thiers realized that a peace was then possible—painful without doubt, but not as painful as the one which would be forced upon them later on. He decided to proceed to Paris immediately to try and obtain the acceptance of such a peace, but Bismarck advised him not to do so, since he would certainly not escape from the madmen who ruled Paris. Thiers considered these dangers, although very real, to be exaggerated, and told Bismarck that he could achieve nothing unless he went to Paris himself; so he decided to make a rendezvous with the members of the government at a point which they might select, in order to learn their opinions on a question which constituted the salvation of their country.

He dispatched M. Cochery, who had already succeeded in reaching Paris, and arranged for a meeting at the Bridge of Sèvres. On the following day, Thiers went to that spot, and was taken to an abandoned house, ruined by shells, in the Bois de Boulogne. Here he encountered only Jules Favre and General Ducrot. The former explained that at the moment it was impossible to bring the populace of Paris to a reasonable decision, and though he entirely agreed with Thiers' proposal, which, under the existing unhappy circumstances, he considered to be wise and acceptable, apparently the Paris Commune was already in command of the situation, although the *de facto* government of the capital was not yet in their hands.

Thiers sorrowfully took leave of Jules Favre, and returned to Versailles, where he awaited a final dispatch from the government of the national defense with regard to the discontinuance of these negotiations, which had become quite useless. He left the chancellor greatly perturbed about the continuation of the struggle.

55

January 18, 1871: The New German Empire Is Proclaimed in the Hall of Mirrors at Versailles, and Bismarck, on His Day of Glory, Is Snubbed by His Emperor[25]

"This imperial childbirth was an extremely difficult business. . . ."

With France defeated, Bismarck now turned to the task of fashioning the new Reich or empire. From the beginning Bismarck knew that its head had to be called kaiser. For him the imperial title was a political necessity. As a historical image it would encourage "unity and centralization among the people." The German princes

25. Account contributed by the editor.

would resent being subjected to a "King of Prussia," but they would accept in good grace the title of "German Kaiser." Bismarck was most concerned that national institutions not appear as extensions of the Prussian state.

But William was adamant. He would not put aside the ancient Prussian title. He would be called the "Grand King of Prussia" or perhaps "King of Greater Prussia," but not "German Kaiser." The argument raged for weeks. On January 17, 1871, the day before the official proclamation of the empire, a three-hour conference was held in which William stubbornly held to his position. The old man grew increasingly angry. He began to sob and lamented that he would have to bid farewell to dear old Prussia. At length he broke off the discussion, declared that he would not hear another word about it, and threatened to abdicate.

The next day the ceremony took place as scheduled in the glistening Hall of Mirrors at Versailles, where a succession of French kings had once held court. There were sixty standard bearers, six hundred officers, and others of rank and distinction. Present were the German ruling princes with the exception of the kings of Saxony, Bavaria, and Württemberg. No one knew what William would do and what symbol he would use as emperor. There was some confusion as to where the colors and standards should be placed.

Finally, William mounted the platform and ordered that there be placed behind him the colors of the first regiment of the Guards (his regiment when he entered the army), the flag of his own grenadier regiment, and the flag of the *Landwehr* battalion he had commanded for many years. His face was white with fatigue, his expression moody, almost angry. He asked his fellow princes to stand on the same level as himself.

The pastor had been warned to deliver a brief invocation, but he straightway launched into a polemic against Louis XIV. The king made a short address of welcome.

Bismarck then stepped forward. He wore a dark-blue uniform and his great cuirassier's boots. (In the famous Anton von Werner painting Bismarck is erroneously depicted as wearing a white gala uniform.) In his hands he held the proclamation. One eyewitness present stated that when Bismarck uttered the first words, "his breast was heaving with excitement, his face was pale, and his ears were so bloodless that they were almost transparent." Another observed that the chancellor was business-like and read out the statement in a low voice and tone as if he were anxious to get the whole affair finished as soon as possible.

It was a highly dramatic scene as Bismarck began to read: "We, William by the grace of God, King of Prussia, and after the German princes and free cities have unanimously appealed to us to renew the imperial dignity, which has been in abeyance for more than sixty years, to reestablish the empire and to take charge of it, . . . hereby inform you that we regard it as our duty to the whole fatherland to respond to this summons of the allied German princes and free cities and to assume the German imperial title."

As the prince of highest rank present, the Grand Duke Frederick of Baden, William's son-in-law, was assigned the honor of hailing William with the new title. No one knew what title he would use. As the company was assembling, he hastily discussed the matter with both William and Bismarck. Neither one had changed his mind. It was a perplexing situation, but Frederick found his own solution. As soon as Bismarck finished his proclamation, Frederick cried out: "Long live his Imperial and Royal Majesty, Kaiser William!" There were cheers from the onlookers.

Then William left the platform. Directly before him stood the chancellor, the proclamation still in his hands. Everyone expected William to exchange handclasps with the man who had brought him from the verge of abdication to this glorious position. Instead, the old man ignored Bismarck, stalked past him without a glance, and gave his hand to the generals only. No one could possibly overlook the affront.

Bismarck was infuriated by this treatment. It was he who had consummated this blending of Hohenzollern authoritarianism, Prussian militarism, and German nationalism. He was the one who had brought the imperial title to William. And here he was being treated as if he were a rejected lackey.

That night he revealed his anger by raging against the clergyman whose sermon at the ceremony had been suffused with "Prussian self-idolization." Several days later he wrote to his wife, Johanna: "Forgive me for not having written to you for so long, but this imperial childbirth was an extremely difficult business. Kings at such times have strange cravings, just like women before they give to the world that which they cannot retain within them. I, who had to play the *accoucheur,* felt often enough like a bomb which was about to burst and lay the whole structure in ruins."

William soon became reconciled to the situation. Once again, as on many previous occasions, he began to see that his great chancellor was right. He became reconciled to the title Bismarck had selected for him.

6 A Frenchman Recommends the Assassination of Bismarck

"The blood which he spills fructifies our country."

The people of Paris, who had suffered starvation and misery under the Prussian siege, cursed the man they regarded as responsible for their plight. It was not surprising that a French journalist, whose style "savors of Victor Hugo's school," should call for Bismarck's assassination. Moritz Busch recorded the story.[26]

I return to what the journal has to tell of events in Versailles on February 4, 1871:

This morning the chief had more time and interest than usual recently for the papers. I was sent for six times before noon. At one of them he gave me a lying French *brochure:* "War as made by the Prussians," and remarked thereupon, "I should like you, please, to write to Berlin. They must draw up something similar on our side, with reference to the cruelties, barbarities, and breaches of the Convention (of Geneva) committed by the French. But not too long, or no one will read it, and it must appear quickly." The next time the question was of several newspaper cuttings "for my collection." Then again, he showed me a small paper, published by a certain Armand le Chevalier, 6 Rue Richelieu, with a woodcut portrait of the chancellor on the frontispiece, and said, "Look here, here is a recommendation with reference to Blind's attempt to assassinate me, and my portrait is given too—like the photographs of the *francstireurs.* You know that in the forests of the Ardennes, photographs of such of our skirmishers as were to be shot were found in the pockets of the *francstireurs.* Luckily no one can say that my likeness is specially well hit off in this—nor for the matter of that my biography either. This passage" (he read it aloud and then handed me the paper) "should be sent to the papers with a moral to it, and then appear as a pamphlet."

Finally he gave me some more French newspapers, saying, "Just look whether there is anything there for me or the king. I shall be off, or the gentlemen from Paris will catch me again."

In M. Chevalier's paper it is in fact stated in rather plain terms by a certain "Ferragus," that France would welcome with ap-

26. Busch, *Bismarck in the Franco-Prussian War . . . ,* II, 310–313.

proval the chief's assassination, although he is, properly speaking, a benefactor to the French. The author, whose style savors of Victor Hugo's school, says:

"Bismarck has probably done better service to France than to Germany. He has worked for a false unity in his own country, but very effectually for a regeneration of ours. He has freed us from the empire. He has restored to us our energy, our hatred of the foreigner, our love for our country, our contempt for life, our readiness for self-sacrifice, in short, all the virtues which Bonaparte had killed in us.

"Honor therefore to this grim foe who saves us, when seeking to destroy us. Meaning to kill us he summons us to immortality, at the same time adding impetus to our earthly life. The blood which he spills fructifies our country; the twigs which he lops off allow the tree to absorb more sap. You will see how much greater we shall be when we escape from these fearful but wholesome toils. We have to expiate twenty years of forgetfulness of duty, of luxury, and of servility. The visitation is severe, but the result will be glorious. I call to witness the manly attitude of Paris, and the hunger after justice and honor with which our bosoms swell. Today when one passes the door of the opera house, one is smitten with shame. Those nudities, which were so brightly illumined by the sun of the empire, shock the modesty of the republic; we turn away from this typical memorial of another age, another grade of civilization. It is Bismarck who has imbued us with this puritan pride. Let us not thank him for it, but pay back with manly hatred this involuntary benefit from a man who, mightier to destroy than to construct, is more easily cursed than hailed with applause. Prussia has made him its great man, but on the 8th of May, 1866, the whole country mourned the fate of a young fanatic, a student, who seeing in Bismarck an enemy of freedom, fired five pistol shots at him.

"Bind [as the author further on calls Blind's stepson] belonged to that class of inspired people, represented by Karl Sand, the murderer of Kotzebue, Stapss, who tried to stab Napoleon at Schönbrunn, and Oscar Becker, the author of the attempt upon the king of Prussia. Bind was not deceived when he gave himself credit for a Roman soul, for he behaved like a Stoic after his capture, and himself opened the artery in his neck, to rob the executioner of his victim.

"If we were to hear today that a more successful attempt had been made upon Bismarck, would France have the generosity not to applaud it? So much is certain that this frightful question of political assassination will always remain one of relative morality, until it is eradicated from the minds of nations together with capital punishment and war. At this time, in October 1870, one would hail as savior a man, who, three months before, would have been branded as a common 'murderer,' "—a fine sign truly of the regeneration, which, according to the opening words of the article, is supposed to have taken place in France, and of the hunger after justice and honor, with which the writer sees his countrymen's bosoms swelling.

The war was finally ended by the Treaty of Frankfort, May 10, 1871. A humiliated France was required to cede Alsace and a part of Lorraine (including the fortresses of Metz and Didenhofen) to Prussia and to pay an indemnity of one billion dollars (five billion francs) within three years. Pending payment, the eastern departments of France were to be occupied. This time there was no generosity in the Prussian terms.

German unification was now completed. The historian Heinrich von Sybel wrote passionately: "Tears run down my cheeks. By what have we deserved the grace of God, that we are allowed to live to see such great and mighty deeds. What for twenty years was the substance of all our wishes and efforts, is now fulfilled in such an immeasurably magnificent way." The North German Confederation was abolished, to be succeeded by the new German empire consisting of Prussia and the North and South German states.

Historians differ on the matter of responsibility for the outbreak of the Franco-Prussian War. Almost all German scholars insist that the war was forced on Bismarck by an envious France, and that he acted merely to defend the honor of the German nation. A. J. P. Taylor, on the other hand, states that Bismarck deliberately provoked war with France over a trumped-up issue. Erich Eyck is even more emphatic: "Responsibility for the war rests in the first instance with Bismarck. He is, of course, not the only person responsible. The unscrupulous French journalists and politicians who frivolously cried: 'À Berlin,' *the Empress Eugénie, who influenced her husband in favor of war, Napoleon himself and Gramont, who threw away a splendid chance because they did not know where to stop—they all have to bear their share of responsibility. But they were all rather driven than driving. Bismarck alone kept the initiative by knowing beforehand how the others would react to his moves. He made them his tools, and they did what he wanted them to do. His superiority towers above them, head and shoulders. Therefore, the primary responsibility rests with him alone."*[27]

27. Erich Eyck, *Bismarck and the German Empire* (London, 1950), pp. 173–174.

From a painting by C. Wagne

BISMARCK IN VERSAILLES, 1871.
Bismarck announces peace terms to the Frenchmen, Faure and Thiers.

PART V

The Master Ruler of the Second German Empire, 1871-1888

57 The Era of Bismarck: A Legend in His Lifetime, the Master of Realpolitik Reveals some Suprising Superstitions

"But God only knows!"

The period of nearly twenty years from the foundation of the German empire in January 1871, to Bismarck's dismissal in March 1890, is often called the Era of Bismarck. During this time he was the fulcrum not only of German but also of European politics. With a powerful army, an efficient bureaucracy, and a loyal bourgeoisie, Bismarck was able to prevent any revolutionary outbreaks. His domestic policy was to consolidate a centralized union under Prussian domination and to promote the prosperity of the new German empire. In order to maintain German military supremacy he required all citizens to be conscripted for training. He proposed new civil and criminal laws, organized an imperial bank, unified the railroad system and introduced a national system of coinage.

At first the only support Bismarck received in the Reichstag came from the National Liberal party. To the left the Progressive party cooperated in matters of unity, but in other matters was less willing to compromise with the government. The Center party, formed in 1870, was designed to give political representation to Catholics. The Prussian conservatives opposed Bismarck on the ground that the events of 1866 and 1871 had diluted Prussian strength. The conservatives split into two groups, one of which, the Reich party, for a time supported Bismarck. In general, however, Bismarck was firmly opposed to any internal rivals and insisted that all opposition to the Prussian conception of the state be crushed.

Bismarck's foreign policy was simple—to consolidate the position he had won for Germany. In the first period of his administration, from 1862 to 1871, he had waged three wars, enhanced Prussia, and unified Germany under the Prussian crown. Now Germany was saturiert. *Bismarck regarded it as his vital task to maintain what Germany had acquired.*

Even men of great intellect can be prone to superstition and its attendant anxieties. Bismarck was no exception. In this man of genius there were mysterious depths. Moritz Busch, who knew him well, related several examples of Bismarck's superstition, unexpected in this man who was a realist in politics.[1]

Even the greatest intelligences are susceptible to something besides religious belief that enlightened people are accustomed to designate as "superstition," and which, although only partially the offspring of Christianity, generally keeps up a certain connection with religion. It is not infrequently encountered in extremely clever men, lacking alike in imagination and religious instinct, in generals, like Napoleon I, politicians, like Gambetta, and even in diplomatists. Symptoms of superstitiousness—and not a few—are apparently manifest in Prince Bismarck.

Somewhere in East Prussia there is an uninhabited castle, which stands empty because its owner is convinced that it is haunted by the ghost of a lady who, during her life committed a crime within its precincts. The specter in question is said to be visible in broad daylight. This story was told to Bismarck one day in the presence of some friends, one of whom began to turn it into ridicule; whereupon the prince remarked, very gravely, that "it was better not to scoff or jest at such matters; there might very well be something true in the tale, for he himself had undergone a similar experience." He refrained, at the time, from saying any more upon the subject; but what he referred to was an occurrence at Schönhausen, recorded by Hesekiel as follows:—

"One night Herr von Bismarck (then not yet minister-president) was lying abed in the very room * in which he had been born; a party of his friends was staying in the castle, among them a Herr von Dewitz, and a shooting expedition had been arranged for the morrow, on account of which orders had been given to a servant to awaken the gentlemen at an early hour. All of a sudden Bismarck started up from his slumbers; he heard in the next room a door open that communicated with the library, and then footsteps. At first he thought it must be the servant, come to call him; but immediately afterwards he heard Herr von Dewitz, three rooms off, exclaim 'Who's there?' He jumped out of bed, the clock struck twelve; nobody was there."

After the battle of Gravelotte, during dinner at Pont à Mousson, we were talking about what would happen after the French should have been completely vanquished; and the chancellor concluded

1. Moritz Busch, *Bismarck: Sketches for a Historical Picture,* trans. by William Beatty-Kingston (New York, 1891), I, 158–163.

* It should be observed that the windows of the bedroom referred to look out upon a neighboring churchyard.

the exponence of his views with the remark "Do not, however, let us talk about the skin of the bear until we have shot him. I confess to being superstitious in this regard." At Rheims, on another occasion, Count Bismarck-Bohlen was counting the places at table before dinner, and muttered to himself: "We are surely not thirteen? No. So much the better; for the minister does not like that at all." Another time we really were thirteen at table, and when I mentioned it to Bucher, who sat next to me, he begged me not to say it aloud, as it would certainly annoy the chief. On the 14th October 1870, General Boyer came to Versailles, on a mission from Bazaine; but Bismarck transacted no serious business with him that day. He asked in the office, "What is the day of the month?" "The fourteenth, your Excellency." "Indeed; so were the days of Hochkirch and Jena; we must not attempt to do anything important on the 14th."

Perhaps it also occurred to him that the 14th in question was also a Friday, which is a day of the week, in the opinion of many people, unpropitious to the transaction of business and in every respect unlucky. In 1852 he wrote to his wife from Halle: "I have been seriously thinking that yesterday—when I started on my journey—must have been a Friday after all; anyhow, it was a *dies nefastus,*" in proof of which he proceeds to recapitulate a whole string of traveling annoyances,—a hotel "full of bugs and infamous coffee, peddlers and tiptop ladies of pleasure from a notorious haunt of vice," and "an obtrusive privy-councillor" in his compartment of the train. In November of the same year he wrote home from Blankenburg. "I had not such good sport in Letzlingen this time as three years ago; it was Friday." During dinner on October 26, 1870, at Versailles, he observed: "Yesterday I was persecuted by a whole series of mishaps, one after another. First of all a person (Odo Russell) who had important business with me asked to see me. I sent a message to him, asking him to wait two minutes, as I was engaged upon a matter of urgent importance. When I asked for him a quarter of an hour later he was gone; and the peace of Europe may possibly depend upon my seeing him or not. Then I went off to the king at midday—earlier than usual—and consequently fell into the hands of ——, who compelled me to listen while he read me a letter, and thus caused me to lose a whole hour, at the expiration of which I sent off several important telegrams, which, through being delayed till then, perhaps have not reached even today the persons to whom they were addressed. In the meantime decisions may have been arrived at and circumstances may have changed, the results of all which may prove very serious and altogether alter the political situation. And all of this comes of Friday!" he added; "Friday negotiations! Friday measures!" In January 1871 he remarked to the governmental-president, von Ernsthausen, "Today is the 13th and Friday into the bargain. That won't do, Sunday will be the 15th,—Wednesday, the 18th, on which the Ordensfest is always held—that will be a good day on which to issue the proclamation (one concerning the emperor and empire) to the German people."

During tea time one evening at Versailles (November 23, 1870) he began to talk about his own death, and indicated the exact age he was predestined to attain, and the year appointed for his decease. "I know it," he wound up, saying, after some of those present had remonstrated against his assertions; "it is a mystic number." Seven years later he repeated this assurance to me at Varzin, adding, however, "But God only knows!"

Finally, it may be mentioned that the chancellor is firmly convinced of the moon's influence upon all growing things, and especially upon hair and plants. "You are looking as young again as usual, privy-councillor," he observed jestingly one day at dinner to Abeken, who had just had his hair cut. "Moreover, you chose exactly the right time to be shorn, for the moon is waxing. And it is just the same with trees as it is with hair. If you want beech roots to strike out and grow again, you must fell the tree during the first quarter of the moon; if they are to be uprooted, in the last. There are plenty of learned people and schoolmasters who will not believe this; but our foresters know it well enough, and the Administration of Woods and Forests as well."

The clearest of thinkers, upon political questions more profound and farseeing than any of his contemporaries, always hitting off the right conclusion, free from prejudice, far above conventionalities; and yet a ghost seer, a chooser of days, a believer in mystic numbers!

Really! But no; with the exception of the Schönhausen episode, it is all pretense or jest. In the autumn of 1883 he expressed himself thus upon the subject. "All that nonsense about my superstitiousness has no more solid foundation than mere jokes or my consideration for other people's feelings. I will make one of thirteen at dinner as often as you please; and I transact the most important and critical business on Fridays, if necessary." *

And the affair at Schönhausen? Was that really superstition? Well, there are things between heaven and earth that are not

* The Berlin Congress, presided over by Prince Bismarck, was both opened and closed on a 13th.

dreamed of in our philosophy.* This sentence may be read in either of its two meanings. I would rather accept it in that intended by Shakespeare. It is open to powerful minds to interpret it otherwise. The public, itself strong-minded, will probably do as they do.

58

Motley Comes to Varzin to Celebrate the Bismarcks' Silver Wedding Anniversary, 1872

"This is the great Bismarck—the greatest living man, and one of the greatest historical characters that ever lived."

Motley's visits gave Bismarck his happiest days. After eight years of absence, Motley wrote to Bismarck and asked if he could come to Varzin to celebrate the twenty-fifth wedding anniversary of the Bismarcks. "You are a thousand times welcome," Bismarck wrote, "and doubly if accompanied by your ladies, who, I am sure, have never seen a Pomeranian on his native soil. . . . The Pomeranian gods will be gracious enough for me to give you a sunny day, and in that case I should order an open carriage, and one for luggage."

There had been changes since the two friends last met. A unified Germany, the dream of centuries, was at last a reality. Motley was sympathetic to the German cause. "These are not dynastic victories," Motley wrote to Oliver Wendell Holmes, "military combinations, cabinet triumphs. They are national, popular, natural achievements, accomplished almost as if by magic by the tremendous concentrated will of one political giant, aided by a perfected military science such as I suppose the modern world never saw before. At least, I fancy that such enormous results were never before reached with so little bloodshed in comparison. Four or five hundred thousand soldiers taken in two or three nets and landed high and dry, to be thrown all alive again into the sea of population when the war is over—this is superior to butchering the same numbers. It is for such considerations as these that I have always felt an intense sympathy with the German movement. Intellect, science, nationality, popular enthusiasm are embodied in it. They must unquestionably lead to liberty and a higher civilization. Yet many

* It may here be remarked (not superfluously, as far as our materialistic physicists are concerned) that the word "philosophy," as Shakespeare understood it and as it was used in the older English language, had a much more comprehensive meaning than the one now attached to it. It included all the natural sciences, and, indeed, specially dealt with them. The above passage from *Hamlet* might, therefore, be also rendered "Things not dreamed of in your physical science."

people are able to see nothing in it but the triumph of military despotism."

The following correspondence describes the visit in detail. The first letter, from Bismarck to Motley, contains the warm invitation. In the other letters Motley tells his wife and daughter about the reception by his good and great friend.[2]

From Prince Bismarck

VARZIN,
July 6th, 1872

MY DEAR MOTLEY,—I was the more agreeably surprised in seeing your handwriting, as I guessed before opening the letter that it would contain the promise of a visit here. You are thousand times welcome, and doubly if accompanied by your ladies, who, I am sure, never have seen a Pomeranian on his native soil. We live here somewhat behind the woods, but Berlin once reached, the journey is not a difficult one. The best train leaves Berlin in the morning between eight and nine o'clock—I believe 8:45, Stettiner Bahnhof, fifteen or twenty minutes to drive from any hotel about the Linden. You go by railway as far as Schlawe, where you arrive at about four o'clock afternoon, and from where a trumpet-sounding postilion brings you to Varzin just in time for the dinner bell, before six o'clock. If you will have the goodness to send me a telegram on your departure from Berlin, or the evening before, I shall make everything ready for you at Schlawe, so that you only have to step from the wagon to the *Wagen*. The Pomeranian gods will be gracious enough for me to give you a sunny day, and in that case I should order an open carriage, and one for luggage. Only let me know by the telegram your will about this and about the number of in- or outside places wanted.

My wife is still at Loden. I expect her to be back on the 9th instant, but *la donna è mobile!* At all events, she will not be detained by female frailty beyond the end of the week. She will be equally glad to see you again; your name is familiar to her lips, and never came forth without a friendly smile. The first day that you can dispose of, at all events, is the best one to come to see us, though we think to remain here until the end of summer. You do not mention that Mrs. Motley will accompany you, and by this silence I take it for granted that she will, as *Mann und Weib sind*

2. *The Correspondence of John Lothrop Motley,* ed. by George William Curtis (London, 1889), II, 339–349.

ein Leib. We will be happy to see her with you, and *en attendant* give my most sincere regards to her and to Mrs. Ives.

Most faithfully your old friend,

v. BISMARCK

To His Wife

VARZIN,
July 25th, 1872

MY DEAREST MARY,—I had better write a line to tell you that we have arrived in safety, although I fear that I shall hardly be able to say much just now, as I wish to go downstairs to the breakfast room. Lily told you all there was to say of Berlin. We had a pleasant half hour with the Bancrofts,[3] who were very cordial, and we promised to go and see them on our return. We left Berlin at a quarter to nine yesterday morning; reached Schlawe station at half-past four.

We had an hour and a half's drive from the station to Varzin. As the postilion sounded his trumpet and we drove up to the door, Bismarck, his wife, M——, and H——, all came out to the carriage and welcomed us in the most affectionate manner. I found him very little changed in appearance since 1864, which surprises me. He is somewhat stouter, and his face more weather-beaten, but as expressive and powerful as ever. Madame de Bismarck is but little altered in the fourteen years that have passed since I saw her. They are both most kind and agreeable to Lily, and she feels already as if she had known them all her life. M—— is a pretty girl, with beautiful dark hair and grey eyes—simple, unaffected, and, like both father and mother, full of fun. The manner of living is most unsophisticated, as you will think when I tell you that we were marched straight from the carriage into the dining room (after a dusty, hot journey by rail and carriage of ten hours), and made to sit down and go on with the dinner, which was about half through, as, owing to a *contretemps,* we did not arrive until an hour after we were expected. After dinner Bismarck and I had a long walk in the woods, he talking all the time in the simplest and funniest and most interesting manner about all sorts of things that had happened in these tremendous years, but talking of them exactly as everyday people talk of everyday matters—without any affectation. The truth is, he is so entirely simple, so full of *laissez-aller,* that one is obliged to be saying to one's self all the time, "This is the great Bismarck—the greatest living man, and one of the greatest histori-

3. George Bancroft, the historian, United States minister to Germany.

cal characters that ever lived." When one lives familiarly with Brobdignags it seems for the moment that everybody was a Brobdignag too, that it is the regular thing to be; one forgets for the moment one's own comparatively diminutive stature. There are a great many men in certain villages that we have known who cast a far more chilling shade over those about them than Bismarck does.

In the evening we sat about most promiscuously—some drinking tea, some beer, some seltzer water; Bismarck smoking a pipe. He smokes very little now, and only light tobacco in a pipe. When I last knew him, he never stopped smoking the strongest cigars. Now he tells me he couldn't to save his life smoke a single cigar. He has a disgust for them. A gentleman named von Thadden and his wife are the only guests, and they go this afternoon—a Pomeranian friend. He made the campaign of Königgrätz, and Bismarck was telling innumerable anecdotes about that great battle, and subsequently gave some most curious and interesting details about the negotiations of Nikolsburg. I wish that you could have heard him. You know his way. He is the least of a *poseur* of any man I ever saw, little or big. Everything comes out so offhand and carelessly; but I wish there could be an invisible, self-registering Boswell always attached to his buttonhole, so that his talk could be perpetuated. There were a good many things said by him about the Nikolsburg Conference confirming what I had always understood.

The military opinion was bent on going to Vienna after Sadowa. Bismarck strongly opposed this idea. He said it was absolutely necessary not to humiliate Austria, to do nothing that would make friendly relations with her in the future impossible. He said many people refused to speak to him. The events have entirely justified Bismarck's course, as all now agree. It would have been easy enough to go to Vienna or to Hungary, but to return would have been full of danger. I asked him if he was good friends with the emperor of Austria now. He said Yes, that the emperor was exceedingly civil to him last year at Salzburg, and crossed the room to speak to him as soon as he appeared at the door. He said he used when younger to think himself a clever fellow enough, but now he was convinced that nobody had any control over events—that nobody was really powerful or great, and it made him laugh when he heard himself complimented as wise, foreseeing, and exercising great influence over the world. A man in the situation in which he had been placed was obliged, while outsiders for example were speculating whether tomorrow it would be rain or sunshine, to decide promptly, it will rain, or it will be fine, and to act accordingly with all the forces at his command. If he guessed right, all the world said, "What sagacity—what prophetic power!" if wrong, all the old women would have beaten me with broomsticks.

If he had learned nothing else, he said he had learned modesty. Certainly a more unaffected mortal never breathed, nor a more genial one. He looks like a Colossus, but his health is somewhat shattered. He can never sleep until four or five in the morning. Of course work follows him here, but as far as I have yet seen it seems to trouble him but little. He looks like a country gentleman entirely at leisure.

The woods and park about the house are fine, but unkempt and rough, unlike an English country place. We have had, since I began to write, long walks and talks in the woods—an agreeable family dinner—and then a long drive through the vast woods of beeches and oaks of which the domain is mostly composed. I don't intend to Boswellize Bismarck any more. It makes me feel as if I were a *New York Herald* interviewing reporter. He talks away right and left about anything and everything—says among other things that nothing could be a greater *bêtise* than for Germany to attack any foreign country—that if Russia were to offer the Baltic provinces as a gift, he would not accept them. As to Holland, it would be mere insanity to pretend to occupy or invade its independence. It had never occurred to him or to anybody. As to Belgium, France would have made any terms at any time with Germany if allowed to take Belgium. I wish I could record the description he gave of his interviews with Jules Favre and afterwards with Thiers and Favre, when the peace was made.

One trait I mustn't forget, however. Favre cried a little, or affected to cry, and was very pathetic and heroic. Bismarck said that he must not harangue him as if he were an Assembly; they were two together on business purposes, and he was perfectly hardened against eloquence of any kind. Favre begged him not to mention that he had been so weak as to weep, and Bismarck was much diverted at finding in the printed account afterwards published by Favre that he made a great parade of the tears he had shed.

I must break off in order to commit this letter to the bag. Of course I don't yet know how long we shall stay here; I suppose a day or two longer. I will send you a telegram about a change of address, so don't be frightened at getting one.

Ever yours,

J. L. M.

To His Wife

VARZIN,
July 27th, 1872

MY DEAREST MARY,—I sent a telegram this morning to ask you to let me have a line at Berlin, where we shall stop a couple of days, in spite of the probable heat, in obedience to your orders with regard to a tailor. On the day we arrived, I ordered a few things, which I daresay will be as hideous as anything else I get, although made by the smartest *Schneider* in Berlin. We shall leave day after tomorrow morning, and sleep that night at the Hôtel du Nord. We have been having a most delightful visit, quite as agreeable as we expected, and that is saying a great deal. It has done me much good to be with Bismarck, so familiarly and pleasantly all this time. We have had long, long talks about the great events in which he has been the principal actor, and he goes on always so entirely *sans gêne,* and with so much frankness and simplicity, that it is a delight to listen. How I wish you could be listening to him too! I find him little changed or aged, but his nervous system is a good deal shattered, and he suffers much from insomnia. She looks very much as she did, but is a good deal of an invalid; and when I tell you that she is by nature as anxious a person as you are, and was always in a state of alarm if the slightest illness occurred to her husband or any of the children, you may imagine what she must have endured in all these campaigns. Tomorrow is their silver (twenty-five years) wedding. His brother and wife and son have just arrived, and another old friend, a certain Pomeranian squire, M. von Blankenburg. I thought that perhaps we might be *de trop,* as they had taken particular pains to let the public know nothing of the occasion, but he wished much that we should stay over the day.

The house is not large—a very moderate sort of *château,* but the woods and walks and drives are very pleasant, and there is room I believe for the company, although I don't feel very comfortable at occupying the best rooms in the house, when so many others are here. I don't mean this to be a descriptive letter from "Your own correspondent," and so I will not put down any more of his talk, which, when noted down, loses most of its point, as a matter of course. We have just returned from a two hours' drive through the woods. We breakfast at any hour, dine generally at about half-past three, he not being allowed to dine late, and after dinner we make these sylvan excursions, and go to bed after a scrambling, promiscuous supper about twelve.

We have promised to dine with Bancroft. He sent me a letter here asking me to name a day, and I sent him a telegram this morning fixing Tuesday. The next day we expect to go as far as Brunswick, and then to make a three or four days' excursion in the Harz. This is about the extent of our ambition, and I have no doubt that when we get away from here, we shall begin to be very homesick.

The weather is very fine and cloudless, without being excessively hot. The atmosphere is pure and invigorating, the country being covered with pine forests, so that one might imagine one's self in New Hampshire.

God bless you, dear, and with love to Susie,

Ever your loving

J. L. M.

My most devoted remembrances to H.M. the Queen.

To His Youngest Daughter

VARZIN,

July 30th, 1872

MY DEAREST SUSIE,—It is an infinite pleasure to listen to Bismarck's conversation, to hear the history of Europe during the last most eventful half-dozen years told in such an easygoing, offhand way by the man who was the chief actor and director of that amazing history. Without giving you, however, a *cours d'histoire contemporaine,* I could hardly undertake to give you much of his conversation. . . . He does not dislike Louis Napoleon, and said that he had long been of opinion that his heart was much better and his head less powerful than the world was inclined to believe.

The *Silberne Hochzeit* was very interesting. Letters and telegrams of congratulation kept coming in all day—from the emperor and crown prince down to students' clubs in all parts of Germany, *Schützenvereine,*—all sorts of individuals and associations of men and women. We went to church in the morning, drove in the forest for several hours, and dined at six. There was no company but his brother, wife, and son, and one other old friend, and some of the adherents and officials of the household. In the midst of the repast M—— suddenly said to me, "You must propose the toast to papa," and forthwith she rapped on a glass, stopped the whole conversation, and called general attention to my oration. It was a masterly effort in the German tongue, lasted twenty-five seconds, and ended with much clicking of glasses and hip, hip, hurraying. After dinner Bismarck made some little speeches to the villagers and the musicians. In the evening a mighty bowl of punch was brewed, and we smoked and made merry until past midnight. I believe the telegrams of congratulation have been counted, and they amount to about two hundred.

. . . Tomorrow morning we leave the house at half-past eight, and arrive at Berlin at 6 P.M., having spent here a most delightful week.

Ever your most affectionate
J. L. M.

To His Wife

Hôtel du Nord, BERLIN,
Thursday, August 1st, 1872

MY DEAREST MARY,—I feel as if I had neglected you and written very few letters. But the promiscuous way in which life went on at Varzin made it very difficult to get a reasonable hour or two for the purpose of writing. And I thought that it would be as well to talk over with you all that we talked about in the woods, and at the breakfast and dinner table, or on the veranda, as to try to record all the slip-slop, *décousu,* but profoundly interesting conversation which we have been so much enjoying.

The way of life is very simple at Varzin, but the irregularity of the hours is great. I usually came downstairs, as well as Lily, between nine and ten; Madame de Bismarck, M——, and the sons came in promiscuously and had breakfast with us. Bismarck came down about eleven. His breakfast is very light—an egg and a cup of coffee—and then he has a meerschaum pipe. While he is sitting there and talking to all of us, his secretary hands him the piles of letters with which he is goaded in his retirement, and with a lead pencil about a foot long makes memoranda as to the answers and other disposition to be made. Meanwhile the boys are playing billiards in another part of the same room, and a big black dog, called "Sultan," is rampaging generally through the apartment and joining in everybody's conversation. I was very sorry that Susie could not have been with us; M—— said a great deal about her, and was extremely sorry not to see her; and I am sure Susie would have liked her very much, she is so full of fun and nonsense and good humor, and much petted but not spoiled. After breakfast Bismarck and I always took a long walk, during which he was always talking—generally about the events of the French war. I have given so many specimens in my letters to you and Susie and Mary that it would be foolish to attempt sending any more small bricks as specimens of the house. The nominal dinner hour was three, but we rarely sat down earlier than a quarter to four. No dinner dressing nor evening costume. Dinner always good and simple; wine excellent.

On the courtyard side the house consists of a main building, two stories high, with two long windows projecting from the house, in which are servants' rooms and offices, making three sides of an open quadrangle. On the lawn or wood side there is a long veranda running in front of the main house. Inside is a square hall, with wide staircase leading to a large hall above, out of which open four spacious bedrooms. On each side of the hall below are a suite of one or two rooms, which are the family and reception rooms, besides his library and the private rooms of the ladies of the family. The estate is about 30,000 morgens, equal to 20,000 acres. A great part —certainly two-thirds—is forest, pine, oak and beech. Of the rest, a small farm, some 200 or 300 acres, is in his own hands. The rest is let in large farms of 800 or 900 acres. The river Wipper, which runs through the property, is a valuable water power. He has built two or three mills upon it, one of which is already let and in operation. The other and larger one is not yet finished. Both are pasteboard mills, pine wood being the raw material, which, of course, furnishes a great demand from his estate.

The Lauenburg property is about of the same dimensions, but much more valuable. This was given to him by the king when he made him prince. Both his sons are manly, active, well-mannered, good-looking. The intense affection which he has for his wife and children is delightful to contemplate, and, as you may imagine, he is absolutely worshipped by them. The week passed here is something for Lily and me to remember for the rest of our lives. The parting was painful to me, *for heaven knows when I shall ever see him again.* He sent most affectionate messages to you, and they were all very sorry you could not come, and Susie also.

I am sorry that I telegraphed so soon for you to write to the Hôtel du Nord. Nothing had been said about the limit of our visit, but when on Sunday night I spoke of ordering the post chaise next morning to take us to the railway station, Bismarck remonstrated so vehemently about it that we were only too glad to postpone our departure two more days; and I think I mentioned to you that Bismarck telegraphed to Bancroft asking him to postpone his dinner for us until Thursday. *I never can* adequately express to you how kind and affectionate they have *all been to us.* She is kindness and cordiality itself, and we have felt all the time as if we were part of the family. As for Bismarck himself, my impressions of his bigness have increased rather than diminished by this renewed intimacy. Having been with him constantly fourteen or fifteen hours a day for a whole week, I have certainly had opportunity enough to make up my mind. . . .

Mr. Bancroft came this morning and made us a long visit. He is excessively cordial. We dine with him today at six, and he has invited some people to meet us.

Pray give my devoted and affectionate respects to the queen when you see her.

Love to Susie, who I hope will not abuse my new clothes got on purpose to please her.

Ever, dearest, lovingly yours,
J. L. M.

59

The Kulturkampf: Convinced that He Must Destroy All Domestic Enemies, Bismarck Begins a War Against the Catholic Church and Loses a Battle on the Home Front

"We shall never go to Canossa, either actually or in spirit."

In 1864 Pope Pius IX issued his Syllabus of Modern Errors, *in which he proclaimed civil marriage and secular education as "modern errors." The Vatican Council of 1870 announced that the pope was "infallible" when speaking* ex cathedra *on matters of faith and morals. These two proclamations angered Bismarck, but because he needed the support of the Catholic south German and Rhenish states in the war situation with France, he decided to await a more propitious moment before accepting the papal "challenge."*

Once the unification of Germany was completed, Bismarck decided to settle the issue with the Vatican to his own satisfaction. He was soon embroiled in the Kulturkampf *("struggle for civilization").*

In 1872 the Cardinal Hohenlohe-Schillingsfürst was appointed as German ambassador to the papacy. Pius IX was asked in the usual fashion whether or not the prince would be acceptable for the post. The pontiff replied in the negative. In the Reichstag there was a debate on the expenses of this post in the budget. Bismarck made the following speech which set off the struggle with the Church.[4]

I can readily understand how the idea may arise that the expenses for this embassy have become unnecessary, because there is no longer a question here of protecting German subjects in those parts. I am, nevertheless, glad that no motion has been made to

4. Translated by Edmund von Mach in *The German Classics* (New York, 1914), X, 191–195.

abolish this position, for it would have been unwelcome to the government.

The duties of an embassy are in part, it is true, the protection of its countrymen, but in part also the mediation of the political relations which the government of the empire happens to maintain with the court where the ambassador is accredited. There is no foreign sovereign authorized by the present state of our legislation to exercise as extensive rights within the German empire as the pope. While these rights are almost those of a sovereign, they are not guarded by any constitutional responsibility. Considerable importance, therefore, attaches to the kind of diplomatic relations which the German empire is able to maintain with the head of the Roman Church, who exerts such a remarkably strong and, for a foreign sovereign, unusual influence among us. Considering the prevailing tendencies of the Catholic Church at the present time, I scarcely believe that any ambassador of the German empire would succeed in inducing his Holiness the Pope, by the most skillful diplomacy and by persuasion, to modify the position which he has taken, on principle, in all secular affairs. There can, of course, be no question here of forceful actions, such as may occur between two secular powers. In view of the recently promulgated doctrines of the Catholic Church, I deem it impossible for any secular power to reach a concordat without effacing itself to a degree and in a way which, to the German empire at least, is unacceptable. You need not be afraid, we shall never go to Canossa, either actually or in spirit.

Nevertheless, I cannot deny that the position of the empire as regards its religious peace is somewhat shaken. It is not my duty here to investigate motives, or to ask which one of the two parties is at fault, but to defend an item of the budget. The united governments of the German empire are searching eagerly and, in justice to their Catholic and their Evangelical subjects, diligently for means which will secure a more agreeable state of affairs than the present, and which will do so as peacefully as possible, and without unnecessarily disturbing the religious relations of the empire. I doubt whether this can be done except by legislation—I mean general and national legislation, for which the governments will have to ask for the assistance of the Reichstag.

But you will agree with me that this legislation should proceed with great moderation and delicacy, and with due regard for every one's freedom of conscience. The governments must be careful to avoid anything which will render their task more difficult, such as errors of information or ignorance of the proper forms, and must strive to readjust their internal peace with tender regard for religious sensibilities, even those which are not shared by all. In this connection it is, of course, necessary that the Holy See should be at all times well informed of the intentions of the German governments, certainly more so than has been the case heretofore. One of the chief causes of the present disturbance in religious matters is, I believe, the misinformation which has reached his Holiness the Pope concerning the conditions in Germany and the intentions of the German governments, and which has been due either to excitement or to the wrong color given it by evil motives.

I had hoped that the choice of an ambassador, who possessed the full confidence of both parties, would be welcome in Rome, of a man who loves truth and deserves confidence, and whose character and bearing are conciliatory; in short, of a man like the well-known prince of the Church whom his Majesty the Emperor had appointed to this post. I had hoped that this choice would be regarded as a pledge of our peaceful attitude and willingness to make advances, and would serve as a bridge to a mutual understanding. I had hoped that it would give the assurance that we should never ask anything of his Holiness the Pope but what a prince of the church, allied to him by the most intimate ties, could present and convey to him, and that the forms would always be in keeping with those which characterize the intercourse of one prince of the church with another. This would have avoided all unnecessary friction in a case which is difficult enough.

Many fears were expressed both by the Protestants and the liberals concerning this appointment, based, I believe, on an erroneous interpretation of the position of an envoy or an ambassador. An ambassador really is a vessel which reaches its full value only when it is filled with the instructions of its master. In such delicate matters as these, however, it is desirable that the vessel should be agreeable and acceptable, and that it should be incapable of containing poisons or potions without immediately revealing them, as people used to say of ancient crystals. Unfortunately, and for reasons which have not yet been given, these intentions of the imperial government could not be carried out because they met with a curt refusal on the part of the Holy See. I can truly say that such a case does not often happen. When a sovereign has made his choice of an ambassador, it is customary for him to inquire, from courtesy, whether the ambassador will be *persona grata* with the sovereign to whom he will be accredited, but the receipt of a negative reply is most unusual, for it necessitates the repeal of an appointment already made. What the emperor can do toward the appointment he does before asking the question. In other words he has made the appointment before he asks the question. The negative reply, therefore, is a demand that a step once taken shall be repealed, a declaration which says: "You have made a wrong choice!"

I have been foreign minister for about ten years, and have been engaged in questions of higher diplomacy for twenty-one years, and I am not mistaken, I believe, when I say that this is the first and only case in my experience where such a question has been answered in the negative. I have known more than once of doubts expressed concerning ambassadors who had served for some time, and of courts confidentially conveying their wish that a change be made in the person accredited to them. In every case, however, the court had had the experience of diplomatic relations with the particular person through several years, and was convinced that he was not qualified to safeguard the good relations which it wished to maintain with us. It explained, therefore, in a most confidential and delicate way, generally by means of an autograph letter from one sovereign to the other, why it had taken this step. Such requests are rarely, if ever, made unconditionally. In recent times, as you know, a few cases have occurred, one of which at least was a very flagrant one, when the recall of an ambassador was demanded; but as I have said, I do not remember another instance where an ambassador was refused when he was to be newly appointed.

My regrets at this refusal are exceedingly keen, but I am not justified in translating these regrets into a feeling of vexation, for in justice to our Catholic fellow citizens the government should not relax its exertions in trying to find ways and means of regulating the dividing line between the spiritual and the secular powers. Such a division is absolutely necessary in the interest of our internal peace, and it should be brought about in the most delicate manner, and in a way which will give least offense to either confession. I shall, therefore, not be discouraged by what has happened, but shall continue to use my influence with his Majesty the Emperor to the end that a representative of the empire may be found for Rome who enjoys the confidence of both powers, if not in equal measure, at least in measure sufficient for his duties. I cannot, of course, deny that our task has been rendered decidedly more difficult by what has happened.

In foreign affairs Bismarck had been brilliantly successful, but his campaign against the Catholic Church was to end in near disaster for him. After expelling the Jesuits from Germany, he put through the May Laws (1872–1878) in the Prussian Landtag *by which the state was given complete control over marriage and education, the Catholic press was muzzled, Church property was confiscated, and recalcitrant priests, monks, and nuns were persecuted. Archbishops, bishops, and priests were deposed, imprisoned, and expelled. An inevitable result was the rapid development of the Catholic Center party as a new and vital political power. The fast growth of the Socialists in Germany convinced Bismarck that the "red international" was considerably more dangerous as an enemy of the empire than the old "black international." The accession of the moderate Pope Leo XIII (1878) facilitated Bismarck's change of heart. The chancellor abandoned the* Kulturkampf. *By 1887 virtually all the anti-Catholic laws were repealed, and Bismarck sought clerical support in his battle against the Socialists.*

0 Beginning of the Bismarckian Treaty System: The Three Emperors' Conferences, 1872–1873

". . . the two European directions which Napoleon called republican and cossack."

The Russian and Prussian armies had fought together against Napoleon Bonaparte, an important factor in the traditional bonds of friendship between the two countries. Still more, both countries were dedicated to the task of preventing the reestablishment of Polish independence, which would have deprived them of areas received in the three partitions of Poland in the late eighteenth century. Bismarck always considered it essential to his foreign policy that friendship be maintained with Russia. In September 1872 he arranged a meeting of the three rulers of Germany, Austria-Hungary, and Russia at Berlin, at which an informal union, later known as the Dreikaiserbund *(Three Emperors' League) was discussed. Though no written agreement was signed, there was established an "understanding" as a basis for the league formed later (1881).*

The following excerpt from Bismarck's autobiography reveals his fears that a conflict might develop between the principles of monarchy and the forces of radicalism.[5]

5. Otto von Bismarck, *Gedanken und Erinnerungen* (Stuttgart and Berlin, 1898), II, 514–515.

The triple alliance, which I at first sought to negotiate after the peace of Frankfort, and concerning which I had already sounded out Vienna and St. Petersburg, from Meaux, in 1870, was an alliance of the three emperors, with the additional idea of bringing into it monarchical Italy. It was designed for the conflict which, as I feared, was upon us—between the two European directions which Napoleon called republican and cossack, and which I, in consonance with our present ideas, should designate on the one hand as a system of order on the basis of monarchy, and on the other as the social republic to the level of which the antimonarchical development tends to sink, either slowly or by leaps and bounds, until the situation thus evolved becomes intolerable, and the disappointed people are ready for a violent return to monarchical institutions in Caesarean form. The task of escaping from this *circulus vitiosus* or, possibly, of relieving the present generation and their children from an entrance into it, should be more closely dependent on the strong existing monarchies, especially those monarchies that still maintain a vigorous life, than any rivalry over the fragments of nations which inhabit the Balkan peninsula. If the monarchical governments do not understand the necessity for uniting in the interests of the political and social order, but, on the contrary, become subservient to the chauvinistic impulses of their subjects, I fear that the international revolutionary and social conflicts which must be fought out will be all the more dangerous, and take on a character which will make the triumph of the monarchical order all the more difficult. Since 1871 I have sought for the most precise assurance against those conflicts in the alliance of the three emperors, as well as in the effort to give the monarchical principle in Italy firm support by that alliance. I was not without hope of a lasting success at the time when the meeting of the three emperors took place at Berlin in September 1872. This was followed by the visits of my emperor to St. Petersburg in May, by the visit of the king of Italy to Berlin in September, and by the visit of the German emperor to Vienna in October of 1873. The first dark clouds over that hope were caused in 1875 by the provocations of Prince Gortschakoff, who spread the falsehood that we intended to strike at France before she recovered from her wounds.

This was the beginning of Bismarck's involved system of alliances designed to maintain Germany's hegemony on the European scene. His aims were to isolate France, conciliate Great Britain, and keep Russia as a friendly power. In 1879 Bismarck concluded the Dual Alliance with Austria-Hungary, by which the signatories were bound to assist one another in the event that either ally was at-

tacked by Russia. In 1881 he set up the Three Emperors' League. In 1882 he expanded the Dual Alliance into the Triple Alliance including Italy. In 1887 he concluded the Reinsurance Treaty with Russia. With this complicated combination of alliances Bismarck was certain that no power or group of powers would dare attack Germany. In fact, there were no major wars between the Great Powers as long as Bismarck remained in power as chancellor from 1871 to 1890.

61 Bismarck Accompanies Emperor William I on a Scintillating Tour to Moscow, 1873

"The statesman disappeared, and gave place to the courtier and the man of the world."

Always worried about the nightmare of a two-front war, Bismarck did everything he could to maintain friendship with the Russians. On April 27, 1873 he accompanied Emperor William I on a ceremonial visit to Moscow. It was a twelve-day triumphal tour, filled with a succession of troop reviews, parades, illuminations, balls, banquets, concerts, and gala performances. The following contemporary account describes the share of the populace in the proceedings, as well as the meeting between Bismarck and Gortchakoff.[6]

The result was a secret military agreement, by which Russia and Germany promised military aid to one another in the event of an attack by a third European power. Several weeks later, Tsar Alexander II went to Austria and signed with Francis Joseph I an agreement whereby they would consult one another on questions on which they differed. Bismarck's treaty structure was in process of formation.

On the evening of the 29th of April . . . a gigantic *fête* was given in the palace square. The two sovereigns witnessed the mammoth concert from the palace balcony.

As they stepped on to the balcony the huge square was suddenly lighted up by five electric lights, with such intense brilliancy that the features of every face in the immense crowd were easily distinguishable, and the orchestra struck up the national Prussian hymn. Fifteen hundred and fifty performers took part in this, besides 600

6. M. Julian Klaczko, *The Two Chancellors—Prince Gortchakoff and Prince Bismarck*, trans. from the French by Mrs. Tait (London, 1876), pp. 317–321.

trumpeters and 350 drummers. The Prussian air was followed by the "March of King Frederick William III," and then by a whole series of military marches—the "Steinmetz March," the *"Wacht am Rhein,"* the "March of the Guards of 1808," to the tune of which the Russian regiments had re-entered St. Petersburg after the Eylau campaign; and the "March of Paris," which had once resounded in the ears of the allied armies as they triumphantly entered the capital of France.

The military prayer, "How great is the Lord in Zion," produced a tremendous effect. It is a little difficult to understand how Weber's plaintive air "The Praise of Tears" (*Lob der Thränen*) wandered into the midst of these strains consecrated to Mars and Vulcan; unless as a discreet homage to the well-known sensibility of the veteran Hohenzollern, authentic evidences of which will be found by history in hundreds of his speeches, letters, and telegrams. Indeed, he did not leave St. Petersburg without displaying this characteristic sensitiveness. As the two sovereigns were bidding each other *adieu* in the imperial saloons of the Gatchina terminus, William of Germany was obliged to hurriedly break away, to prevent himself from yielding to his emotion. With bent head and twitching features he left the saloon with hasty footsteps, and buried himself in his railway carriage, *without once looking back.*

If, however, during this Prussian visit to the banks of the Neva the honors were all for the tsar's uncle, the eager and almost feverish curiosity of the public was a good deal more occupied with the celebrated minister whose white cuirassier's uniform lent an extra emphasis to his conspicuous stature—with the famous German chancellor, who in one brief lustrum had known how to found an empire on the ruins of two other ones. St. Petersburg had not yet had time to forget the free-spoken diplomatist, who, from 1859 to 1862 had astonished and amused Russian society by his abuse of his own court, by his ridicule of the "*perruques* of Potsdam" and the "Philistines of the Spree"; and who sometimes quoted—always taking care, however, to be the first to laugh—M. Prudhomme's famous saying, "If I were the government!"

Now he was, indeed, the government—he was even the master of Europe; and before his star those of a Hapsburg and a Napoleon had paled their ineffectual fires! The topic was in truth one that suggested many a striking comparison, many a piquant reminiscence; nor was it one that refused to lend itself to idle comments, to the *plerisque vana mirantibus* alluded to by the immortal historian when speaking of striking changes of fortune.

As the great ladies in the Winter Palace looked at the man of the five milliards, they remembered an ambassadress of ten years ago who was heard one day to roundly declare that she really could not afford to pay forty rubles for a dish of early asparagus; and who, on another occasion, very candidly owned that her new diamond earrings were the result of the exchange of a valuable snuff-box, an old gift of the Prince of Darmstadt.* This ambassadress was the wife of M. de Bismarck, then only a baron, now a prince, tempered, lively, and obliging as when he was envoy. He inquired after his friends, after his acquaintances, after both the great and little people he used to meet; and seemed as though he were taking up the thread of intimacies interrupted but a day ago. The statesman disappeared, and gave place to the courtier and the man of the world. We are told by a sagacious observer that even with Prince Gortschakoff he made a point of stepping out of the foreign minister, and appearing in the undress of an old companion, almost a fellow countryman. M. de Bismarck paid his Russian colleague the affectionate deference of a friend to an elder friend, of a disciple to his master, artlessly enough said his flatterers, forgetting the old saying, *discipulus supra magistrum;* though Alexander Mikhaïlovitch, a good Latin scholar, probably remembered it.

The pair often appeared side by side in public at *fêtes* and receptions: the one conspicuous by his great height and remarkable head; the other easily recognizable by his more delicately-cut features, by his keen, witty, and slightly cunning expression. Obeying the ingenious precept of court etiquette first introduced by good old Homer when he made Glaucus and Diomede exchange armor, the Russian minister wore the Order of the Prussian Black Eagle, and the Prussian minister that of St. Andrew of Russia. In truth, this interchange of orders seemed typical of the community of views which had so long united these illustrious diplomatists.

Such a cordial, stable understanding between a couple of statesmen at the helms of two different empires was assuredly an unusual spectacle. It was certainly a striking one, and amidst the solemn pomp of St. Petersburg, it gave reflecting minds much food for thought. The annals of the past were ransacked in vain for such an enduring and brilliant instance of harmonious action. A few celebrated political intimacies, such as those between Choiseul and Kaunitz, Dubois and Stanhope, Mazarin and Cromwell, were only called to mind to be instantly recognized as comparatively misleading and merely apparent analogies.

* From the *St. Petersburg Gesellschaft,* II, 89.

62 The Arnim Affair: A Specialist in Hate, Suspecting a Friend of Disloyalty, Proceeds Methodically to Destroy Him[7]

"At this very desk . . . you will see—even that isn't worth a damn!"

Bismarck's will to power was so intense that he could tolerate no rivalry. He turned angrily on Harry von Arnim, a companion of his youth. Arnim had gradually worked his way up in the diplomatic service until he was considered by many to be Bismarck's successor. He did all he could to confirm that impression. To Bismarck this was treachery. When the chancellor suspected Arnim of mutinous behavior, he hounded him out of office. After a sensational trial, Arnim was found guilty of appropriating secret papers from the German embassy at Paris. He escaped to Switzerland where, in 1876, he published a bitter pamphlet directed at Bismarck. His career ruined, Arnim died in 1881 in a Nice hotel without seeing his homeland again. The depressing affair revealed Bismarck's overwhelming compulsion to cling to power.

. . . A most sensational trial began before the Berlin Criminal Court. The accused was no less a personage than the former ambassador of his Imperial Majesty in Paris, his Excellency the Privy-Councillor Count Harry von Arnim. Some months before, in October 1874, all Europe was startled by the news that his Excellency had been arrested and flung into prison in Berlin like a common felon. What was his crime? High treason? Conspiracy? No, nothing of the kind. He had refused to give up certain documents which the foreign office regarded as its own property but which he considered were his.

In the ordinary way such a difference of opinion would never have been brought before the criminal court. But this was, in fact, the culmination of a bitter political and personal feud between the chancellor and the ambassador.

Arnim and Bismarck had known each other from their youth. Arnim, indeed, claimed that they had been friends. When Bismarck took over the Prussian foreign office, he sent Arnim to Rome as

7. Erich Eyck, *Bismarck and the German Empire* (London, 1950), pp. 210–213.

Prussian envoy to the Holy See. During the Vatican Council they had not seen eye to eye about the policy to be adopted towards the Council. But in spite of this difference of opinion, Bismarck sent Arnim to France after the war to represent the empire in the negotiations about the implementation of the armistice, and when the peace treaty was signed he made him ambassador in Paris. This was certainly the key post in the whole German diplomatic service. One would suppose that Bismarck would entrust it only to a man in whom he had complete confidence. But it is now known that, at the same time, he wrote to the emperor that Arnim had "an uncertain and untrustworthy character."

The political differences between the chancellor and the ambassador centered on the attitude towards Thiers and the republican form of the French state. After Thiers' overthrow by the monarchist majority in the French parliament in May 1873, Bismarck reproached Arnim with cutting across his policy by supporting, not Thiers but the monarchists. For, as we have already seen, Bismarck wished to keep Thiers in power and the Republic in being in order to make France *bündnisunfähig,* as he put it; that is, incapable of forming alliances. As foreign minister, Bismarck certainly had the right to lay down the lines of foreign policy which every ambassador had to follow. To this extent he is right in his famous saying: "My ambassadors must fall into line like soldiers." But Arnim, although he did not share Bismarck's views, denied that he had done anything to help or promote monarchist reaction. What he complained of was that Bismarck demanded that he should accommodate to his chief's views not only his actions but also his *dispatches.* This is, indeed, a most dangerous doctrine, as was seen many years later, when the German ambassador in London, Count Metternich, was dismissed because his pessimistic reports about the bad impression made in Britain by the expansion of the German navy displeased the Emperor William II. In Arnim's case his reports displeased Bismarck because they impressed the old kaiser. In essence, therefore, Bismarck was blaming Arnim because his arguments, that republican developments in France would threaten the monarchic principle in Europe, found favor with William.

The tone in which Bismarck rebuked the ambassador is sharp and insulting to a degree. Why? Because Arnim enjoyed the favor of the emperor and, more than that, of the Empress Augusta. Bismarck knew that Arnim also criticized the *Kulturkampf,* just as Augusta did, and Arnim, as a former minister in Rome, could speak with some authority on these questions. But the worst of it was that

Arnim was spoken of in some conservative circles as a possible chancellor, and in Bismarck's eyes, of course, that was the unforgivable sin. True, Bismarck's position was so firm and unshakable that he could have ignored rumors and rivals alike, but he was not cast in that mold. He was extremely suspicious of every rival—likely or unlikely. In the last conversation he had with Arnim, he told him bluntly: "You are plotting with the empress and you will not stop intriguing until you sit at this very desk where I am sitting now—and then you will see—even that isn't worth a damn!"—a truly Bismarckian phrase.

To compass Arnim's downfall, Bismarck sent a spy to Paris. This was Baron Fritz von Holstein, then a councillor of legation at the Paris embassy, later for many years of William II's reign the most influential member of the Wilhelmstrasse. Holstein was base enough to do this dirty work. During the Arnim trial he went through what was probably the worst hour of his life, when in the witness box, in spite of all his shufflings and evasions, he could not deny that he had spied on his chief. These revelations in open court affected the whole course of Holstein's life. They made him for some years a social pariah; they had much to do with the development of that tortuous turn to his character which was to prove so fateful for German policy. It was a sort of nemesis that the first man to desert Bismarck in his hour of distress in 1890 was Baron von Holstein.

Arnim admittedly made some serious mistakes and so forfeited the confidence of the old emperor, who at last allowed Bismarck to remove Arnim from Paris and ultimately to expel him from the diplomatic service altogether. But Bismarck's thirst for vengeance was unquenchable and he instituted criminal proceedings against the ambassador which completely ruined him. The trial before the Berlin court in December 1874 was a political triumph for Bismarck, who handled matters with supreme skill. He had some of his most masterly dispatches read out, and they made an immense impression on the public, while Arnim's letters and notes appeared feeble by comparison. But the critical observer could not help feeling that Bismarck's tactics of personal attack and prosecution were as relentless and unscrupulous as they were clever. But this did not help Arnim, who had to go into exile. Some pamphlets which he wrote defending his attitude and attacking Bismarck gave rise to a fresh prosecution. In the end he was condemned *in absentia* to five years' penal servitude, a verdict which so grossly outrages justice that even Bismarck in his *Reminiscences* disclaims all responsibility for it. But even here Bismarck makes fresh insinuations against the unfortunate adversary, who had long since died in exile.

53 Another Assassination Attempt: A Cooper's Apprentice, Infuriated by the War on the Catholic Church, Tries to Kill Bismarck at Kissingen, July 13, 1874

". . . the providential escape of the chancellor."

Bismarck was to learn in an unpleasant way how deep were the passions raised by the Kulturkampf. *On July 13, 1874, as he was driving through the streets of Kissingen in an open carriage, another attempt was made on his life. A bullet grazed his cheek and wounded him in the hand. The would-be assassin was a young cooper's apprentice named Kullmann, who, as a Catholic, was convinced that Bismarck was threatening the very existence of his church.*

The sensational event was reported in The New York Times *in the following series of dispatches.*[8] *The story was essentially correct, although it misspelled the name of the assailant and also hinted at a conspiracy. While not altogether certain, it was probable that Kullmann had acted on his own without accomplices.*

Bismarck took full advantage of the incident. He interviewed Kullmann twice in his cell in an effort to find out why the young man wanted to kill him. In December Bismarck, still angered, attacked his Catholic enemies in a speech before the Reichstag:

> *The man, with whom I myself have spoken, is in full possession of his faculties. Indeed, we have medical testimony to this effect. . . . Repudiate the assassin as you please, he still holds on to your coat-tails, says he belongs to your political party. . . . He said: "I wanted to kill you because of the ecclesiastical laws. . . . You have injured my political party. . . . I mean the Center party in the Reichstag."*

LATEST NEWS BY CABLE
ATTEMPTED ASSASSINATION OF PRINCE BISMARCK
HE IS FIRED ON WHILE OUT DRIVING—THE BALL GRAZES HIS WRIST—ARREST OF THE CULPRIT

KISSINGEN, July 13. While Prince Bismarck was driving in the country toward the Saline Springs, at noon today, he was fired at by a young man.

8. *The New York Times,* July 13–15, 1874.

The ball grazed his wrist. The wound is insignificant. The would-be assassin was promptly arrested.

He has not been identified. At 1:00 P.M. Prince Bismarck drove through Kissingen, and showed himself to the people.

The populace were with great difficulty prevented from lynching the man after his arrest.

THE IDENTITY OF THE WOULD-BE ASSASSIN ESTABLISHED

BERLIN, July 13. The identity of the would-be assassin of Prince Bismarck has been established. His name is Kullman. He belongs to Magdeburg, and is a cooper by trade. He is a member of the Catholic Journeyman's Society of that city, and has been observed of late frequently in the company of a Catholic priest.

[Editorial in *The New York Times,* July 14, 1874]

Prince Bismarck has had the honor, seldom enjoyed by anyone but crowned heads, of having two attempts made on his life. Young Blind gave him the benefit of four pistol balls, only one of which slightly wounded the statesman, in May 1866, and now a Magdeburg cooper has failed at Kissingen in a somewhat less determined attempt on his life. It was to the fury of German radicalism that Prince Bismarck was to be offered as a sacrifice in 1866; it is from the fanatical hatred of Roman Catholicism that the promptings to his assassination have come in 1874. Bismarck on the eve of the war with Austria, and Bismarck on the eve of the decisive struggle against the papacy, present two historical figures which will be all the better remembered because of the pistol bullets that passed by them.

ENTHUSIATIC RECEPTION OF PRINCE BISMARCK

KISSINGEN, July 14. Prince Bismarck appeared in the public gardens last evening, and was received with the utmost enthusiasm. The musical societies, accompanied by a great crowd of people, subsequently serenaded him at his residence. In response to the demands of the concourse, the chancellor appeared and made a speech. After expressing his thanks for the demonstration, he said the attempt on his life was not aimed at his person but at the cause he represented. In conclusion he proposed cheers for the German Empire and the allied German princes.

The people responded, giving repeated cheers for Bismarck.

There is to be a thanksgiving service in the Protestant Church today for the providential escape of the chancellor.

It is reported that Kullman has confessed that he intended to assassinate the prince, and that he has used expressions indicating that others are implicated in his scheme. A priest named Hanthaler has been arrested at Schweinfurt under the belief that he was an accessory to the shooting. He came from Kissingen yesterday.

PRINCE BISMARCK'S PATRIOTIC DECLARATION

KISSINGEN, July 14. The King of Württemberg and the Italian government have telephoned congratulations to Prince Bismarck over his escape from assassination.

The prince, in his speech at the public gardens last night, referring to the peril in which his life had been placed, asked, "Why should I not be ready to die for the unity and freedom of the Fatherland like so many of my fellow citizens during the late war?"

FURTHER DETAILS OF THE ATTEMPT TO ASSASSINATE BISMARCK

LONDON, July 15. Kullman, who attempted Bismarck's life, is considered a mere tool. He confesses he was acting in concert with others.

Hanthaler, the priest arrested for connection with the plot, belongs to the village of Walchsee, in the Austrian Tyrol. He checked Bismarck's horses by stepping in front at the critical moment.

Immediately, on hearing of the affair, the king of Bavaria sent congratulations to Prince Bismarck in his fortunate escape.

The Berlin press declare the attempted assassination proves the necessity of repressing ultramontane teachings.

HOW THE PARIS PRESS REGARD THE ATTEMPT

PARIS, July 14. Some of the Paris journals affect to consider the attempt on Bismarck's life a plot concocted by the German police.

64

During the Decade Following National Unification in 1871, the Chancellor Is Gradually Converted to the Cause of a Protective Tariff Policy

"We have placed our tariffs at too low a rate."

Bismarck became convinced that the acute sufferings of German industries and the depression of prices had been due in large part to the government's moderate free-trade practices. In reaching this decision, he was undoubtedly influenced by the views of his confidential assistant, Lothar Bucher, who warned him that Germany was being swamped by the surplus production of foreign nations, and who considered the Manchester free-trade movement as "the most colossal and the most audacious campaign of political and economic deception which the world had ever seen."

Bismarck's shift from laissez-faire *liberalism to economic nationalism was not an easy one. A battle took place between proponents of* laissez faire *(parliamentarians, liberals, bankers, and merchants) and protectionists (agrarians and manufacturers). Finding himself unable to convert the National Liberals, Bismarck negotiated with the Center, which agreed to support him if he dropped the* Kulturkampf. *His success reflected the relative decline of the National Liberal and Progressive parties (strongly free trade) and the enhanced position of the Conservatives (strongly paternalistic).*

The effect of the new tariff schedule, adopted on June 12, 1879, was that Germany became a world power instead of a purely European power. Her prosperity increased steadily. The change in basic economic policy coincided with the beginning of Germany's great industrial development, which contributed to the international economic and political friction culminating in the world wars of the twentieth century.

Bismarck appeared before the Reichstag on May 2, 1879, and delivered a long speech in which he opposed the whole theory of free trade. Pertinent extracts from this speech are given below.[9]

. . . The only country [which persists in a policy of free trade] is England, and that will not last long. France and America have departed completely from this line; Austria, instead of lowering her

9. Adapted from *Stenographische Berichte über die Verhandlungen des Reichstages, 1879*, II, 297.

tariffs, has made them higher; Russia has done the same, not only through the gold standard but in other ways also. Therefore, to be alone the dupe of an honorable conviction cannot be expected of Germany forever. By opening wide the doors of our state to the imports of foreign countries, we have become the dumping ground for the production of those countries. Anything can be palmed off on us just now, and it has, when it arrives in Germany, a higher value always than in the country of its origin—at least, so everybody thinks. Since we have been swamped by the surplus production of foreign nations, our prices have been depressed; and the development of our industries and our entire economic position has suffered in consequence.

Let us finally close our doors and erect some barriers, as we have proposed to you, in order to reserve for German industries at least the home market, which, because of German good nature, has been exploited by foreigners. The problem of a large export trade is always a very delicate one; there are no new lands to discover, the world has been circumnavigated, and we can no longer find abroad new purchasers of importance to whom we can send our goods. . . .

It is a fact that we find ourselves today in a sorry position, much worse, I am convinced, than that of any of our neighboring countries which have adopted a policy of protection. If the danger of protection were as great as we are told it is by enthusiastic free traders, France would have become impoverished long ago, for she has had a policy of protection since the time of Colbert, and she would have been ruined by theories which have guided her economic policies. . . .

In all questions such as these, I have regarded scientific theories with the same doubt with which I view the theories applied to other organic formations. Medical science, as compared with anatomy, has made but little progress in the last two thousand years with regard to those parts of the body that the eye cannot reach; today, the riddle of organic changes in the human body is as great as it was years ago. It is the same thing when we consider the organism of the state. I am left completely cold by the *dicta* of abstract science. I make my judgments on the basis of practical experience of the time in which we are living. I see that those countries which have adopted protection are prospering, and that those countries which have free trade are deteriorating. Mighty England, that powerful athlete, after she had strengthened her muscles, stepped out into the open market and said: "Who will fight me?" I am prepared to meet anybody. Yet, England herself is preparing to return slowly to protection, and, in a few years, she will do it to save for herself at least the home market.

In my opinion, since we have placed our tariffs at too low a rate (and I blame myself for that, too), we have been slowly bleeding to death because of insufficient protection. This process was arrested for a while by the billions we received from France after the war. In my view, this situation should not be complicated by personal sensitiveness. I would, therefore, beg that all personal sensitiveness be set aside in this matter, as well as all political differences; the question that lies before us is not a political but a clearly economic one. We shall see how the German body recovers when we give it the power of regular circulation of the blood. My personal request, and a most urgent one, is that we drop all questions of political parties and political tactics in the face of this matter of general importance to all Germans. . . .

65

Ulysses S. Grant, Hero of American Unity, Comes to Berlin to Visit the Statesman Responsible for German Unification [10]

"What always seemed so sad to me . . . was that you were fighting your own people."

In the summer of 1878 the American general and former president Ulysses S. Grant, making a world tour, came to Berlin. There was a mutual bond of interest between Bismarck and Grant. On Grant's inauguration on March 4, 1869, Bismarck had sent a congratulatory note by cable and the same evening, although ill and overworked, attended a dinner in Berlin arranged by George Bancroft, the American ambassador, in celebration of the event. At this dinner he delivered a toast "in German wine . . . to the victorious commander in the service of the United States. . . . This inauguration has a special claim to the sympathetic interest of Prussia." During the Franco-Prussian War, Grant had been an outspoken friend of the German cause, a fact that had raised a storm of objection in France. Grant had the utmost contempt for Louis Napoleon III, whom he had denounced as "usurper and charlatan." Such convictions were heartily endorsed by Bismarck.

The coming of so important a political personage as General Grant gave Bismarck the opportunity to reassert the friendly relations existing between the United States and Germany, although

10. John Russell Young, *Around the World with General Grant* (New York, 1879), I, 412–418.

he was engaged just at this time in pressing duties connected with the Congress of Berlin. As soon as Bismarck heard of Grant's arrival during the latter part of June, he made two calls at the visitor's hotel, but on each occasion found him absent. Finally a meeting was arranged. The American general walked to the Frederick Palace where Bismarck was living. As he entered the courtyard, the sentinels presented arms. A Prussian military man could recognize a soldier. Grant smiled, returned the salute, and walked quietly to the door. Two liveried servants, astonished by the unusual lack of ostentation, which they had not expected of so dignified a person as a former president of the United States, rushed to the huge doors and swung them open.

Bismarck came through the portals and with both hands extended welcomed the American. Clad in an officer's uniform, the chancellor led his visitor into the library. He had expected to meet a much older man, he said, but a comparison of ages showed that Grant was but eleven years Bismarck's junior. "That shows the value of a military life," Bismarck said, "for here you have the frame of a young man, while I feel like an old one." Grant smiled at the compliment, saying that he was at that period of life when one enjoyed being called a young man.

Bismarck sat at a swivel chair in the spacious library, with its walls of gray marble and plain furniture. One of the chancellor's dogs lay cozily on a Turkish rug, eyeing his master devotedly.

Bismarck said that the emperor himself was disappointed in not being able to see the general.

"His Majesty," said the prince, "has been expecting you, and evinces the greatest interest in your achievements, in the distinguished part you have played in the history of your country, and in your visit to Germany. He commands me to say that nothing but his doctor's orders that he shall see no one, prevents his seeing you."

The general said, "I am sorry that I cannot have that honor, but I am far more sorry for the cause, and hope the emperor is recovering."[11]

"All the indications are of the best," answered the prince, "for the emperor has a fine constitution and great courage and endurance, but you know he is a very old man."

11. In May 1878 a would-be assassin had fired at the eighty-year-old emperor, who was out driving. Fortunately, the old man escaped. Three weeks later, from a window in Unter den Linden, a second attempt was made on the emperor's life. This time a Dr. Nobiling, an erratic intellectual, discharged a shotgun at the emperor, who was struck by thirty pellets and seriously wounded. Bismarck insisted that both assailants were Socialists, and he used the incidents to push through his anti-Socialist laws.

"That," said the general, "adds to the horror one feels for the crime."

"It is so strange, so strange and so sad," answered the prince, with marked feeling. "Here is an old man—one of the kindest old gentlemen in the world—and yet they must try and shoot him! There never was a more simple, more genuine, more—what shall I say—more humane character than the emperor's. He is totally unlike men born in his station, or many of them at least. You know that men who come into the world in his rank, born princes, are apt to think themselves of another race and another world. They are apt to take small account of the wishes and feelings of others. All their education tends to deaden the human side. But this emperor is so much of a man in all things! He never did any one a wrong in his life. He never wounded any one's feelings; never imposed a hardship! He is the most genial and winning of men—thinking always, anxious always for the comfort and welfare of his people—of those around him. You cannot conceive a finer type of the noble, courteous, charitable old gentleman, with every high quality of a prince, as well as every virtue of a man. I should have supposed that the emperor could have walked alone all over the empire without harm, and yet they must try and shoot him."

The general said that it was a horrible thing, and referred to Lincoln—a man of the kindest and gentlest nature—killed by an assassin.

"In some respects," said the prince, continuing as if in half a reverie, and as if speaking of a subject upon which he had been thinking a great deal—"in some respects the emperor resembles his ancestor, Frederick William, the father of Frederick the Great. The difference between the two is that the old king would be severe and harsh at times to those around him, while the emperor is never harsh to any one. But the old king had so much simplicity of character, lived an austere, home-loving, domestic life; had all the republican qualities. So with this king; he is so republican in all things that even the most extreme republican if he did his character justice would admire him."

The general answered that the influence which aimed at the emperor's life was an influence that would destroy all government, all order, all society, republics and empires.

"In America," said General Grant, "some of our people are, as I see from the papers, anxious about it. There is only one way to deal with it, and that is by the severest methods. I don't see why a man who commits a crime like this, a crime that not only aims at an old man's life, a ruler's life, but shocks the world, should not meet with the severest punishment. In fact," continued the general, "although at home there is a strong sentiment against the death penalty, and it is a sentiment which one naturally respects, I am not sure but it should be made more severe rather than less severe. Something is due to the offended as well as the offender, especially where the offended is slain."

"That," said the prince, "is entirely my view. My convictions are so strong that I resigned the government of Alsace because I was required to commute sentences of capital nature. I could not do it in justice to my conscience. You see, this kind old gentleman, that emperor whom these very people have tried to kill, is so gentle that he will never confirm a death sentence. Can you think of anything so strange that a sovereign whose tenderness of heart has practically abolished the death punishment should be the victim of assassination, or attempted assassination? That is the fact. Well, I have never agreed with the emperor on this point, and in Alsace, when I found that as chancellor I had to approve all commutations of the death sentence, I resigned. In Prussia that is the work of the minister of justice; in Alsace it devolved upon me. I felt, as the French say, that something was due to justice, and if crimes like these are rampant they must be severely punished."

"All you can do with such people," said the general quietly, "is to kill them."

"Precisely so," answered the prince.

Prince Bismarck said the emperor was especially sorry that he could not in person show General Grant a review, and that the crown prince would give him one. "But," said the prince, "the old gentleman is so much of a soldier and so fond of his army that nothing would give him more pleasure than to display it to so great a soldier as yourself."

The general said that he had accepted the crown prince's invitation to a review for next morning, but with a smile continued: "The truth is I am more of a farmer than a soldier. I take little or no interest in military affairs, and, although I entered the army thirty-five years ago and have been in two wars, in Mexico as a young lieutenant, and later, I never went into the army without regret and never retired without pleasure."

"You are so happily placed," replied the prince, "in America that you need fear no wars. What always seemed so sad to me about your last great war was that you were fighting your own people. That is always so terrible in wars, so very hard."

"But it had to be done," said the general.

"Yes," said the prince, "you had to save the Union just as we had to save Germany."

"Not only save the Union, but destroy slavery," answered the general.

"I suppose, however, the Union was the real sentiment, the dominant sentiment," said the prince.

"In the beginning, yes," said the general; "but as soon as slavery fired upon the flag it was felt, we all felt, even those who did not object to slaves, that slavery must be destroyed. We felt that it was a stain to the Union that men should be bought and sold like cattle."

"I had an old and good friend, an American, in Motley," said the prince, "who used to write me now and then. Well, when your war broke out he wrote me. He said, 'I will make a prophecy, and please take this letter and put it in a tree or a box for ten years, then open it and see if I am not a prophet. I prophesy that when this war ends the Union will be established and we shall not lose a village or a hamlet.' This was Motley's prophecy," said the prince, with a smile, "and it was true."

"Yes," said the general, "it was true."

"I suppose if you had had a large army at the beginning of the war it would have ended in a much shorter time."

"We might have had no war at all," said the general; "but we cannot tell. Our war had many strange features—there were many things which seemed odd enough at the time, but which now seem providential. If we had had a large regular army, as it was then constituted, it might have gone with the South. In fact, the Southern feeling in the army among high officers was so strong that when the war broke out the army dissolved. We had no army—then we had to organize one. A great commander like Sherman or Sheridan even then might have organized an army and put down the rebellion in six months or a year, or, at the farthest, two years. But that would have saved slavery, perhaps, and slavery meant the germs of new rebellion. There had to be an end of slavery. Then we were fighting an enemy with whom we could not make a peace. We had to destroy him. No convention, no treaty was possible—only destruction."

"It was a long war," said the prince, "and a great work well done —and I suppose it means a long peace."

"I believe so," said the general.

The prince asked the general when he might have the pleasure of seeing Mrs. Grant. The general answered that she would receive him at any convenient hour.

"Then," said the prince, "I will come tomorrow before the Congress meets."

Both gentlemen arose, and the general renewed the expression of his pleasure at having seen a man who was so well known and so highly esteemed in America.

"General," answered the prince, "the pleasure and the honor are mine. Germany and America have always been in such friendly relationship that nothing delights us more than to meet Americans, and especially an American who has done so much for his country, and whose name is so much honored in Germany as your own."

The prince and the general walked side by side to the door, and after shaking hands the general passed into the square. The guard presented arms, the general lit a fresh cigar, and slowly strolled home.

"I am glad I have seen Bismarck," the general remarked. "He is a man whose manner and bearing fully justify the opinions one forms of him. What he says about the emperor was beautifully said, and should be known to all the Germans and those who esteem Germany."

56 To Prevent a General European Conflagration, Bismarck Calls the Congress of Berlin in 1878 and Acts as an "Honest Broker" between Quarreling Russia and Great Britain

"Bismarck is an amazing man."

In late 1877, Russia, in line with her policy of Pan-Slavism, attacked in the Balkans. The Russo-Turkish War of 1877–1878 was ended by the Treaty of San Stefano, which left Constantinople to the Turks but took from them most of the rest of the Balkan peninsula. The British, who in 1853–1856 had gone to war against Russia in the Crimea to prevent this kind of Russian penetration into the Mediterranean, refused to accept the settlement of San Stefano. Europe was on the verge of another great war. In this dangerous situation Bismarck, who regarded the preservation of peace at this time as vital for Germany, offered Berlin as a seat for a congress over which he would preside. He became, as he informed the Reichstag, an "honest broker" between the powers. The leading world's statesmen came to Berlin to revise the Treaty of San Stefano and achieve a balance in southeastern Europe. The main lines of the settlement lasted for thirty years, but Russia, forced to relinquish some of her booty, thereafter blamed Bismarck for it. The lighter side of the Congress of Berlin was described in Bismarck's Table Talk.[12]

"As for the Treaty of San Stefano," said Bismarck, "I think the whole situation might thus be summed up: Russia has swallowed more than she can digest, and the Congress must try to give her relief."

At the close of the Congress, the chancellor remarked to Lord Salisbury: "I have conducted this conference sometimes like a gentleman, and sometimes like a sergeant-major." . . .

About the beginning of its sittings, Bismarck, the "honest broker," the president of the Congress, gave a dinner to the members, the parole on this occasion being, "Not a word of politics!" And yet the Greek minister, M. Rhangabé, deftly succeeded in evading this rule, and in giving full expression to the national aspirations of his countrymen. The *menu,* like the music, was of an international character, and there was one course of vegetables *"à la Macédonie."* On this dish being handed round, M. Rhangabé passed it on without helping himself.

"But, Excellency, why don't you take some Macedonia?" asked Bismarck, to whom the Greek minister sat opposite.

"Only *some,* your Serene Highness? Why, I should like the whole of it!"

The crown prince wished to give a farewell "peace-dinner" to the members, and Bismarck took occasion to ask Lord Beaconsfield whether the next Thursday would suit him for this purpose.

"Your Highness already speaks of peace and parting, but is that not selling the bear's skin before it is killed?"

"Well," rejoined the chancellor, "it is for you to kill the bear" [Russia].

"That is precisely what I mean to do," replied the British premier.

Some time after the Congress, Herr von Dietze-Barby asked Bismarck which of the plenipotentiaries he regarded as the first diplomatist.

"Ah, that I cannot tell you," answered the chancellor; "but certainly the second was Lord Beaconsfield."

Shortly after the Congress, Lord Ampthill was conversing with Bismarck on the character of the first English plenipotentiary, when the chancellor pointed out that the only three works of art which adorned his room were portraits of his wife, the emperor, and Lord Beaconsfield!

12. *Bismarck's Table Talk,* ed. by Charles Lowe (London, 1895), pp. 250–255.

On the other hand this was what was written by Bayard Taylor, American minister in Berlin: "I made the acquaintance of all the members of the Congress. After Gortschakoff . . . I was most impressed by Beaconsfield. . . . But Bismarck is still a head higher than all these. . . . Think of seeing and talking with Bismarck, Gortchakoff, Beaconsfield, Andrassy, Waddington, Mehemet Ali Pasha, Curtius, Mommsen, Lepsius, Helmholtz, Grant, etc., etc., the same day! They are all pleasant and accessible people, but Bismarck is an amazing man."

And again: "Yesterday, when I had my first interview with Bismarck, he began with, 'I read one of your books through with my wife during my late illness.' I passed an hour with him alone, in the garden behind the palace, and felt in ten minutes as if I had known him for years. I was astounded at the freedom with which he spoke, but I shall honor his confidence, and say nothing for years to come. . . .

"On Saturday I had an hour's talk with Bismarck in the garden behind his palace; he being accompanied by a huge black dog, and I by a huge brown bitch. I tell you he is a *great* man! We talked only of books, birds, and trees, but the man's deepest nature opened now and then, and I saw his very self."

At one of his parliamentary *soirées* shortly before the outbreak of the war, which was followed by the Berlin Congress, Bismarck said that he had known exactly for two years already how the Eastern question could best be solved.

At this there was a sudden silence in the room, and all pricked up their ears to listen. But this silence was followed by peals of laughter when the prince added:

"At the same time, as Germany has no interest in the Eastern question, I would rather say nothing about it."

Indeed, according to the chancellor, the direct interest of Germany in this question was so slight as not to be worth "the healthy bones of a Pomeranian musketeer"; and that was why he did all he could to limit the area of the inevitable war to Russia and Turkey. As for England's intervention, he did not see that much could come of it. He might compare a struggle between England and Russia to a fight between a fish and a wolf—or rather, between a whale and a bear—which never could get at each other properly, and had to use long poles for the purpose—a metaphor of a rather mixed kind.

The only thing that could induce Germany to abandon her attitude of strict neutrality would be the necessity of going to the assistance of Austria should this power see fit to take the field against Russia, and be worsted in the encounter. Germany could never stand idly by and behold Austria receive a deadly or even a dangerous wound. The maintenance of this state was an absolute necessity for the balance of power in Europe, and in no circumstances could Germany afford to let its integrity be impaired. The German provinces were the cornerstone of the dual monarchy, which could not hold together but for these, and hence the stupidity of those who represented him as hankering after these provinces for Germany. No; these provinces were as absolutely necessary for the stability of the dual monarchy as the continuance of this monarchy was essential to the safety of the general situation in Europe, so let him hear no more about his own lust of conquest in this direction. Friendship with Russia if possible, but friendship with Austria at all costs—such, in brief, was the principle which would always determine his attitude to the Eastern question.

"First of all," he said, upon another occasion of the same kind, "we have to look after our own interests, then those of Austria which coincide with ours; and after that we must continue to live on as good a footing as may be with Russia." Volumes could not have better expressed the chancellor's principles of international policy.

Bismarck followed the war with the critical glance of a soldier, as well as with the vigilant eye of a diplomatist. "If I were the tsar," he remarked after Plevna, when the fortune of arms seemed to be against the Russians, "I would lead my troops back to the left bank of the Danube, and there remain for the winter. I would, however, at the same time issue a manifesto to the powers declaring that, if necessary, I was prepared to continue the war for seven years, even if I should be reduced to carry it on with peasants armed with dungforks and flails. I would then begin next spring by taking a few of the large fortresses on the Danube, and gradually work my way farther."

Talking with Dr. Carl Braun of Wiesbaden, Bismarck remarked: "Frederick the Great used to say of Kaiser Joseph II that he always wanted to take a second step before finishing his first. Take care that the same isn't said of us. Germany has great tasks—above all things, that of preserving the peace of Europe. This must be our guiding principle in the Eastern crisis."

67 The Jews: Bismarck Overcomes the Prejudice of His Youth and Disassociates Himself from Irrational Anti-Semitism

"I am no enemy of the Jews."

Bismarck was aware of his prejudices: "I have sucked them in with my mother's milk." In the United Diet of 1847 he spoke against the complete civil emancipation of the Jews. Yet two decades later he promoted a law for Jewish emancipation. Somewhere between these years he cast off the bigotry of his early life. Now he began to see the Jews in another light: he extolled them for their conjugal fidelity, respect for parents, and usefulness in society. He advocated marriage between the Prussian nobility and Jews: rather than have Jewish males marry into Junker families, he thought it best "if one brought together a conjunction of a Christian stallion of German breed with a Jewish mare." He entrusted both his health and property to Jewish professional men. Drs. Cohen and Schweninger, both Jewish physicians, were devoted friends. The Jewish banker Gerson von Bleichröder acted as Bismarck's confidential business agent and had the power of attorney for administering Bismarckian property. By no means was the chancellor responsible for rising anti-Semitism in Germany, although Hitler's propagandists took his words out of context to prove his anti-Semitism. The following accounts are closer to the truth.

Moritz Busch: Bismarck on the Jews [13]

We must now endeavor to render intelligible the attitude assumed by the chancellor towards the Jews and the Jewish question recently brought upon the *tapis* anew; to which end the best we can do is to let him speak for himself.

In the first United Diet on June 15th, 1847, . . . he declared himself opposed to the unrestricted emancipation of the Jews. "I am no enemy of the Jews," he said; "and should they be foes of mine, I forgive them. I even like them—under certain circumstances. I would also accord to them every imaginable right, except that of holding authoritative office in a Christian realm." The idea that a Jew might be qualified to encounter him in the capacity of

13. Busch, *Bismarck: Sketches for a Historical Picture*, trans. Beatty-Kingston, I, 149–153.

a representative of his Majesty the King produced a depressing and discouraging effect upon him. He must, however, have found it necessary to become reconciled to this idea later on, although I do not suppose he has ever quite liked it; for he offered no opposition to the measures granting equality of rights to Jew and Christian, incorporated, firstly, in the constitution of the North German Confederation, and secondly, in that of the German Empire; indeed, he supported them, although we can scarcely imagine that they enlisted his sympathies to any great extent. Sitting at table with us in Ferrières, on September 25, 1870, he said (speaking of the Jews):—"As a matter of fact they have no real home. So to speak, they are European in a general sort of way; cosmopolitans—in a word, nomads. Their fatherland is Zion (here he turned towards Abeken), Jerusalem. Outside that, they belong, as it were, to the whole world, and hang together all over the earth. The petty Jew alone experiences anything like a feeling of local patriotism. Among Hebrews of that class may be found some decent, honest people. There was one such in my part of the country (Pomeranian) who dealt in skins and such matters. His affairs could not have been very flourishing, for he became a bankrupt. Upon that occasion he came to me, begging me to let him off easy and not to take out proceedings upon my claim against him, for he would surely pay me what he owed, a little at a time, as soon as he could. As had been my wont of old in such cases, I agreed to his proposal; and he really *did* pay up. Long after, when I was envoy to the Confederation at Frankfort I was still receiving installments from him at intervals; and I believe that I lost far less by him than did his other creditors—if, indeed, I lost anything at all. Perhaps there are not many Jews of that sort to be found nowadays.

"Even Jews, however, have their good qualities; they are renowned for respect to their parents, conjugal fidelity and benevolence." On December 19th, 1870, after having been for a drive about the environs of Versailles with Simson (afterwards president of the Imperial Supreme Tribunal), he observed to us:—"I thought he would have taken some interest in the park and its pretty views; but he manifested none whatsoever. It seems that he has no sense of the picturesque. That is the case with a vast number of Jews. As far as I know there are no Jewish landscape painters, and but few Jewish painters of any description." Meyerheim and Bendemann were mentioned. "Yes," he replied, "I grant you Meyerheim; but it was only Bendemann's grandfather and grandmother who were Jews. There have been plenty of Jewish composers—Meyerbeer, Mendelssohn, Halévy; but as for painters—well, a Jew will paint, but only in case he is not compelled to get his living by his brush." A few days later (December 23rd) we were all talking at table about the arrests of Social Democratic demagogues which had taken place in Germany a short while previously, and Count Lehndorff asked if anything serious was to be apprehended from the imprisonment of Bebel and Liebknecht—if it might be expected to arouse a great deal of excitement? "No," replied the chancellor, "there is nothing to be feared on that score." Lehndorff: "But Jacoby's arrest gave rise to no end of noise and clamor." The chancellor: "He was a Jew and a Königsberger. If you only catch hold of a Jew, forthwith an outcry arises from every nook and corner."

Shortly afterwards (January 10th, 1871) the conversation at table turned upon the names Meier and Kohn, of common occurrence among the Jews, and I offered an explanation of that circumstance, winding up with the remark that the patronymic Kohn (originally signifying a priest) had now and then suffered transformation into Kuhn, Kahn and Hahn.

This brought the chancellor to the subject of Jews who had been converted to Christianity, and later on to that of mixed marriages between Christians and Jews—of which he seemed not to disapprove. "Indeed," he continued, "I am of opinion that Jews must be improved by crossing their breed. The results are really not so bad." He mentioned a few noble families which had assimilated Semitic blood by marrying some of their male members to Jewesses, and added, "They are all quite intelligent, nice people." Then, after reflecting awhile—omitting to give words to a passing thought anent the union of noble Christian damsels, German baronesses and countesses, to wealthy and talented Israelites—he added with a smile: "On the whole it is better the other way—I mean, by the conjunction of a Christian stallion of German breed with a Jewish mare. The Jews' money is thus brought into circulation again; and the result of the cross is a very fair breed. I really do not know what I shall advise my sons to do, one of these days." This was a jocular utterance *inter pocula,* but not altogether devoid of a serious *substratum.* It certainly did not justify the assumption that the chancellor entertains any prejudices against the Semitic race.

Of late years the Jewish question has been again and again *à l'ordre du jour,* and voices have been publicly heard to recommend the partial abrogation of the civil and political rights conceded to the Israelites by the constitution; but the chancellor has forborne from giving utterance in public to his views with respect to the agitation in question, its causes and aims. We have reason to believe, however, that the anti-Semitic movement appeared to him by no means difficult to account for, but somewhat untimely, and therefore inconvenient. That was the opinion expressed in tolerably plain words by the *Norddeutsche Allgemeine Zeitung*, which also observed that the Jews were indebted to the chancellor for his assistance in obtaining their emancipation, but failed to display any gratitude towards him—on the contrary, for the most part they sustained and strengthened the opposition in its hostility to his policy. It is well known that this assertion is correct. The prince himself once repeated it to me in the course of private conversation, with the remark: "Men who own property of any kind pay their taxes, abstain from writing democratical leading articles, and do not frequent barricades. It is the other sort of people that does these things."

Heinrich von Poschinger: Conversation on the Jews [14]

He did not see any way by which the aims of the anti-Semites might be realized. If one questioned them about the practical execution of their plans, they became like the Social Democrats; they were unable to propose anything that could be practically carried out; their recipes were not applicable to the organism of the state of today. Moreover, what could one do? Measures like Bartholomew's Eve or the Sicilian Vespers could hardly be proposed even by the anti-Semites themselves. Nor could the Jews be expelled without grave injury to the national welfare. Any measures by which the Jews would be excluded from judicial and other positions in the state would only increase the evil which the anti-Semites thought they had to do away with. For then the same Jewish intelligence, to which public careers would be closed, would embrace those fields in which the overweight of the Jews is already said by the anti-Semites to be intolerable, *i.e.* those of commerce.

The prince then stated his opinion that the Jewish movement sprang less from religious and social instincts than from economic reasons. He mentioned as a fact that the Jews are greatly superior to the other elements of the population in making money. Their superiority rests on qualities which, whether they are pleasing or not, cannot be removed by measures of state. The Jews, by reason of their natural dispositions, were generally more clever and skillful than Christians. They were also, at any rate so long as they had not made their fortunes, if perhaps not more industrious at least more frugal and saving than their Christian competitors. To this must be added the fact that the Jew would risk something

14. *Conversations with Bismarck,* collected by Heinrich von Poschinger, ed. by Sidney Whitman (New York and London, 1900), pp. 164–166.

more readily once in a way in order to gain a commercial advantage, and in applying his methods to gain his object, would also act more kindheartedly than his Christian competitor. All this gives him an advantage in commerce which could not legally be taken away. Even the anti-Semites had up till then been unable to suggest anything which might paralyze this advantage and its effect on the economic life of the nation. Their proposals had hitherto been impracticable, and no government would be found able to carry them out. It was also inadvisable for the state to put obstacles in the way of the pursuit of gain and fortune, for the other elements of the population would thereby suffer equally, and the national wealth would decrease.

It is not necessary on that account to allow the Jews to dominate, or to make one's self dependent on them financially, as is the case in some states. In his own dealings, as a minister, with the *haute finance,* he had always placed them under an obligation to him.

He considered the Jews to be useful members of the state of today, and thought it unwise to molest them. The rich Jew especially was generally a regular taxpayer and a good subject.

Finally the prince spoke about his personal relations with Jews, and remarked *inter alia* that he had really reaped ingratitude at their hands. No statesman had done more for their emancipation than he had; yet, in spite of this, it was just the progressive and radical papers, in the hands of the Jews, which attacked him most violently. But he did not take that too much to heart; the reason was, probably, that the owners of the papers considered it due to their liberal or radical spirit not to allow the memory of that, for which they as Jews had to thank him, to influence the attitude of their papers with regard to him and his policy.

58 Battle of the Bulging Waistline: The Man of Gargantuan Appetite Finds It Difficult to Control His Desire for Food and Drink with Predictable Repercussions

"Just as you told me . . . a couple of bottles each day with my dinner."

All his life Bismarck was indiscreet in matters of food and drink. He was good at rationalizing his weaknesses: he insisted that he could sleep only after eating large quantities of caviar to promote thirst. One visitor to his home reported that, while complaining of bad digestion, he ate in order: soup, eels, cold meat, prawns, lobsters, smoked meat, raw ham, roast meat, and pudding.[15]

[Bismarck] admitted smilingly that his appetite was hereditary. "In our family we are all large eaters. If there were many of the same capacity in the country the state could not exist; I should emigrate. . . . I admit that I eat too much, or rather too much at one time. I cannot rid myself of the folly of having only one meal in the day. Formerly it was even worse, for then I only drank tea in the early morning and ate nothing at all until 5 P.M., though I smoked incessantly, and that did me a great deal of harm. By doctor's advice I now eat at least two eggs in the morning and smoke but little. But I am to have several meals—today one and a half beefsteaks and a few slices of pheasant. That sounds rather much, but it is not much, for as a rule it is my only meal. I breakfast, it is true, but the meal only consists of two eggs and a cup of tea without milk. After that nothing till the evening. If I eat a quantity then I am like a boa constrictor, but I cannot sleep."

Looking at the menu one day he laughingly remarked, "There's always one dish too many. I am resolved to ruin my digestion with duck and olives, and now there is Rheinfelder ham, of which I must now eat too much for fear of not getting my share (the chancellor was absent from breakfast that day, December 22, 1870), and there is also wild boar from Varzin." Ham seems to have been a favorite dish of the chancellor, for on another occasion when he was to dine with the crown prince, he remained at his own table until the Varzin ham was brought in, having told the footman, "Bring it in while I am here; it must be consumed with my cooperation—with thoughts of home." . . .

"I could eat marenas every day, in fact I almost prefer them to trout, which I only like when they are medium-sized, about half a pound in weight. There is not much to be said in praise of the large ones, which it was customary to serve at the Frankfort dinners. They generally come from the Heidelberg Wolfsbrunnen, and are expensive enough, so they must appear on the menu."

Good mutton and brisket of beef were among the favorite dishes of the prince's table, while filet and roast beef were not much relished. Of hares he observed, "A French hare is really nothing in comparison to a Pomeranian hare; it does not taste like game at all. How different are our hares which get their good flavor from heather and thyme."

15. *Ibid.*, pp. 270–273.

At the time the Parisians were compelled to turn to horses and other animals for their food, Bismarck inquired one day at table, "Is that *du cheval?*" and on receiving the answer that it was honest ox, continued, "It is curious that one does not eat horseflesh unless compelled to, like the people in Paris who soon will have little else to eat. The probable reason is because the horse is more akin to us than other animals. As a rider, we are, as it were, a part of it. It's the same with the dog. *Du chien* is said to taste quite nice, and yet we don't eat it. The more familiar a thing is to us the less we like to eat it. It must be very disgusting to eat monkeys, whose hands look human! Neither does one care to eat *carnivora*—animals of prey, wolves, lions, even bears; though the latter live less on flesh than on plants. I do not even like to eat a chicken that has been fed on meat—not even its eggs."

Bismarck's favorite fruit was cherries, and blue plums stood next in his estimation. As the Gruyère was being handed round, some one asked the chancellor whether cheese and wine went well together. "Different kinds to different wines," was the reply; "sharp tasting cheeses, like Gorgonzola and Dutch cheese, do not, but others certainly do. At the time when there was much drinking in Pomerania, two centuries ago, the Rammin family were the hardest drinkers. One of them got some wine from Stettin which he did not care about, and so he complained to the wine merchant. He received the following reply, 'Eat cheese with your wine, Herr von Rammin; the wine will then taste the same in Rammin as it does in Stettin.'" This anecdote led to the subject of drinks in general. When the chancellor and his staff were in St. Avold, the possibility of finding themselves without beer was mooted, but Bismarck thought that would not be a great loss. "The vastly increasing consumption of beer is to be deprecated. Beer makes a man stupid, lazy, and incapable. It is the cause of all the democratic political discussions to which men listen. A good corn brandy would be preferable." A glass of brandy at dinner reminded the chancellor of the following *dictum:* "Lately—if I am not mistaken it was at Ferrières—a general enunciated the following maxim regarding the beverages of mankind: claret for children, champagne for men, brandy for generals."

Andrew W. White, American ambassador to Germany from 1879 to 1881, was in a good position to hear the gossip of diplomatic circles in Berlin. He, like many others, was entranced by the stories of Bismarck's appetite. In his autobiography White repeated two stories he had heard from Dr. Rudolf von Gneist, Professor of Roman Law at the University of Berlin.[16]

Among the striking characteristics of Bismarck was his evident antipathy to ceremonial. He was never present at any of the great court functions save the first reception given at the golden wedding of the Emperor William I, and at the gala opera a few evenings afterward.

The reason generally assigned for this abstention was that the chancellor, owing to his increasing weight and weakness, could not remain long on his feet, as people are expected to do on such occasions. Nor do I remember seeing him at any of the festivities attending the marriage of the present Emperor William, who was then merely the son of the crown prince. One reason for his absence, perhaps, was his reluctance to take part in the *Fackeltanz,* a most curious survival. In this ceremony, the ministers of Prussia, in full gala dress, with flaring torches in their hands, precede the bride or the groom, as the case may be, as he or she solemnly marches around the great white hall of the palace, again and again, to the sound of solemn music. The bride first goes to the foot of the throne, and is welcomed by the emperor, who gravely leads her once around the hall, and then takes his seat. The groom then approaches the throne, and invites the empress to march solemnly around the room with him in the same manner, and she complies with his request. Then the bride takes the royal prince next in importance, who, in this particular case, happened to be the prince of Wales, at present King Edward VII; the groom, the next princess; and so on, until each of the special envoys from the various monarchs of Europe has gone through this solemn function. So it is that the ministers, some of them nearly eighty years of age, march around the room perhaps a score of times; and it is very easy to understand that Bismarck preferred to avoid such an ordeal.

From time to time, the town, and even the empire, was aroused by news that he was in a fit of illness or ill nature, and insisting on resigning. On such occasions the old emperor generally drove to the chancellor's palace in the Wilhelmstrasse, and, in his large, kindly, hearty way, got the great man out of bed, put him in good humor, and set him going again. On one of these occasions, happening to meet Rudolf von Gneist, who had been, during a part of Bismarck's career, on very confidential terms with him, I asked what the real trouble was. "Oh," said Gneist, "he has eaten too

16. *Autobiography of Andrew D. White* (New York, 1905), I, 589–591.

many plover's eggs (*Ach, er hat zu viel Kibitzeier gegessen*)." This had reference to the fact that certain admirers of the chancellor in the neighborhood of the North Sea were accustomed to send him, each year, a large basket of plover's eggs, of which he was very fond; and this diet has never been considered favorable to digestion.

This reminds me that Gneist on one occasion told me another story, which throws some light on the chancellor's habits. Gneist had especial claims on Americans. As the most important professor of Roman law at the university, he had welcomed a long succession of American students; as a member of the imperial parliament, of the Prussian legislature, and of the Berlin town council, he had shown many kindnesses to American travelers; and as the representative of the Emperor William in the arbitration between the United States and Great Britain on our northwestern boundary, he had proved a just judge, deciding in our favor. Therefore it was that, on the occasion of one of the great Thanksgiving dinners celebrated by the American colony, he was present as one of the principal guests. Near him was placed a bottle of Hermitage, rather a heavy, heady wine. Shortly after taking his seat, he said to me, with a significant smile, "That is some of the wine I sent to Bismarck, and it did not turn out well." "How was that?" I asked. "Well," he said, "one day I met Bismarck and asked him about his health. He answered, 'It is wretched; I can neither eat nor sleep.' I replied, 'Let me send you something that will help you. I have just received a lot of Hermitage, and will send you a dozen bottles. If you take a *couple of glasses* each day with your dinner, it will be the best possible tonic, and will do you great good.' Sometime afterward," continued Gneist, "I met him again, and asked how the wine agreed with him. 'Oh,' said Bismarck, 'not at all; it made me worse than ever.' 'Why,' said I, 'how did you take it?' 'Just as you told me,' replied Bismarck, '*a couple of bottles* each day with my dinner.' "

All this, of course, had a deleterious effect on Bismarck's health. From September 1880 to October 1884, the Hamburger physician, Dr. Eduard Cohen, acted as family doctor for the Bismarcks. In this capacity he kept careful records of his most important patient, then in his mid-sixties. Following are excerpts from Dr. Cohen's records.[17]

17. Condensed from *Aufzeichnungen von Dr. E. Cohen*, unpublished papers in Hamburg ownership, as quoted in *Bismarck: Die gesammelten Werke*, VIII, ed. by Willy Andreas (Berlin, 1926), 376, 384, 389, 404, 448, 474, 480, 484, 496, 512. Translated by the editor.

September 16, 1880: Bismarck said that it was a wonder that his nervous system had not been ruined.—As a sixteen-year-old student, and as a seventeen-year-old at the university, he lived recklessly, drank much, and carried on this way until his marriage. He drained his emotions in eighteen years of politics. In St. Petersburg as ambassador he was exasperated by Prussian politics—he often wrote reports until four in the morning, and on many occasions he was distressed to tears—later, continuous friction with the king, the court, and the Free Masons. In 1866 he made enormous efforts to get the king to go along with him. At Nikolsburg terrible battles with the generals. Same thing in Paris.

November 2, 1880: Bismarck in a good mood—he has slept well for two nights and has had no more heartburn. But he protests that his diet takes the joy out of life. He had hoped to be like his father, who at the age of seventy-five could still go hunting and could hold his own in drinking.

December 5, 1880: Bismarck on doctors. He can't stand them, because they always make a mountain out of a molehill. It had a political tinge: because if the sick man dies, then the doctor has predicted it, but if he became well, then the doctor has made a marvelous cure. Then he can't give anatomical details about the illness, because that only makes the patient more nervous.

December 13, 1880: Only a short conversation. Bismarck in extraordinarily good condition, almost merry because today he was able to do some heavy physical duties with complete ease. He feels as elastic and strong as he did years ago.

April 3, 1881 [*in Berlin*]*:* Bismarck seems very well, but complains about weakness in his legs. He recently had a heavy catarrh.

May 12, 1882: Bismarck feels that he has become older and that his bodily machine won't respond any more. He intends to stop the type of life he has been leading, and would be quite happy to devote whatever energy he has left to writing his reminiscences. He recently proposed to the emperor that he be made an adjutant general and be relieved of his ministry. The emperor smilingly replied: "Then where will I get a new minister?"

July 5, 1883: The prince just returned two days ago from Berlin to Friedrichsruh. He suffers miserably from a cold in the stomach and jaundice. Doesn't talk much, but complains continually about the political parties.

October 13, 1883: Bismarck very cheerful and talkative.

November 1, 1883: Bismarck quite ill. Did not come to the table to eat. Very upset about court intrigues by people who have no political sense. He loves his Fatherland too much to allow stupidities to happen. The emperor has little to do with it, but the crown princess is behind it with her marriage plans for her daughter.

November 5, 1883: Although I had an appointment to make my visit today, I found Schweninger[18] there. Bismarck told me when I arrived that his wife had written to Schweninger yesterday and bid him come; he himself had not known that I was to make my visit that day. At this the princess said: "You must have misunderstood or forgotten, because we certainly talked about it." From that I got the impression that Bismarck himself had arranged the invitation to Schweninger, and now was shifting the blame to his wife. The reason was simple—to allow morphine to be injected, which I opposed and which Schweninger immediately executed. I made no secret of my resentment about the recklessness of this procedure, and I was silent in a very obvious way. I left with the words: "I can only leave my good wishes with you." Bismarck did not respond to that, and his face seemed glum and dark. That was, indeed, my last professional visit.

December 14, 1883: On December 12 I got a telegram signed by Bismarck himself in which he invited me to dine with him on either the 13th or 14th. The princess received me with extraordinary kindness and surprised me with the gift of a Lenbach sketch of her husband, signed by the prince. While I was thanking her, Bismarck came in and said that he was delighted that the picture gave me pleasure. Both were so completely friendly and warm that I could only have the impression that they wanted to make up for the lack of consideration they had shown me [on November 5].

October 11, 1884: Invited to dinner with Count Wilhelm Bismarck.[19] Bismarck extraordinarily cheerful, loquacious, and friendly, seems well, but he has put on weight.[20]

18. Dr. Ernst Schweninger took over responsibility for Bismarck's health. (See pages 291–293.)
19. Bismarck's second son, Bill.
20. Dr. Cohen died shortly after this entry.

69

Press Agent Moritz Busch Describes His Master's Rib-tickling Humor and Penchant for Practical Jokes

"I sought consolation in some capital beer."

Bismarck's Boswell was press agent Moritz Busch, who painstakingly put on paper everything he heard in the great man's presence. A cheerful man, Busch found Bismarck excruciatingly funny. To present-day readers these examples of Bismarck's humor may seem a bit heavy-handed and ponderous, but to Busch they revealed a jovial Falstaffian disposition. Certainly they show another side of the Bismarckian personality.[21]

In private conversation the chancellor does not always give his thoughts expression fluently and in well-arranged, smooth sentences, especially when serious matters are in question. But he is an admirable *raconteur*. The rich humoristic vein that runs through his nature, his keen perception of the comic aspects of men and things, a certain frivolous turn, sometimes *naif* and sometimes sly, his capacity for taking a semi-ironical, semi-jovial view of circumstances, events and persons, make him the most agreeable *causeur* that ever entertained a company *inter pocula* or by the fireside. Many of his letters are real gems of fanciful narrative and description.

I subjoin a selection of his utterances, illustrating the above characteristics, which will prove that as a humorist, Bismarck need not fear comparison with the best of his contemporaries in that line. He has no faculty for punning, much practiced by our Jewish jesters and appreciated by the masses, but in reality, a very distant connection of true humor. His humor is rather that of the people; but he is not averse to *jeux de mots,* for he takes notice of the Berlin comic papers, and frequently alludes to their jokes in conversation.

Once, when a referendary, he observed with reference to some unfair expropriation, "No money will compensate me for the conversion of my father's park into a carp pond, or, of my deceased aunt's grave into an eel swamp." The position of certain Pom-

21. Busch, *Bismarck: Sketches for a Historical Picture,* trans. Beatty-Kingston, II, 248–257.

eranian districts being under discussion, he said: "The principality of Cammin hangs over that of Belgard like a pair of breeches." During one of his parliamentary evening parties he remarked: "While I was sitting opposite the Emperor Napoleon for nearly an hour in the parlor of the weaver's cottage at Donchery, I felt exactly like a young man at a ball who has engaged a girl for the *cotillon,* has not a word to say to her, and heartily wishes that someone would take her away." As I was taking leave of him for some considerable time in March 1873, he said to me: "My health, indeed, is by no means good. Last year I was away for nearly six months, but to no purpose. I am not what I was of old—only the Ziska-drum, you know, nothing but skin and noise." While we were fishing one afternoon at Varzin the prince, pointing to me, said to Privy-Councillor Tiedemann: "Stuff in the loop of his coat collar that is sticking out; he looks as if he ought to be hung up by it, which he has not deserved to be." In April 1878, when the chancellor wished to resign office he indicated his feelings towards his projects of economic and social-political reform as follows: "I am like a weary hunter who has been following the chase all day long without result, and who, worn out and faint with fatigue, sinks to the ground and resolves to give up sport altogether. All of a sudden the beaters light upon a couple of splendid boars; forthwith his old passion revives in his breast; he springs to his feet as fresh as ever, and hurries off to the chase anew. It is thus with me just now. Weary of business that I cannot get transacted, and worried by unproductive colleagues, I would fain have done with the whole thing and go home. But, were any of the departmental ministers to bring me a really good scheme, I would take to my work again with renewed vigor and energy." Speaking to me (March 1880) about the Russian attempt to conspire against us with the French government through General Obrutscheff, he observed: "But the French would not have it, and told us all about it, just as a virtuous woman tells her husband when anybody makes indecent proposals to her." With reference to a personage supposed to be a candidate for the premiership of a ministry *in nubibus,* he said: "There are plenty of candidates for the chancellorship, because it is such an easy post to fill! That reminds me of what happened when the elector of Hesse sent his body surgeon to Bernburg to find what was the intellectual condition of the last reigning duke. The doctor found his Highness worse than he had expected, and reported on his return that the duke had become an idiot. 'Good God! an idiot'; exclaimed the elector, 'why then he is incapable of reigning.' 'Oh, he can reign well enough for all that!' rejoined the doctor." He then reverted to the opposition offered to him on all sides during his eighteen years' tenure of office: "Sometimes they attacked me several at a time, and from all quarters. My position was like that of Gerstæcker, as depicted in a comic paper, when an anaconda, a lion, a crocodile and a bear were all making for him simultaneously, and he was exclaiming 'What a capital article for the *Augsburger Allgemeine Zeitung*!' But, seriously speaking, I am not good enough for these people, who fancy they know every thing better than I do, and think my successor would manage things so much more cleverly. *Contenti estote,* make the best of your black bread!"

I could add to the above many striking remarks made by the prince in the course of conversations with me, but must keep them by me, with other matters of the sort, until they shall become powerless to harm any one.

A fountain of wit and humor sparkles in many of Bismarck's letters, as well as throughout his speeches. He wrote to Manteuffel in December 1854: "It is not easy to keep touch with General von Reitzenstein; he sits stiffly upon his lieutenant general's horse, and is much exercised respecting the independence of his position." A year later he wrote to Gerlach: "Unless we get hold of the helm of German politics forthwith, the ship will be driven into a French harbor by the breeze of Austrian intimidation and the tide of Western influence, we playing the part of a mutinous cabin boy." Again, writing to Manteuffel upon the subject of Austria's policy, he observed: "The Vienna cabinet will play the part of Don Juan to all the other cabinets, if it can secure the services of so sturdy a Leporello as Prussia; true to that *rôle,* it will always contrive to get out of scrapes at our cost, and leave us in them." . . .

In a letter to his sister, complaining of all sorts of country life grievances, he says: "There is Johann outside steadfastly whistling an infamous *Schottische* out of tune and I am not hard-hearted enough to tell him to leave off, because he is doubtless endeavoring to assuage the pain of his love-sorrows by music. The ideal of his dreams was recently persuaded by her parents to marry a wheelwright." On another occasion he wrote to the same person: "Yesterday I looked on at a dance in Plathe and drank a lot of Montebello; the former gave me acidity in the stomach, the latter cramp in the calves." Again, complaining of being coerced into taking his family to the seaside, he wrote: "Johanna (his wife) who is just now reposing in the arms of Lieutenant Morpheus, will have told you what awaits me. The boy yelling in the major, the girl in the minor, two singing nursemaids all over wet napkins and feeding bottles; myself in the character of an affectionate *paterfamilias.* I fought against it long, but, as all the mothers and aunts were agreed that nothing would do poor little Mary any good but salt water and sea air, had I positively refused I should have been compelled to listen to reproaches for my meanness and paternal barbarity—such as 'You see how it is! If the poor child had only been allowed to get the benefit of the sea!' every time my daughter might happen to catch a cold up to her seventieth year."

Concerning a trip on the Danube between Gran and Pesth in the summer of 1852, he wrote to his wife: "Picture to yourself Odenwald and the Taunus close together, and the interval filled up with Danube water. The shady side of the voyage was the sunny side; for it was burning hot enough to make Tokay grow upon the deck, and there was a crowd of passengers; but, only imagine, no English. They cannot have discovered Hungary yet." Writing the same evening from the Royal Castle at Ofen, he observed: "May angels watch over you! In my case a bearskinned grenadier is doing so. I see six inches of his bayonet sticking up above the windowsill, two arms' lengths off. He is standing on the terrace overlooking the Danube, and probably thinking of his Nanny." In Amsterdam the chimney pots struck him as resembling "men standing upon their heads and stretching out their legs wide apart," and Holland itself as "a vast meadow, always flat and always green, upon which bushes grow, cattle feed, and towns cut out of old picture-books stand." From Pskoff he wrote (1859) to his wife: "Russia has become elastic beneath our wheels; the versts have all had young ones." "Green," he writes from Moscow, "has every right to be the Russian national color, as it is. I slept through forty of the hundred (German) miles hither; but the remaining sixty were all shades of green." Writing from Vienna (July 22, 1864) he observed: "I was wet through and listened to music in the Volksgarten today for two hours. The people stared at me as though I had been a new hippopotamus for the Zoological Gardens. I sought consolation in some capital beer."

His dislike of shams and humbug, conceit and mock pathos, has found expression in many satirical word-sketches of courtiers, diplomatic colleagues, generals, deputies, men of science and the like, extremely amusing, but far from flattering for the personages in question. In a letter addressed to Manteuffel from Frankfort he wrote: "With the exception of a few subordinate intrigues connected with the fortresses, the press and the federal exchequer, we have been living a non-political idyll here since the 21st ult."—In the autumn of 1858 Prince Hohenlohe was placed at the head of state affairs; and it was reported that the new Liberal ministry would recall Bismarck from Frankfort and appoint him to another post. About that time he wrote to his sister: "If they wish to get rid of me in order to oblige place-hunters, I will retire under the guns of Schönhausen and watch how Prussia can be governed with the support of majorities of the Left, endeavoring meanwhile to do my duty in the Upper House. Variety is the soul of life, and I hope to feel myself younger by ten years when I again take up the position in the order of battle which I occupied in 1848–9. As soon as I find the *rôles* of gentlemen and diplomatist incompatible with one another, the pleasure or trouble of spending a large salary handsomely will not weigh in the balance with me for a moment. I have as much as I want to live upon; and if God will, as heretofore, keep my wife and children well, I shall say *vogue la galère,* no matter on what waters. Thirty years hence it will be all one to me whether I now play the part of a diplomatist or of a country squire; and up to the present time the prospect of a free, fair fight, unhampered by any official restraints, has had just as great a charm for me as that of a protracted regimen of truffles, dispatches and Grand Crosses."

On occasion Bismarck could revert to a kind of primitive cruelty. In Versailles in 1871 he ordered Prussian troops to fire on starving women and children from Paris who approached the besieging soldiers. "Corpses," he said, "need no shelter or food. France's African troops, the Turcos and Zouaves, should be killed out of hand, and all franctireurs *should be hanged." Along with this cruelty was a peculiar sense of mischief, which went back to his youth and his university days. Moritz Busch recorded specimens of the great man's practical jokes.*[22]

Bismarck played many practical jokes some forty odd years ago when he had turned his back upon the state service and was farming at Kniephof. His guests now and then underwent strange and startling surprises. One day, while he was chatting to his fair cousins, the door of the drawing room suddenly opened and four young foxes rushed in, jumping upon the sofas and chairs and tearing their coverings to tatters. Male visitors had need of steady nerves; for it not infrequently happened that when they had fallen asleep, soothed by a comfortable nightcap lined with porter and champagne, they were suddenly aroused from their slumbers by pistol shots, and the bullets, striking the ceiling above their heads, brought down showers of plaster upon them.

22. *Ibid.*, II, 266–273.

A lively specimen of his peculiar humor at that period was related to me by the chancellor himself. Once he had a young lieutenant of hussars staying with him at Kniephof, who was called upon to pay a visit to a worthy old uncle in the neighborhood—a venerable gentleman extremely tenacious with respect to etiquette and elegant manners, who had invited a party of relatives and friends of his own kidney to a grand birthday feast. On the eve of this occasion Bismarck persuaded the youthful warrior to drink a great deal more than was good for him; and next morning conveyed him in a springless cart to his uncle's castle. The roads were not good at any time; but heavy rains had transformed them into mud lakes, so that the two gentlemen arrived desperately besplashed. The lieutenant's moral and physical condition was a dismal one, for the consequences of his debauch overnight had been seriously aggravated by the shaking and jolting of the cart, and expressed themselves in somewhat alarming symptoms. The company that greeted them on their arrival, consisting of about forty persons—the ladies *en grande toilette,* the gentlemen in tail coats and white ties—contemplated them with mingled amazement and horror. The hussar soon became invisible; but Junker Otto, despite the loathing with which the highly proper, stiff and respectable people regarded him, sat down to dinner with them as coolly and cheerfully as though nothing out of the way had taken place. Everybody said how astonishing, how extremely astonishing it was that he had no notion, not the shadow of a notion, what an unpleasant person he was. . . .

After he had resumed his official career, and was serving as referendary to the Potsdam government, one day his chief, ignoring his presence in the office, walked to the window and began to drum with his fingers upon one of the panes. Forthwith Bismarck betook himself to the window also, and performed the *"Old Dessauer's March"* on another pane for the special entertainment of his Excellency the President of the government. This was the amiable official who one day made his referendary wait in the antechamber for an hour, and then, calling him in, asked him roughly, "What do you want?" Bismarck replied, "I came to ask for a few days' leave; now I beg to notify my resignation."

Regarded from a certain standpoint there was a great deal of practical humor in the way he misled Benedetti and Napoleon III in 1866 with respect to his willingness to fall in with French projects of aggrandizement, induced the ambassador to show his hand, and, when the opportune moment arrived, brought his comedy of errors to a close by publishing the document recording Napoleon's secret plans, of which he had obtained possession by dexterous maneuvering. He began by bamboozling Bonaparte into believing that he was not *un homme sérieux;* then he amused himself for several years with Napoleonic delusions; finally, he duped him and caused him to make a fool of himself. All this constituted the comic *lever de rideau* preceding the great war tragedy.

In Ferrières the king had prohibited shooting in the park behind Rothschild's *château,* which contained several thousand pheasants. Unaware of this, I asked the chancellor one evening why he did not sally forth, once in a while, and shoot a few of these toothsome birds for our table. "Why not, indeed?" he replied with a smile. "True, shooting is strictly prohibited; but what can they do to me if I turn out and knock over a brace or two? I can't be taken up, for there is no one to do it." An entry in my diary upon September 28, says: "Today the king drove out to visit the cantonments before Paris. At midday I had a communication to make to the prime minister; but in the anteroom they told me he was not at home. 'Ridden out, I suppose?' 'No; the gentlemen have gone out to shoot a few pheasants. Engel (the chancellor's *chasseur*) was told to follow them!' 'Have they taken their guns with them?' 'No; Podbielski sent them on ahead!' " At 2 P.M. the chief was back. He, Moltke and Podbielski had been shooting pheasants in the coverts adjoining the park, so as not to sin against his Majesty's commands. A strain of *naif* humor ran through the whole incident.

Another example of Bismarck's practical humor was afforded by the method he adopted of enlightening the major-domo of Ferrières with respect to the virtue of hospitality. Baron Rothschild, the hundredfold millionaire—who, moreover, had been Prussian consul-general in Paris up to the outbreak of the war—had instructed his major-domo to refuse us the wine we needed, which would have been paid for like other provisions supplied to us. Summoned before the chancellor, this audacious fellow persisted in his refusal. First of all he denied that there was a drop of wine in the house; then he admitted that he had "a couple of hundred bottles of thin claret in the cellar" (there were seventeen thousand), and finally declared that he would not let us have any of it. The chancellor began by pointing out to him how rudely and shabbily his master acknowledged the honor conferred him by the king's condescension in using his house; then, as the stubborn major-domo seemed about to become insolent, he asked him curtly whether he knew what a straw halter was. The man seemed to guess at his meaning, for he turned as white as chalk. He was then informed that a straw halter was a thing with which stiff-necked and impertinent major-domos were bound in such sort that, when laid upon the ground, their faces were not uppermost—he might imagine the rest. Next day we had all we wanted, nor had we subsequently any reason to complain; on the contrary, a daily improvement became manifest in the behavior of the previously recalcitrant major-domo. He even supplied our table with champagne. Practical humor had effected his complete conversion.

"Oh, Keudell," exclaimed the chancellor suddenly, one day at Versailles, "it just occurs to me that I must get some plenary powers from the king—in German, of course. The German emperor must write nothing but German; his minister may be guided by circumstances. Official intercourse with diplomatists must be carried on in the language of the country, not in a foreign tongue. Bernstorff was the first who tried to bring this about at home. He wrote in German to all the foreign representatives in Berlin; and they all answered him in their respective mother tongues—Russian, Spanish, Swedish and I know not what besides, so that he was obliged to have a whole swarm of translators at the ministry. That was how I found matters when I took office. Soon afterwards Budberg sent me a note in Russian. I could not stand that. If the Russians wanted to take their revenge upon us they should have made Gortchakoff write in Russian to our envoy at Petersburg. That would have been all right. But, to answer my German letter in Russian at Berlin was not fair. So I settled that whatever should reach us written in any language but German, French, English or Italian, should be relegated to a cupboard. Budberg, however, went on writing reminder after reminder, always in Russian. At last he called upon me in person, and asked why I did not answer him. 'Answer?' I ejaculated, with an amazed look; 'answer what? I have not seen any communication from you.' 'Why, a month ago, I wrote so and so to you, and have reminded you of it several times since.' 'Oh, of course, now I remember,' I rejoined; 'there is a whole bundle of papers in Russian character lying downstairs; your letters will be among them. But not a soul here understands Russian; and everything that reaches us in an incomprehensible idiom is put away.' "

One anecdote more, relating to a mysterious arrangement in the building added to Varzin Castle. The chancellor had just been showing me his new study, and we passed into his adjoining bedroom, just opposite which a few steps lead down into a bathroom on the right hand in the dimly lighted corridor. Close to the bathroom door is another, hidden in the wall, and opening upon a dark winding staircase. "The castle dungeon?" I enquired. "My sallyport," replied the prince. "By these stairs I steal off quietly and unobserved, and get safe into the park by an underground passage when undesirable visitors come in sight. In the park I have a nook of refuge, where my people let me know when the coast is clear. We call the arrangement Senfft-Pilsach, because his garrulity is so wearisome." How far the secret passage went on subterraneously, or where it returned to the upper air, I never learned; and if I knew I would not tell, for to do so would be to frustrate its purpose. Let my partial revelation serve as a warning to those who may still feel themselves alluded to by the chancellor's term "undesirable." It no longer applies to Herr von Senfft-Pilsach, who has departed this life, and is now probably a peculiarly hallowed member of the old Conservative party in the heavenly Parliament, whom "indiscreet books" can no longer vex or annoy.

70

Journeys into Pessimism: The Great Man Complains that Life Has Brought Him Little Satisfaction and Joy—Nothing but Vexation, Care, and Trouble

"How weary . . . the uses of this world."

Throughout his life Bismarck had intervals of low spirits, periods of excessive irritability and anxiety. At these times he was depressed in spirit, discontented, and dissatisfied with his achievements and his destiny. Moritz Busch relates one such incident.[23]

It was twilight at Varzin, and he was sitting—as was his wont after dinner—by the stove in the large back drawing-room, where Rauch's statue of "Victory Casting Wreaths" is set up. After having sat silent for a while, gazing straight before him and feeding the fire, now and anon, with fir cones, he suddenly began to complain that his political activity had brought him but little satisfaction and few friends. Nobody loved him for what he had done. He had never made anybody happy thereby, he said; not himself, nor his family, nor any one else. Some of those present would not admit this, and suggested "that he had made a great nation happy." "But," he continued, "how many have I made unhappy! But for me, three great wars would not have been fought; eighty thousand men would not have perished; parents, brothers, sisters, and

23. *Ibid.*, I, 114–115.

widows would not be bereaved and plunged into mourning . . . . That matter, however, I have settled with God. But I have had little or no joy from all my achievements—nothing but vexation, care, and trouble." He continued for some time in the same strain. His guests kept silence; and those among them who had never before heard him say anything of the kind were somewhat astonished. It reminded one of Achilles, speaking to King Priam in his tent before Ilion. . . .

This speech of the chancellor—the "character of iron," the spirit one had accustomed oneself to think of as proudly and sternly certain of itself—sounded (especially with relation to the statue of Victory, stationed in the corner opposite his seat, and making as though it would cast laurel wreaths at his feet) like an echo of the feeling running through the soliloquy, "To be or not to be," in the course of which Hamlet exclaims:—

> How weary, stale, flat and unprofitable
> Seem to me all the uses of this world!
> Fie on't! O fie! 'tis an unweeded garden
> That grows to seed; things rank and gross in nature
> Possess it merely! [24]

Still more keenly did all this pessimism of his remind one of that passage in the *Koheleth,* the author of which makes the royal preacher complain in the following terms: "But when I looked at all my works which my hand had wrought, and at the trouble that I had taken, behold, it was all vanity and vexation, and nothing more under the sun."

What was the cause of his melancholy? Possibly it resulted from physical suffering, which conjures up painful dreams even to the wakeful mind, from excessive irritability caused by overmuch thinking and anxiety, by lassitude, by discords in his nervous system, or perhaps—and this seems to me most probable—by an unwitting outburst and overflow of Christian feeling. One thing is certain—that of late years he has repeatedly expressed himself in words almost identical with those above quoted, and that, upon such occasions, no arguments have availed to soothe him.

24. Moritz Busch erred when he attributed this exclamation by Hamlet to the "To be or not to be" soliloquy. The latter appears in Act III, Scene I, while the lines quoted by Busch are in Act I, Scene II.

71

When a Liberal Opponent Predicts that the Chancellor Will Ruin both Himself and His Country, Bismarck Proclaims His Political Philosophy

"[My] only . . . lodestar . . . the welfare of the State."

On February 24, 1881, when the budget of the empire was under discussion, Eugen Richter, leader of the Progressives, called upon his liberal colleagues to help curb Bismarck's power. "If this is not possible, and if we go on as things are going, the chancellor will ruin himself, and he will ruin the country." Bismarck replied in the following speech, in which he protested that his guiding star had always been the salus publica*—welfare of the state.*[25]

The remarks of the previous speaker have hardly touched on the subject under discussion, the budget, since I have been here. Consequently I am excused, I suppose, from adding anything to what the secretary of the treasury has said. The previous speaker has mainly concerned himself with a critique of my personality. The number of times the word "chancellor" appears in his speech in proportion to the total number of words sufficiently justifies my assertion. Well, I do not know what is the use of this critique, if not to instruct me and to educate me. But I am in my sixty-sixth year and in the twentieth of my tenure of office—there will not be much in me to improve. You will have to use me up as I am or push me aside. I, on my part, have never made the attempt to educate the Honorable Mr. Richter—I do not think I am called upon to do it; nor have I endeavored to force him from his sphere of activity—I should not have the means of doing this, nor do I wish it. But I believe he in his turn will lack the means of forcing me from my position. Whether he will be able to compress me and circumscribe me, as toward the end of his speech he said was desirable, I do not know. I am, however, truly grateful to him for the concern he expressed about my health. Unfortunately, if I wish to do my duty, I cannot take such care of myself as Mr. Richter deems desirable—I shall have to risk my health.

When he said that every evil troubling us, even the rate of interest and I know not what else, was based on the uncertainty of our conditions, and when he quoted the word of a colleague of a "hope-

25. Translated by Edmund von Mach in *The German Classics*, X, 210–220.

less confusion"—well, gentlemen, then I must repeat what I have said elsewhere and in the hearing of the Honorable Mr. Richter: Make a comparison and look about you in other countries! If our conditions with their ordered activities and their assured future at home and abroad constitute a "hopeless confusion," how shall we characterize the conditions of many another country? I can see in no European country a condition of safety and an assured outlook into the future similar to that prevailing in the German empire. I have already said on the former occasion that my position as minister of foreign affairs made it impossible for me to be specific. But everyone who will follow my remarks with a map in his hand, and a knowledge of history during the past twenty years, will have to say that I am right. I do not know what is the use of these exaggerations of a "hopeless confusion" and "a lack of assurance and uncertainty of the future." Nobody in the country believes it; and isn't that the chief thing? The people in the country know perfectly well how they are off, and all who do not fare as they wish are pleased to blame the government for it. When a candidate comes up for election, and says to them: "The government—or to quote the previous speaker—the chancellor is to blame for all this," he may find many credulous people, but in the majority he will find people who will say: "The chancellor surely has his faults and drawbacks"—but most people will not be convinced that I am to blame for everything. . . .

On the whole you will agree with me that the tone of our public debates is less elevated than that of our social gatherings, especially when our ministers are addressed, but at times even among fellow members, although of this I am no competent critic. I do not even criticize the behavior toward the ministers, for I am hardened by an experience of many years and can stand it. I am merely describing the reasons why no minister clings to his post, and why you do me an injustice if you believe that it takes an artful effort to make a minister yield his place. Not many of them have been accustomed to see a totally ignorant correspondent tear an experienced minister to pieces in the press as if he were a stupid schoolboy. We see this in every newspaper every day, but we can stand it. We do not complain. But can anyone say that the members of the government—the bureau chief's frequently fare even worse—meet in the parliamentary debates with that urbaneness of demeanor which characterizes our best society? I do not say "no," leaving it to you to answer this question. I only say that the business of being a minister is very arduous and cheerless, subject to vexations and decidedly exhausting. This brings it about that the ministers are habitually in a mood which makes them readily give up their places as soon as they have found another excuse than the simple: I have had enough, I do not care for more, I am tired of it.

The changes of ministers, however, have not been so many nor so quick with us as they are in other countries, and this I may mention to Mr. Richter as a proof of my amiability as a colleague. Count, if you will, the number of ministers who have crossed the public stage since I entered office in 1862, and sum up the resignations due to other than parliamentary reasons, and you will find a result exceedingly favorable to the accommodating spirit of the German minister, when it is compared with that of any other country. I consider, therefore, the insinuating references to my quarrelsome disposition and fickleness distinctly wide of the mark.

In this connection I shall take the liberty of referring with one more word to the reproaches, often occurring in the press and also in the Reichstag, that I had frequently and abruptly changed my views. Well, I am not one of those who at any time of their life have believed, or believe today, that they can learn no more. If a man says to me: "Twenty years ago you held the same opinion as I; I still hold it, but you have changed your views," I reply: "You see, I was as clever twenty years ago as you are today. Today I know more, I have learned things in these twenty years." But, gentlemen, I will not even rely on the justice of the remark that the man who does not learn also fails to progress and cannot keep abreast of his time. People are falling behind when they remain rooted in the position they occupied years ago. However, I do not at all intend to excuse myself with such observations, for *I have always had one compass only, one lodestar by which I have steered:* salus publica, *the welfare of the state.* Possibly I have often acted rashly and hastily since I first began my career, but whenever I had time to think I have always acted according to the question, "What is useful, advantageous, and right for my Fatherland, and —as long as this was only Prussia—for my dynasty, and today—for the German nation?" I have never been a theorist. The systems which bind and separate parties are for me of secondary importance. The nation comes first, its position in the world and its independence, and above all our organization along lines which will make it possible for us to draw the free breath of a great nation.

Everything else, a liberal, reactionary, or conservative constitution—gentlemen, I freely confess, all this I consider in second place. It is the luxury of furnishing the house, when the house is firmly established. In the interest of the country I can parley now with one person, now with another in purely party questions. Theories I barter away cheaply. First let us build a structure secure on the outside and firmly knit on the inside, and protected by the ties of a national union. After that, when you ask my advice about furnishing the house with more or less liberal constitutional fittings, you may perhaps hear me say, "Ah well, I have no preconceived ideas. Make your suggestions, and, when the sovereign whom I serve agrees, you will find no objections on principle on my part." It can be done thus, and again thus. There are many roads leading to Rome. There are times when one should govern liberally, and times when one should govern autocratically. Everything changes. Nothing is eternal in these matters. But of the structure of the German empire and the union of the German nation I demand that they be free and unassailable, with not only a passing field fortification on one side. I have given to its creation and growth my entire strength from the very beginning. And if you point to a single moment when I have not steered by this direction of the compass needle, you may perhaps prove that I have erred, but you cannot prove that I have for one moment lost sight of the national goal.

72 Bismarck Goes to Battle in a Customs War against the American Pig and Accuses It of Undermining German Health and Profits[26]

"We do not greet each other when we pass in the street!"

The new course of protectionism had a vital effect upon German-American relations. The metamorphosis of Germany from a food-exporting to a food-importing country, a result of German industrialization, profoundly affected the attitude of German agrarians to imports from America. Bismarck's tariff of 1879 embodied an agrarian, as well as an industrial, protective policy. Two conflicting interests had to be served: it was necessary to protect German farmers against the large imports of American grain, livestock, and foodstuffs, and yet at the same time German industrialists had to receive raw materials, including foodstuffs, at a price low enough to enable them to compete with foreign manufacturers in the final selling of their products.

In 1880 Bismarck precipitated a quarrel with the United States by banning the importation of American pork and pork products. For a decade thereafter the bitter controversy threatened to develop into a customs war.

26. Account adapted from Louis L. Snyder, "The American-German Pork Dispute, 1879–1891," *The Journal of Modern History*, XVII, No. 1 (March, 1945), 16–28.

The pork dispute between Germany and the United States began with an imperial decree of June 25, 1880, prohibiting the importation from the United States of all sorts of pork except hams and sides of bacon. The reason given was that a recent epidemic of trichinosis had been due to the eating of diseased pork. Hams and sides of bacon were exempted from the decree because these could be inspected properly for trichinosis. In 1882 the request of the United States for a modification of the decree for the benefit of the meat products of two large American packing companies was refused.

Sensing victory in the campaign against American pork, German agrarians began to apply pressure on the government for total exclusion. On March 27, 1882, a circular was addressed to agricultural societies in Germany by a committee appointed by the Congress of German Agrarians, asking that petitions be prepared and sent to the chancellor and the *Bundesrat* demanding prohibition of all American cattle, meat, and meat preparations. Through the spring and summer of 1882 Bismarck's office was deluged with petitions. It became apparent that the chancellor intended to go ahead with the prohibition edict. The *Berliner Tageblatt,* alarmed by the probability of the decree, warned against the step: "Should this prohibition go into effect we should have cause to regret it, for the reason that it would result in making meat dearer to the mass of people, or even restrict them in its consumption. American meat undoubtedly is, and always was, cheaper than the domestic article, and the claim that it is unwholesome is not sufficiently proved to justify its exclusion from our market." Nevertheless, on November 21, 1882 Bismarck transmitted a memorandum, together with the exclusion bill, to the *Bundesrat,* characterizing meat inspection in America as unsatisfactory.

From December 1882 to March 1883 there was an acrimonious debate in the German press and in the Reichstag over the question of the total exclusion of American pork and pork products. The chambers of commerce of all German seaports, which expected to be hard hit, protested against the contemplated legislation. Westphalian farmers, who imported a large quantity of American bacon and hams, which appeared on the market as Westphalian *Schinken,* sent a deputation to protest to Bismarck. The *Berliner Tageblatt* again warned that the prohibition would be "disastrous"; the *Weser Zeitung* expressed fear of retaliation; and other opposition newspapers termed the measure "injurious" and "ill-advised."

On January 9, 1883, a debate on the pork question took place in the Reichstag following an interpellation addressed to the chancellor by the opposition parties. According to Ambassador Aaron A. Sargent's account, the arguments of deputies Eugen Richter,

Dr. Friedrich Kapp, Dr. Wilhelm Theodor Barth, and Gerhard Ahlhorn, in summary, were: (1) the previous prohibition of American pork had been injurious; (2) the chancellor had made no efforts to collect or present any evidence of the unsoundness of American pork; (3) cases of trichinosis arose from the use of German chopped meat, fresh from the butchers; (4) the poorer classes were deprived of a source of cheap food on flimsy and sensational evidence; (5) the *Bundesrat* had no right to make the prohibition under the tariff law of 1839; and (6) it was undesirable to disturb the good relations with the United States, which was then engaged in reducing tariffs.

Bismarck arrived in the midst of the debate. Excusing himself, on the basis of ill-health, from speaking at length, he indicated that he was not moved by the pleas of the opposition and dismissed the matter sarcastically by terming pork "the poor man's trichinae."

It was clear that Bismarck was determined to prohibit American pork despite all opposition. Therefore, President Chester A. Arthur, on February 15, 1883, directed that the imperial government be informed of his intention to appoint an impartial and competent commission to examine the raising of hogs and the curing and packing of hog products in the United States. The proposal also invited Germany to send her own commission of experts to cooperate with the American experts, who were "scientists of known probity." The suggested investigation by German experts might well have shown that American methods were as careful, and American pork as healthful, as the German.

A complicating factor in the dispute was Bismarck's personal animosity to Aaron A. Sargent, who had been American minister in Berlin since March 2, 1882. Formerly the chancellor had always enjoyed cordial relations with American ministers. With the historian George Bancroft, the poet Bayard Taylor (translator of *Faust*), and the educator Andrew D. White, Bismarck had maintained close personal relations, reminiscent of his intimate friendship during his student days at Göttingen with John Lothrop Motley. But the chancellor disliked Sargent, and it is not all unlikely that Bismarck's somewhat bad-tempered handling of the pork issue was influenced, to some extent, by his attitude toward the American minister. Sargent, like Bismarck, was a man of strong and forceful personality, aggressive in political contests, untiring and persevering in pursuit of his ends, a good German scholar, and an able debater. Unlike his predecessors at Berlin, Sargent was a masterful machine politician; and undoubtedly in some of his actions he stepped beyond the bounds of effective diplomacy.

Soon after arriving in Berlin, Sargent worked to forestall any further action by the German government against American pork and pork products. In a series of dispatches to Washington he criticized the German position.

Throughout the controversy Bismarck contended that American pork was infected with trichinae, that the prohibition concerned problems of public health, and that the "Federal Council could not take the trichinae of the poor under their special protection." From the chancellor's viewpoint the prohibition was a measure of internal legislation found necessary "after careful investigation on sanitary grounds." But Bismarck deliberately utilized a smoke screen to hide his real intentions. The interdiction of American pork was much less a sanitary than a protectionist measure.

There were, indeed, cases of trichinosis in Germany which could be traced to the eating of pork; but most of these cases of death or disease had resulted from the use of freshly slaughtered German, Russian, or Hungarian pork. The German (and also European) practice of eating pork unboiled was undoubtedly responsible for the sporadic outbreaks of trichinosis which the German government attributed to American swine. In an interview with an American newspaperman, Professor Rudolf Virchow, the eminent German pathologist, condemned the prohibition against American pork as "utterly illogical, unnecessary, and unjustifiable on the ground of sanitary reasons."

An indication of Bismarck's real motive in banning American pork may be found in his remark to an American journalist in July 1884: "It is absolutely necessary for us people of Europe to protect ourselves in time against your competition, for whenever the point arrives that the United States is not checked in its inroads on our agriculture, complete ruin will overtake our landholding classes." Bismarck considered the large landowners as pillars of the monarchy, as men of noble lineage, whose sons formed the flower of the German army. He was anxious to shield them from foreign competition, especially if their status as a class were endangered.

There was considerable resentment in the United States when it became clear that Bismarck did not intend the prohibition to be a temporary measure. During 1884, members of Congress received numerous letters from their constituents urging retaliatory action against Germany. Anger over a wide section of the country was indicated by a series of bills and resolutions introduced into both the house and the senate bearing on the problem of retaliation. Both President Arthur and Secretary of State Frelinghuysen believed, however, that a customs war with Germany was undesirable and that it was wiser to move slowly. In his message to Congress

(December 1883) Arthur suggested "equitable retaliation," but he alluded in general to invidious distinctions against American products by foreign governments and not specifically to the prohibition of American pork by Germany. Frelinghuysen felt that the mere introduction of legislative bills would have a sufficient effect and advised against any retaliatory legislation.

By 1885 Germany imposed additional duties on wheat and rye and had contemplated measures hostile to American petroleum. A house resolution called for instructions to the committee on foreign affairs to "inquire into and report whether the interests of the United States do not demand the adoption of like discriminatory measures against such principal articles imported from the German Empire as are grown or manufactured in the United States."

The dispute stimulated a famous American cartoon called "Avenging the American Hog," which appeared in *Frank Leslie's Illustrated Newspaper* on March 1, 1884. Bismarck is shown bearing a great porcelain pipe in one hand and a foaming jug of beer in another, with a pretzel hanging from his cap. Passing in the opposite direction is a huge hog, whose belly is wrapped in an American flag and from whose tail the Stars and Stripes wave proudly. The caption reads: "We do not greet each other when we pass in the street!"

Another cartoon in the April 5, 1884 issue of the same magazine was titled "President Arthur Apologizes." Bismarck is shown seated on a throne, the legs of which are beer mugs. The hands and feet of a hog were substituted for Bismarck's legs. Covering the pedestal is an American flag. President Arthur is shown bowing before Bismarck humbly and apologetically. On the wall is a sign stating: "We have enough hogs—Bismarck."

Two related developments finally led to the end of the pork dispute. The first one, initiated by the American Congress, was designed to meet the German government halfway by agreeing to inspect American meats before exportation. In 1886 a bill was introduced in the Senate (S. 1644) providing for an inspection of meats for exportation. On March 3, 1891 Congress passed an act making microscopic inspection of meat compulsory. Thus, one of the critical objections of the Germans to American pork was removed, and the German government was given an opportunity to lift the ban without losing face.

Of greater importance was the prospect of American retaliatory action. Although the American government until this time had avoided such legislation, it became evident that retaliation was imminent. The victory of Benjamin Harrison over Grover Cleveland in the presidential elections of 1888 resulted in the dominance of the protective tariff party. According to the McKinley Tariff of October 1, 1890, the president, under section 3, had the power to reimpose a duty on German sugar and sugar products imported into the United States after January 1, 1892. Germany at this time exported large quantities of beet sugar to the United States. During the illness of Count von Arco Valley, the German minister to the United States, the German *chargé d'affaires,* Mumm von Schwartzenstein, sought to forestall this prospective action by intimating the intention of his government to accept the inspection law as satisfactory and revoke the prohibition of American pork. The American president replied, with a touch of sarcasm, that the two questions were unrelated, since American pork had been shut out because it allegedly exposed German consumers to disease.

Nevertheless, an agreement was reached in the form of an exchange of declarations, since called the "Saratoga agreement." Germany agreed to import American pork and pork products into Germany with an official certificate stating that the meat had been examined and found free from qualities injurious to health. In return, the American government agreed not to take advantage of the clause in the McKinley Tariff regarding German sugar. With this *quid pro quo* the pork dispute was terminated.

Significantly, the Saratoga agreement was not negotiated until after Bismarck's resignation in 1890. Bismarck rarely changed his course. In retirement at Friedrichsruh he expressed dissatisfaction with the Saratoga agreement, holding that "it attached officially the same trustworthiness to a foreign certificate as to that heretofore only enjoyed by a domestic certificate." To the retired chancellor the American hog remained unacceptable.

73 The Chancellor Seeks to Take the Wind Out of the Sails of Socialism by Promoting Governmental Labor Reforms

"A human being . . . treated worse than a dog in his own house!"

To Bismarck, socialism was evil. If there were to be any revolution in Germany, he would see to it that it came from above. He would extract from the Socialist program "those parts that are reasonable and right, and then incorporate these into the existing state system." There was method in his policy: "One who can look forward to an old age pension is far more contented and much easier to manage."

Bismarck realized that the working class would be alienated by his anti-Socialist laws. He would, therefore, avoid discontent by promoting the workers' welfare himself. In April 1881 he proposed to establish an Imperial Insurance Office to insure against accidents all workers in mines and factories whose income was not more than 2,000 marks a year. His defense of this measure, reprinted here, reveals his most effective oratorial style.[27]

This was the beginning of a comprehensive program which in a sense atoned for the anti-Socialist laws. The Sickness Insurance Law of 1883, the Accident Insurance Law of 1884, and the Old Age and Invalidity Law of 1887 were enacted during Bismarck's chancellorship. Later, in 1911, these acts were unified in a great social insurance code which set a standard for the world.

The field of legislation—justly pronounced by Deputy Richter to be one commanding a vast perspective—opened up by this measure has to do with a question which, in all probability, will not vanish from the order of the day very speedily. For the last fifty years we have been talking about the social question. Since the Socialist Law was passed, I have been repeatedly reminded, in high quarters as well as low, of the promise I then gave that something positive should be done to remove the causes of socialism. Hints of this sort have been imparted to me *toto die;* but I do not believe that our sons, or even our grandsons, will be able finally to solve the question. Indeed, no political questions can ever be mathematically settled, as books are balanced in business; they crop up, have their time, and give way to other questions propounded by history. Organic development wills that it shall be so. I consider it my duty to take up these questions without party feeling or excitement, because I know not who is to do so, if not the imperial government.

Deputy Richter has pointed out the responsibility of the state for what it is now doing. Well, gentlemen, I feel that the state should also be responsible for what it leaves undone. I am not of opinion that *laissez faire, laissez aller,* "pure Manchester policy," "everybody takes care of himself," "the weakest must go to the wall," "to him who hath shall be given, from him who hath not shall be taken even that which he hath," can be practiced in a monarchically, patriarchically governed state. . . .

27. Busch, *Bismarck: Sketches for a Historical Picture,* trans. Beatty-Kingston, II, 219–223.

The legislation we propose does not go far enough for Deputy Richter. Well, if he will only have patience enough, we shall be able later on to meet his expectations and wishes; but not too quickly or all at once. Such laws are not founded upon the basis of a theoretical whim, but have a genesis, an antecedent history of their own, from which they directly emanate.

The reason we have come forward today with a bill for insurance against accidents is that this method of assisting the poor and weakly had already been warmly recommended at a time when I was looking closely into the whole question. I found all manner of suggestions and schemes with respect to this measure, which seemed by documentary evidence to be most urgent; and I gave my attention to it. I felt at first, in proportion to the theory it represented, it was not nearly comprehensive enough. I was tempted to substitute the words "every German" for "every workingman" in the first paragraph, dealing with compensations for accident. But the insurance question is surrounded by serious difficulties—for instance, when it touches the independent workingman, who suffers injury when he is working on his own account, and the first thing that we had to think about (it troubled us a good deal more than the two hours' speech of a deputy does) was: How far should this measure extend, without involving us in a blunder at the very inception of our legislative experiments? . . .

Deputy Richter had his statistics all ready respecting the exact percentages of each branch of human occupation, and imparted them to us with great positiveness. I should be grateful to him if he would acquaint us with the source from which he derived that valuable information. We did our best; our prefatory studies were compiled most carefully from authentic *data,* not imaginary ones based upon conjecture; and if we had lighted upon the statistics which Deputy Richter seems to have discovered with a mere glance of his more perceptive eye—if they had been accessible to us and we had found them correct—we might have gone further in our proposals than we have actually done. . . .

For my part, I should not have the courage to proceed with this measure if the outlay it involves were to be exclusively borne by industrialists. Were state assistance, in every form now obtaining, to be cut off, I should not venture to assume the responsibility of imposing the bill upon German industry. We may limit the state subvention to a period of three years, or otherwise, as you please; but, without having made any experiment by which we can appraise what is before us, I do not feel justified in saddling our industrialists with the whole cost of these state institutions, or in burdening them more heavily than heretofore with the outlay for injured operatives that has hitherto been defrayed by local poor relief, and will at some future time be disbursed to a greater, completer, and more dignified extent by the insured themselves in partnership with the state. . . .

The invalid workman is saved from starvation by the measure we now advocate. That, however, is not sufficient to make him look forward contentedly to old age. And the bill is animated by a desire to keep alive the sense of human dignity, which I hope the poorest German will preserve, and which prescribes that he should not be forced to accept eleemosynary assistance (to which he has no right) but should be entitled to something of which nobody can dispose but himself, and of which nobody can deprive him; that doors, hitherto closed to him, should open readily when he knocks, and that better treatment should be accorded to him in his place of refuge by reason of the additional means he brings into it with him.

Whosoever has looked closely into the state of the poor in large towns, or into the arrangements made for paupers in country communes, and has seen for himself how—even in the best-managed villages—a poor wretch is sometimes treated when weakly and crippled, must admit that any healthy operative, contemplating that spectacle, is fully justified in exclaiming: "It is simply horrible that a human being should be treated worse than a dog in his own house!" I say, therefore, our first object in bringing forward this bill is to ensure kindlier treatment to this class of the poor; and next year I will do my best to give Deputy Richter full satisfaction as to the extent of the provision proposed to be made by the state for the better usage of the unemployed. For the present this measure must be regarded as an experiment—an attempt to find out the depth of the financial water into which we ask the country to plunge. . . .

An appropriate title for our enterprise would be "Practical Christianity," but we do not want to feed poor people with figures of speech, but with something solid. Death costs nothing; but unless you will put your hands in your pockets and into the state exchequer, you will not do much good. To saddle our industry with the whole affair—well, I don't know that it could bear the burden. All manufacturers are having hard times. . . .

74

The Family Autocrat Threatens Suicide to Prevent the Marriage of His Eldest Son, Herbert, to Princess Elizabeth Carolath, Connected with the Detested Anti-Bismarck Fronde [28]

Herbert Bismarck: "I cannot marry without permission."

Herbert Count von Bismarck-Schönhausen (1849–1904) entered the foreign service in 1874 at the age of twenty-five and remained with it until 1881. For the next several years he represented his father on diplomatic or special missions in London, Paris, St. Petersburg, The Hague, and Vienna. In London, as the unofficial link between his father and English political circles, he played an important role in the involved negotiations of the undercover struggle by which Germany obtained her first foothold in Africa. In 1885 Herbert became undersecretary in the foreign office. From 1886 to 1890 he was foreign secretary, resigning along with his father in 1890. Later he served several terms in the Reichstag.

There was a deep mutual affection between father and son. What Herbert did with success was to act as an instrument of his father, almost an extension of the older man's personality. This brought the character of his services almost down to the level of a private secretary, but he did work which no one else could have done and which was of great importance to Bismarck.

Ironically, the son's private happiness was ruined by a father who loved him deeply. After his unfortunate love affair in 1881, Herbert was left embittered, rough, and overbearing. The marriage fiasco was also responsible in all probability for his increasing addiction to alcohol, which helped bring about his death just short of his fifty-fifth birthday.

A painting by Gustav Richter shows Princess Elizabeth Carolath as a beautiful, radiant young lady with dark brown hair and blue eyes. She was then the eighteen-year-old daughter of Prince Hatzfeldt-Trachenberg and a member of what many regarded as an eccentric family. Her marriage to Prince Carolath-Beuthen had been an unhappy one. Herbert von Bismarck had met her in the seventies and had been promptly smitten. Courting her with typi-

28. Account condensed from Louis L. Snyder, "Political Implications of Herbert von Bismarck's Marital Affairs, 1881, 1892," *The Journal of Modern History*, XXXVI, No. 2 (June, 1964), 156–162.

cally Bismarckian fire, he urged her to divorce her husband and become his wife. The ambitious young lady was immensely attracted by the idea of becoming the chancellor's daughter-in-law.

Unfortunately for her future, Elizabeth Carolath was connected too closely with the anti-Bismarck fronde. One of her sisters was married to Baron Walther von Loë, and the other to Count Alexander von Schleinitz, treasurer of the court household. Both her brothers-in-law were leaders of the anti-Bismarck faction. The chancellor regarded them as among his most bitter political enemies and calumniators. The Hatzfeldt-Loë-Schleinitz crowd, according to the Bismarcks, was a part of the Augusta party, the real front against the Bismarcks. Augusta in 1881 was the German empress and queen of Prussia.

Born the princess of Saxe-Weimar, Augusta was a woman of great beauty, but dictatorial in manner. Until her death in 1890, the chancellor had to bear what he called Augusta's "intolerable accessory and opposition government." His conflicts with Augusta he spoke of as "the hardest fought battles of my life."

The Bismarck-Augusta feud began as early as the revolution of 1848 at a time when Augusta had been married for nearly twenty years to Prince William of Prussia, brother of the king, Frederick William IV (1795–1861). The two clashed about the problem of succession to the throne. From this point on the ambitious Junker and the strong-willed queen were bitter enemies. In Bismarck's letters and conversations there were many attacks upon the woman he regarded as an obstacle both to himself and to the progress of Prussia-Germany. He was certain that his unwanted transfer from Frankfort to St. Petersburg in 1859 was due to her machinations. Max Lenz reported that Augusta opposed Bismarck's appointment as minister-president in 1862 because of "his attitude in the March days of 1848, his reactionary views as diplomat and politician, and his frivolous and arrogant personality." In 1866 Augusta and her clique worked feverishly against the war with Austria. In Bismarck's view, Augusta's tactics in those days were definitely antinational. According to Lothar Bucher, Bismarck's assistant, Augusta, in an outburst of pique following the end of the Franco-Prussian war, held up the victory celebration in Berlin for several weeks while she took the cure at Baden-Baden. On May 14, 1875, Bismarck, in a letter to Count Georg zu Münster, the German ambassador in London, complained about Augusta's private correspondence with Queen Victoria. He accused her of playing politics and of hampering the work of responsible ministers. Bismarck suspected Augusta of passing state secrets to Princess Victoria, wife of Crown Prince Frederick, heir to the German throne. He was sure that Princess Victoria was giving these secrets to her mother, Queen Victoria. To the chancellor this was treason.

The feud between Augusta and Bismarck became more intense when she and her adviser, Alexander von Schleinitz, joined hands to support the anti-Bismarck fronde. Schleinitz worked with Bismarck's enemies, the Catholic leader Ludwig Windthorst and the diplomat Count Harry von Arnim in opposing Bismarck and Bismarckian policies. All three were favorites of Augusta, who, through them, sought to embarrass the chancellor.

Little wonder then that the chancellor regarded a marriage linking his adored son with the Augusta clique as a catastrophe to be avoided at all costs. His reaction was violent. Not only was the Princess Carolath a divorced woman, but she was also a Catholic. The father was unimpressed with the son's plea that his intended bride was willing to become a Protestant. In the chancellor's view this intention was not sufficient to excuse the facts that the Augusta-Hatzfeldt-Loë-Schleinitz cabal had conspired secretly against the Bismarckian political program, and that it had slandered and libeled the Bismarck family by circulating false rumors about it to the press. It was just too much. The angered Bismarck would not allow this camarilla to invade the sanctity of his home. His wife, Princess Bismarck, added her agreement: "I'll fight tooth and nail to see that the society of Loë, Schleinitz and Hatzfeldt do not come to our table!" The clash of wills left all three principals sick and miserable. When the Bismarck family physician, Dr. Eduard Cohen, visited the chancellor on April 3, 1881, he found him to be suffering from a strong catarrh and in a high state of nervousness which the doctor attributed to Bismarck's "misunderstanding with his son."

In early April 1881, when she heard the shocking news of the chancellor's opposition to her marriage, Princess Carolath fled to Venice, where she collapsed. "I was so sick," she wrote to Eulenburg on April 14, "that it was believed I wouldn't live, and even now I am so weak that I can scarcely take a few steps. . . . I shall try to regain my strength and seek to begin a new life." The rejected lady maintained an embarrassed and inconclusive correspondence with Herbert. On April 20 Herbert urged Eulenburg to write to the princess "because the poor woman has no one to whom she can talk from the heart." He added that he intended to go to Venice in May. "When I come back, I shall make a final attempt with my father. My present feeling is that it is a matter of life and death, and what will happen God knows! I seem to be faced by the absolute impossibility of devoting to the princess what remains to me of life."

Father and son now had several painful interviews which left both shattered. At the first meeting, on April 28, 1881, the elder Bismarck, with tears in his eyes, informed his son that he was determined absolutely not to go on living if the marriage took place. At the second interview, two days later, Bismarck warned his son that it was incompatible with his honor that his name be connected with those of Hatzfeldt, Loë, and the others. He beseeched Herbert to remember that he did not bear the Bismarck name for himself alone, that anything which affected his father's name affected him and his brother, William as well. He would, therefore, oppose Herbert's marriage *"mit Zähnen und Nageln"* ("with tooth and nail").

The chancellor now placed additional pressure on his son. He was Herbert's superior in governmental service, and as such his permission was necessary for the marriage. He hinted at the possibility that Herbert might be disinherited if he went through with his plans. Herbert described this development in a plaintive letter dated April 31, 1881:

> In the meantime, I am forbidden to leave the service. Therefore, I cannot marry without permission (there is no legal possibility until after the lapse of ten months). In addition, I must remember that I have nothing to offer the princess, since, according to the terms of the law of primogeniture, as recently changed with the emperor's approval, any son who marries a divorced woman is automatically disinherited. Since my father has nothing except the two great entailed estates, I should have no inheritance whatever. This would be all the same to me, since I would not live very long after the marriage anyhow; the split with my parents and their ruin would be the death of me.

In the same letter Herbert wrote that his father had said again that "if the princess were to bear his name, it would drive him to suicide."

A week later, on May 6, Princess Carolath wrote to Herbert that she expected him in Venice by the middle of May. She did not wish to live any longer. Herbert's father had no heart. She quoted the Bible: "For this cause shall a man leave his father and mother, and shall cleave unto his wife." When apprised of the contents of this letter, the infuriated chancellor demanded that his son pledge upon his honor that he would not go to Venice. If he made the pilgrimage, he would have to accept the company of his father. "I have your own fortune and the prevention of the marriage more at heart than the whole empire."

The hapless Herbert was caught in a dilemma. He knew that it was impossible to keep the proposed journey to Venice a secret. The anti-Bismarck cabal would exaggerate the marriage hegira out of all proportion. The Bismarcks would be ridiculed mercilessly, probably with cartoons showing the chancellor in a gondola speeding to rescue his son from the arms of a designing woman.

Herbert bared his heart in his letters to his friend Prince Philip zu Eulenburg. A selection of his thoughts reveals his terrible inner conflict. "I wonder whether or not I have lost my reason." "I feel that I am one of those unfortunates being torn apart by four horses." "I regard it as a point of honor that I should marry her, even though my love for her were gone." "I blame myself for all that has happened, and am loathsome to myself." "The rest of my life stretches out before me in prospect like an interminable avenue of trees leading to a flat, sandy waste." As tactfully as possible, Eulenburg advised Herbert not to separate himself from his parents. Eulenburg equated filial loyalty with patriotism. "In all seriousness," he wrote, "I feared for the life of Prince Bismarck, whose health was degenerating. If the marriage took place, it would have meant the withdrawal of the chancellor from all affairs of state and his retirement to Friedrichsruh to await death. . . . I did my duty with a bleeding heart."

In the end Princess Carolath broke off the marriage plans. She wrote Herbert crisply that she despised him, and let him know through others that she would have nothing further to do with the house of Bismarck. Never again did she send a word, a letter, or a greeting to the man who had deserted her. "Suffering the fate of Ariadne," wrote von Bülow, "she was left to languish on Naxos." Apparently, she retained her beauty for some time. She turned to a brilliant social circle in Venice, where natives and visitors alike were apt to point out her private gondolas with the black-gold livery as belonging "to the woman scorned by the Bismarcks." She survived for thirty-three years in the Palazzo Modena, where she died in January 1914.

The outcome of the affair gave a large amount of fuel to the anti-Bismarck camarilla. Herbert Bismarck was denounced as a shameful lout who had arranged Princess Carolath's divorce and had then betrayed her. Said General von Loë, reacting with what he believed to be proper military spirit: "If Herbert were not the son of the almighty chancellor, he would be brought before a court of honor and it would be a farewell appearance."

Herbert was the real loser. The marriage tragedy left permanent effects on him. From a clever, confident, rising diplomat, aged thirty-two, he became a hard misanthrope who hated people and earned their hatred and contempt in return. He was never able to rid himself of feelings of guilt. He was now open to accusations of cowardice. He was denounced as a weakling who was overpowered by fear of his father, as a selfish rascal who had no taste for being disinherited, and as a man completely lacking in a sense of independence.

The chancellor emerged shaken and scarred from the ordeal. A classic hater, he was caught between two conflicting emotions—his love for his son and his overwhelming hatred for his enemies, "that mob of vile conspirators." If there were a matter of honor concerned, then the honor of the Bismarcks was by far the weightier. Having won his victory, the elder Bismarck tried to dismiss it from his mind. In a letter dated December 27, 1881, to A. W. Hildebrandt, a former servant, he avoided details: "My sons are, unfortunately, not yet married. Herbert is at the embassy in London, and the youngest works here under me; both, thank God, are in good health, which, unfortunately, I cannot say about my wife."

75 William I, Royal Master, and His Faithful Paladin Exchange Notes on Their Respective Dreams

"The wall of rock collapsed like a scene in the theater."

The relationship between William I and Bismarck was an intimate one. Though he often complained about his old master, Bismarck knew that he would always receive William's consent for any important action. On his side the old man admitted frankly that his decisions were made for him by his brilliant minister. However, it was often hard. "At best," he once said, "it is not easy to be an emperor under such a chancellor." In the following exchange of letters the two friends tell about their dreams.[29]

William I to Bismarck

BERLIN, *December* 18, 1881

I must tell you of an extraordinary dream I had last night, which was as clear as I now relate it.

The Reichstag met for the first time after the present recess. On Count Eulenburg's entrance the discussion abruptly ceased; after a long interval the president called on the last speaker to continue the debate. Silence! The president thereupon declared the sitting adjourned. This was the signal for a great tumult and

29. *The Correspondence of William I and Bismarck, with Other Letters to and from Bismarck,* trans. by J. A. Ford (2 vols., London, 1903), I, 207–209.

clamor. No order, it was urged, should be bestowed on any member during the session of the Reichstag; the monarch may not be mentioned during the session. The House adjourns till tomorrow. Eulenburg's appearance in the Chamber is again greeted with hisses and commotion—and then I awoke in such a state of nervous excitement that it was long before I recovered, and I could not sleep from half-past four to half-past six.

All this happened in the House in my presence, as clearly as I have written it down.

I will not hope that the dream will be realized, but it is certainly peculiar. I dreamed it after six hours of quiet sleep, so it could not have been directly produced by our conversation.

Enfin, I could not but tell you of this curious occurrence.

Your

WILHELM

Bismarck to William I

BERLIN, *December* 18, 1881

I thank your Majesty most respectfully for the gracious letter. I quite believe that the dream owed its origin, not exactly to my report, but to the general impression obtained during the last few days from Puttkamer's* oral report, the newspaper articles, and my report. The pictures we have in our minds when awake do not reappear in the mirror of our dreams until our mental faculties have been well rested by sleep. Your Majesty's communication encourages me to relate a dream I had in the troublous days of the spring of 1863. I dreamed, and I told my dream at once to my wife and to others the next morning, that I was riding along a narrow Alpine path, to the right an abyss, and to the left rocks; the path became narrower and narrower, until at last my horse refused to take another step, and there was no room either to turn or to dismount. I then struck the smooth rocky wall with my riding whip in my left hand, and invoked God; the whip became interminably long, and the wall of rock collapsed like a scene in the theater, opening up a wide pathway, with a view over hills and forests such as one sees in Bohemia. I also caught sight of Prussian troops, with their banners, and, still in my dreams, wondered how I could best report this quickly to your Majesty. This dream was realized, and I awoke from it glad and strengthened.

The bad dream from which your Majesty awoke nervous and agitated can be realized only in so far that we shall still have many stormy and noisy parliamentary debates, which must unfortunately

* Minister for the interior, and vice-president of the ministry of state.

undermine the prestige of the parliaments and seriously interfere with state business. Your Majesty's presence at these debates is an impossibility; and I regard such scenes as we have lately witnessed in the Reichstag regrettable enough as a standard of our morals and our political education, perhaps also our political qualifications, but not as a misfortune in themselves: *l'excès du mal en devient le remède.*

Will your Majesty pardon, with your accustomed graciousness, these holiday reflections, which were suggested by your Majesty's letter; for from yesterday till January 9th we have holidays and rest.

BISMARCK

6 With His Health in a Chaotic State, Bismarck Declines Rapidly Until a Strong-willed Young Bavarian Doctor Conquers the Cantankerous Patient and by Force of Will Changes His Whole Way of Living [30]

"Then please consult a veterinary surgeon; he asks no questions!"

In 1883, in his sixty-eighth year, Bismarck was a candidate for early death. He had begun to show the effects of a lifetime of too much food, drink, and smoking. Plagued by shattered emotions, distressed by Herbert's unhappy love affair, he complained of a variety of illnesses, including neuralgia, headaches, insomnia, varicose veins, and swelling of the legs. One doctor after another gave up in disgust after facing him. Some believed him to be perfectly healthy and said his symptoms were psychosomatic. Others, repelled by the nervous tension generated in the Bismarck household, refused to visit him.

Then came the most successful practitioner of the lot, a thirty-three-year-old Bavarian physician, a man of strong character and keen intelligence. Dr. Ernst Schweninger took his autocratic patient in hand and wrought a "miracle cure," which consisted primarily in keeping him from ruining his own health by over-indulgence in food and drink.

Schweninger . . . had been introduced to the chancellor by the latter's second son, Count "Bill," who, having grown enormously

30. *Bismarck's Table Talk,* ed. Lowe, pp. 276–279.

stout for a man of his age, had successfully submitted to a Banting process of maceration at the hands of the Munich doctor. In 1881 Schweninger went with his patient, Count "Bill," on a visit to Varzin, and on this occasion he was secretly consulted by the princess regarding the prince, and by the prince regarding the princess. His stay was prolonged until he had to remind the prince that the duties of his profession in Munich summoned him away. Before he went, however, the chancellor had poured out his whole plaint to him. No sleep, aches and pains in nerves and veins, disordered digestion—doctors and prescriptions all of no use! The doctors, he said, had told him that he was worn out; that he must lie on a sofa and stay indoors; that he must avoid all excitement; virtually, in fact, that he must patiently await the arrival of death for release.

Schweninger listened patiently to all this tale of woe, but he refused to prescribe unless he were permitted to undertake the whole treatment and the whole responsibility. He declared his opinion that unless "the chancellor's whole way of living were changed, unless he practiced strict self-command, and allowed his diet, exercise, repose, etc., to be submitted to a most scrupulous and minute control, he might drag along as he was doing for some six months longer, but that nature would then imperiously assert her rights."

Six month later, when Schweninger passed through Berlin on his way to Danzig, Bismarck had been given up by the doctors, whose diagnosis wavered between cancer of the liver and cancer of the stomach. His powers were failing, and he lost in weight daily. Schweninger, on being consulted informally, still confined his replies to precepts of a general nature. But he had scarcely arrived in Danzig when a telegram summoned him back to Berlin. The prince's family was in despair; the prince had resolved to entrust himself unreservedly to Schweninger's care. But the difficulty lay in the impossibility of controlling or dictating to the chancellor, who was accustomed to command rather than to obey.

There was a very dramatic scene—the prince walking up and down in a state of alternate acquiescence and rebellion, Schweninger calmly eyeing him and awaiting his decision. At an early stage of this first consultation the prince was said to have lost his temper and to have growled, "Don't ask so many questions"; to which Schweninger replied, "Then please consult a veterinary surgeon; he asks no questions!" When, at the close of the interview, Bismarck tugged at the bell, the doctor was in doubt as to whether he was not to be shown out into the street. But the command was, "Fetch the doctor's things from the station," and thenceforth Schweninger continued to be the chancellor's body physician—

almost, indeed, a member of his household. Schweninger was actually the hundred-and-first doctor who had tried his skill on Bismark, who said, "The difference between Schweninger and my former doctors lies in this: that I treated them, while Schweninger treats me."

At first Schweninger found it impossible to persuade his patient to go to bed at ten, and used, therefore, to call punctually at that hour for a long time to make sure that he had really retired. This was well known in the circles which Schweninger frequented; and when he disappeared at the usual hour, people used to say, "He has to go and put the prince to bed first." . . .

[Bismarck] had always been a . . . heavy smoker. In his earlier days, indeed, he was what the Germans call a "chain smoker"—a species of the weed-consuming genus whose morning and night is connected by a cable of cigars, each link of which is lighted at the stump of its predecessor. Bismarck once related that in this way he had, for example, smoked all the way from Cologne to Berlin, a railway journey of about ten hours. "Happy man!" once sighed Gambetta to a friend who was talking to him about the German chancellor. "Happy man! Beer and smoke agree with him." But the time came when he could not even look at a cigar. "I have not given up cigars," he once said; "it is they who have given up me."

But not even Schweninger could wean him from his love of good drink—Schweninger, of whom his illustrious patient once said: "The nearer one is to Rome, the more he may sin."

7 How the Reich Chancellor, Who Had Avoided the Acquisition of Colonies Because They Were a Costly Luxury, Changes His Mind and Embarks on a Colonial Policy[31]

"The German government expected their rights to be respected."

"A colonial policy for us would be just like the Polish noble families who wear silken sables but have no shirts." This was Bismarck's early attitude toward colonies before 1871. Colonies, he was sure, only provided sinecures for officials. They were too costly for the nation as a whole. But by the 1880's the situation had

31. Adapted from Louis L. Snyder, "The Angra Pequena Negotiations between Germany and Britain, 1880–1885," *The Journal of Negro History,* XXV, No. 4 (October, 1950), 435–452.

changed. The Kulturkampf *was at an end, the French policy of* revanche *was softened, and Germany's position in Europe was strengthened by the Triple Alliance. Bismarck was now in a position to defy England on the matter of colonies. Impatient at British delays, he let it be known that his support for British claims on Egypt could be had only at a price—colonies for Germany. How he relied on his son, Herbert, to bring England to terms shows the Bismarckian* modus operandi *at its best.*

The Bay of Angra Pequena, located along the southwest African coast at 26.38 degrees south by 15 degrees east, was discovered by Bartholomew Diaz in 1487. In 1796 a Captain Alexander landed there with a British ship and took possession of the bay in the name of Great Britain. In 1805 a group of German missionaries, in the service of the London Missionary Society, landed at a small village on the coast, and in 1814 a settlement was founded at Bethany, a village 125 miles east of Angra Pequena Bay. In 1842, a German missionary, Knudsen, representing the Rhine Missionary Society, settled at Bethany, and other Germans established homes in the Walfisch Bay area on the coastline to the north. In 1877, the governor of the Cape Colony, Sir Henry Bartle Edward Frere, uncomfortable because of the settlement of so many Germans in the Angra Pequena and Walfisch Bay areas and annoyed by the numerous disputes between the German missionaries and the natives, vainly urged his home government to place both Damaraland and Namaqualand, i.e., virtually all of southwest Africa, under the British empire. In March 1878, the British government placed under its protection Walfisch Bay and the surrounding territory for fifteen miles. With no help coming from Britain the German missionaries protested to Berlin, which sent a German warship to Walfisch Bay in August 1881.

As a result of the Rhine Missionary Society's requests for protection, Count Münster, the German ambassador in London, communicated a note to the British government asking for the extent of British sovereignty in southwest Africa. On November 29, 1880, Lord Granville, the British foreign secretary, replied that:

> Her Majesty's government cannot be responsible for what may take place outside British territory, which only includes Walfisch Bay and a very small portion of the country immediately surrounding it.

A month later, on December 30, 1880, in a note from the Colonial Office, London, to the Cape government, Britain defined the extent of her claims:

> Her Majesty's government are of the opinion that the Orange River should be maintained as the northwestern limit of the Cape Colony, and they will give no countenance to schemes for the extension of British jurisdiction over Great Namaqualand and Damaraland.

The British had cause to regret these two declarations of 1880, for soon it became obvious that Bismarck had embarked seriously on a policy of colonization.

By this time the missionary issue had been complicated by more important economic matters. Trading possibilities in Africa had interested the German Hansa merchants, especially F. A. E. Lüderitz, the head of a large mercantile house in Bremen. In 1876 Lüderitz, as spokesman for a merchant group, unfolded to Bismarck a complete scheme for founding a colony in South Africa, but his plan was for the moment rejected as impractical. Lüderitz was not discouraged. In 1881 he founded a factory at Lagos on the African Guinean coast, and with trade increasing rapidly, gradually developed the idea of setting up more factories as the nucleus for a German colony. On November 16, 1882, Lüderitz asked his own Foreign Office whether he would receive imperial protection for his factory and for his contracts with African chieftains. With a secret agreement from Bismarck that he would be given imperial protection if he could acquire a harbor in which no other nation could assert a claim, Lüderitz decided to go ahead in his plans.

On February 4, 1883 Bismarck opened the negotiations by addressing a note to Britain through his son, Count Herbert Bismarck, then *chargé d'affaires* in London, asking if Britain exercised any authority over the Angra Pequena region. Britain replied on February 23, 1883 that:

> The Cape Colony government has certain establishments along the coast, but without more precise information as to the exact location of Lüderitz's factory, it is impossible for the British government to say whether it could afford this protection in case it were required.

This was an evasive and even procrastinating reply, inasmuch as Britain had already declared that this part of the coast was outside her jurisdiction. Lüderitz, with his secret promise of protection from Bismarck, now acted. He sent his agent, Heinrich Vogelsang, in April 1883 to Angra Pequena, where a landing was effected, a treaty signed with the Africans, and the German flag hoisted on May 2, 1883.

This news was greeted in German colonial circles with undisguised joy, in England with ridicule. In the Cape Colony it was received with indignation and incredulity. The Cape Colony, which hitherto had shown no desire to occupy Angra Pequena, even now did not choose to show the slightest intention of seizing the unoccupied remainder of the coast. Apparently neither Britain nor the Cape Colony realized that this was the founding of the first German colony in Africa.

On August 18, 1883, the German government notified the German consul at the Cape that if the rights of other nations were not interfered with thereby, they would be prepared to give protection to Lüderitz's settlement, and a German gunboat took up a permanent station in the Bay of Angra Pequena. A German corvette, the *Carola,* appeared in the bay and gave notice to the commander of the British gunboat, the *Boadicea,* which had arrived from the Cape, that he was in German territorial waters.

Britain's definite reply to Bismarck's inquiry, which finally came after nearly nine months, stated that, although British sovereignty had been proclaimed at Walfisch Bay and the islands off Angra Pequena, any claim to sovereignty or jurisdiction by a foriegn power between Angola and Cape Colony would infringe Britain's legitimate rights. Bismarck's note of December 31, 1883 was hard in tone and demanded by what rights or title Britain could claim sovereignty over a territory formerly considered independent. Britain did not reply to this note.

From December 1883 to April 1884 the thermometers of public indignation and national chauvinism rose steadily and rapidly in Germany, to Bismarck's not altogether disinterested delight. On April 24, 1884, the German chancellor sent a telegram to the German consul at Capetown declaring officially that Lüderitz's settlement was under imperial protection, thus officially inaugurating the German colonial empire. The old Kaiser William I could now say happily: "Now I can look the Great Elector in the face when I cross the long bridge in Berlin."

So far, so good—from the Bismarckian viewpoint. The chancellor had proceeded cautiously and cleverly and had been successful in quieting any British suspicions of German colonial aspirations. Although the correspondence of 1880 had definitely delimited British claims, it did not prevent Bismarck from continuing his inquiries at London as a means of maintaining Germany scrupulously in the right. Thus far British indifference, pusillanimity, and procrastination had played into Bismarck's hands. But now the issue was getting serious. There were embarrassing inquiries in the House of Lords about rumors that "Germany intended to steal

Angra Pequena from Great Britain," and the British press spoke of "insults to the Home Country." The chancellor's diplomacy was put to a hard test. How to complete the negotiations on Angra Pequena without losing the main objective and without goading the British too far became for Bismarck a matter of prime importance.

From Bismarck's viewpoint the proper presentation of his own views to the British was complicated by his belief that the German ambassador in London, Münster, was "more English than German" and had been content to allow the question of Angra Pequena to hang fire. Eccentric both physically and mentally, with a disproportionately large head that reminded Bülow of "a pumpkin on a long stalk," Münster was by nature courteous and considerate, qualities which Bismarck considered of doubtful value in negotiations at a high level with British diplomats on a critical issue. Münster's personal connections with England, both by birth and marriage, made him anxious to interpret the unpleasant communications, of which he was at this time frequently the bearer, in the most conciliatory manner possible. Often he took it upon himself to soften down the asperities of Bismarck's notes in the interest of maintaining cordial relations, thereby increasing the number of his enemies at the German Foreign Office, who clamored for his recall so that Herbert Bismarck might replace him. Münster on his side had only contempt for the German Foreign Office under Bismarck, to whom he referred as the "Central Ox." Although an Anglophile, Münster believed that Germany had nothing to fear from British statesmen, who impressed him as "wealthy amateurs who live from hand to mouth, without really understanding the situation." From April 27, 1884, when he returned to his London post, to the first week of June, Münster made a number of serious mistakes which made him *persona non grata* with the "Central Ox." Clearly, then, Bismarck was not satisfied with Münster as an intermediary in the delicate negotiations.

In this emergency Bismarck turned to his son, Herbert, whom he had already tested by sending him on a mission to London in 1881–1882 and had been satisfied by the results. On November 20, 1881, the chancellor sent a personal message through Bleichröder, his secret agent, to Lord Ampthill, the British representative at Berlin, saying that he had decided to send his eldest son as second secretary to London and that he personally hoped and flattered himself that it might be regarded as a compliment and as an earnest desire to wipe out the painful impression made by a scandal which had taken place the previous summer at the German embassy in London. Several days later Bismarck wrote Ampthill, asking him as a personal favor to recommend his son, Herbert, "to Lord Granville's benevolence." The British ambassador promptly reported to London:

> Bismarck adores this son, who is a remarkably clever youth, and hopes to make a great stateman of him. He has often told me in confidence that Herbert, young as he is, would already make an abler ambassador than all the members of the German diplomatic body taken together.

Knowing full well that he and his family were not "in *ordeur* [*sic*] of sanctity" in high quarters, Bismarck kept Herbert's visit to England a secret at the palace from all except the emperor, until the newspapers revealed his arrival.

Lord Granville, the British foreign secretary, received the young Bismarck with warm hospitality, giving him a magnificent reception despite a "Berlin letter" sent him by the queen painting Herbert Bismarck in black colors. He found Herbert "clever, well-informed, bright, and easy to please," and was certain that the visit would do much to dispel "the want of knowledge of each other which some politicians display." Granville was almost pathetically eager to lionize the young cub as a means of softening the heart of the growling father. Similarly, members of English society vied with one another to give Bismarck's son a hearty welcome. Regarding the visitor as the political as well as personal heir of the dynasty the British hosts tried to flatter the paternal vanity of the great man whose power was then at its zenith.

Herbert Bismarck himself was not a little astonished by the cordiality of his reception, both by the official world and by society, and he allowed that he had never been made so much of before. He quickly assumed a position which made it clear that he was the representative, though not officially accredited, of his father. Without consulting his nominal chief, Münster, he sent his father, Holstein, and Rantzau private reports of the gossip he picked up in London clubs, which were then forwarded to the emperor and occasionally made use of in the press. Bismarck and his wife were delighted. They thanked Granville and Lady Granville through Ampthill for the cordiality of the reception to their beloved boy, whereupon Ampthill reported to London that "He (Bismarck) said he could never be sufficiently grateful for the reception his son had met with in England." And again: "Princess Bismarck never ceases to talk in grateful and eloquent language" about Granville's kindnesses to her son.

It was a happy state of affairs: the British had invested their kindness politically, Bismarck seemed to have a growing preference for England, and relations between Britain and Germany seemed to be improving.

This love feast was rudely disturbed in 1884 by the shadows of Angra Pequena. Feeling that the time was right for a showdown with Britain, Bismarck decided to use his trump card—the threat of withdrawing his support for Britain's policy in Egypt. On June 14, 1884, just before a debate in the Reichstag, he informed Ampthill that he "deplored the delay in answering his questions, which had been respectfully and loyally put," and feared that "public opinion in Germany would resent the fact that after six months delay the Cape government had been wedged in between German aspirations and interests and Angra Pequena."

In the meantime Herbert Bismarck had arrived in London on a special mission for his father to deal with the Angra Pequena question. Bismarck planned his attack well: on the same day that he was discussing the matter with the British ambassador at Berlin, June 14, 1884, his son Herbert was having his first long conversation with Granville in London. Herbert first complained of the long delay in answering his father's inquiries, to which replies might have been given in a few days. He then insisted that the German government would negotiate only with the Foreign Office and not with the Colonial Office, and then accused Lord Derby, the colonial secretary, of double dealing by taking advantage of the delay to press the government of the Cape Colony to take action anticipating actions of the German government.

Herbert Bismarck then made clear the importance that his father attached to Angra Pequena and stated that his father intended to set up an arrangement at Angra Pequena that would preclude the possibility of the annexation of that place by any other power.

With the groundwork prepared, Herbert Bismarck now produced his father's sharpest weapon. While Prince Bismarck still entertained the same friendly feelings toward her Majesty's government and was desirous of supporting its policy in Egypt, he thought it right that Granville should be warned that the feeling in Germany as regards these colonial questions was so strong that, with the best of wishes, he felt he would be unable to afford Britain the same friendly assistance as hitherto, unless he could give some satisfaction to public opinion on the subject. To this Granville replied that he "objected to anything in the nature of a bargain between us. Each question ought to be discussed on its own merits." Herbert Bismarck then insisted that he did not raise any question of a bargain, but that "the German government expected their rights to be respected." "We have the painful impression," he informed Granville, "that you will evade the question and are awaiting reports, whether you can want the thing." Granville denied this strenuously and said: "If it is your *right* you will see England at your feet at once."

On June 17, 1884 Herbert Bismarck and Granville met for the second time. This interview proceeded along the same lines as the previous one, although there were differing accounts by the participants. Herbert Bismarck reported that Granville had said that in England it was the opinion that the national possessions were already too great and that England had not the slightest reason to oppose German colonization. Granville wrote to Ampthill that he had asked Herbert Bismarck to let him know definitely what Germany claimed: "Did they wish, I said, to protect the German settlers only, or were they desirous of undertaking the protection of both the German and the British settlers, or thirdly—did they claim to extend protection to all settlers of whatever nationality who might obtain concessions?"

During these two interviews Herbert Bismarck adopted a policy of calculated rudeness which appears to have been planned well in advance. Thus, in the first conference of June 14, 1884, Granville said that since the problem of Angra Pequena affected his colleagues more than it did him, he would be pleased if Herbert Bismarck would confer, in his presence, with Lord Derby and Lord Kimberley. Herbert curtly refused the invitation. In the second interview of June 17, 1884, Granville brought up the question of sovereignty at Angra Pequena. Herbert Bismarck, who had been prepared for this very question by his father in an exchange of telegrams, retorted not over-politely that he thought it "a question of mere curiosity if you ask about sovereignty: it can be all the same to you, what another power does in a country not belonging to you." Moreover, he was sure that "my government would decline to give an answer in a matter that is of no concern to you." This was an extraordinary way for a thirty-five-year-old diplomat to address the seventy-year-old minister of a great power, but the elder Bismarck was delighted with his son's toughness. Herbert Bismarck seemed to be carried away with his role of tough negotiator; he sent home scornful reports on almost all the British ministers. The British, on their part, were not unaware of the policy of rudeness adopted by the two Bismarcks. Thus, Sir Charles Dilke reported that he attended a cabinet meeting at Lord Granville's house at a time when Herbert Bismarck was in the house. "He (Herbert Bismarck) had been very rude to Lord Granville about Angra Pequena, which was mentioned to the Cabinet, which could do nothing."

Here is an excellent illustration of Bismarckian diplomacy in high gear. From the beginning Bismarck was sure of his ground. The British were taken in a trap and he was well aware of it. Eighty-eight years previously British troops had been landed on the southwest African coast, yet Britain had never claimed it or set up a government. British diplomats handled the Angra Pequena matter with varying amounts of indifference, delay, expressions of ignorance, and the earnest hope that somehow in some way southwest Africa could be saved either for Britain or the Cape Colony, and the embarkation of German colonialism in Africa discouraged or prevented. Bismarck met these tactics with brusqueness and rudeness, carefully planned for its effect and executed by his son. The idea was to convince the British Foreign Office that he was serious. Thoroughly disgusted with the temporizing methods of British ministers and convinced that Münster had not represented German interests with sufficient energy, Bismarck sent his son to London with explicit orders to carry on diplomacy-by-irritation.

On June 22, 1884, another confidential conference was held between Herbert Bismarck and Granville, during the course of which the British foreign minister said that the Cabinet, having thoroughly examined the Angra Pequena question, had come to the conclusion that Britain was not in a position to question the right of the German government to afford protection to its own subjects who had settled there. Thus, in three interviews Herbert Bismarck had achieved a preliminary settlement of the southwest Africa issue, with the British government giving Bismarck all that he had wanted. Britain had been forced to admit that the German protection over the mainland acquired by Lüderitz was justified, and she had been compelled to withdraw her claims to this area of Africa, with the exception of Walfisch Bay.

It was bitter medicine for the proud British, but the fact that they gave in eventually to Bismarck's demands was another indication that realism and not sentiment ruled the Foreign Office. It would seem that the only satisfactory answer to Herbert Bismarck's rough diplomacy-by-irritation should have been equally harsh and stiff-necked treatment, but the British were by now well aware of the weakness of their own position and the corresponding strength of Bismarck's. It was felt that the chancellor's support in Egypt was well worth the loss of Angra Pequena. In London there was much criticism in the press about "this ignominious chapter in the colonial history of England" as well as a good deal of pride-swallowing among chagrined ministers; in Berlin the press happily applauded "the clever manipulating and use of great patience" by the Bismarcks, father and son, who joyfully toasted each other in mutual admiration.

There were some further repercussions, although the matter was basically settled. In July 1884, the Cape Colony suddenly declared that, with Lord Derby's sanction, she had annexed southwest Africa. Bismarck promptly dispatched three warships to the spot, and on August 7, 1884 the German flag was hoisted. Britain had no desire to go to war about Angra Pequena, hence she explained that the annexation order referred only to such lands as were not actually occupied by the Germans. Germany's great colonial adventure was under way.

78

The Lasker Affair: Bismarck Rejects a Resolution of Sympathy by the American House of Representatives on the Death of a Despised Political Opponent[32]

"Am I to make myself my enemy's postman?"

To Bismarck hatred was as great an incentive in life as love. We have seen how Count Harry von Arnim, whom Bismarck suspected of seeking the chancellorship, was driven from his ambassadorial career and hounded to the day of his death in 1881. Several years later came another manifestation of the Bismarckian will-to-vengeance.

Eduard Lasker, parliamentarian and co-founder of the National Liberal party, was a man with an unlimited drive for work, a devastating debater, a distinguished statesman who held firmly to free and liberal ideas. A man utterly devoted to his career, without hobbies, he was absorbed completely by his role in the Reichstag. At night he studied the publications of the house, in the mornings he sat on committees, afternoons he attended meetings, and evenings he spent with his party colleagues. He was one of the most important, popular, and able leaders in Germany.

But Bismarck was repelled by Lasker, whom he dubbed "the sickness of Germany." The battle of words between these political opponents was carried on with great personal bitterness, irritability, and vindictiveness. Bismarck complained that he could never have a bill passed in the Reichstag without a Lasker amendment, which resulted in giving Bismarck's measures more of a liberal flavor than he liked. Above all, Bismarck resented Lasker's at-

32. Account contributed by the editor.

tempts to strengthen parliamentary government in Prussia-Germany.

Veit Valentin described the rivalry between the two politicians in this passage:

> They had little in common, the little Jew of Jaroczin and the reactionary Junker of old Prussia who had become a revolutionary, a destroyer, a master of political intrigue, the builder of the new German Reich, the creative genius of the period, the man of destiny, the pioneer of the German future. . . . The development of this feud is an amazing chapter of German political psychology.[33]

In the summer of 1883, the frail Lasker, worn out by his labors, went to the United States in search of rest and health. After visiting a brother in Texas, he came to New York City. During the evening of January 4–5, 1884, while on the street on his way home from a dinner party, he complained of illness and in a few minutes was dead of a heart attack.

The news of the death of the German parliamentarian was received with sorrow in both Germany and the United States. The press of both countries praised him for his "pure character," his "devotion and unselfishness," "his extraordinary talents and remarkably steady industry." The *New York Tribune* described him as "pre-eminently the greatest lawyer" and concluded that "German liberalism loses one of its most distinguished leaders."

On January 9, 1884, the House of Representatives of the American Congress passed this resolution:

> *Resolved,* That this House has heard with deep regret of the death of the eminent statesman, Eduard Lasker.
>
> That his loss is not alone to be mourned by the people of his native land, where his firm and constant exposition of and devotion to free and liberal ideas have materially advanced the social, political, and economic conditions of those peoples, but by the lovers of liberty throughout the world.
>
> That a copy of these resolutions be forwarded to the family of the deceased as well as to the minister of the United States resident at the capital of the German empire, to be by him communicated through the legitimate channel to the presiding officer of the legislative body of which he was a member.

This address of sympathy was handed to Bismarck, who thereupon refused to transmit it to the Reichstag and sent it back to the

33. Veit Valentin, "Bismarck and Lasker," *Journal of Central European Affairs,* III, No. 4 (January, 1944), 402.

United States through the German ambassador in Washington. The American press reacted angrily against this "fantastic performance, malicious, resentful, and ill-mannered."

Bismarck refused to retreat. "I would have presented the resolution to the Reichstag," he said, "had I not been prevented by its form. It was not confined to a general expression of sympathy, but it expressed the conviction that Herr Lasker's labors had been very useful to Germany. This clause was directed against the policy, which, in the emperor's name, I have been pursuing for years. Now, the question arises whether Herr Lasker was right. If he was, then the emperor's policy, my policy, was wrong. . . . Herr Lasker introduced himself in America as the champion of German freedom against a government of despotic tendencies impersonated in the chancellor. . . . Am I to make myself my enemy's postman?"

Bismarck's sarcastic speech caused an explosion of indignation in the United States. Congressmen complained that there was never more than an intention to compliment the people of Germany by paying a tribute of respect to one of Germany's greatest statesmen.

That was the end of the matter. Bismarck had only contempt for Lasker as a political enemy. Let others wallow in laudatory obituaries and praise for the dear departed. Bismarck despised the dead Lasker as much as he had resented the live opponent. He was certain that his political enemies were even using Lasker's death to continue the battle against his own policies. Not even death could salve Bismarck's hatred.

79

The Battenberg Affair: Alexander of Bulgaria, Handsome Extrovert, Seeks to Marry into the Prussian Royal Family Only to Find His Way Barred by an Angered, Determined Bismarck

"I would recommend that you marry an orthodox millionairess."

At the Congress of Berlin in 1878 Russia was given temporary control of Bulgaria until a ruler was named. In April 1879, at the instigation of Tsar Alexander II, Prince Alexander von Battenberg, of German lineage, was called to the Bulgarian throne. A strikingly handsome officer of the Garde du Corps, *Alexander lived on the fringe of fashionable society and was adored by the ladies. As soon as he ascended the Bulgarian throne, he began a foreign policy directed at Russia. In 1882, at the age of twenty-five, he visited Berlin, where he met Princess Victoria, daughter of the crown prince and crown princess of Prussia. The young princess was overwhelmed by her romantic suitor, and the two became secretly engaged. The crown princess and her mother, Queen Victoria, motivated by both sentimental and political reasons, endorsed the union.*

In early 1884 rumors about the romance reached Bismarck, who was anxious to avoid any worsening of Russo-German relations. He went to Emperor William and, in a long, impassioned interview, expressed his hostility to the union. William reluctantly decided to veto the marriage. Several days later, on May 12, 1884, Bismarck received the Bulgarian ruler in a formal audience. At first he tried to sound out Alexander on the contemplated union, but receiving no information, he stated bluntly what was on his mind. A verbatim report of the interview follows.[34]

"The rumors of the union of your Highness with a Prussian princess have made the most painful impression in Berlin. I hope to receive directly from your Highness the calming assurance that you have not been contemplating such a marriage."

Prince Alexander: "I heard about such rumors for the first time here in Berlin."

Pause.

At this point Bismarck spoke ironically: "Well, since your Highness seems to know so little about the matter, permit me to say that this union has been discussed seriously and in such a manner that it has led to violent scenes in the palace. Her Imperial Highness, the crown princess, and the English court are all for it, but the emperor and empress have declared that they cannot give their permission. As chancellor of the Reich I have told his Majesty: Germany has no interest in Bulgaria. Our aim is peace with Russia. Above all else it is most necessary that Russia have the conviction that we do not have any interests in the Near East. On the day on which a Prussian princess becomes princess of Bulgaria, Russia will become distrustful and disbelieve such assurances from us. This marriage will cause me political embarrassment. I cannot relent on this matter, and I have declared to his Majesty that, as long as I am chancellor of the Reich, this marriage will not take

34. Quoted in E. G. Costi, *Fürst Alexander von Battenberg* (Vienna, 1920), pp. 165 ff. Translated by the editor.

place. At the same time I have assured the emperor that he will not find any successor to me who would act differently."

Pause.

"I hold it my duty to urge your Majesty to think anew about this problem. His Majesty arranged to have you stay in Wiesbaden because he did not want to see you in Berlin. I regret that you have seen fit to come here. I just cannot understand why you wish to marry a Prussian princess. The Princess Beatrice of England or the Princess Helene of Mecklenburg would be a more suitable partner for you. I would recommend that you marry an orthodox millionairess. That would secure your status in Bulgaria, because in the Near East ruling means bribery, and for that, money is needed. One is not concerned with morality there.

"I believe that it is high time that you make a choice: German or Bulgarian. Until recently you have been German, but that ended with your departure. In your place I probably would have remained German, because I know it must be difficult for an honorable, upright gentleman such as you to deal with Orientals. But if you wish to remain in Bulgaria, for better or worse you must turn to Russia. If it be necessary, then by all means take an anti-German position! However, I believe the very existence of Bulgaria to be problematical. It will eventually become an object of compensation to some country. Sooner or later, in your high position, you will be reminded of your stormy youth. They know our views in St. Petersburg. I strongly advise you to take every opportunity you can to return to the good graces of Russia. Your Majesty has the full sympathy of influential German circles. I myself have a high regard for you. But I am the chancellor of forty-five million Germans, whose interests I cannot sacrifice for a single German. I have chanced the danger of incurring your disfavor by speaking as frankly as I can.

"And now to come once again to the Princess Victoria, I must add this," said Bismarck further. "I have informed his Majesty that if this marriage is a matter of ardent desire on your part, your Majesty can revert to your old status as a Prussian general and a German prince. If, after you do that, you still wish to become the emperor's son-in-law, then I, Bimarck, would become the first person to raise my hat to this marriage."

Until now Prince Alexander had said scarcely a word. Bismarck had been carrying the conversation all alone. Now Prince Alexander spoke: "I have learned with dismay that Russians have been working against me in a way in which decent people do not act. In Vienna and Berlin it has been rumored that my private life has been scandalous, that I have numerous debts, and that in St.

Petersburg there are papers whose publication I am supposed to fear. To these rumors I must reply and declare unequivocally: All papers which concern me can be published. I can only profit from it. I do not now have any debts. As far as my private life is concerned, you can learn all about it from German sources. I live in the glare of publicity and everyone can come to see me day or night. Every Bulgarian knows how soberly and impeccably I live and recognizes this gratefully."

"I know that," responded Bismarck, "and, moreover, not one of us has ever given any credence to these rumors, which have been passed on to me through my son Herbert, among others. We pay no attention to such means here."

With that the interview came to an end. Both the adversaries took leave of each other in the most courteous way.

Alexander was unfortunate—he had unwittingly opened the Near Eastern question at an inconvenient time and thereby incurred Bismarck's enmity. Two years later he was kidnapped by Bulgarian officers and taken out of the country. He returned briefly but was again forced into exile by Tsar Alexander III, who had conceived a violent dislike for him. Such was the unhappy fate of one who risked Bismarck's wrath.

30

April 1, 1885: His Majesty William I of Hohenzollern Congratulates Bismarck on His Seventieth Birthday and Expresses His Warmest Gratitude [35]

"I shall always have the fullest confidence in you."

Bismarck's seventieth birthday was greeted enthusiastically throughout Germany. The great man received many valuable presents, not the least of which was the purchase deed to the ancestral estate of Schönhausen (when in difficulties in the past the family had sold this deed). A committee of the people collected more than a million marks and placed it at Bismarck's disposal. The chancellor used part of it for scholarships for needy students. Among the 3,500 telegrams and 2,100 letters was the following telegram from Emperor William. The picture referred to in the text was a

35. *The Correspondence of William I and Bismarck,* trans. Ford, pp. 227–228.

reduced copy of Anton von Werner's painting of the "Proclamation of the Empire at Versailles."

BERLIN, *April* 1, 1885

MY DEAR PRINCE,

When such an ardent desire is shown by the German people to manifest to you on your seventieth birthday that all you have done for the greatness of the fatherland is still held in grateful remembrance, I feel impelled from my heart to tell you today how much I rejoice that such a current of thanks to and admiration of you is passing through the nation. I am glad of this, as it is an acknowledgment that you have abundantly earned, and it cheers my heart to see these feelings manifested in such a general manner. It is an ornament to the nation in the present, and a good augury for its future, when it shows its appreciation of the true and the great, and when it does honor to its deserving men. It is an especial pleasure to me and my house to participate in such a celebration, and we desire to express by means of this picture with what feelings of grateful remembrance we do this. For the picture represents one of the greatest moments in the history of the Hohenzollern house, a moment which no one will ever recall without at the same time thinking of your great services.

You know, my dear prince, that I shall always have the fullest confidence in you, and entertain the most sincere affection and the warmest gratitude towards you! I am therefore telling you nothing new, and I think that this picture will be a testimony to your descendants that your emperor and king, with his house, are fully aware of what we owe to you.

With these sentiments I end this letter, and remain, even beyond the grave,

Your grateful, truly devoted
Emperor and King,
WILLIAM

KISSINGEN, *June* 23, 1885

I thank your Majesty most humbly for the gracious telegram with which your Majesty has honored me. The losses which your Majesty has sustained recently, by the death of faithful servants, are numerous and heavy, and exhort us who are left behind to fill, by increased devotion in the sovereign service and to your Majesty's person, the empty places of those to whom your Majesty was attached. It is especially painful to me that my state of health does not permit me to manifest my most respectful sympathy in your Majesty's affliction by my presence. I am permitted to hope, however, that my "cure" this year will have an especially favorable effect, and already feel traces of increased vigor when taking bodily exercise. This result is to a great extent due to the decreased burden of work; the slowness with which the English ministerial crisis is developing has produced a stillness in diplomatic intercourse which is unusual even during the summer. No reports entailing much work are coming in from any ambassador. The duke of Cambridge's wishes, on which I report today officially, have already been fully replied to by your Majesty, and everything was then said to the duke that is to be said; your Majesty has thus amply fulfilled all the demands of *courtoisie,* the *business* side of the affair is not in your Majesty's hands, but in those of the Federal Council and the Brunswick Ministry. . . . May God give his blessing to your Majesty's "cure" at Ems and especially at Gastein this year as in former years.

v. BISMARCK

Two years later, in 1887, on the fortieth anniversary of his marriage, Bismarck sent Johanna a telegram thanking her for "14,610 days, 2,088 Sundays, and ten 29th of Februarys, of good and bad, but much more good!"

New York Public Library Picture Collec

PART VI

)ecline and Fall: The Final Decade, 1888-1898

81

Pride Goeth: At the Pinnacle of Power, Bismarck, in a Speech on February 6, 1888, Calls for Still More Military Strength to Be Equal to All Contingencies

"We Germans fear God, but nothing else in the world."

Convinced that France was bent on a war of revenge and that additional danger threatened from Russia, Bismarck called for increased armaments. On December 9, 1887, a bill to this effect was introduced in the Reichstag, and on January 31, 1888, another act proposed to procure the money for an increase in armaments. Bismarck opened the discussion with the following speech, the effect of which was electric.[1] *The Reichstag passed both bills by unanimous vote.*

When I say that we must constantly endeavor to be equal to all contingencies, I mean by that to claim that we must make greater exertions than other powers in order to attain the same result, because of our geographical position. We are situated in the middle of Europe. We have at least three fronts of attack. France has only its eastern frontier, Russia only its western frontier, on which it can be attacked. We are, moreover, in consequence of the whole development of the world's history, in consequence of our geographical position, and perhaps in consequence of the slighter degree of internal cohesion which the German nation as compared with others has thus far possessed, more exposed than any other people to the risk of a coalition. God has placed us in a situation in which we are prevented by our neighbors from sinking into any sort of indolence or stagnation. He has set at our side the most warlike and the most restless of nations, the French; and he has permitted warlike inclinations, which in former centuries existed in no such degree, to grow strong in Russia. Thus we get a certain amount of spurring on both sides, and are forced into exertions which otherwise perhaps we should not make. The pikes in the European carp pond prevent us from becoming carps, by letting us feel their prickles on both our flanks; they constrain us to exertions which perhaps we should not voluntarily make;

1. Quoted in Charles Dudley Warren, ed., *Library of the World's Great Literature* (New York, 1896), V, 1955–1958.

they constrain us Germans also to a harmony among ourselves that is repugnant to our inmost nature: but for them, our tendency would rather be to separate. But the Franco-Russian press in which we are caught, forces us to hold together, and by its pressure it will greatly increase our capacity for cohesion, so that we shall reach in the end that state of inseparableness which characterizes nearly all other nations, and which we still lack. But we must adapt ourselves to this decree of Providence by making ourselves so strong that the pikes can do no more than enliven us. . . .

The bill gives us an increase in troops trained to arms—a possible increase: if we do not need it, we need not call for it; we can leave it at home. But if we have this increase at our disposal, and if we have the weapons for it, . . . then this new law constitutes a reinforcement of the guarantees of peace, a reinforcement of the league of peace, that is precisely as strong as if a fourth great power with an army of 700,000 men—and this was formerly the greatest strength that existed—had joined the alliance. This powerful reinforcement will also, I believe, have a quieting effect upon our own countrymen, and lessen in some degree the nervousness of our public opinion, our stock-market, and our press. I hope it will act upon them as a sedative when they clearly comprehend that from the moment at which this law is signed and published the men are there. The armament, too, may be said to be ready, in the shape of what is absolutely necessary: but we must procure a better, for if we form an army of triarians of the best human material that we have,—of the men above thirty, the husbands and fathers,—we must have for them the best weapons there are. We must not send them into the fight with an outfit that we do not regard as good enough for our young troops of the line. The solid men, the heads of families, these stalwart figures that we can still remember from the time that they held the bridge of Versailles, —these men must have the best rifles on their shoulders, the completest armament, and the amplest clothing to protect them from wind and weather. We ought not to economize there.

But I hope it will tranquilize our fellow citizens, if they are really thinking of the contingency (which I do not expect to occur) of our being attacked simultaneously on two sides,—of course, as I have pointed out in reviewing the events of the last forty years, there is always the possibility of any sort of coalition,—I hope it will tranquilize them to remember that if this happens, we can have a million good soldiers to defend each of our frontiers. At the same time we can keep in the rear reserves of half a million and more, of a million even, and we can push these forward as they are needed. I have been told, "That will only result in the others going still higher." But they cannot. They have long ago reached their limits. . . . In numbers they have gone as high as we, but in quality they cannot compete with us. Bravery, of course, is equal among all civilized nations; the Russian and the Frenchman fight as bravely as the German: but our men, our 700,000 new men, have seen service; they are soldiers who have served their time, and who have not yet forgotten their training. Besides—and this is a point in which no people in the world can compete with us—we have the material for officers and under-officers to command this enormous army. It is here that competition is excluded, because it involves a peculiarly broad extension of popular culture, such as exists in Germany and in no other country. . . .

There is a further advantage that will result from the adoption of this law: the very strength at which we are aiming necessarily makes us peaceful. That sounds paradoxical, but it is true. With the powerful machine which we are making of the German army no aggression will be attempted. If I saw fit—assuming a different situation to exist from that which in my conviction does exist—to come before you here today and say to you, "We are seriously menaced by France and Russia; the prospect is that we shall be attacked: such at least is my conviction, as a diplomatist, on the basis of the military information that we have received; it is to our advantage to defend ourselves by anticipating the attack, and to strike at once; an offensive war is a better one for us to wage, and I accordingly ask the Imperial Diet for a credit of a milliard or half a milliard, in order to undertake today the war against our two neighbors,"—well gentlemen, I do not know whether you would have such confidence in me as to grant such a request. I hope not. But if you did, it would not be enough for me.

If we in Germany desire to wage a war with the full effect of our national power, it must be a war with which all who help to wage it, and all who make sacrifices for it—with which, in a word, all the nation—must be in sympathy. It must be a people's war; it must be a war that is carried on with the same enthusiasm as that of 1870, when we were wickedly attacked. I remember still the joyful shouts that rang in our ears at the Cologne station; it was the same thing from Berlin to Cologne; it was the same thing here in Berlin. The waves of popular approval bore us into the war, whether we liked it or not. So it must be, if a national force like ours is to be brought fully into operation. It will be very difficult, however, to make it clear to the provinces, to the federal states and to their people, that a war is inevitable, that it must come. It will be asked: "Are you so sure of it? Who knows?" If we finally come to the point of making the attack, all the weight of the imponderables, which weigh much more than the material weights, will be on the side of our antagonist whom we have attacked. "Holy Russia" will be filled with indignation at the attack. France will glisten with weapons to the Pyrenees. The same thing will happen everywhere. A war into which we are not borne by the will of the people —such a war will of course be carried on, if in the last instance the established authorities consider and have declared it to be necessary. It will be carried on with energy and perhaps victoriously, as soon as the men come under fire and have seen blood; but there will not be back of it, from the start, the same dash and heat as in a war in which we are attacked. . . .

I do not believe—to sum up—that any disturbance of the peace is an immediate prospect; and I ask you to deal with the law that lies before you, independently of any such idea or apprehension, simply as a means for making the great force which God has lodged in the German nation completely available in the event of our needing it. If we do not need it, we shall not call for it. We seek to avoid the chance of our needing it. This effort on our part is still, in some degree, impeded by threatening newspaper articles from foreign countries; and I wish to address to foreign countries especially the admonition to discontinue these threats. They lead to nothing. The threat which we receive, not from the foreign government, but in the press, is really a piece of incredible stupidity, if you think what it means—that by a certain combination of words, by a certain threatening shape given to printer's ink, a great and proud power like the German Empire is assumed to be capable of intimidation. This should be discontinued; and then it would be made easier for us to assume a more conciliatory and obliging attitude toward our two neighbors.

Every country is responsible in the long run, somehow and at some time, for the windows broken by its press; the bill is presented some day or other, in the ill-humor of the other country. We can easily be influenced by love and good will,—too easily perhaps,—but most assuredly not by threats. We Germans fear God, but nothing else in the world; and it is the fear of God that makes us love and cherish peace. But whoever, despite this, breaks it, will find that the warlike patriotism that in 1813, when Prussia was weak, small, and exhausted by plunder, brought her whole population under her banners, has today become the common heritage of the whole German nation; and whoever attacks the German nation will find it united in arms, and in every soldier's heart the firm faith "God will be with us."

82

The Affair of the Emperor's Diary, 1888: Infuriated to the Point of Apoplexy, Bismarck, in a Lamentable Performance, Defends His Place in History [2]

"I consider the diary in its present form not to be genuine."

In March 1888, Emperor William I, who had passsed the age of ninety, died. His son, the crown prince at the age of fifty-six ascended the throne as Frederick III. This tragic Hohenzollern suffered from a fatal disease, cancer of the throat: his reign lasted just ninety-nine days. Married to the eldest daughter of Queen Victoria, Frederick had been impressed by British constitutional institutions. With him died the great hopes of German liberals.

In September 1888 a highly respected journal, the Deutsche Rundschau, *published extracts from the diary which Frederick had kept during the Austro-Prussian War of 1866 and the Franco-Prussian War of 1870–1871. It told of the struggles in the German headquarters at Versailles over the nature of the new German empire. It revealed Frederick as a supporter of the national idea and the liberal organization of the future Reich. It also criticized Bismarck as too hesitant and wavering.*

Bismarck was appalled by the publication of these notes. He was still further annoyed when the opposition press began to praise the diary. With William II's consent, Bismarck issued an "Immediate Report," printed in full below. The opening sentences virtually accused Frederick of treason, an almost unbelievable slander. The incident showed that Bismarck would stop at nothing if anyone, including the royal family, dared attack his place in history.

Bismarck was so angered that he had criminal proceedings started against the dead emperor's friend, Professor Heinrich Geffcken, who had edited the diary. The unfortunate professor was jailed for three months and then released after it was decided that the indictment was untenable. Bismarck was thus defeated legally. Politically, on the other hand, it was a severe blow to his prestige.

FRIEDRICHSRUH, *Sept.* 23, 1888

In obedience to your Majesty's commands I have the honor to make the following report with reference to the alleged diary of

2. *The Emperor's Diary of the Austro-Prussian War 1866 and the Franco-German War 1870–71,* ed. by Henry W. Lucy (London, 1888), pp. 126–139.

the late emperor as published in the *Deutsche Rundschau:*—

I consider the diary in its present form not to be genuine. It is true that his Majesty, the then crown prince, in 1870 stood outside the sphere of political negotiations, and was therefore liable to be incompletely or inaccurately informed about many incidents. I did not possess the permission of the king to talk with his Royal Highness on esoteric questions of our policy. His Majesty dreaded on the one hand, the indiscreet revelations which might thus be made to the English court, full of French sympathies, and, on the other, was apprehensive lest detriment might accrue to our relations with our German allies by reason of the far-reaching aims and the violence of the means which were recommended to his Royal Highness by political councillors of doubtful ability. Thus the crown prince stood without the sphere of all business negotiations.

At the same time it is scarcely possible that, if the impressions he received had been recorded daily, so many mistakes of fact and especially of time could have crept into his diary. It seems rather as if the daily notes themselves, or at least later additions to them, had originated with someone in the *entourage* of the crown prince. At the very beginning of the diary it is said that on the 13th of July, 1870, I looked upon peace as secured, and therefore wanted to return to Varzin. As a matter of fact—which can be proved by documentary evidence—his Royal Highness knew at the time that I regarded war as necessary, and was resolved to go to Varzin only after retiring from office if war were avoided. His Royal Highness was at one with me about this, as appears from the alleged entry on the 15th of July, where it is said that the crown prince completely agreed with me that peace and concession were already impossible.

Nor is it right that his Majesty the King had not much objection to the mobilization. His Majesty continued to believe, as the crown prince knew, that he could still preserve peace and spare the nation war. His Majesty was in Brandenburg, and during the whole of the railway journey from there to Berlin withstood my advocacy of mobilization. But after hearing M. Ollivier's speech, which was read to him at the Berlin station, and commanding it to be read to him a second time, he considered it as tantamount to a French declaration of war, and without more ado the king, *proprio motu,* decided to mobilize. It was then that the crown prince, who had already the day before agreed with me as to the necessity of a complete mobilization, put an end to further wavering by announcing the royal decision to the public—*i.e.,* to the officers present, with the words, *"Krieg, mobil."*

Further, judging from conversations I then had with the crown prince, it is not possible for his Royal Highness to have foreseen after this war a pause in the era of battles and bloodshed (as recorded under date of the 1st of August), seeing that his Royal Highness shared the general conviction, and expressed it too, that whatever might be the issue of this war it would inaugurate a series of wars, and that a warlike century was inevitable.

Again, it is impossible that the crown prince could have said that he had some difficulty in persuading the king to confer the Iron Cross on non-Prussians also, seeing that when at Versailles, months afterwards I was repeatedly commissioned by the king to beg the crown prince himself to proceed with the conferring of the Iron Cross on non-Prussians. I did not find the crown prince readily inclined to do so, and it required the repeated intervention of his Majesty to get the order attended to.

Especially remarkable in one's examination of the genuineness of the alleged diary is the chronological error implied in the statement that a lively discussion between the crown prince and me with reference to the future of Germany and the relations of the kaiser to his fellow-sovereigns, took place no earlier than at Versailles. This conversation between us was held at Donchery on the 3rd of September, and part of it even on previous occasions, several hours at a time, of which I only remember that we were on horseback, and therefore probably at Beaumont or Sedan.

At Versailles there were no longer any discussions or differences of opinion between his Royal Highness and me as to the future constitution of Germany. I may, I think, rather assume that his Royal Highness had by this time convinced himself that the line of the attainable marked out by me was the correct one, for on the few occasions when the future of Germany and the kaiser question came up for discussion, in presence of both father and son, I enjoyed the agreement of his Royal Highness in combating the scruples of his Majesty. The assertion of the diary that his Royal Highness could have thought of employing force against our allies, and of thus breaking the treaties which had been faithfully kept by them, and sealed with their very blood, is a calumniation of the deceased prince. Such ideas, which are equally contemptible from the standpoint of honorable feeling and from that of policy, may have found advocates among the *entourage* of the crown prince, but they were too dishonorable to find an echo in his heart, and too clumsy to appeal to his political sense.

And just as little consonant with the facts is what is said in the diary with reference to my attitude to the kaiser question in 1866, or to those of infallibility, an Upper House, and imperial ministries. The crown prince never entertained the idea that empire (*Kaiserthum*) would have been possible or profitable in 1866, knowing that a North German kaiser might have passed for an emperor, but would never have been a historic representative and instrument of the national regeneration of Germany. Similarly, the Upper House idea was disposed of by us at Donchery on the 3rd of September, the crown prince being convinced that the German kings and sovereigns would never be got to lend themselves to anything like the Prussian House of Lords (*Herrenhaus*).

As for infallibility, that is a question to which I was always indifferent. I regarded it as a false move on the part of the then pope, and begged his Royal Highness to let this question alone, during the war at least. But an impression that I meant to take it up after the war can never have been gathered by his Royal Highness and entered in a diary that was written up daily.

In one place (under date September 1) it is stated that his Majesty the King dictated to Count Hartzfeldt the draft of his reply to the letter of Napoleon. The crown prince was standing by when the king ordered me to draft the answer, and this rough draft was read out to the king for his Majesty's approval. Here, therefore, also, it is not credible that such a mistake could have occurred if the entries in the diary had been made daily.

In view of all this, I hold the diary, in the form in which it is published in the *Rundschau,* to be spurious. If it were genuine, it would, in my opinion, come under Article 92 of the Penal Code, which runs thus:—

"Whoever wilfully makes public state secrets, or intelligence whereof the secret keeping is essential to the welfare of the German empire," &c.

If there were any state secrets at all, they would primarily include the fact, if fact it was, that when the German empire was in course of re-establishment, Kaiser Frederick advocated the idea of breaking faith and treaties with the South German States, and using force with them. A number of other passages, such as those recording the opinion of his Royal Highness the crown prince as to their Majesties the kings of Bavaria and Württemberg, and referring to the alleged intentions of the Prussian government in the matter of papal infallibility, such passages, if true, would most unquestionably fall within the category of state secrets and intelligence of which the publication would imperil the existence and future of the German empire, which to a great extent depends upon the unity of its sovereigns; and, therefore, within the scope of Article 92 of the Penal Code.

If the publication is held to be genuine, Article 92, sec. 1, applies to it. But if, as I assume it to be, the publication is a forgery, it will primarily, perhaps, come under Article 92, sec. 2. And if there are any legal doubts as to its applicability, then, apart from Article 189 referring to libellous assaults on the memory of deceased persons, I think there are other clauses which may form the basis of a judicial investigation whereby, at least, light may be thrown on the origin and aims of this publication, which forms a calumniation of the deceased Emperors Frederick and William. That this should be done is in the interest of your Majesty's two predecessors, whose memory forms a valuable possession of the people and of the dynasty that should be preserved from the disfiguring tendencies with which this anonymous publication, accomplished in the interest of revolution and domestic discord, is primarily directed against the Emperor Frederick.

In this sense I respectfully pray your Majesty graciously to empower me to convey to the minister of justice your Majesty's commands to direct the public prosecutor to take criminal action against the *Deutsche Rundschau* and the authors of the publication complained of.

VON BISMARCK

To His Majesty the Emperor-King

83

The Family Is Entranced by Edison's Phonograph, 1889

"It is a clever instrument."

On October 7, 1899, a Herr Wangenheim, German representative of the Edison Company, brought a phonograph to Friedrichsruh for demonstration. The recent invention of the American, Thomas A. Edison, was an object of wonder for the Bismarck family, as reported in the daily press.[3]

At the request of Princess Bismarck, Mr. Wangenheim played a roll with the voice of the crown prince, which the chancellor and his wife heard with the heartiest joy.

When Mr. Wangenheim asked the prince to say something for the German people, Bismarck said: "I'd prefer not to just now; they would only ridicule it." All the same, in order to excite his

3. Condensed from *Tägliche Rundschau*, issues 236 and 237, October 9 and 10, 1889 in *Bismarck, Die gesammelten Werke*, VIII, ed. by Willy Andreas (Berlin, 1926), 664–665. Translated by the editor.

wife, he recorded his own voice on the instrument. First he sang the American folk song: "In Good Old Colony Times";[4] then he repeated the opening lines of Uhland's verse about the Emperor Barbarossa; and finally the first verse of *"Gaudeamus igitur."* Then followed several words directed to his son, Count Herbert, which ran as follows: "Be moderate in work, moderate in eating, and also a bit moderate in drinking. That is the advice of a father to his son."[5] Count Herbert was supposed to say whether or not he recognized the voice of his father through the apparatus. The princess and the councillor von Brauer, as well as Bismarck's three young grandsons (sons of Count Rantzau) immediately recognized the voice, but naturally the chancellor himself did not do so. When the Princess Bismarck, to satisfy the family, said a few words for the instrument, Bismarck applauded and said jokingly: "I have to be careful not to cry out 'Bravo!' when my wife speaks!" The chancellor, who chatted in lively and spirited fashion, remarked that it must have taken an enormous amount of work to achieve this success. He described the Edison phonograph in English as "a clever instrument" and predicted a great future for it. To him it looked like the realization of the Baron Munchhausen legend, in which the tone froze in a horn and then began to come out. But this was even greater than Munchhausen, for one could hear the same tone ten thousand times. The phonograph demonstration went on for another hour and a half.

34 Fall of the Titan, 1890: In an Irreconcilable Clash of Personality and Policy between Royal Master and Powerful Chancellor, Bismarck Submits His Letter of Resignation

". . . I am unable to execute the command of your Majesty."

Frederick III's son and successor, William II, who ascended the throne at the age of twenty-nine, presented a sharp contrast to his liberal father. The young emperor was an extraordinary individual, whose character embraced a world of contradictions. Though intelligent, talented, and cultivated, he was inclined to act at times in a highly erratic manner. On occasion, he could be

4. Bismarck had been taught "In Good Old Colony Times" by his American friend, John Lothrop Motley, in Göttingen in 1832. (See page 132.)
5. There was irony in Bismarck's words: Herbert, unfortunately, had turned out to be a notoriously heavy drinker.

a most engaging person, but he could easily change into an impatient, fickle, and clumsy boor. Although aware of the responsibilities of his position, he was, nevertheless, susceptible to the flattery of courtiers. Both as prince and ruler he tried to study all the problems of business, art, science, and government. Possessing a remarkable memory and the willingness to learn, he surrounded himself with leading scholars, industrialists, and artists. At the same time, his nature was so impulsive that he scarcely penetrated deeply into any of the problems he studied and almost invariably gained only superficial impressions.

A sincere patriot, William II was convinced that his high position was entrusted to him by God. He believed it to be his duty to maintain the monarchy that had been bestowed on him by Divine Providence. "I regard my whole position," he said, "as given to me direct from Heaven and I have been called by the Highest to do his work; by One to whom I must one day render an account." In another speech he proclaimed: "Remember that the German people are chosen by God. On me, as the German emperor, the spirit of God has descended. I am His weapon, His sword, His vicegerent." To his friend "Nicky" (Nicholas II, tsar of Russia) he wrote: "A sacred duty is imposed by Heaven on us Christian kings and emperors—to uphold the doctrine of the divine right of kings."

William II's nationalistic, bombastic, and warlike utterances were probably compensatory gestures for what was in reality a weak, uncertain personality. The arrogant young monarch, and the elder statesman, found it difficult to work together in harmony. William feared that his chancellor intended to create a Bismarck dynasty in the person of his son, Herbert, whose career had been assiduously promoted. In foreign policy, Bismarck wanted to renew the Reinsurance Treaty with Russia, while the emperor desired closer relations with England. On the domestic scene, Bismarck recommended that the Anti-Socialist Laws be made permanent, while William insisted that the disaffection of labor could be removed by remedial measures.

The differences between the two came to a head on a constitutional issue. Bismarck, annoyed by the fact that the emperor was discussing problems of administration with colleagues without informing him, reminded William of the cabinet order of 1852. This latter decree had been enacted as a means of giving the then minister-president the complete control that was necessary if he were to be responsible for the whole policy of the government. William ordered Bismarck to reverse the decree. Bismarck refused, on the ground that his position would be degraded by such an action. William then forced Bismarck's dismissal, although he sought to give it the tone of a resignation.

The first document below reprints the cabinet order of 1852; the second, Bismarck's letter of resignation; the third is the text of the order by which William suspended the order of 1852.

The Cabinet Order of 1852 [6]

I find it imperative that the minister-president, in order to maintain a more than hitherto general view over the various branches of domestic administration (thus making possible, according to his position, a unity of action), should give me information on all important administrative measures on my demand. For this purpose I have decided on the following procedures:

1. On all important administrative measures, which, according to existing regulations, do not require a preliminary decree of the ministry of state, the respective department chief must come to an understanding, either orally or in writing, with the minister-president. The minister-president may feel free, according to his judgment, to call a consultation in the ministry of state and, also, may deem it advisable to report on it to me.

2. When the administrative measure is such, according to existing regulations, that it necessitates my approval, then the requisite report must be submitted beforehand to the minister-president, who, with whatever remarks he cares to make, shall place it before me.

3. If a department chief finds it necessary to obtain an audience with me in a matter of immediate importance, he must inform the minister-president beforehand in time enough so that the latter, if he finds it necessary, can attend the conference personally. The regular audiences of the war minister are exempted from this order.

Charlottenburg, September 8, 1852

FREDERICK WILLIAM
MANTEUFFEL

Bismarck's Letter of Resignation, March 20, 1890 [7]

In the audience graciously granted to me on 15th instant your Majesty commanded me to lay before you the draft of an order canceling the royal order of September 8, 1852, which has hitherto regulated the position of a minister-president with regard to his colleagues. I beg leave most humbly to submit the following account of the origin and significance of the order in question.

6. Adapted from Georg von Eppstein, *Fürst Bismarcks Entlassung* (Berlin, 1920), Note 62.
7. Otto von Bismarck, *Gedanken und Errinnerungen* (Stuttgart and Berlin, 1898, 1919), III, 650–654. Trans. in William Jacks, *The Life of Prince Bismarck* (Glasgow, 1899), pp. 456–462.

In the days of absolute monarchy there was no necessity for the office of a president of the state ministry, and it was first at the united Diet of 1847 that the then Liberal deputies pointed out the necessity of paving the way for constitutional government by the nomination of a minister whose task it should be to undertake to maintain the uniformity of the policy of the entire responsible ministry. In the year 1848 this constitutional usage came into existence in Prussia, and "presidents of the state ministry" were appointed in the persons of Count Arnim, Camphausen, Count Brandenburg, Baron von Manteuffel, and Prince von Hohenzollern, not for one department only, but for the entire policy of the cabinet—that is, of all the departments together. Most of these gentlemen had no department of their own, but held the presidency only like my immediate predecessors, Prince von Hohenzollern, Minister von Auerswald, and Prince von Hohenlohe. But it was incumbent upon the president to uphold in the ministry of state and in its relations to the monarch that unity and continuity without which ministerial responsibility, as determined by the very nature of a constitutional régime, is impracticable.

The relations of the state ministry and of its respective members to the new institution of a minister-president very speedily required to be regulated more definitely in conformity with the constitution; and, accordingly, in agreement with the then state ministry, the cabinet order of September 8, 1852, was issued. This order has ever since remained authoritative with regard to the attitude of the minister-president towards the state ministry, and it alone gave the minister-president the authority to take upon himself that measure of responsibility for the entire policy of the cabinet which is expected of him by the diet and by public opinion. If each individual minister, without any previous agreement with his colleagues, is able to promulgate enactments of the monarch, a consistent policy for which some particular person may be held responsible is impossible. No minister, and especially no minister-president, can possibly continue to bear the constitutional responsibility for the entire policy of the cabinet. A regulation such as was contained in the decree of 1852 could be dispensed with in the days of absolute monarchy, and would not be required at the present day were we to return to absolutism without ministerial responsibility. But according to the constitutional institutions existing by law a presidential control of the ministry is indispensable on the basis of the decree of 1852.

Regarding this point, as was confirmed yesterday at the sitting of the state ministry, all my colleagues are now in accord with me, and they also agree that none of my successors as minister-president could undertake the responsibility in the absence of the authority which the decree of 1852 confers upon him. The need of this authority will be more and more felt by each of my successors than it has been by me, because none of them will at once possess the advantage of the authority which has been conferred upon me in virtue of my having held the presidency for long years, and of having enjoyed the confidence of both the late emperors. I have never hitherto felt the necessity of appealing to the order of 1852 against any one of my colleagues. Its existence and the certainty that I enjoyed the confidence of the late Emperors William and Frederick were sufficient to ensure my authority in the council of my colleagues. This certainty no longer exists either for my colleagues or for myself. I am, therefore, compelled to resort to the order of the year 1852 in order to ensure the necessary unity in your Majesty's service.

For the above-mentioned reasons I am unable to execute the command of your Majesty, according to which I myself am to effect and to countersign the repeal of the order of 1852 which I have called to mind, while I am, nevertheless, to continue to hold the presidency of the state ministry. After the communications made to me yesterday by General von Hahnke and the *Geheimekabinetsrath* Lucanus, I can no longer doubt that your Majesty knows and believes it to be impossible for me to repeal the order and yet to remain a minister. Your Majesty has, nevertheless, upheld the command communicated to me on the 15th instant, and has led me to understand that your Majesty will accept my resignation, which has thereby become necessary.

From former conversations which I have had with your Majesty regarding the question whether my continuance in office would not be in accordance with your Majesty's desires, I might infer that it would be agreeable to your Majesty were I while resigning my position in your Majesty's Prussian service to remain in the service of the empire. In examining this question more carefully, I took leave most humbly to call attention to certain serious consequences that such a separation of my offices would entail. I particularly referred to the necessity that the chancellor should be able to adopt a rigorous attitude in the Reichstag. I forbear from recapitulating here all the consequences which a separation of that nature between Prussia and the imperial chancellor would involve. Your Majesty was thereupon pleased to grant that in the meantime things should remain as they were. But, as I have already had the honor of explaining, it is impossible for me to continue to hold the office of minister-president after your Majesty has repeatedly ordered the *capitis diminutio* which is involved in the repeal of the order of 1852. Your Majesty was further pleased at the audience graciously granted me on the 15th instant, to set such limits to my official rights as do not leave me that measure of participation in the business of the State and in its supervision or that degree of freedom in my ministerial decisions, and in my intercourse with the Reichstag and its members, which I require if I am to undertake the constitutional responsibility for my official activity.

But, even were it feasible to carry on our foreign policy independently of the domestic and external policy of the empire, and so independently of the Prussian, as would be the case if the imperial chancellor stood in the same independent relation to the policy of Prussia as to that of Bavaria or Saxony, and had no share in the manipulation of the Prussian vote in the Federal Council in its relation to the Reichstag, I should still consider it impossible for me to undertake the execution of your Majesty's injunctions in the matter of foreign policy after the most recent decisions of your Majesty with regard to the trend of our foreign policy as summarized in the autograph letter with which your Majesty yesterday accompanied the reports of the consul in ——. Were I to undertake this, I should be imperiling all the successes of importance for the German empire which our foreign policy, framed in accordance with the views of both your Majesty's late predecessors, has achieved in our relation with —— in spite of unfavorable circumstances. The great importance of these successes, beyond all expectation, —— has confirmed to me, since his return from P——.

In view of my attachment to the service of the royal house and to your Majesty, and after having accustomed myself by the habit of many years to circumstances which I had hitherto considered to be permanent, it is very painful to me to abandon my old relations to your Majesty and to the whole policy of the empire and of Prussia. But after conscientious consideration of the intentions of your Majesty, which I should have to be prepared to execute if I remained in office, I can but humbly beg your Majesty graciously to relieve me of the offices of imperial chancellor, of minister-president, and of Prussian minister of foreign affairs with the statutory pension. From my impressions during the last few weeks, and from the information conveyed to me yesterday in the communications emanating from the civil and military cabinets of your Majesty, I may humbly assume that by tendering my resignation I am meeting the wishes of your Majesty and that I may safely count upon its being graciously accepted. I should have tendered the resignation of my offices to your Majesty long ago had I not been under the impression that your Majesty desired to utilize the experiences and abilities of a faithful servant of your predecessors. Now that I know that your Majesty has no longer any use for these, I may retire from political life without any apprehension that my resolution will be judged inopportune by public opinion.

VON BISMARCK

To His Majesty the Emperor and King

William II's Suspension of the Order of 1852 [8]

Since the utilization of the order of September 8, 1852, by his late Majesty the King, Frederick William IV, concerning the relationships of the president of my state ministry and the state ministry itself, has given rise to doubts, I decree the suspension of this order under the following considerations:

It is the task of the president of my state ministry to bear the responsibility for the uniform and equal implementation of the basic principles decided by myself as authoritative for the guidance of all administration. In order to fulfill this task, it is imperative that the department chiefs, after previous understanding with the president of my state ministry, obtain my decision on all matters which diverge from the above-mentioned basic principles, or which are of essential importance. Where there are differences of opinion, both the minister-president and the department chief are to come to me in common audience. At the same time, I want to clarify my order of May 2, 1889, by noting that, in cases where members of my state ministry are concerned with changes or the initiation of proposals which reach the parliamentary bodies for debate, the aforementioned obtaining of my decision shall be required only insofar as the point of view represents a divergence from the basic principles approved by me or follows a direction which casts doubt on my interpretation.

WILHELM R.
CAPRIVI

William accepted the resignation in a few hurried lines written in pencil: "The grounds which you have adduced for your decision convince me that further attempts to persuade you to withdraw your resignation have no prospect of success." Only this answer was published. The German people were led to believe that Bis-

8. Cabinet order of April 14, 1890, quoted in O. Gradenwitz, *Bismarcks letzter Kampf, 1888–1898, Skizzen nach Akten* (Berlin, 1924), p. 114.

marck had voluntarily offered his resignation and that the emperor had tried in vain to dissuade him. The text of the resignation was only published years later when Bismarck was already dead: Moritz Busch, Bismarck's faithful assistant, made the letter public on August 1, 1898, one day after the chancellor's death.

85

Enraged, Describing His Honors as "a First-Class Funeral," the Fallen Chancellor Leaves Berlin, March 29, 1890

"Nor could I have believed that so severe and somber a class of people could ever portray so much downright emotion."

William II tried to ease the dismissal by raising Bismarck to the rank of general of cavalry in the army. The fallen chancellor was unimpressed. On March 29, 1890, on his departure from Berlin, a great demonstration took place in the streets, as described by a special correspondent of the Times, *London.*[9]

Thousands upon thousands had crowded to the Wilhelmstrasse to catch a final and a farewell glimpse of the great statesman who was to leave the spot where his mighty spirit had ruled and brooded so long. Prince Bismarck had spent the last few days in paying and receiving farewell calls, and among the most interesting of the former was a drive to Charlottenburg. The ex-chancellor had already taken personal leave of all the royal princes, but on Friday there still remained one member of the Hohenzollern family to whom he owned his *devoir,* and this was the emperor—King William I, now lying in marble state beside his royal parents in the mausoleum at Charlottenburg.

Quietly driving out here towards the gloaming, the chancellor entered the solitary vault, and laid a few roses on the tomb of the monarch whom he had served so long and nobly, and loved so well. Sad and overpowering must have been his thoughts as, rising from his knees, he took a final farewell of the man whom he made an emperor, and who had kept his vow to cling to him to the last. That was a touching farewell; but a more overwhelming leave-taking still awaited the prince, when, in his accustomed cuirassier uniform, with his son, Count Herbert, at his side, and his wife

9. The *Times,* London, March 30, 1890.

and daughter and their son in a carriage following, he left the Radziwill palace and began his progress through the densely-crowded and excited streets to the Lehrter station, here to take train for Friedrichsruh.

As if the funeral of some great and deep-mourned man were afoot, Berlin had poured out all the best elements in its population to weep and wildly wave their hats and handkerchiefs, to scatter flowers, and to struggle to shake and kiss the hand of the man who was about to pass from their midst and be lost to them. This is not the language of exaggeration, but the sober record of incidents which I saw with my own eyes. I have never seen so respectable a crowd in Berlin, which contained none of the usual constituents of a mob, but was recruited from all the best circles in Berlin society, especially the official world; nor could I have believed that so severe and somber a class of people could ever betray so much downright emotion.

It was only with the utmost difficulty that the mounted constables escorting the chancellor's open carriage could cleave a passage for it through the encompassing throngs of those who pushed toward him to offer him the choicest of spring flowers, and seize his hand to shake or kiss it. It was no wonder that all this spontaneous demonstration of popular devotion almost unmanned its object, and made the man of blood and iron almost melt into tears. This was the scene which presented itself all along the prince's route between his forsaken palace and the railway station. In they burst, and packed themselves on the platform around and behind the dismounted squadron of cuirassiers which, with standard and trumpets, had been sent by the emperor to act as a guard of honor to the departing prince, who, it must be remembered, carries with him into his rural retirement the rank of *General-Oberst* of cavalry and field-marshal general.

But, in addition to this unusual guard of honor, the emperor had also sent his personal *aides-de-camp* with his final *adieux,* accompanied by a magnificent device in flowers. The high officials formed the nucleus of a brilliant crowd of all that was foremost in the official world of Berlin—all the ministers and ambassadors, including those of England and France, and the whole array of those who had ever owned the chancellor as friend, or master, or hero, or all three in one. Every one sought to get a final word with him, or, at the very least, to press his hand; but in the midst of all this overflowing emotion and enthusiasm it was too much to expect anything like appropriate or coherent answers from the prince, who really looked as if, for the very first time in his life, he had fairly lost his head.

Cheer after cheer, each louder and more thrilling than the other, went up and made the vaulted station ring, as the prince showed himself at the window of his carriage, or in converse with some friend. In the intervals of the cheering the crowd struck up the *"Wacht am Rhein,"* or *"Deutschland, Deutschland uber Alles."* At last the excitement reached its culmination when the whistle shrieked the signal for departure, and when, amid a final salvo of frantic cheers, blended with the sound of the cuirassiers' trumpets, the train slowly steamed out of the station, Prince Bismarck shaking hands from the window all the while. Then the crowd slowly dispersed, and as some of its members neared the Brandenburger Tor they encountered the young emperor placidly trotting home from his afternoon ride in the Tiergarten.

86

The Dismissed Chancellor, Angered by the Vagaries of Human Beings, Turns for Solace to His Dogs

"The animal does not seem to please you?"

Bismarck's misanthropy had grown in geometrical pattern. The circumstances of his retirement embittered him to such an extent that he turned more and more to his dogs. They, at least, were loyal friends. For years he had been the master of a series of iron-gray or black hounds, all like their owner, huge and highly strung creatures. On the death of his old and faithful companion, "Sultan," gift of a Moroccan prince, Bismarck almost collapsed with grief. A few days after his resignation, the chancellor told a Bavarian editor about his dogs.[10]

On the arrival of Prince Bismarck at Kissingen after his dismissal, I received a telegram to say that he was expecting me. I proceeded to Kissingen at once, and arrived at the Upper Saline about 1:45 P.M., just as lunch was being cleared away.

The prince's secretary, Dr. Chrysander, to whom I had sent my name, informed me that the prince would receive me immediately. Since, however, I was clad in a gray jacket and had left my portmanteau in my hotel, I said that I would drive there as soon as possible to put on a black suit. This was of no importance; the

10. Interview on August 16, 1890 at Kissingen with Anton Memminger, editor of the *Neue Bayerische Zeitung*, as quoted in *Conversations with Bismarck*, collected by Heinrich von Poschinger, ed. by Sidney Whitman (New York and London, 1900), pp. 117–120.

prince wished to see me, and not my wardrobe. Everything happened so quickly, that, without more ado, I was forced to step from the dining room to the prince's study.

The prince stood erect before me in his simple black coat, gazing earnestly at me with his great eyes. I stepped up to him without hesitation and grasped his proffered hand, as he returned the pressure with the words, "You are heartily welcome." I then thanked him for his invitation, and was about to add a few polite words, when he interrupted me. "You have nothing to thank me for; you are a self-made man. I confess I did not imagine you to be such a Pomeranian grenadier. Why, you are as broad and heavy and almost as tall as I am. Please take a seat; I have several matters to discuss."

The prince settled himself on the sofa in such a position that he could rest his head and back against its high wing, and, stretching one leg, remarked, "You will not take it amiss if I make myself comfortable; I often feel twinges in my legs now that I am no longer quite free from gout. I am also old: age is the worst malady that I endure and will kill me some day, perhaps just at the moment when I am most plagued by curiosity to see what turn events will take in the world. We really live in a most interesting age—an age which may become still more interesting, since unpleasant times and events will certainly come sooner than many a wise augur predicts."

I had taken an easy chair opposite the prince, and moved a little to one side, as the sun shone into my eyes. Tyras, who was lying close to my chair, growled, and I told him to be quiet. The prince, who also forbade him to growl, must have noticed that I did not think much of the dog, for he said, "The animal does not seem to please you?"

"No, your Highness; he has a stupid head."

The prince laughed aloud. "You speak openly, which pleases me; but I must tell you that you are the first visitor who has failed to admire the dog. Every one else, and especially the ladies, who have met him in the streets, have hitherto thought him wonderfully beautiful and charming."

"But I think the dog as ugly as he is stupid."

"Why, this is even better," laughed the prince. "Take care that you utter no insult and are locked up again."

"Oh no, your Highness; I have no such thought. How can I commit an offense in not considering a cur more beautiful than he really is?"

"You are quite right," replied the prince. "I have never thought the dog good-looking or clever; at first one could hardly bear to look at him. Everywhere and always one can find people who do not deny their simian descent, and who tender homage to their cousin, the dog. Why, there are even foolish ladies who wish to possess hairs of this animal to carry about in golden lockets as treasured remembrances and talismans in the place of 'lucky pigs.' If they only knew that this dog is a present from the emperor! And you cannot have known this either, or you would have spoken more considerately and euphemistically of Tyras. Of course you have no wedding garment and no knee breeches, only a Bavarian peasant's coat."

"Your Highness, I speak as I think, and it's all the same whether I am in a Bavarian coat or appear as a *Salon Tyroler* before the emperor or the tsar, the pope or the sultan!"

Again the prince laughed. "It's all the same—that is your motto. I have already noticed it in your paper, and I must say that Marcus Aurelius could not have found a better inscription for his *Stoa.* In certain situations—for instance, on the day of my dismissal, and since then—I also adopted a similar motto. I therefore retain this dog of the emperor's. It's all the same! I had a fine hound, a gray bitch, Rebecca, of the same breed as my old dog, Tyras I, who was a gift from the Munich Dog Fanciers' Association. Tyras was really an excellent dog, under whose protection I was much safer than under that of the whole secret police of Berlin. The loss of that dog, in fact, grieved me as much as that of my former *Reichshund,* Sultan, who was poisoned by a miserable scoundrel and a faithless *employé.* As my birthday happened to be coming around, the emperor asked Minister —— how he could give me pleasure, and, on being told of the death of Tyras and my grief, he at once ordered, 'See that you get him a new *Reichshund.*' The minister, who understands about as much about dogs as certain diplomats do about statesmanship, went to the celebrated dog breeders, *Caesar und Minka,* and ordered a new 'imperial' dog. Immediately afterwards—now listen—I received a letter from *Caesar und Minka,* in which they requested permission to assume the title of 'Purveyors to Prince Bismarck' in return for supplying a rare and magnificent specimen of a dog. Such coolness went against the grain, and I sent them an answer which they certainly will never sell to an autograph collector." . . .

37 Retreat to Friedrichsruh: In His Great Estate Surrounded by Pine Forests the Great Man Growls in Retirement

"They shall not silence me."

The seventy-five-year-old chancellor, forced against his will to return to everyday life, came back to Friedrichsruh, his magnificent estate just twenty miles from Hamburg. William Harbutt Dawson described the milieu.[11]

No perfume is sweeter than that of the pines when warm spring sunshine falls upon the tall forest spires. No woodland way is fairer than that which lies through crackling cones and yellow spikes and tangled heather. We in England have lost our forests. Germany is wiser and preserves hers. To the larger forests of Germany belong the Schwarzwald, the Thüringer Wald, the Fichtenwald, and to the smaller Sachsenwald, in Lauenburg, for over twenty years the possession of Prince Bismarck. It is a comely estate, in the center of which are the hamlet and the *château* of Friedrichsruh, and it lies but twenty miles from Hamburg. From the cluster of houses which adjoin the castle park a rich pine forest extends for miles in all directions. Here and there it is intersected by sandy highways and grassy byways and pleasant glades that give the trees breathing space. Excepting for the presence of a railway—for Friedrichsruh lies on the main line between Hamburg and Berlin—the spot would be one of ideal calm, and even with the iron way it is charming to look upon, one of those homes of sylvan beauty and tranquillity from which one draws the wholesome reminder that whoever makes the big, black, smoky towns, it was God who made the country. It was a handsome gift, this great forest estate, for Emperor William I to make to his trusty chancellor as compensation for a direct share in the French milliards.

Yet the external appearance of the *château* in which so many statesmen have been entertained since Bismarck became its lord—Count Kalnoky, M. de Giers, Prince Orloff, Count Schouvaloff, among them—is not prepossessing. The architecture is exceedingly simple and unassuming. The *Schloss* would in England at best pass muster for the mansion of a well-to-do country gentle-

11. William Harbutt Dawson, *Germany and the Germans* (London, 1894), II, 335–337.

man. But the house was here before Bismarck came to the estate, and though it was too small for his use he preferred rather to mend it than end it. Hence a building of disparate style and unpretentious both within and without. But the park redeems the mansion. It is surrounded on two sides by a high brick wall, on two by plantations and hedges. Noble trees rise on every side, a broad stream flows sluggishly through the demesne, and there is a pretty lake fringed with tall willow and rush. The landscape's charm is also increased by the presence within the park boundaries of several quaint cottages of the brick and wood kind so often found on the Rhine. In the *château* are treasured many of the tokens of honor, favor, and popularity which have been bestowed upon the prince during the many years of his service to king and Fatherland. Here, too, most of Prince Bismarck's restful days were passed while still in office, and here he lives for the greater part of the year—only changing this retreat for Varzin—now that his work is done.

The shock of retirement hit the old man with tremendous impact. It was a lonely life for one inured to sensational political drama. Bismarck was astonished to see the state he had fashioned go on functioning as if he himself no longer existed. The man of power, the man of action, groped helplessly in emptiness. These were sullen, undignified days.[12]

No reconciliation or accommodation was now possible. The emperor did all he could to make it appear that the resignation was voluntary and friendly. He conferred on the retiring chancellor the highest honors: he raised him to the rank of field marshal and created him duke of Lauenburg, and publicly stated his intention of presenting him with a copy of his own portrait. As a soldier, Bismarck obediently accepted the military honor; the new title he requested to be allowed not to use; he had never been asked whether he desired it.

No outward honors could recompense him for the affront he had received. What profited it him that the princes and people of Germany joined in unanimous expression of affection and esteem, that he could scarcely set foot outside his house for the enthusiastic crowd who cheered and followed him through the streets of Berlin?

12. James Wycliffe Headlam, *Bismarck and the Foundations of the German Empire* (New York and London, 1899), pp. 456–461.

For twenty-four years he had been Prussian minister and now he was told he was in the way. His successor was already in office; he was himself driven in haste from the house which so long had been his home. . . .

The rest he had so often longed for had come, but it was too late. Forty years he had passed in public life and he could not now take up again the interests and occupations of his youth. Agriculture had no more charms for him; he was too infirm for sport; he could not, like his father, pass his old age in the busy indolence of a country gentleman's life, nor could he, as some statesmen have done, soothe his declining years by harmless and amiable literary dilettantism. His religion was not of that complexion that he could find in contemplation, and in preparation for another life, consolation for the trials of this one. At seventy-five years of age, his intellect was as vigorous and his energy as unexhausted as they had been twenty years before; his health was improved, for he had found in Dr. Schweninger a physician who was not only able to treat his complaints, but could also compel his patient to obey his orders. He still felt within himself full power to continue his public work, and now he was relegated to impotence and obscurity. Whether in Varzin or Friedrichsruh, his eyes were always fixed on Berlin. He saw the state which he had made, and which he loved as a father, subjected to the experiment of young and inexperienced control. He saw overthrown that carefully planned system by which the peace of Europe was made to depend upon the prosperity of Germany. Changes were made in the working of that constitution which it seemed presumption for anyone but him to touch. His policy was deserted, his old enemies were taken into favor. Can we wonder that he could not restrain his impatience? He felt like a man who sees his heir ruling in his own house during his lifetime, cutting down his woods and dismissing his old servants, or as if he saw a careless and clumsy rider mounted on his favorite horse.

From all parts of Germany deputations from towns and newspaper writers came to visit him. He received them with his customary courtesy, and spoke with his usual frankness. He did not disguise his chagrin; he had, he said, not been treated with the consideration which he deserved. He had never been accustomed to hide his feelings or to disguise his opinions. Nothing that his successors did seemed to him good. They made a treaty with England for the arrangement of conflicting questions in Africa; men looked to Bismarck to hear what he would say before they formed their opinion; "I would never have signed the treaty," he declared. He quickly drifted into formal opposition to the government; he even made arrangements with one of the Hamburg papers that it should represent his opinions. He seemed to have forgotten his own principle that, in foreign affairs at least, an opposition to the policy of the government should not be permitted. He claimed a privilege which as minister he would never have allowed to another. He defied the government. "They shall not silence me," he said. It seemed as though he was determined to undo the work of his life. Under the pretext that he was attacking the policy of the ministers, he was undermining the loyalty of the people, for few could doubt that it was the emperor at whom the criticisms were aimed.

In his isolation and retirement, the old uncompromising spirit of his ancestors once more awoke in him. He had been loyal to the crown—who more so?—but his loyalty had limits. His long service had been one of personal and voluntary affection; he was not a valet, that his service could be handed on from generation to generation among the assets of the crown. "After all," he would ask, "who are these Hohenzollerns? My family is as good as theirs. We have been here longer than they have." Like his ancestors who stood out against the rule of the Great Elector, he was putting personal feeling above public duty. Even if the action of the new government was not always wise, he himself had made Germany strong enough to support for a few years a weak ministry.

More than this, he was attempting to destroy the confidence of the people in the moral justice and necessity of the measures by which he had founded the empire. They had always been taught that in 1870 their country had been the object of a treacherous and unprovoked attack. Bismarck, who was always living over again the great scenes in which he had been the leading actor, boasted that but for him there would never have been a war with France. He referred to the alteration in the Ems telegram, . . . and the government was forced to publish the original documents. The conclusions drawn from these disclosures and others which followed were exaggerated, but the naïve and simple belief of the people was irretrievably destroyed. Where they had been taught to see the will of God, they found only the machinations of the minister. In a country where patriotism had already taken the place of religion, the last illusion had been dispelled; almost the last barrier was broken down which stood between the nation and moral skepticism.

Bismarck's criticism was very embarrassing to the government; by injuring the reputation of the ministry he impaired the influence of the nation. It was difficult to keep silence and ignore the attack, but the attempts at defense were awkward and unwise. General

Caprivi attempted to defend the treaty with England by reading out confidential minutes, addressed by Bismarck to the secretary of the minister for foreign affairs, in which he had written that the friendship of England and the support of Lord Salisbury were more important than Zanzibar or the whole of Africa. He addressed a circular dispatch to Prussian envoys to inform them that the utterances of Prince Bismarck were without any actual importance, as he was now only a private man. This only made matters worse; for the substance of the dispatch quickly became known (another instance of the lax control over important state documents which we so often notice in dealing with German affairs), and only increased the bitterness of Bismarck, which was shared by his friends and supporters.

For more than two years the miserable quarrel continued; Bismarck was now the public and avowed enemy of the court and the ministry. Moltke died, and he alone of the great men of the country was absent from the funeral ceremony, but in his very absence he overshadowed all who were there.

38 The Interviews Begin: To Friedrichsruh from All Corners of the World Come Distinguished Reporters to Record Their Impressions of the Ex-Chancellor

"I am under a regular boycott."

Friedrichsruh was like a magnet for the world's journalists and distinguished travelers. They came from everywhere in a steady stream to ask for the prize of an interview with the retired chancellor. Bismarck was not averse to this publicity. He was already beginning to miss the routine of his political career. In the old days he had complained about life in Berlin, but now that he was out of office he found it almost impossible to adapt himself to his new leisure. Many visitors had to be content with wandering around the village, but those fortunate enough to get to Bismarck's presence generally got a good story. Bismarck readily complained to them about the "young chap who discharged me." An American industrialist of German background, Henry Villard, was among those who came away with a story after visiting Bismarck in the summer of 1890, shortly after the chancellor's resignation.[13]

13. Henry Villard, "A Visit to Bismarck," *The Century Magazine*, No. 5 (March, 1904), 665–668.

Professor Schweninger and a servant in livery received me at the station, which was only a few hundred yards from the mansion. The latter proved to be a very plain building, being really only an enlarged country inn, and neither the exterior nor the interior revealed the splendor which the fame and wealth of the owner led one, not unnaturally, to expect.

I was shown into a commodious chamber on the second floor, and was just making my ablutions when I heard heavy steps approaching the door, and immediately there appeared in it the erect form of the prince, dressed in black, with a slouch hat of the same color,—the same costume in which Lenbach painted his best portrait of him,—with a heavy stick in his right hand, and followed by two large Danish dogs. The prince welcomed me heartily, and when I apologized for being in my shirt sleeves and for not offering my wet hands, the prince said:

"Just go on with your toilet. I will sit down, and we can talk while you wash and dress."

One of the dogs, encouraged, no doubt, by his master's friendly words, now approached me, standing up before me and putting his paws on my shoulders and trying to lick my face.

"There is another hearty greeting for you," the prince remarked, calling the animal off. "I am really glad you came," he said: "first, because you are a German who has gained a high position in a foreign country, a sort of success which I have always especially admired, because I know how difficult it is to achieve; and, secondly, because I like company, and you are the only visitor I have had in a week except Schweninger."

On my expressing my astonishment at this, he said:

"Yes, it is just as I state it. The fact is that I am under a regular boycott. Ever since I lost my position, everybody is afraid to have anything to do with me, for fear of displeasing the young chap who discharged me. Why, formerly my trouble was to keep people away from here. Everybody wanted to come, especially the officials who needed my good will. Now none of the latter dare come, lest their names should appear in the newspapers as my visitors and be seen by the new man on the throne. I know that men travel by here every day who, a few months ago, would have no more dared to pass this place without paying their respects than they would have ventured to pass me on the street in Berlin without saluting me. But I ought not to have expected anything else, for hounds follow those who feed them."

This outburst was a clear indication of what was uppermost in the prince's mind, and prepared me for what was to follow on the same line during my stay.

My toilet being finished, the prince and the dogs led the way to the rear of the mansion, where we took seats on a sort of veranda. Professor Schweninger joined us, followed by Bismarck's private secretary, the princess, her married daughter, Countess Rantzau, and the latter's children. The prince, noticing the gouty formations on my hands, said:

"I see you are suffering from gout. How long have you had it?"

When I replied, "For nearly twenty years," he pointed to the professor:

"That is the man to help you. But for him I should have been obliged to retire from office long ago. Perhaps it would have been better for me if I had done so. All the medical professors had practiced their arts upon me without doing me any good. He alone gave me relief and made life tolerable for me. You had better try him, although he is a great tyrant and exacts strict obedience. I found it hard to change my habits of life, but he made me do it. I now eat and drink only what he sees fit to allow me. See how gentle he looks. But I tell you he can be as rough [*grob*] as any old Bavarian [*Altbaier*], of which stock he comes."

The prince then began to question me regarding myself, about my early life in Germany, how long I had been in the United States, and about the course of my career there. He wanted to know how many miles of railroad I had built, in what time it had been done, how many steamships had been under my control, how many men I had employed, being very much surprised that fifteen thousand Chinese had been among them, and saying: "Why, you had a whole army corps under your command!" He asked how much capital I had been obliged to raise and how it was raised, and about the relative value of white and of Chinese labor. He inquired whether I had named Bismarck, the capital of Dakota, after him, to which I had to reply that the place had been founded and baptized before I had anything to do with the Northern Pacific. Bismarck remembered that he had received thence telegraphic greetings from the German participants in the Northern Pacific opening excursion, and asked whether it had a future.

In reply, I had to confess that it was not then very prosperous, and I explained that all the capitals of the several American states were, as a rule, of slow growth. This the prince could not understand, in the light of the contrary European experience. He remarked that what I had accomplished in a foreign country I never could have done in the Fatherland, owing to tradition and to the clinging to accustomed ways so characteristic of old countries. Did I not encounter a great deal of prejudice among native Americans against me as a foreigner in the pursuit of my undertakings? To this I replied that, on the contrary, I had found my chief financial backing and my main support among them, and that there was no people on earth among whom enterprise and energy prevailed to a greater extent, or that more readily appreciated those who possessed such qualities.

To this the prince said that he was well aware that the Americans were the most progressive people in the world, for which he admired them, but it was new to him that they were so free from national jealousies in appreciating merit.

An early dinner ended this first talk. The prince sat at one end of the table, the princess at the other. I was on his right, Professor Schweninger on his left. The secretary and the Rantzau family formed the rest of the party. Behind the host, at a distance of about six feet, lay the two dogs, watching the proceedings eagerly, but not stirring until toward the end of the repast, when, upon a sign from their master, they approached and sat on their haunches on each side of him. Then from time to time the prince threw morsels into their open jaws. The table talk was of an ordinary kind, but one amusing incident is worth remembering. The prince drank one glassful of light Rhine wine, and then called for another. Schweninger at once interposed, saying:

"Your Highness, you have had your allowance for one meal, and you can't have any more."

The prince looked at me quizzically, and remarked:

"Now you see how I am treated. I have to submit, but at times when the censor is not here I jump the traces. He doesn't know, but I will tell him now [and he chuckled heartily] that I celebrated my last birthday by enjoying several bottles of wine and several glasses of beer."

"Yes, you did," retorted the doctor; "and when I came here a few days afterward, you growled dreadfully over fresh neuralgic pains."

After dinner the prince excused himself for his afternoon nap, after inviting me to go with him on his usual four-o'clock drive. Punctually at that hour we set out for a tour of the Sachsenwald, or Saxon Forest, as the extensive woods adjoining the mansion grounds are called. They consist largely of grand old oak trees free from all undergrowth, under the canopy of which the carriage passed, now following roads, now regardless of them.

After describing his estate, the prince began speaking English, "so that that fellow," pointing to the coachman, "may not understand us," and surprised me by his fluency, his command of idiomatic expressions, and his very slight accent. He began with these words, "Since I have been kicked out of office," which so astonished me that I begged pardon for interrupting him and said: "Prince, that is an Americanism; where did you pick it up?" He answered that he did not remember where, but the expression fitted his case exactly, for the manner of his dismissal was but the equivalent of an application of the toe of a boot. He then proceeded to tell the story of his forced resignation.

Such a rapid flow of keen wit, of cutting sarcasm and bitter denunciation, as followed for half an hour I had never heard before and never heard again. It was a strange mixture of eloquence and loquaciousness. Bismarck's voice seemed not as deep and strong as his stature led one to expect, but it had a pleasant sound. A most intense sense of the wrong and ingratitude he claimed to have suffered made itself manifest. As an example of his unjust treatment, he recounted what he had done to unify the nation and to aggrandize the Hohenzollern dynasty. There was not only an unhesitating assertion of his own deserts as the founder of the German empire, but an almost sneering and even contemptuous depreciation of other performers in the historic drama of his time, including even the old Emperor William, the unfortunate Emperor Frederick, and the Empress Augusta. His language became a perfect diatribe when he referred to the present emperor and some of his ministers, whom he held responsible for his removal. His expressions regarding them were not only amazing, but embarrassing to me, as I had close social relations with many of the ministerial objects of his scorn. "Some of those rogues I picked out of the very gutter," he once said. Fortunately, he did not stop for any word of assent, but went right on until his pent-up wrath was expended. As he remarked, when it was all spent:

"It was quite a relief to me to have this opportunity to speak without restraint to a gentleman who, I am sure, will honor my confidence."

Even were it not for this restriction, some of the sayings I heard and noted down at the time were so extraordinary that, if they were repeated, their reality would probably be doubted, and certainly the lese majesty they involved would render it unsafe for me to venture again on German soil.

The prince's countenance during the excited delivery of his philippic was a study. The working of every vein and muscle of the face showed his intense feelings. The play of his great eyebrows was also very remarkable. Most impressive of all were the spirit and light shining from his wonderful eyes. No one ever came into the presence of the chancellor without a deep sense of the mind power reflected from those large gray-blue orbs. Their flashing brilliancy and the piercing penetration of the glances shot from them were never to be forgotten. They seemed incapable of expressing affection, and their steel-like hardness only inspired awe for the towering intellect, the irresistible will, the defiant courage, the fiery energy of their owner. To watch the lightning changes of expression mirrored in them, reflecting the strong emotions evoked by humble pride, wounded ambition, and thwarted selfishness, and, above all, by the loss of his absolute sway, was indeed an enviable privilege. . . .

I took my leave of the prince on the second evening, as I was to start for home in the morning before he would be up. I assured my host of my lasting gratitude for the generous hospitality received, and was told in return that I should be welcome again at any time. I left Bismarck with the fixed impression that the prince never would or could forget or forgive those who caused his compulsory abdication from power, that he felt nothing less than implacable hatred toward them, that any apparent reconciliation on the prince's part to the new regime that might follow would be only a stage show and not a reality, that his thirst for revenge would not be quenched as long as he lived, and that he would improve every opportunity to gratify it. That this judgment was correct will be confirmed by those intimate with him during the last years of his life.

Bismarck was disturbed by some visitors, but to others he took a liking and granted them extensive interviews. Among the favored newspapermen was Sidney Whitman, an American, who was invited back several times. Following is Whitman's report of his first visit to Friedrichsruh in April 1891.[14]

. . . It is customary to call the building a *Schloss,* and for brevity's sake this may pass. But in reality the residence of Friedrichsruh, as of many a German noble family, is what we term a manor house—be it big as a barn or small as an attic, in the form of a square, a parallelogram, or triangle—in short, the house of the lord of the manor—his mansion—and that lord was Prince Bismarck. The Germans do not possess the exact term, for which the only rendering would be *Das Herren Haus.* As such, however, no building could have been better suited to Prince Bismarck. The house itself, let alone the princely estate, possessed the one *sine*

14. Sidney Whitman, *Personal Reminiscences of Prince Bismarck* (London, 1902), pp. 32–37.

qua non condition of distinction—the dignity of space. With the extensive view from the dining room the possessor could indulge at will in the sense of the unlimited nature of his property, a feeling those can best appreciate who have lived much in broad scenery, far from the busy crowd of town life.

In curious contrast to the extent of the estate, one side of the *Schloss* abutted upon the high road in direct touch with all the publicity of railroad and village life. This contiguity with the outer world was congenial to Bismarck, even though at times it had its inconveniences. Throughout the greater part of his life his official position had made it difficult for him to walk unobserved in town or country. He was able to do this more or less in Friedrichsruh, and he liked to mingle with the country folk round about him. He also enjoyed the contrast between the solitude of the wood and the bustle of the road. Had this been otherwise, he would never have decided that his last resting-place should be near a railway station, a vicinity which people of his caste and position usually affect to dislike. Perhaps the fact that the dignity and affluence of the family were not painfully contrasted by the dirt and poverty of humble villagers, as is often the case of noblemen's estates in some countries—notably, but not only in Bohemia—this possibly had something to do with Bismarck's liking for the village. Friedrichsruh is a favorable specimen of a German village; it reflects a high civilization. I never once saw a pauper, a beggar, or a shabbily dressed person during all my visits to Friedrichsruh.

In the course of the morning Count Herbert asked me whether I would like to ride out with him and his cousin Count August Bismarck, and before long we were all three in the midst of the Saxon Forest careering at a gallop over *Stock und Stein.* Count August Bismarck was something of a steeplechase rider, and such a ride in his company was a thing to look back upon thankfully when once over and uninjured bones allow of our doing so.

On our return we met Prince Bismarck in the grounds, and I accompanied him for a stroll through the village. He took me to see the *Försterei,* the dwelling of the head forester, Lange. Bismarck told me that he himself had lived there for some time, and had received visits from ambassadors while there, when he first came to Friedrichsruh and his present residence was being altered to his taste. His head forester was a fine-looking man, with a long, black beard plentifully streaked with gray. Prince Bismarck told me that he was a gay fellow, who was a great favorite with the fair sex in the village.

Every day a crowd collected about the gates to catch a glimpse of the prince as he left the *Schloss* for his afternoon drive. People came from all parts, and especially on holidays; Friedrichsruh even at that time had become a shrine for pilgrims. Sometimes they vented their feelings in loud cheers; at others they uncovered in silent reverence. This was only one of the many indications of the prince's hold upon the heart and imagination of a vast section of the German people that I noticed during my first visit to Friedrichsruh. Whereas the foreign press, and, more particularly, a part of the German press, endeavored to make the world believe that the sentiments of his countrymen towards him were of a totally different nature. Scarcely a day passed but telegrams arrived embodying good wishes and expressions of devotion from some social gathering throughout the country. When the train stopped at Friedrichsruh every head was put out of the carriage windows in the hope of catching a glimpse of the "retired" statesman. And should he happen to be on the platform to welcome a friend or bid *adieu* to a visitor, a forest of hats waved in deferential greeting.

One of the sincerest tributes of those days came from Bavaria, in the somewhat cumbersome shape of barrels of Bavarian beer. There was no end to them, sent by Bavarian brewers in the hope of receiving an autograph letter in acknowledgment, expressing appreciation of the excellence of the brew. For whereas Prince Bismarck's closer countrymen had quietly acquiesced in him being put on the list of the "played out" (*Auf dem Aussterbe Etat*) as one whose opinions were of no further consequence, the shrewd Bavarians had still the most implicit faith in his judgment on a matter of far more importance to them than politics or even religion—the quality of their beer.

The interior of the *Schloss* itself, however, supplied perhaps the most tangible proof of the place Prince Bismarck held in the hearts of his countrymen. The rooms were full of presents sent to him, and I was told that it was the same at Varzin and Schönhausen, his other seats. Among them were a number of books dealing with his career, portraits, busts, illuminated addresses, presentation pieces of furniture sent to the prince by trade guilds or other corporations and societies. A large oak chest stood against the wall of the morning room. It was the gift of a paper manufacturer, and contained enough writing material for generations to come. I also noticed an imposing oak chime clock, which might well sound the hours of joy and sadness in the family for many a year yet.

Two mammoth iron safes contained the recent presentation of the German manufacturers. It consisted of a silver dinner service, said to represent a money value of about a quarter of a million marks. While we were inspecting this, a servant brought two sets of massive gold drinking cups, gifts from the German residents of Moscow and Odessa.

I was rather struck by the small amount of attention bestowed upon these costly offerings. Princess Bismarck, for instance, seemed to think more of a telegram from an obscure but kindly well-wisher than of any of these tributes in gold or silver. As for the prince, I do not think that he ever saw half the presents that were sent to him. He certainly never referred to them. Even Lenbach's beautiful portraits of him—two of which hung upon the walls, and called forth the admiration of every visitor—seemed hardly to exist for him.

On one occasion I mentioned this fact to Count Herbert Bismarck, and added that I felt his father was extremely indifferent towards the decorative side of life; that of all things, decorations would be the least likely to possess much value in his eyes; that there were only two such which I could fancy him prizing. These were the medal for saving human life, *Die Rettungs-Medaille,* and the Prussian Order *Pour le Mérite.*

"It is strange," he replied, "that you should mention this, for they were indeed the first and last distinctions conferred upon my father."

There were exceptions, however, to the prince's indifference toward the offerings of his admirers. Among the treasures of Friedrichsruh I was shown a silver tankard—a so-called *taler-beaker*—in which a number of old and new German coins were let in. It was a present from a publisher of Oldenburg of the name of Schwartz, who was also the proprietor of a periodical entitled the *Volksboten.* Bismarck was much impressed by this man's patriotic sentiments, and was pleased with his gift. When later on most of the presents were sent to Schönhausen, he insisted on keeping this particular one by him at Friedrichsruh. He cared not for things, but valued the sentiments they were intended to convey.

Bismarck had no intention of taking his dismissal without protest. Two years after his resignation he was busily writing or inspiring articles filled with harsh criticisms against such individuals as Karl von Boetticher, Freiherr von Biberstein, and Count von Caprivi. In the year 1892 at least a hundred articles from his pen were published in the Hamburger Nachrichten, *which opened its columns to his invective. On May 31, 1892, Dr. Hans Kleser, editor of the* Westdeutsche Allgemeine Zeitung, *interviewed Bismarck at Friedrichsruh and wrote a detailed account for his newspaper. The old man played the game of protesting that he certainly had nothing against the emperor, but it was clear that he felt exactly the opposite of what he was saying. There was no forgiveness in him for what he regarded as the shabby circumstances of his dismissal.*[15]

Shortly after the conclusion of lunch we sat down in the prince's study (he smoked his usual long pipe, while I enjoyed the fragrant "Bismarck Bock" which he handed me). Conversation at once opened by the prince returning to my speech about him in Cologne. "One must not think that I bear a self-consuming grudge against the emperor, or any one else. I am far removed from that. Here in Friedrichsruh I feel happier and more contented since my dismissal, apart from bodily pains from time to time, than ever during my official life. The people who have brought about my fall are really entitled to my gratitude." In reply to a query as to whether the order for his dismissal did not appear to make his retirement a voluntary and desired one, the prince observed, "My departure was no voluntary one. To the last I opposed rather passively the ever plainer attempts of the emperor to induce me to tender my resignation. The first signs that the emperor wished to be rid of me date further back than is generally accepted. It was not always my wish to be spared a railway journey from here to Varzin, Berlin, or Potsdam whenever important matters were to be discussed, and for a long time I had noticed, and they let me notice it, that every extension of my stay in the country would be welcome. The real insistence on my removal dates from New Year, 1890. Even then I still evaded it. The emperor noticed it, and so he became still more plain, at first with the pretext secretly conveyed to me of separating the presidency of the Prussian ministry from the imperial chancellery. We had such bad results from this separation under Roon, who was assuredly an excellent man, that I believed such a plan could at most be resorted to after my death. But if a smart general, proposed by me—and in conversation I mentioned Caprivi as an example—were to be placed at the head of the Prussian ministry of state, I declared myself ready to continue as chancellor of the empire alone. For just then the political situation was fraught with such momentous decisions, that I did not consider myself justified by my conscience in resigning at that juncture. But even this proposal was distasteful to the emperor;

15. Visit to Friedrichsruh, May 31, 1892, by Dr. Hans Kleser, of the *Westdeutsche Allgemeine Zeitung,* in *Conversations with Bismarck,* coll. von Poschinger, ed. Whitman, pp. 152–163.

he wanted me to be put aside completely, and his immediate *entourage* no longer treated this as a secret.

"Even Windthorst heard of it and sought an audience of me, and this I granted him, as I have always done as far as possible to any member. If Windthorst has reported that I mentioned Caprivi to him as my successor, it is an error of Windthorst's. Perhaps he heard from some one in the emperor's *entourage* that I had hinted at a solution by making a general—perhaps Caprivi—president of the Prussian ministry. At the time Windthorst was with me, I was not aware that Caprivi would be particularly welcome to the leader of the Center. It is true that Windthorst said to me that he sincerely wished me to continue in office. Perhaps he even meant it; but stipulations for the event of my remaining were not discussed.

"The emperor then made strong representations to me because I had received Windthorst without asking him (the emperor). I had to deny the justice of this censure; but I saw from this occurrence that the emperor wished to remove me at all costs from the direction of even the imperial affairs. Nevertheless, for conscientious reasons I continued my passive resistance, but without abandoning the institutions, for without them it is impossible to carry on the affairs of the empire and the presidency of the Prussian ministry with security. I did not approve, therefore, of the cancellation of the cabinet order of 1852, which directs the departmental ministers only to communicate with the king through the president of the ministry. A council of the ministry took place on the 16th of March, at which the situation was discussed, and it was unanimously resolved that the situation demanded that I should be requested to remain in office. A member of the council of the ministry was found who reported the resolution, declared to be secret, and on the 17th, General Hahnke appeared at my house, without any direct commission from his Majesty, so he said, to make known his Majesty's expectation that I would send in my resignation. I informed the general that if the emperor considered that he had no further use for me, he was able to dismiss me. No move on my part was required for that. It was impossible for me to apply for my retirement myself, since I was obliged to consider it a serious damage to German policy under the existing circumstances.

"On that very day Lucanus arrived with the direct royal commission. He sweetened it by mentioning the emperor's wish to create me duke of Lauenburg, and stated that he, Lucanus, believed himself able to assure me that if I doubted my ability to support a ducal household on my income, the emperor would be gracious enough to take this into consideration. That, indeed, was the last thing wanting—to be placed on the retired list, like a zealous, worked-out postman, with a special remuneration! I declared that I could not ask for an elevation in rank, which I might have had before, as I did not desire it. I answered Lucanus that, since the emperor expected to receive my application to retire immediately I was prepared to sign my simple resignation at once, but that for an application of such importance a certain amount of time was required. I agreed to send the document to his Majesty as soon as I was able. I composed it on the 18th and during the night of the 19th. It contains about twenty pages, and explains why I could not officially be personally responsible for my retirement under the present conditions. According to my thinking, the emperor could hardly have read this, my last official document, attentively when I received the decree of dismissal, the wording of which you know. So long as I live, my application to retire which really was the opposite of an application to retire, will not be published; but if the government press of today, in order to falsify history, constantly points to my application to retire and to the gracious acceptance of the same, please demand that my application be published word for word officially by the government."

The chancellor then proceeded to discuss in general terms the difficulties of the situation, which prevented him from retiring voluntarily.

"In the first place, there were our relations with Russia, and the uncertainty whether any successor of mine would be able to maintain them in the then existing sincerity and friendship. It is true that Alexander III is averse to German ideas, and is even an enemy of Germany. But he is a prudent ruler, and does not allow himself to be swayed in his foreign policy by a certain well-known feminine influence. Since the tissue of lies which Gortschakoff had spun round my person at the tsar's court has been destroyed, Germany, so long as I was at the head of affairs, was on a good and sound footing with Alexander III which means with Russia. Alexander III is naturally suspicious; but still there was one politician in the world whom he believed and trusted in unconditionally, and that was I. Today it is different, as I had foreseen. They have abandoned my foreign policy at its most vital point."

On his attention being drawn to the alleged danger of the pan-Slavonic movement in Russia, Bismarck observed, "I do not understand why a Russia holding Constantinople should be more dangerous to us than the present one with Petersburg, Warsaw, and Odessa. From Germany's point of view, I should not have put any difficulties in the way of Russia if she had wanted to take Constantinople. From an egoistic point of view, I should even consider a Russia in possession of Constantinople, *i.e.* which had made one step from Odessa across the Black Sea, to be less dangerous to us than the present one. So far as pan-Slavism is concerned, I consider that official Russia, nay, even the real Russians, are not at all pan-Slavonic. The pan-Slavonic leading articles in the Russian papers, which fill the Western Europeans with such fears, are not written by Russians at all, but chiefly by Poles, whose aim it is to incite Slav and Teuton against each other in the hope of creating a new Polish kingdom at their expense, no matter which side be victorious.

"There is by nature a fundamental difference between Russians and Poles. At the bottom of his temperament the Russian is a dreamer and an enthusiast, if you will, a silent romanticist; the Pole is an intriguer, hypocritical, untruthful and unreliable, quite incapable of maintaining a state organization—today he overflows with *Jescze Polska,* tomorrow it is *Waschlapski* and *Krapulinski.*

"The Russian is therefore as hateful to the Pole as is the Teuton, but that does not interfere with his working with either, nor from being in the pay of both. As I have already said, those who champion the pan-Slavonic ideas in the Russian papers are Poles. What I have said does not imply that there are not individuals of eminent learning and high character among them. I am speaking of the general character, and particularly of the political character, of the Pole. During my official career I have had to conquer many obstacles and annoyances created for me by Poles. The youthful love of the Emperor William for a Princess Radziwill resulted in the creation of a multitude of Polish connections, which the emperor, with this chivalrous tenderness, maintained during his life. All kinds of Polish political intrigues were carried on at court, against which I have often had to fight a hard battle. The Pole is always engaged in proselytizing, and the Polish women are untiring therein and also successful. Therefore the suppression of Poledom, which is everywhere political and *'Great-Polish,'* must not be lost sight of. To favor Poledom would also put us on a bad footing with Russia. Unfortunately, this favoritism came into full swing immediately after my dismissal. The appointment to the Archbishopric of Gnesen of a well-known champion of the ideas of Great-Poledom was especially weak and reprehensible, both as a matter of foreign and domestic policy."

After a digression to discuss the characteristics of the old emperor, Dr. Kleser asked the prince, in connection with the chancellor's great speech in February 1887, whether there had been any difference of opinion between him and Moltke on the question of a declaration of war with France.

"Certainly," replied Bismarck, "and Moltke's view found more support than mine, which did not gain the day so easily. In my Reichstag speech I gave my reasons why I was against a so-called preventive war with France. My personal conviction, gained from the study of history, is that it is unwarrantable to enter upon a war with a weaker opponent at an apparently suitable date, merely because the opponent at that time threatens to attack you as soon as he is strong enough to do so. Some of the French who threatened us five years ago are already dead today, and in all probability hardly one of them will be alive at the time when France may see her chance of attacking us. But I will go still further, and maintain that, if Germany retains only semi-capable statesmen, France will never have such an opportunity. During my time in office she certainly did not have one, and by herself alone she can hardly ever catch us up in a military sense. Moreover, Providence, or, if you will, the course of the history of the world, often takes care that, when a warlike feeling prevails, circumstances prevent its gratification. There was a time, after the Peace of Berlin, when Russia appeared anxious for war. But the progress we had made in the manufacture of guns and projectiles and the preparation of powder, which Russia could not equal quickly enough, prevented the possibility of war until the desire for war had vanished. Moreover, a personal argument in favor of peace existed for me in the thought of my old master. Where should we have left the emperor during a war? At his age he could not have gone through the campaign; and do you think he would have remained behind in Berlin and have allowed the army to march out of the Brandenburg Gate without him? It would, I believe, have been possible for me, in spite of his deep-seated aversion to the horrors of a new war, to induce him to consent to such if I had given him the assurance that I was convinced that the war was unavoidable to secure the future of Germany, for he would then have felt it his duty to consent to it. Since I did not then possess this conviction, which I have not even today—in spite of the deterioration of our relations since my dismissal, Germany simply remained on the side of peace. No one in the world believes that we did this on account of weakness."

Reference was then made to the rumors that Bismarck wished to be "reconciled" to the emperor before going to Vienna, where his son's marriage was to take place.

The prince remarked, "These communications proceed from the present government, and have no further object than to invest me with the appearance of feeling guilty in some respect towards the emperor, by inventing a desire for reconciliation. The words 'reconciliation with the emperor' are in themselves an absurdity, were it only for the reason that a situation does not exist which a 'reconciliation' presupposes—at least, not on my part. My criticism is solely directed against the wrong political methods which my successor and his colleagues have adopted, for they fill me with anxiety for the empire. Seldom, perhaps never, have I been so deceived in a man's capabilities as I was in Caprivi's. Perhaps, after all, there can be no more unsuitable preparatory career for the direction of the affairs of the state secretariate in the Foreign Office than that of a state counsel. The king is above all criticism; no remark of mine is directed against him, and I beg you, as well as all visitors, who publicly support my political views, to leave the personality of the emperor out of the question as far as possible, but in any case not to attack him. During my stay in Berlin to treat about taking over the presidency of the Prussian ministry, thirty years ago, I learned with real horror that the king of Prussia was only saluted in the streets of his capital by a couple of hair dressers and a few court tradesmen. I then made a vow to myself to do what lay in my power to effect a change in this. I have done so, and reached my goal; and though it strikes me at times that I may have even overshot the mark, this is less serious than the other condition would be. Therefore, not a word against the king. But the ever-recurring insinuations as if I were stretching out my hand, or ought to take the first step towards a reconciliation, are meant to serve no other purpose than to create the impression that I have to make something good to the king—in fact, to beg his pardon. There can be no idea of that. Whether I am in the king's good graces or not I do not know; I have done nothing to forfeit them, and therefore I can do nothing to regain them. Now and again there comes a visitor, who thinks he must needs tell me that the emperor wishes to approach me again. These expressions of opinion I judge from the same point of view; they are apocryphal because they are absurd in themselves. According to my conviction, the emperor does not desire any other relations with me but those which he himself has created.

"The circumstances under which I had to quit the chancellor's palace were indeed most insulting to me and my family. Contrary to all custom, I was not even left in office until my successor was appointed, so as to give me sufficient time to move my things, such as any small citizen's family might expect. Nay, hardly had my successor been appointed, than he took possession of the chancellor's palace, and obliged us to pack up on the stairs and landings. We were turned into the street like thieves, and lost many a bit of property by the hasty packing of our things. But all that does not affect me personally; it leaves me calm, and least of all does it excite me against the emperor. If, therefore, the present relations between the emperor and myself are represented as if I desired to see them changed, it is intended either to show the world that others are free from blame as regards myself, or, in the event of a 'reconciliation' taking place, I should be represented as the party that has begged off. For nothing in the world will I allow this suspicion to be thus cast upon me, as if I had committed some fault, or even shown a want of respect toward the reigning emperor. Probably the people who spread such reports know that they can only call forth a denial on my part, thus making the so-called 'reconciliation' impossible on my side. That, perhaps, is the reason why these reports always crop up again, but they do not move me."

Then the prince continued—

"I had long foreseen that things were bound to happen with the emperor and me as they came about, and only from a pure sense of duty did I hold out, by the exercise of great self-control, and put off my retirement as long as I could. I was, therefore, not taken by surprise, though, on the other hand, I do not conceal from you that I was grievously disappointed in the German people. I thought they possessed more political judgment. It is not the faithlessness and defection of a few that pained me, but the complete inertia of the whole nation, which is apparently not able to perceive what drives me to criticism. It is not a personal grudge, nor revenge, nor even a wish to regain power, but the anxiety, the heavy anxiety, which robs me of many a night's rest, about the future of the empire founded with such costly and heavy sacrifices."

Dr. Kleser assured the prince that only a slight opportunity was necessary to rouse the deep-seated feeling of the nation from its apparent apathy.

The prince was skeptical, but his interviewer proved to be right, for only a fortnight later the "Urias" letter of Count Caprivi to the German ambassador at Vienna caused the sentiments of the German nation to be proclaimed with no uncertain voice.

9 Official Boycott and Public Acclaim: Bismarck Comes Out of Retirement to Witness the Marriage of Herbert and the Countess Hoyos in Vienna [16]

"My duty is to be silent."

In 1881 Bismarck interfered in the marriage plans of his son, Herbert, and broke up his contemplated union with the Princess Carolath.[17] *Eleven years later, in 1892, the retired chancellor finally saw his son married in Vienna. Even here the nuptials were marred by an imbroglio between the Bismarck and William II. The seventy-seven-year-old Bismarck, officially stigmatized by the emperor and court circle, fought back to defend his name, rank, and honor. It was an old story—whatever Bismarck touched turned into a personal battle.*

At the instigation of his father, Herbert became engaged to a Hungarian heiress, the Countess Marguerite Hoyos, whose mother was English and whose father was half-Austrian, half-Hungarian. The elder Bismarck was delighted by the match. He had encouraged the courtship on the ground that a union of his eldest son with a representative of a people who owed him so much was desirable, thus repeating in the domestic life of the Bismarck family the alliance between Prussia and Hungary.

On May 5, 1892, when the engagement was announced, William II sent this telegram of good wishes to Herbert:

> Best thanks for your friendly announcement and heartiest wishes for your happiness on the occasion of your engagement to Countess Marguerite Hoyos.
>
> WILHELM, *Imperator Rex*

There was little spontaneity or warmth in this communication. Despite his battle with the Bismarcks, William II considered it to be good manners as well as good politics to pretend that he was delighted by the news of the forthcoming wedding.

16. Account adapted from Snyder, "Political Implications of Herbert von Bismarck's Marital Affairs, 1881, 1892," *The Journal of Modern History*, XXXVI, No. 2 (June, 1964), 162–168.
17. See pages 284–289.

The young emperor might not have been so quick to send congratulations had he known that the elder Bismarck himself intended to go to Vienna for the ceremony. The news brought excitement to Berlin. Word spread through the anti-Bismarckian court circle and among Wilhelmstrasse officials that the fallen chancellor had sinister political designs in making the journey to the Austrian capital. One rumor had it that Bismarck on one occasion had remarked that he would "open the eyes" of Francis Joseph to the young kaiser. There would be a triumphant procession of the Bismarcks through German cities. Once in Vienna, the dangerous lion and his cub could be counted on to mend their political fences and prepare the way for a return to power. To the uncomfortable monarch and his advisers this was but an extension of the concerted effort to arouse popular enthusiasm for the Bismarck dynasty, thus embarrass the emperor, force him to oust General Leo von Caprivi, Bismarck's successor as chancellor, and then recall Bismarck.

Bismarck's own advisers, especially his confidential agent, Gerson von Bleichröder, urged him not to make the trip and argued that it would be interpreted as a new venture into the political arena. But the old man would not listen. Had not Herbert already ascertained that the Austrian emperor would receive him? Was he not assured of an audience and a welcome in Vienna? Further, as was the privilege of any father, he was determined to go to Vienna "to please the family of the daughter-in-law."

When it became obvious that nothing could deter Prince Bismarck from making the trip to Vienna, it was decided at the highest level to stigmatize him officially as a person not to be received and also to arrange a social boycott of the family. On June 9, 1892, a letter signed by Chancellor Caprivi was dispatched to Prince Heinrich VII von Reuss, the German ambassador in Vienna:

> After an audience with his Majesty, I inform your Excellency of the following concerning the forthcoming marriage of Count Herbert Bismarck. The rumors of a reconciliation of Prince Bismarck and his Majesty do not take into account the indispensable presumption of a first step upon the part of the prince. But even if this did take place, the reconciliation could never go so far that public opinion would take it that the prince had won any kind of influence in the leadership of national affairs. His Majesty requests your Excellency that, should the prince or his family make any approach to your Excellency's house, you limit yourself to the conventional forms, and avoid accepting any invitation to the wedding. His Majesty will not accept any notice of the wedding. You are instructed to inform Count Kálnoky [foreign minister of Austria-Hungary] of this fact in whatever

> manner may seem best to you. These indications as to behavior apply to the staff of the embassy as well as to yourself.

It is probable that Freidrich von Holstein, from 1878 to 1906 councillor (*Vortragender Rat*) in the political department of the German Foreign Office, had a hand in drafting this communication. Eulenburg's biographer, Johannes Haller, states categorically: "This unfortunate step was wholly Holstein's work." Otto Gradenwitz wrote that Holstein had a double purpose in mind: to boycott Bismarck and at the same time to prepare the way for Eulenburg's appointment as ambassador in Vienna.

On June 12, 1892, three days after the official dispatch had been sent to Vienna, William II sent a handwritten communication to Francis Joseph:

> At the end of the month Bismarck goes to Vienna, . . . in order to receive planned ovations from his admirers. . . . You are aware that one of his masterpieces was the secret treaty *à double fonds* with Russia, which, negotiated behind your back, was annulled by me. Since his retirement, the prince has carried on a most perfidious war against me and Caprivi, my minister. . . . He seeks, with all the art and shrewdness he possesses, to twist matters so that the world shall believe that I am making advances to him. The main feature of his plan is that he had asked you for an audience. . . . Therefore, I venture to beg you not to complicate my situation in my own country by receiving this unruly subject of mine before he has approached me and said *peccavi*.

It was impossible to keep communications of this kind secret in the Berlin atmosphere, suffused as it was with gossip and intrigue. The "unruly subject" soon learned about the contents of these two insulting letters. At first he reacted as if he were still a student at Göttingen: He would challenge Caprivi to a duel. The seventy-seven-year-old Bismarck would defend his name, rank, and honor. "But when I turned the matter over in my mind I remembered that I am an officer, and that the affair would be submitted to a court of honor composed of elderly generals. I should never have got him to face my pistol." Still, it took great effort by the family to calm down the furious old man. Privately, Bismarck denounced the emperor's communication, which he called a *Uriasbrief* (Uriah letter), as "a contemptible piece of effrontery." *

The Bismarcks left for Vienna on June 18. The *Norddeutsche*

* "Letter of Uriah" (II Sam. 11:15), a treacherous letter, proclaiming friendship but in reality meant as a death warrant. It refers to the biblical story of Uriah the Hittite, a captain in David's army, who was sent to the most dangerous area of the battle line, where he was killed. David then took as his wife Bathsheba, who had been Uriah's spouse.

Allegemeine Zeitung announced erroneously that the former chancellor and his party would arrive in Berlin at the Lehrter station, whereas they actually came in at the Anhalter station. Nevertheless, a huge mob was at the Anhalter station clamoring for a speech. "My duty is to be silent," said Bismarck. An onlooker countered: "When you keep silent, then will the stones speak!" City officials met the Bismarck party at the station in Dresden. The city was in banner, the Bismarcks' private car covered with flowers. "Our unity is unbreakable," said Bismarck in a speech. That night, from his rooms at the Hotel Bellevue, he reviewed 13,000 torchbearers and 1,600 singers. At 10:30 P.M. on the evening of June 19 the party arrived at Vienna, where the reception was so stormy that Bismarck and Herbert were nearly trampled by the crowds. By the next day, however, it became obvious that there was an official and social boycott. Unimportant mayors and representatives of prominent citizens did wait upon the Bismarck family, but there were no invitations from kings and princes. The nobility, "the true aristocracy," remained aloof.

Emperor Francis Joseph, unwilling to disturb political relations with Berlin, did not receive the Bismarcks at court. Reuss found himself in an embarrassing position. He had been instructed not to receive the Bismarcks. He was not even to allow the German *Gesangverein* in Vienna to take part in any demonstrations for the visitors. Since he could not very well disobey his emperor, Reuss took to his bed and became diplomatically ill. However, his wife, daughter of Grand Duke Alexander of Saxony, proclaimed loudly and boldly that *she* was not in the diplomatic service; she would receive the ex-chancellor and his family with great deference in her home. On the afternoon of June 20 Bismarck left his card with Kálnoky at the Foreign Office. That evening there was a gala party at the home of Count Palffy, a relative of the bride's family, with whom the Bismarcks were staying. The guests included Kálnoky, the ambassadors of Russia, England, and Italy, and the military attaché of the German embassy in Rome.

The humiliation of the Bismarcks went to almost ludicrous proportions. Neither the resigned chancellor nor his son was supposed to wear a military uniform because such attire could be worn in foreign countries "only with permission." The old man was infuriated by this ban. "I don't know about rules on uniforms," he wrote to his son, William, "and I do not believe they are in effect. Think of it, at my age, to have to ask what I should wear!" However, when Bismarck was driven to the church on the morning of June 21, he was dressed in the uniform of a cuirassier.

Despite the plethora of premeditated insults, the ceremony went off happily at noon on June 21 at the Helvetian Reform Church. There was no official representation at the wedding. The ex-chancellor gave a toast at the wedding dinner: "To the political unity of the two great powers." At 5:00 P.M. that afternoon the couple, orange blossoms in hand, went off on their honeymoon.

The elder Bismarck remained in Vienna for two more days. Despite his age, he visited the Prater, the Rathaus, and mounted the 158 steps of the Festsaal. On June 23, aching for battle, he carried out his carefully made plan for revenge. In a long interview with M. Benedikt, editor of the *Neue Freie Presse,* he openly attacked the German government and accused it of stupidity:

> Austria, in the commercial treaty, has, of course, turned to account the weakness and ineptitude of our negotiators. This result must be ascribed to the fact that in our country men have come to the front whom I had formerly kept in the background—the reason being that everything had to be changed. . . . For my part, I am no longer under any obligations toward the personalities now in office, or toward my successor. All the bridges have been broken down. . . . The tie which used to connect us with Russia has been severed. Personal authority and confidence are lacking in Berlin.

This tough talk created an uneasy sensation in Berlin. Something had to be done to discredit the "garrulous old man." Eugen Richter, leader of the Progressives, referred to legal paragraphs which could be used against Bismarck for this interview, and even reckoned how many years the ex-chancellor would have to serve in jail.

The return journey of the Bismarcks was made by way of Munich (June 24), Augsburg (June 26), Kissingen (June 27), Jena (July 30), Berlin (August 6), and Varzin (August 8). The German public, aware of the shabby treatment accorded Bismarck in Vienna, greeted him with an outburst of enthusiasm. Never in his active political life had the Junker of Friedrichsruh enjoyed such popularity. He was astonished: "My six weeks' journey was a triumphal tour—such as I had never dreamed. . . . Everywhere the people greeted me joyfully." Crowds of many thousands met him at the railway stations. There were torchlight parades and choirs. Hans Blum, with commendable *Gründlichkeit,* reported that during his five weeks in Kissingen, Bismarck received 320 dispatches totaling 10,000 words. At Jena, where the Bismarcks had breakfast, a golden tablet was placed on the wall: "Here lived Prince Bismarck on 30 and 31 July 1892."

Bismarck exploited the situation with a series of political speeches. He called the German people to war against their government. In the past, he admitted, the "inner building" of the Reich demanded a certain dictatorial activity: "Now, however, one need not look upon dictatorship as a lasting institution of a great empire." According to Johannes Ziekursch, "The man who had done everything to lessen the influence of the Reichstag in the 1880's, the man who had broken political parties, now spoke in terms of a majority in the Reichstag."

All Europe was amused by the press battle which followed. While the Bismarcks were in Kissingen, the *Norddeutsche Allgemeine Zeitung* sharply attacked the ex-chancellor for his interviews and speeches. It recognized with horror that "his memory is failing him." It accused him of "wounding the monarchical sentiment and of undermining respect for the kaiser." Bismarck replied vigorously in the *Hamburger Nachrichten* that the attacks on him were "tasteless absurdities." On July 7, 1892, Caprivi published the text on his June 9 communication to Reuss. Undoubtedly, this "vassal-like act of loyalty" was an effort to turn the scorn of an angered public from the kaiser to himself. Every German now had the opportunity of reading how the new chancellor had humiliated his predecessor.

90

Stream of Visitors, 1893: Bismarck Enjoys Access to World Opinion through More Newspapermen and Eminent Foreigners

". . . and then the fire dying out only to flame up again."

The stream of foreign reporters and visitors continued year after year, both in Friedrichsruh and in Kissingen, where the Bismarcks went in summers to take the waters. Invariably those who were invited to meet him wrote a sympathetic account of the interview, which is precisely what Bismarck wanted. Among the best portrayals was this report by a British journalist.[18]

I had last seen Prince Bismarck in 1888, in the Reichstag; and on various occasions before that, notably one evening in his palace in the Wilhelmstrasse—the old one—of which I have many memories. But never till now had I seen him except in uniform, whether in public or private, in parliament or in the street, or as a figure in

18. G. W. Smalley, "A Visit to Prince Bismarck," *The Fortnightly Review*, CCCXIX (July 1, 1893), 4–7, 22–27.

a military parade. I don't know that he ever appeared or spoke, whether in the Prussian diet or in the Reichstag, otherwise than in a soldier's dress. Soldier he has always been, and still is, and nothing seems to be dearer to him than the military character, as, indeed, it is to most Prussians. . . . Prince Bismarck, when I first saw him in 1866, was a major of cuirassiers. He has risen—slowly, inasmuch as he has had other things than soldiering to do—to be general, and that is his rank in the army today.

He was now in black from head to foot; black double-breasted frock coat, buttoned to the throat across the chest, relieved by no order or decoration, or any touch of color, except that he wore around his neck a pale yellow, or perhaps cream-colored, soft silk neckcloth, something like the cravat which prevailed in England in the earlier part of the century, but less voluminous and tied carelessly. He wore no collar. He wore his coat like a uniform. It set off the breadth of the shoulders, the depth of the chest, and the whole huge framework and vast body which of itself seemed to fill the room, whether he stood or sat. He towered far above everybody. His manner when he walked down the room as we came in was, above everything, that of the host anxious to welcome his guests. Almost his first word was a regret that the clocks at Friedrichsruh did not keep what he called mid-German railway time; an artificial sort of time, based on an average of differences for the zone in which it is observed, and extremely helpful to the punctuality and smooth working of the German railway system. "Still," said he, "here in Friedrichsruh we must have the real time." All his life long he has clung to realities, the make believe having no attraction for him nor, to his mind, any validity in public or private affairs. . . .

The face and head which rose out of the black coat and soft pale yellow neckcloth are known to everybody by pictures and photographs, and also by description, and yet they are not known. . . . Every view is a new view. The power of the head and face is what it was. Age has altered, not impaired it. The firmness of outline remains. The muscles of the neck have not lost their elasticity, the head rises aloft and alert; in the carriage of it something haughty, something almost defiant and victorious, as of one who all his life long has had enemies to deal with, and the habit of overcoming them. The lines and outlines are drawn with a free hand and a wide sweep; with the breadth to which nature more often attains when she works on a great scale, as in fashioning a mountain range or shaping a continent. The actual measurements of the skull must be extraordinary. I do not know what they are, but no figures could express the sense of intellectual force and force of character.

Herr Lenbach once spoke of the face as faultless. Nothing, he thought, could be added or taken away without injuring it; all the features were perfect. This is stating the matter too strongly. Herr Lenbach has painted Prince Bismarck often and well; no one else so well; the world of the hereafter will owe much to him; for photographs may not last forever, nor do photographs always tell you what you most want to know about a face. Perhaps, by long study and admiration, Lenbach has in his own mind idealized his sitter. He does not idealize him on canvas, except in the sense that he paints character as well as the external facts of face and figure. If the features were, as he said on that occasion, faultless, they would be, in Tennyson's phrase, faultily faultless. They are nothing of the kind. They are not regular, not classic, not molded to any known type or accepted standard, or not all of them. The face is the man, with all his individuality, and the eyes are the man. They are deep blue—the blue seems to have grown deeper with years—large, full, wide apart, beautiful in repose and capable of expressing, without any help from the other features, the most various moods—authority, tenderness, anger, and many others. The dry light of pure intelligence seems their natural expression till it changes into some other, and when they are turned upon an individual or a parliament in a spirit of inquiry they look through and through the individual or the parliament. The power of penetrating character, of judging men, has ever been one of his gifts and one of his sources of mastery in public affairs, and this also you see in these piercing orbs, the light of which is the next moment peaceful and kindly. The eyebrows, which are very heavy, are not so much tangled as interwoven; the full tufts of white hair braiding themselves into strands. The moustache, which overhangs without concealing the mouth or much altering the expression of the lips, follows the lines of the mouth, which at either end it closely embraces.

The masterful strength of all the lower part of the face is but the counterpart of the upper; the capaciousness of the brain and the willfulness of the character are each indicated clearly; neither is out of proportion; there is neither excess of intelligence nor excess of firmness; the two are in harmony, and you would never fear that mere activity of mind should turn into particularism, or that mere determination should paralyze the thinking faculties; nor has either of these catastrophes occurred in actual life. The work of his life has, of course, left its mark upon the worker. The figure before you, with its simple and beautiful dignity, is the history of Germany for thirty years; a new Thirty Years' War, as beneficent as the old man was destructive. Prince Bismarck, and not the youthful Hohenzollern at Potsdam, is the incarnation of imperial Germany. . . .

He spoke throughout in English, not without a certain effort. His mastery of English, for conversational purposes, and upon a wide range of topics, is tolerably complete. It is not professor's English, nor that of the student, but idiomatic, vigorous, often colloquial, and ever the English of the man of affairs and of the world. Language is to him an instrument, to be used as he uses other instruments—for his own ends. He has audacities of speech as well as of act. What is wanting to him in English is practice. He had of late, he said, no occasion to speak English more than twice a year, and his fluency was less than it had been. But if he sometimes had to search for the word, he always found it, and always the right word, and sometimes a picturesque one where greater familiarity might have led him or another to use a commonplace one. It was all the more instructive to behold him struggling amid these linguistic difficulties; you saw the machinery at work, as when on a great steamship you look through a glass partition at the engines doing their twenty knots an hour. Still, the medium sometimes hampered him; but when a change was suggested, he refused. It seemed as if it were part of his conception of his duties as host to express himself in the native tongue of his two guests. . . .

The talk flowed on for another hour, the prince choosing his own topics, dismissing one with a flashing sentence, enlarging upon another, the face radiant at times, the eyes burning, and then the fire dying out only to flame up again; and sometimes the cold glitter of steel came into them, and then the words cut like steel.

All the while the dogs were about him, appealing to him for the notice they did not often get, except from the caress of his left hand. If he would not respond, they turned to us. They had the frank good nature of the breed, and readily put their huge heads into any friendly hand. Once the prince tossed a biscuit to Rebecca, which she caught cleverly. His gesture, the movement of the arm, the precision, the rapidity of the act, were one more characteristic of the extraordinary man who can do nothing like other men, and who never thought it beneath him to do the least or most trivial thing as well as it could possibly be done. The dogs are magnificent creatures, one blue-black, one of a dense bluish-gray color, with broad heads and amiable piercing eyes, and that kind of powerful slouching movement which one commonly sees behind the bars of a cage, and the gracefulness which comes from tremendous strength. The prince and the dogs were on easy terms; his manner to them and theirs to him was charming, but you could see that discipline was maintained. At night they sleep in his bedroom. . . .

It was interesting to see his pipe brought in, a huge machine, with a porcelain jar two feet high, in which it rested. With it came a round lacquered tray, on which was a collection of instruments, including a lead pencil some fifteen inches long; two silver paper knives in the form of daggers, both sheathed; a silver letter opener, and others which, it presently appeared, were tobacco stoppers, and rods for cleaning the pipe, also sheathed. All these he showed us. . . .

Meantime, all the company except ourselves had slipped away, leaving the prince to talk on to his guests. We had been two hours at table before there came a pause, and then Dr. Chrysander reappeared to suggest that it was time for the siesta which Dr. Schweninger prescribes for his patient. So, with a word of excuse and a half protest against submission, the prince departed. We were shown to our rooms, and then Dr. Chrysander fetched us soon after for a stroll in the forest. The forest is a real forest, of red and white beech and much other good timber, well grown, but not of very great size, and wherever we went an uncleared undergrowth; the whole seamed with roads and opening into sunny glades clothed in a rough turf. The wood is peopled with deer, of which we saw none, and there are wild boar and much other less formidable game; altogether, a royal preserve. The prince loves it, loves the trees, and the stream, and the shady walk, and the views from the terrace, and from the benches along the path. One which takes him by the bank and beyond the sloping meadow to the forester's house is his favorite. He walks there daily, and daily people gather in the road he has to cross, near the bridge, to see him go by. Here, in and about his home, he is loved, and the love and lovers come from all over Germany as well. Not a week passes that there is not a deputation, or a band of students, or some other company of honest Germans with a true reverence for the greatest German of all. Often they arrive daily, sometimes more than one in a day. There had been eight hundred children the day before. There were men waiting by the bridge as we passed. The swans were waiting in their wired-off demesne; a duck with her ducklings, for little bits of floating fluff, smiling by triumphantly, out of all danger from the swans; the living and visible proof of the success of those domestic politics we had heard described at luncheon. . . .

Our walk took us three or four miles through the forest. As we came near the house again, we heard singing, and, turning into the grounds behind the house, saw Prince Bismarck and the family on the balcony, and below it a group of schoolchildren from Hamburg. They were the singers, and sang song after song. There were tables on the grass, and tea and cake and other good things for the children, and the inevitable beer for the masters, and perhaps for the children. We went up on the balcony, to which there is a flight of steps, and tea was going on there, too. What I call a balcony is more like a veranda without a roof, a broad square stone terrace with stone balustrade, and room for thirty or forty persons, beside the tables and seats. This is the scene of the receptions and greetings which occur so often, and here, at any rate, you are remote enough from the outer world—nothing but the house, which encloses two sides of the grounds, and the trees with every tint of spring green against the dark firs, and the flowing stream, and the sloping meadow, and woods, and blue sky—blue with a black thundercloud coming up. The prince had completed his costume with a black soft felt hat with sugar-loaf top and broad brim, and carried a stick on which he leaned a little as he walked. He might not care much for the songs; it is the music of birds he cares for, and he pretends to like the organ in the sitting room—a mechanical organ; likes it because, as he said with quaint kindness, it is good exercise for the princess. But the good little German boys and girls went on singing in good faith, and the prince listened, and stood at the balustrade looking down with a softened face and friendly eyes at his young admirers. The song ceased after a while, and one of the masters made a brief speech, asking his pupils to notice the beauty of the spring and its foliage, and telling them that if they had a Fatherland in which they might peacefully enjoy its beauty, they owed it to the great man who stood there on the terrace. The little creatures cheered with their shrill voices with right good will again and again. Then Prince Bismarck, instead of saying a word or two formally and stiffly from his platform above their little heads, went down the steps and stood among them, and put his hand on those nearest him, and said simply, "I thank you very much, my dear children, and your teacher, for coming here and singing to me. And I hope you won't get wet going home." The heavy drops were already falling, and away went the children. But of rain there was almost none. The prince thought his black, sugar-loaf, broad-brimmed hat a better protection against the rain than an umbrella, which he never carries. He never carried one in politics either. With his hat and the huge blue cloth coat we had seen in the hall, he defied the rain. He came up the steps again, and the party sat down in groups.

Dr. Schweninger had arrived, coming by train from Berlin, to see his patient, from whom he is seldom very long away. It is not that the prince is ill, but that he requires watching if he is to be kept in full health. He still has a little of the neuralgia which has tormented him so long. The seventy-eight years he has completed have not tamed his energy, nor does banishment from the public service mean idleness to him. I fancied, from what I saw and heard, that he was likely to do too much unless hindered. A man who has in times past thought sixteen or eighteen hours a fair day's work does not readily reduce his allowance to within such limits as seem sufficient to the medical mind. Dr. Schweninger thought him tired, and prescribed rest, but the prince said he would take his rest talking.

Lord Randolph Churchill, British statesman and leader of the Tory Democratic movement, was rebellious and somewhat erratic, but at the same time he was a brilliant tactician. He dedicated his life to upholding church, constitution, and conservatism. In 1886, at the age of thirty-seven, he became chancellor of the Exchequer and one of the top men in his party. In the summer of 1893, feeling ill, he came to Kissingen to submit himself to a strict medical regimen in the hope that a quiet, peaceful resort life with its simple routines would restore his health. Here the ailing forty-five-year-old Englishman met the seventy-eight-year-old retired chancellor. The two men had much in common, especially a mutual dislike of Gladstone, as revealed in the following letter from Lord Randolph to his mother. This letter and an account of the meeting appeared in a biography of Lord Randolph by his son, Winston Spencer Churchill.[19]

Lord Randolph's Letter to His Mother

7 *August.*—The sensation of yesterday was the visit of Prince Bismarck. We had left cards on him the day before, and I did not expect he would do more than return them. However, yesterday the weather was showery, and as Jennie was rather seedy we did not go our usual drive. I was reading the papers when a great big *Chasseur* appeared and informed me that the Fürst von Bismarck was in his carriage at the door and was asking for me. I hurried downstairs and met the prince at his carriage. He came up to our rooms—which luckily are on the first floor—and sat down, and we began to converse. I had sent off a message to Jennie, who had gone to the Kurhaus to see a friend. So I had about a quarter of an hour in which to talk to the prince. I will tell you of his appearance. He is seventy-eight—so he told me afterwards—but he looks so

19. Winston Spencer Churchill, *Lord Randolph Churchill* (London, 1906), II, 477–481.

much younger than Mr. Gladstone that in fact you would hardly give him more than seventy-three or seventy-four years. He looked in good health, and came upstairs without the slightest difficulty. We discussed various subjects, which I will go through *seriatim.* We spoke in English; but whether it was for that reason, though he spoke very correctly, he struck me as being nervous. Perhaps it was meeting with a total stranger, because he had never seen me before. However, he was most gracious and seemed very anxious to please. You may imagine that I did my very best to please him, for I thought it a great honor for this old prince to come and see us.

The conversation began on Kissingen—the baths, the waters, etc. He told me he had first come here in 1874, and had been here almost every year since. He gave up drinking the waters about eight years ago, but he continues to take baths, and thinks they do him good. After this I asked him why he never went now to Gastein. He said, laughing, "Oh, Gastein is a peculiar water to some people —sometimes dangerous"; that he knew two of his friends who died of apoplexy when taking the baths; and added that his doctor had told him that Gastein was the last resource; and he remarked, "And I am seventy-eight," and seemed quite pleased about it. Then he talked about the Emperor William on a question as to whether Gastein had not added some years to his life. He quite admitted it, and told me that for many years the emperor used to go to Carlsbad, when he used to accompany him; and this reminiscence seemed very pleasing to him. In talking of the emperor he always used the expression "my old master."

Then I turned the conversation on to Siam, and asked him whether he did not think it was a satisfactory settlement. He appeared to agree and began speaking in this connection of M. Jules Ferry. He regretted his loss, and said that Jules Ferry was the best man that France had had for years, and joked a little about his appearance—long whiskers, etc. Then he went on to say that he thought, if Jules Ferry had remained in power, a very good arrangement and condition would have come about between the Germans and the French. He said that he had nearly concluded an agreement between himself and Jules Ferry that France should remain on friendly and peaceful terms with Germany, and that he (Prince B.) would support France in Tunis and Siam, and generally in her Eastern colonization. Then I remarked about Siam that Rosebery had learned out of his book this principle—to ask for no more than he required, but to insist on getting what he required, and to treat with neglect what was not essential. He said that was so and he went on to praise Rosebery, and described him as a good combination of will and caution, and added that of all English statesmen he was the one who was most modest and quiet in his acts and attitude.

Of course, no conversation would be complete without a reference to Mr. Gladstone, to which I led him. He, of course, began by admitting that Mr. Gladstone was very eloquent; but that he had always been like an ungovernable horse whom no one could ride in any bridle, and was not to be controlled in any way. He used a German adjective to described the horse, which I have forgotten; but seeing his drift, and in reply to his question what was the English expression for the German word, I said "ungovernable and unmanageable and hard to ride" would express it, and I remarked that in England people often called such a horse a "rogue." On which he turned his face to me with a smile, but said nothing, though he clearly understood the allusion. He further in conversation said that he should be very alarmed and anxious if such a man as Mr. Gladstone governed "my country." Then Jennie arrived and he talked mainly to her for a few minutes, when he announced that his son Herbert and his recently married wife arrived that afternoon to stay a few days with him, and that he hoped we should see something of them.

Without doubt this prince and statesman has a most powerful attraction. The whole of his career, from the time when he was first minister of the king and fought the parliament, to the time of the proclamation of the German empire at Versailles, seems to me more intelligible now, and at the same time a work that only this man could have carried out or even conceived the possibility of. I never took my eyes off his face while he was talking to me and kept trying to fix it in my memory. For all his quiet manner his qualities would be apparent to any observer of experience; you can trace the iron will in great emergencies which has so frequently borne him up, all the calm courage for which the North Germans are peculiarly distinguished, and yet with all that—in spite of the recollection of the great things he had done—no trace of pride, no sign of condescension, but perfectly gracious and polite, a true *Grand Seigneur.* He carried himself at his age as erect as a soldier, and for all his long black coat and his rather old black, soft, low-crowned wide-awake hat he looks all over what he is—the combination, so rarely seen in this century, of statesman and general.

Winston Churchill's Further Account

This friendly conversation, proving mutually agreeable, was followed by an invitation to dinner with the Bismarck family. "We dined," so runs the account, "in the hall of an old bishop's palace, on the first floor, which a friend of the prince owns and lends him every year. It was of large and fine proportions. At one end we assembled before dinner; at the other end the table was laid. The dinner was a regular old-fashioned German dinner, a little *bourgeois* (like the Berlin court under the old emperor), but everything was dignified as to the table—the food, the wine, the old servants—and, though very different from our ideas—had realy *un air noble.* All this was greatly added to by the presence of the prince, his impressive appearance, and the combination of respect and affection which all his family, and those friends that were dining, showed him. His good spirits and excellent humor and his sustained support of the conversation—sometimes with Jennie, sometimes with me, sometimes with Herbert and his wife—can never be forgotten by anyone who saw it."

Lord Randolph sat next to Prince Bismarck and was so occupied in observing him and the scene generally that he took but little part in the conversation. The picture was complete—the princess, feeble and broken in health; Count Herbert and his wife; the famous black wolfhounds which once upon a time frightened Gortchakoff so much; Bismarck himself, "speaking English very carefully and slowly, frequently pausing to get the right word, but always producing it, or something like it, in the end"; drinking a mixture of very old hock poured into a needle-glass of champagne—" 'the last bottle [of hock], a present from ——,' a grand duke whose name I cannot remember"—at length arriving at his great pipe, prepared all ready for him by a venerable retainer, "stem two feet in length, curved mouthpiece, bowl long and large in china and standing up square with the stem, lighted by broad wooden safety matches to prevent him burning his fingers; and all the time running on in talk brisk and light, always courtly and genial, never quite serious."

"I did not dare," declares Lord Randolph, "to drink this old hock, and only sipped it. The prince, who was joking, said to Jennie that he was very sorry I had not drunk my share, as it would cause him to drink too much and he would be 'half over the seas.' " Presently he wanted to know about Mr. Gladstone. He would be useful in putting to rights the disorders of German finance. Would the English people exchange him for General Caprivi. "I told him," writes Lord Randolph shamelessly, "that the English people would cheerfully give him Mr. Gladstone for nothing, but that he would find him an expensive present!" So with chaff and good temper the evening passed away—pleasant, memorable, one of the last he was to know.

91

In an Emotional Speech Delivered in 1894 to a Delegation of Visitors from Posen, the Hermit of Friedrichsruh Reveals His Old Fire and Calls for a Strict Sense of Nationality

"They are standing equally firm at the Warthe and the Vistula!"

On September 16, 1894, a delegation of 2,200 Germans from the province of Posen, appeared in Varzin to express their thanks to Bismarck for his devotion to the national idea. The retired chancellor seized the opportunity to review his forty years of Polish diplomacy. Bismarck was old, but there was still fire in his eyes and in his words.[20]

Gentlemen! First I must ask your indulgence, since for two days I have been upset by an unpolitical enemy called lumbago, an old acquaintance of mine for sixty years. I hope to get the better of him soon, and then to be able to stand again fully erect. At present, I must confess, I am hampered by him.

I begin by replying to the words of the previous speaker with thanks for the honor done me, addressing myself first of all to him, but then also to you. The previous speaker is as old as I. We were both born in 1815, and different walks of life have brought us together again here in Varzin after almost eighty years. The meeting gives me great pleasure, although I have not run my course as safe and sound as Mr. Kennemann. When I claim to be an invalid of hard work, he may perhaps claim the same. But his work was possibly healthier than mine, this being the difference between the farmer and the diplomat. The mode of life of the latter is less healthy and more nerve-racking. To begin with, then, I am grateful to you, gentlemen, and I should be even more grateful, if we were all to put on our hats. I have lost in the course of years nature's own protection, but I cannot well cover my head if you do not do the same.

I thank you that you have spared no exertion to show your national sentiments in this way. The exertion was considerable, a night in the train, a second night on the way back, insufficient

20. Translated by Edmund von Mach in *The German Classics* (New York, 1914), X, 276–285.

meals, and inconveniently crowded cars. The fact that you have stood all this and were not deterred by it attests the strength of your national feeling, which impelled you to bear witness to it here. That you did it here greatly honors me, and I recognize in it your appreciation of my part in the work of establishing the conditions which we are enjoying in Germany today, after years of disunion. These conditions may be imperfect, but "the best is the enemy of the good." At the time when we shaped these conditions we never asked: "What may we wish?" but "What must we have?" This moderation in our demands for union was one of the most important preliminaries of success. But following this path we have reached the results which have strengthened the pledge that your home will remain united with the German empire and the kingdom of Prussia. The proportion, in the meanwhile, of Germans in the foundation of our structure to the less reliable—I will not say loose—Polish element has become decidedly more favorable for the Germans. Our national figures are forty-eight million Germans and two million Poles; and in such a community the wishes of the two million cannot be decisive for the forty-eight million, as must be apparent, especially in an age when political decisions are dependent on a majority vote as a last resort. The forces which guarantee the union of these territories are strong enough both in the parliament and in the army to assure it, and no one can doubt that the proper authorities are ready to use these forces at the right time. No one mistakes the meaning, when the announcement is made from the highest quarters: "Ere we shall yield again Alsace, our army will have to be annihilated" (and words to this effect have been spoken). The same thing is true, to an even stronger degree, of our eastern frontier. We can spare neither, Posen even less than Alsace, and we shall fight, as the emperor has said, to the last man, before we renounce Alsace, this protection of our southern states. Yet Munich and Stuttgart are not more endangered by a hostile position in Strasbourg and Alsace than Berlin would be endangered by a hostile position near the Oder. It may, therefore, be readily assumed that we shall remain firm in our determination and sacrifice, if it should become necessary, our last man and the last coin in our pockets for the defense of the German eastern frontier as it has existed for eighty years. And this determination will suffice to render the union between your province and the empire as positively assured as things can be in this world.

We confined our demands to what was necessary for our existence and what enabled the big European nation which we are to draw a free breath. We did not include territories where German used to be spoken, when this had been largely due to a propaganda of the German courts. More German used to be spoken in the East, Northeast, and elsewhere than today. Remember our ally, Austria, and how familiar German was there in the days of Joseph II and of the Empress Maria Theresa, when German was a greater force in parts of Hungary than it is or can be today. But, for everything we gave up in the shape of a linguistic and outward union, we have found rich compensation in the intensity of a closer union. If the older gentlemen will think back to the time before Emperor William I, they will realize that the lack of love among the various German tribes was much greater at that time than it is today. We have made notable progress in this direction, and, when we compare the unequivocal expressions of opinion from Bavaria and Saxony today with the familiar sentiments of earlier times, we must say that Germany, which for the past one hundred years had lagged behind the other people of Europe in national development, has rapidly caught up with them. Forty years ago we were far behind all other nations in national feeling and love of one another. Today we are no longer behind them.

Our fellow countrymen from the Rhine, from the Alpine lake and the Saxon Elbe are attached to one another in affectionate sympathy, not only when they meet abroad, but also at home. A united people has been created in a remarkably short time. This proves that the medical cure which we employed, although it was of blood and iron, lanced only a sore, which had come to a head long ago, and that it gave us speedy comfort and good health. God grant that the cure will be lasting and subject to no change. How far reaching it is has been proved by the testimonials which I have received since I gave up my office. They have come from all people, —from Baden, Bavaria, Saxony, Swabia, Hessen, and from all the districts of Prussia outside the provinces of Frederick the Great. These entirely voluntary manifestations, which were arranged by no one, and which not infrequently came to me at rather inconvenient and inopportune times, have impressed me with the existence of national harmony. Every one of them has given pleasure to my patriotic heart, and has borne witness to a common feeling existing in all German races—this much I wished to say concerning the stability of the political and national union of your province today.

We often sing "Firm is the stand of the faithful guards on the Rhine," but they are standing equally firm at the Warthe and the Vistula. We cannot spare an acre of land in either direction, for the sake of principle if for nothing else. The previous speaker referred to the attempts which had been made, as a result of the movement of 1848, to shake loose the union in which we were then living in Prussia and Germany, and to disregard our boundary lines. These attempts of satisfying the wishes of our Polish neighbors ended with the action of the Prussian General von Colomb, who closed the gates of Posen to the Polish troops which, in response to promises made in Berlin, had been raised under the Prussian General von Willisen. We were obliged to conquer with Prussian troops, and in a bloody war, the army of the insurgents who fought bravely and honorably. I wish to add that even that war was not fought with the Polish people as such, but with the Polish nobility and their following. I remember speaking to some Polish soldiers of the 19th regiment, I believe, in Erfurt at that time, that is in 1850, who called the opponents only *"Komorniks"* —the Polish word for "contract laborers." We should, then, not deceive ourselves into believing that even today the number of those who are opposed to the two races in Posen and in West Prussia living together peacefully is as large as statistics may claim.

This brings me to the second point touched upon by the previous speaker, the two races living together peacefully. I believe that many of you have in your employ laborers and servants who speak Polish, and that you are of the opinion that no danger comes from this lower social stratum of the population. Living together with them is possible, and no disturbance of the peace starts with them. They do not promote any movements hostile to us. I do not even mention the fact that they are possibly of another race than the nobility, whose immigration into the Slavic districts is lost in the obscure past. The statistical numbers, therefore, of those opposed to a peaceful communion of both races must be lessened by the large number of laborers and farmers. The lower classes are, in the bulk, satisfied with the Prussian government, which may not be perfect always, but which treats them with greater justice than they were accustomed to in the times of the Polish republic of nobles. They are satisfied with this. It was not part of my program that the commission on colonization should pay special attention to small holdings of German-speaking settlers. The Polish peasants are not dangerous, nor does it make any difference whether the laborers are Polish or German. The chief thing was to create crown lands among the big estates, and to rent them to men whom the state could permanently influence. The desire for quick sales and colonization emanated from other competent quarters than myself. It was impossible for me to supervise these measures after I had instigated them.

The difficulties which I met in the forty years of my Polish diplomacy did not start with the masses of Polish laborers and peasants, but were, I believe, occasioned largely, if not exclusively, by the Polish nobility with the assistance of the Polish clergy. Perhaps this latter term is too narrow, for I know of instances when German priests assisted in the Polish propaganda for the sake of peace. This is a peculiarity of our race—and I do not exactly wish to condemn it—that we often place our religion above our nationality. The very opposite is true of our opponents, the Poles and the French people, who regard their nationality more highly than their religion. We are suffering from this habit. We possess, however, a certain material counterweight, provided the state government unreservedly supports the German element. The religious element has great weight in the family circle and among women, especially the Polish women, whom I have always greatly admired. The minister has a freer access to them than the local governor or the judge. There will, however, always be a powerful weight in the scales, when the Prussian government exercises its influence with firm determination and so clearly that doubts for the future are impossible. *Vestigia terrent!* we may say, when with 1848, no—not 1848, I mean 1831–32—the attention paid to the Polish nation became almost more pronounced in Germany than that given to the German element. Since then we have surely been able to register progress in our politics. Now I must ask your indulgence for a moment on account of my lumbago. (Voices: "Sit down, your Highness.") Sitting down does not help me. I know this visitor from years of experience. I was speaking of the possibility of having the two races living peacefully side by side. This is not impossible, for in Switzerland we see three different nationalities—the German, Italian, and French Swiss—deliberate quietly and without bitterness on matters of joint interest. In Belgium we see the Germanic Flemish form a united state with the Gallic Walloons, and we perceive that it is possible under circumstances to live peacefully together even with the Poles, when we remember East Prussia, where the Polish Masures, the Lithuanians, and the Germans work together harmoniously. Because nobody has incited the people there, no national ill feeling has appeared among them. It is true, to be sure, that the Catholic priest, with his peculiar interests, is unknown there. But look at your neighbors in Upper Silesia. Have the two races not lived there in peaceful communion for centuries, although the religious differences exist there also? What is it, then, that Silesia has not, and that has made it possible for us to live there, through centuries, in religious harmony? I am sorry to have to say it, it is the Polish nobility and the clergy of the Polish propaganda. The Polish nobles are, no doubt, very influential—more so with the Poles than the Germans—but the statistical figures are much larger than the actual number of our aggressive Polish opponents with whom we have to count.

The nobles are thinking of the time when they were all-powerful, and they cannot give up the memory of conditions when they ruled the king as well as the peasants. The Polish nobles, however, are surely too highly educated to believe that the conditions of the old Polish republic of nobles could ever return, and I should be astonished if the Polish peasants knew the history of Poland so badly that they did not recoil from the possibility of a return to the old state of affairs. The peasants must say to themselves that a "wet year," as the farmers put it, would be their lot if the nobles regained their power. Among the national-Polish representatives that are elected, you generally meet only noblemen. At least I cannot remember having seen a Polish farmer as a representative in the Reichstag or in the diet. Compare this with the election results in German districts. I do not even know whether there are Polish burghers in our sense of the word. The middle classes in the Polish cities are poorly developed. Consequently, when we reduce our opponents to their proper size, we grow more courageous in our own determination; and I should be very glad if I could encourage those who on their part are adding to the encouragement of the Polish nobles. I feel, gentlemen, that I am of one mind with you, who have traveled the hard road hither. I have no influence with other elements, but we shall not give up hope in spite of all vicissitudes.

The address of the previous speaker also referred to vicissitudes and changes. These changes have characterized our entire Polish policy, from 1815 till today. They took place whenever high Polish families gained influence at court. You all know the Radziwill family and its influence at the court of Frederick William IV. If we could make a mental test of the popular feeling of 1831 and of today, we should find that the conviction has greatly increased that we have German fellow countrymen in the grand duchy of Posen. The former and, I am tempted to say, childish cult of the Poles as I knew it in my childhood is no longer possible. Then we were taught Polish songs in our music lessons together with the *"Marseillaise,"* to be sure. The Polish nobleman, therefore, than whom God never created anything more reactionary, was here thrown into one pot with the French Revolution, and liberalism was coupled with the cause of the Poles, because we were lacking in political perspicacity. Such feelings were ingrained in our citizens at that time. I am thinking especially of the citizens of Berlin. If today you ask the opinion of your forty-eight million fellow countrymen, and compare their views and those of the bulk of the German army with the bugbear which had found lodging in German hearts at the time of Platen's Polish songs, you surely cannot despair of further development. We may, you must agree, register progress, although it is slow and there are lapses. It is like climbing a sandy hill or walking in the lava of Mount Vesuvius. One often glides back, but on the whole one is advancing. Your position will grow the stronger the more vigorously developed our sense of nationality will become. I ask of you, do not despair if there are clouds in the sky, especially in this rainy year which has saddened the farmers. They will disappear, and the union of the Warthe and the Vistula with Germany is irrefragable.

For centuries we have existed without Alsace-Lorraine, but no one yet has dared to think of what our existence would be if today a new kingdom of *Poland* were founded. Formerly it was a passive power. Today it would be an active enemy supported by the rest of Europe. As long as it would not have gained possession of Danzig, Thorn, and West Prussia, and I know not what else the excitable Polish mind might crave, it would always be the ally of our enemies. It indicates, therefore, insufficient political skill or political ignorance if we rely in any way on the Polish nobles for the safety of our eastern frontier, or if we think that we can win them to fight anywhere for German possessions, sword in hand. This is an Utopian idea. The only thing which we and you, gentlemen, can do under present conditions, and which we can learn from the Poles, is to cling to one another. The Poles, too, have parties, and used to show this even more unfortunately than we, but all their parties disappear as soon as a national question is broached. I wish the same would come to be true of us, and that in national questions we would belong primarily, not to a party, but to the nation. Let us be of as divergent opinions as we choose, but when in our eastern provinces the question arises: "German or Polish," then let the party feuds be laid aside until, as the Berliners say, "After nine o'clock." Now is the time to fight and to stand together. This is just as it is in military matters—and I am glad to see among you many who have experience in such things. Before joining an attack in war we do not ask: Shall we follow our progressive or our reactionary neighbor? We advance when the drum beats the signal, and so we should in national affairs forget all party differences, and form a solid phalanx hurling all our spears, reactionary, progressive, and despotic alike, against the enemy.

If we agree on this—and the dangers of the future are compelling us to do so—we shall win our women and children for the same strict sense of nationality. And if our women are with us, and our youths, we are saved for all time. This is one of our present tasks, to give a national education to our children. I am confident that the German women possess all the necessary qualifications for this task. I shall ask you, therefore, to join me in a toast: The German Women in the Grand Duchy of Posen! And may the German idea take an ever firmer hold in your country!

A few weeks after delivering this speech, Bismarck was shattered by the death of Johanna at the age of seventy. The barefooted old man went into her room one morning and found her dead; he cried like a child. Bismarck was to live on for four years without the consolation of his beloved wife.

92

April 1, 1895: On His Eightieth Birthday Bismarck Reviews the Battles of the Past and Urges German Youth to Keep Alive the Fire of Unity

"No struggle, no life!"

April 1, 1895 was the occasion of celebrations throughout Germany. More than five thousand young people journeyed to Friedrichsruh to pay homage to the grand old man of Prussia-Germany. After receiving a delegation of students, Bismarck addressed them with the following speech.[21] *Though he ended his talk with the usual toast "Long live the emperor and the empire!" it was clear that the embittered old man meant the office and not William II.*

Gentlemen! I have just heard from the lips of your teachers, the leaders of higher education, an appreciation of my past, which means much to me. From your greeting, I infer a promise for the future, and this means even more for a man of my years than his love of approbation. You will be able, at least many of you, to live according to the sentiments which your presence here today reveals, and to do so to the middle of the next century, while I have long been condemned to inactivity and belong to the days that are past. I find consolation in this observation, for the German is not so constituted that he could entirely dismiss in his old age what in his youth inspired him. Forty and sixty years hence you will not

21. *Ibid.*, X, 286–290.

hold exactly the same views as today, but the seed planted in your young hearts by the reign of Emperor William I will bear fruit, and even when you grow old, your attitude will ever be German-national because it is so today—whatever form our institutions may have taken in the meanwhile. We do not willfully dismiss from our hearts the love of national sentiments; we do not lose them when we emigrate. I know instances of hundreds of thousands of Germans from America, South Africa, and Australia who are today bound to the Fatherland with the same enthusiasm which carried many of them to the war.

We had to win our national independence in difficult wars. The preparation, the prologue, was the Holstein war. We had to fight with Austria for a settlement; no court of law could have given us a decree of separation; we had to fight. That we were facing a French war after our victory at Sadowa could not remain in doubt for anyone who knew the conditions of Europe. It was, however, desirable not to wage this war too soon nor before we had garnered to some extent the fruits of our North-German union. After the war had been waged everybody here was saying that within five years we should have to wage the next war. This was to be feared, it is true, but I have ever since considered it to be my duty to prevent it. We Germans had no longer any reason for war. We had what we needed. To fight for more, from a lust of conquest and for the annexation of countries which were not necessary for us, always appeared to me like an atrocity; I am tempted to say like a Bonapartistic and a foreign atrocity, alien to the Germanic sense of justice.

Consequently since we rebuilt and enlarged our house according to our needs, I have always been a man of peace, nor have I shrunk from small sacrifices. The strong man can afford to yield at times. Neither the Carolina Islands nor Samoa were worth a war, however much stress I have always laid on our colonial development. We did not stand in need of glory won in battles, nor of prestige. This indeed is the superiority of the German character over all others, that it is satisfied when it can acknowledge its own worth, and has no need of recognition, authority, or privilege. It is self-sufficient. This is the course I have steered, and in politics it is much easier to say what one should avoid than to say what one should do. Certain principles of honesty and courage forbid one to do certain things, just as the access to certain fields is interdicted in the army maneuvers. But the decision as to what has to be done is a very different matter, and no one can be sure of it beforehand, for politics are a task which can be compared only to the navigation of unknown waters. One does not know what the weather will be or how the currents will flow, nor what storms will be raging. There is in politics this additional factor of uncertainty that one is largely dependent on the decisions of others on whom one has counted and who have failed. One never can act with complete independence. And, when our friends whose assistance we need, although we cannot guarantee it, change their minds, our whole plan has failed. Positive enterprises are, therefore, very difficult in politics, and when they succeed you should be grateful to God who has given His blessing, and not find fault with details which one or the other may regret, but accept the situation as God has made it. For man cannot create or direct the stream of time. He can sail on it and steer his craft with more or less skill, be stranded and shipwrecked, or make a favorable port.

Since we now have made a favorable port, as I conclude from the predominant although not unanimous opinion of my countrymen, whose approval is all we have worked for, let us be satisfied, and let us keep and cherish what we have won in an emperor and an empire as it is, and not as some individuals may wish it should be, with other institutions, and a little bit more of this or that religious or social detail that they may have at heart. Let us be careful to keep what we have, lest we lose it because we do not know how to appreciate it. Germany once was a powerful empire under the Carolingians, the Saxons, and the Hohenstaufens, and when she lost her place, five, yes, six hundred years passed before she regained the use of her legs—if I may say so. Political and geological developments are equally slow. Layers are deposited one on the other, forming new banks and new mountains.

But I should like to ask especially the young gentlemen: Do not yield too much to the German love of criticism! Accept what God has given us, and what we have toiled to garner, while the rest of Europe—I cannot say attacked us, but ominously stood at attention. It was not easy. If we had been cited before the European Council of Elders before our French affairs were settled, we should not have fared nearly so well; and it was my task to avoid this if I possibly could. It is natural that not everything which everybody wished could be obtained under these conditions, and I mention this only to claim the indulgence of those who are perfectly justified in expecting more, and possibly in striving for more. But, above everything, do not be premature, and do not act in haste. Let us cling for the present to what we have.

The men who made the biggest sacrifices that the empire might be born were undoubtedly the German princes, not excluding the king of Prussia. My old master hesitated long before he voluntarily yielded his independence to the empire. Let us then be thankful to the reigning houses who made sacrifices for the empire which after the full thousand years of German history must have been hard for them to make; and let us be thankful to science, and those who cultivate her, for having kept alive on their hearths the fire of German unity to the time when new fuel was added and it flamed up and provided us with satisfying light and warmth.

I would then—and you will say I am an old, conservative man—compress what I have to say into these words: Let us keep above everything the things we have, before we look for new things, nor be afraid of those people who begrudge them to us. In Germany struggles have existed always, and the party schisms of today are naught but the echoes of the old German struggle between the noble families and the trade unions in the cities, and between those who had and those who had not in the peasant wars, in the religious wars, and in the Thirty Years' War. None of these far-reaching fissures, which I am tempted to call geological, can disappear at once. And should we not be indulgent with our opponents, if we ourselves do not desist from fighting? Life is a struggle everywhere in nature, and without inner struggles we end by being like the Chinese, and become petrified. No struggle, no life! Only, in every fight where the national question arises, there must be a rallying point. For us this is the empire, not as it may seem to be desirable, but as it is, the empire and the emperor, who represents it. That is why I ask you to join me in wishing well to the emperor and the empire. I hope that in 1950 all of you who are still living will again respond with contented hearts to the toast.

LONG LIVE THE EMPEROR AND THE EMPIRE!

93

Continuing Lust for Battle: The Recluse of Friedrichsruh Refuses to Hold His Tongue and Persists in Making Dangerous Revelations to Journalist Maximilian Harden, 1897

"I can accustom myself to most things, but not to being alone."

No one, not even the emperor, could silence the voice from Friedrichsruh. Bismarck's contempt for William II became even more intense as the years went by. He welcomed the emperor's critics to his home. Among them was Maxmilian Harden, a young journalist who had founded Die Zukunft *in 1892. When William sought to end the undignified quarrel by sending Bismarck a consignment of old wine, the latter deliberately drank it in the company of Harden. In September 1897, about ten months before his death, Bismarck gave the following interview to Harden.*[22] *The revelations were embarrassing, even dangerous, but Bismarck did not hesitate to make them, nor did Harden pause before publishing them.*

The prince lives quietly in his house in the Sachsenwald, follows attentively the occurrences of the day, both great and small, makes comments on them according to his custom; but leaves no doubt open that he has no wish whatever to offer official advice or suggestions, or otherwise to interfere with the political affairs of the day. Although he meets the present government with good will, as he would any other which does not force him to fend off obviously hurtful measures, still he would not like to be made responsible for its actions, and placidly, though sometimes a little bitterly, expresses a wish "to be left in peace." Meanwhile, piercing voices scream his name on the boulevards of Paris, and an editor of the *Figaro* mockingly exclaims that he would much have liked to see the face of the terrible man of blood and iron, on reading the speeches made on board the *Pothuau.* Had this heart's wish of M. de Roday been gratified, he would have seen a merry unclouded face. Prince Bismarck does not find in the after-dinner speeches of the Emperor Nicholas and M. Felix Faure any definite proof of a change in the situation, created between Russia and France by the Anglophile inclinations of Caprivism. He remarked on the subject: "*Nations alliées* are by no means an *alliance,* and may sometimes only be a mere politeness, a strengthening and underlining of the unimportant words *nations amies;* I remember, during my political activity, such dubious interpretations which were not unwillingly listened to by the parties concerned. And if an alliance had really been spoken of, one would first have to know its full contents in order to be able to estimate its value and importance. The people in Paris who demand the publication of the text are not far wrong. I do not believe that the contents of the treaty, if one exists at all, would please the French. In any case I have learned that Russian policy is always very cautious, and I cannot think that it would ever embark needlessly on adventures from which it has nothing to gain.

"Count Muravieff, with whom I very willingly consorted officially and personally when he acted as *chargé d'affaires* for my friend Schuvaloff, passed as our friend, and I do not know why he

22. Maximilian Harden, in *Die Zukunft,* September 4, 1897, quoted in *Conversations with Bismarck,* coll. von Poschinger, ed. Whitman, pp. 179–187.

should have changed his opinions. It seems to me today that, in many instances, people exaggerate the importance of journeys, visits, fêtes, toasts—I might say, the decorative element in politics. They have sometimes attempted to use even me decoratively, like a shade of color, but I am already too old for that, and hardly to be utilized for theatrical effects. M. Faure, who is said to have been a capable merchant—not at all a bad school for heads of state—appears to be endowed with all manner of useful qualities for the new method of traveling politics: he is hardened against carriage and cabin fatigues, has a good stomach, and behaves tactfully and cleverly, without harmful exaggerations and excesses of eloquence. If it is true that he has, in dress coat and top hat, greeted the Russian troops in military fashion—his hand to his tall hat,—such a method of saluting was certainly not correct for a civilian. He ought to have taken off his top hat, and, like old Fritz, paid the compliment with his three-cornered hat down to his saddle. On the whole, however, he has obviously got well and tactfully out of the affair. Only one must not believe that pleasant impressions and sympathies are deciding influences in politics; there, in the end, interests decide, and, with my experience, I cannot see what interest the Russians, who in political affairs are generally very cautious, are to have in coming to the aid of the French desire for *revanche,* so long as we do not carry on quite unwisely. 'Tsar's Hymn' and *'Marseillaise':* they do not rhyme. Nevertheless, the French pipkin has now got nearer to the fire, and may boil over more easily than ever, perhaps. That ought to rid our ruling masters of any remaining illusions, and warn them against shifting the base on which our defensive strength rests. It is as well that we Germans can never enjoy the careless ease of the Phæacians, and that the Parisians, who frame French policy, should from time to time awaken us from our all too beautiful dreams by their cries. But they cannot frighten us with *nations amies et alliées:* Russian emperors are nowadays too conscientious to set their soldiers in motion only in order that French vanity may perhaps find gratification.

"The papers now reproach me for having hurt the Conservative party by an expression which was published in a Vienna paper. I cannot now call this expression to mind. I do not know how it got into the paper, and I assume that it referred to events which occurred at my retirement, and during the discussion of the first commercial treaties. Of the present leaders of the Conservatives, moreover, I only know a few who are on friendly terms with my family, and whom I naturally did not wish to hurt; nor do I doubt the personal honor of the others. But it lies in the very nature of this party that it is particularly easily infected by the regrettable customs of party ambition. Officials who have seats, though they do not really belong to parliament, who have to provide for sons, daughters, and grandchildren, and therefore have to have considerations,—many a one would like to climb a step higher in the state; and useful relationships, social and military connections also play a part. Add to this, that my equals in rank are very comfortable, do not willingly overwork themselves, or are much occupied by their agricultural duties; then it is that the hardest strivers, who prepare themselves for the sittings, and are well up in printed matter, seize the reins, and the party notices, perhaps too late, that they have reached a 'crooked plane.' The gentlemen of the *Kreuzzeitung* persuasion made ministerial life thoroughly sour for me; I never was their man, and the worst insinuations always came from this side. They left me in the lurch when the time came, first of all, to put the German empire on its legs before the world. Much would have been different if I had then had Conservative help; but I would much rather have made a compact with Herr Richter than with the friends of Nathusius-Ludom and their kidney. There was much envy because I had got on better than other Junkers had, but there was also much theoretical narrowness and Protestant-Jesuitical zeal. On my being sent away, the same people again had a hand in the game: look at . . . and the like affairs. How matters stand in the party today, I do not know. Their outwardly visible performances do not exactly call for admiration from me. I often have the feeling that these gentlemen confuse the terms 'government' and 'Conservative'; and I sometimes ask myself whether they really know exactly what they want to conserve.

"Incessant arguments take place in the papers about the increase of our fleet. Why such noise? What is necessary, according to the opinion of sober, professional men, must be granted. I believe we want new cruisers; but I am very suspicious of parade ships, which are only to serve in marking our prestige, and which one might call lying ships, because they cannot do anything when affairs become serious. As a minister I lacked every inclination for a policy of colonial conquest on the French pattern, and it seems to me as if the present time was especially unfavorable for that. Our trade must find sufficient protection everywhere, but the flag must follow trade, not precede it. For the present time the most important thing for us is a strong reliable army of efficient soldiers, armed with the best weapons. That was also Moltke's opinion, and he shared the conviction with me, that we shall have to fight the decisive battles (for our colonial possessions) on the continent of Europe. No stinginess, therefore, but also no fantastic plans, in which we might finally embroil ourselves with other people, important for our European situation. *Qui trop embrasse. . . .*

"I am astonished that state assistance has not been given at once, orderly and rationally, in connection with the inundations. Private collections do not make a pleasing impression. As many and as highly placed personages as possible ought to show themselves at once in the affected districts, and talk kindly to the poor people—not merely talk, but also have a decent amount of money in their hands. That is the chief thing, quite apart from the duties of neighborly love, which the state has to exercise; a government should lose no opportunity of making itself beloved in the country. And at present, it seems to me, such opportunities ought to be most particularly welcome.

"The empress took a great part in the wearing away of my nerves. She was herself of a nervous, unstable, and unquiet nature, liked to busy herself in politics, and became fire and flames if one did not, could not, at once agree to her plans. Our frictions were of an early date. When the prince of Prussia was to go to England in 1848, and I wished to see him, to advise him urgently to remain in Potsdam, when the whole army and a large portion of the country population were for him, and his journey would have an evil effect, she would not let me see him. She was excited, and declared to me that she must provide for the future of her son before all things. Later on I heard of a curious plan which was concocted in her palace. Herr von Vincke addressed me in the diet, and said he wished to move a resolution to entrust the princess of Prussia with the regency; what did I think about it? First of all I asked why the prince was not to be regent. The prince, opined Vincke, had become impossible in the country. 'Very well,' said I; 'if you move this, I shall move to have you arrested for high treason.' The resolution fell through because it had no prospect of success without the support of the extreme right. My relations with the princess did not improve thereby, and she could never quite conceal a certain grudge against me, even when she became queen and empress. Her preference for everything French and Catholic also had an effect; and at one time there was in her court a camarilla, which did not always employ scrupulous means to attain its object. I should not have been able to do much if my old master, who moreover did not suffer less than I under these things, had not kept his ground at the crucial moment. But these struggles tried the nervous system, especially when the queen sought to persuade him to abdicate, and I had to seize him, figuratively speaking, by the sword-knot. I may well say these years of feminine warfare have told more on my health than all open fighting in parliament and in the diplomatic service."

A newspaper had observed that the old chancellor would certainly go to Kiel shortly to christen a ship. The prince read the paragraph aloud, and added, "So? People still seem to think that I am like a maid who once said to my wife, in Varzin, 'I can accustom myself to most things, but not to being alone!' I feel all right at home, and am no longer fit for festivals."

4 Portrait in Acid: In the Third Volume of His Memoirs Bismarck Paints so Devastating a Portrait of William II that Its Publication Is Delayed Until after the Emperor's Abdication[23]

"His words flow readily. . . ."

The greater part of Bismarck's autobiography, Gedanken und Erinnerungen (Reflections and Reminiscences), *was published in two volumes in 1898. The third volume was withheld from publication at that time by Bismarck's heirs, primarily because they deemed it important to protect William II. In 1921, following the German revolution, with the kaiser abdicated and in retirement, the third volume was issued. In this volume Bismarck, considered to be the firm supporter of royalty, penned a deadly chapter on William II. Not only did Bismarck attack the man who had forced his resignation, but he also turned his wrath on the entire Hohenzollern family. It was an unexpected polemic which gave additional meaning to Bismarck's judgment: "I have seen three kings naked and often enough the behavior of these exalted gentlemen was by no means kingly." Bismarck's whole career had been dedicated to making the once lowly Prussian kings the most powerful monarchs in Europe; now he sneered at them as "Swabian weaklings."*

The first paragraph below is from Bismarck's chapter on William II as Prince William, while the remainder is devoted to William II as emperor. Unless otherwise noted, the word "kaiser" refers to William II.

When I now look back I assume that the kaiser [William II], during the twenty-one months when I was his chancellor, was only with difficulty able to suppress his inclination to get rid of an inherited mentor; until this inclination suddenly exploded, and a

23. *The Kaiser vs. Bismarck: Suppressed Letters by the Kaiser and New Chapters from the Autobiography of the Iron Chancellor,* trans. by Bernard Miall (New York and London, 1921), pp. 26, 148, 153, 165–170.

separation which, if I had known the kaiser's wish, I would have brought about with an avoidance of all external sensation, was forced upon me suddenly, in an injurious and, I might say, an insulting fashion. . . .

As regards his natural endowment with the characteristics of his forebears, the kaiser had inherited a certain diversity of talents. He has the love of splendor, the leaning toward court ceremonial, enhanced, on solemn occasions, by costume, of our first kings, combined with a lively susceptibility to adroit approbation. The autocratic temper of the age of Frederick I has been essentially modified by the lapse of time; but if it had lain within the legal possibilities of the present period, I believe I should not have been spared the fate of Count Eberhard Danckelmann as the conclusion of my political career. Considering the brief duration of life on which I can count in my old age, I should not have tried to evade a dramatic conclusion of my political career, and I would have endured even this irony of fate with cheerful submissiveness to the will of God. Even in the most serious situations in life I have never lost my sense of humor.

The kaiser displayed inherited sympathies similar to those of Frederick William I, first of all in the superficiality of his predilection for a "tall fellow." . . .

In common with Frederick William IV, the present kaiser has the gift of eloquence and the need of employing it more frequently than is desirable. His words flow readily; but in the choice of them his great-uncle was more discreet and perhaps more laborious and scientific. In the case of the great-nephew the presence of a shorthand writer is not always desirable; but it was very seldom that a grammatical criticism could be brought against Frederick William's speeches. These latter were the eloquent and sometimes poetical expression of ideas which at that time would have been capable of stimulating men to action, had the words been followed by deeds to correspond. I very well remember the enthusiasm aroused by the coronation speech and the king's utterances upon other public occasions. If they had been followed by energetic resolutions of the same emphatic character, they might at that time have produced a powerful effect, all the more as people's feelings were not yet blunted in respect of political emotions. In the years 1841 and 1842 more was to be achieved with fewer means than in 1849. We can form an impartial judgment of those matters now that the then desirable object has been attained, and the need of 1840 is no longer present in the national mind; on the contrary, *Le mieux est l'ennemi du bien* is one of the soundest of proverbs, against which the Germans are theoretically more inclined to trespass than other nations. William II resembled Frederick William IV in this, that the foundation of their policy was rooted in the conception that the king, and he alone, is more closely acquainted with the will of God than other men, governs in accordance with the same, and therefore confidently demands obedience, without discussing his aim with his subjects or announcing it to them. Frederick William IV had no doubt of his specially privileged position in respect of the Deity; his honest belief corresponds with the picture of the high priest of the Jews, who *alone* stepped behind the curtain.

In certain respects we shall seek in vain for any resemblance between William II and his father, grandfather, and great-grandfather; peculiarities which were the principal features of the characters of Frederick William III, William I, and Frederick III were not to the fore in the young sovereign. A certain timid distrust of their own capacity for work had, through the four generations, made way for a certain degree of assured self-confidence, such as we have not seen upon the throne since the time of Frederick the Great; but only, I think, in the person of the reigning sovereign. His brother, Prince Henry of Prussia, seems to possess the same distrust of his own powers and the same secret diffidence as are found, on closer acquaintance, at the bottom of the characters of Kaisers Frederick and William I, despite all their consciousness of their Olympian rank. In the latter his profound and pious trust in God was needed as surety, in the face of his unassuming and humble conception, before man and God, of his own personality, for the steadfastness of those resolutions which he made manifest in the time of conflict. Both rulers atoned by their goodness of heart and their honest love of the truth for their occasional deviations from the current estimation of the practical influence of kingly birth and anointing.

If I seek to paint a portrait of the present kaiser after the conclusion of my relations with his service, I find in him the characteristics of his predecessors incarnated in a manner which would for me possess a strong attractive power, and result in my attachment to his person, if they were animated by the principle of reciprocity between monarch and subject, between master and servant. The Germanic feudal law gives the vassal few pretensions save to the property of the subject, except that the fealty between him and his feudal lord is reciprocal, and the infraction of this fealty by either party is reckoned to be felony. William I, his son, and his predecessors possessed the corresponding sentiment in a high degree; and this is the essential basis of the attachment of the Prussian people to their monarchs, which may be explained psychologically, for the tendency to bestow a *one-sided* affection has no existence as an *enduring* motive in the human soul. In the presence of Kaiser William II, I could not get away from the impression of a one-sided affection; the feeling which is the firmest foundation of the constitution of the Prussian army, the feeling that the soldier will never leave the officer in the lurch, but also that the officer will never leave the soldier in the lurch, a sentiment to which William I conformed in respect of his servants almost to exaggeration, cannot so far be recognized as entering, in any adequate degree, into the mentality of the young sovereign; his pretension to absolute sacrifice, confidence, and unshakable fealty has increased; and the inclination to guarantee a return of confidence and security on his own part has so far failed to make its appearance. The ease with which he dismisses trusted servants, even those whom he has hitherto treated as personal friends, without explanation of his motive, does not promote, but weakens, the spirit of confidence as it has prevailed for generations in the service of the kings of Prussia.

With the transition from the Hohenzollern spirit to the Coburg-English conception an imponderable factor was lost which will be difficult to restore. William I protected and rewarded his servants, even when they were unfortunate or unskillful, possibly more than was profitable, and in consequence of this he had servants who were more attached to him than was profitable to themselves. In particular his warm-hearted good will toward others was unchangeable, if his gratitude for services performed came into play. He was always far from regarding his own will as the sole rule of conduct, nor could he contemplate the wounding of other people's feelings with indifference. His manner toward subordinates was always that of a royal and benevolent master, and alleviated the ill humor arising in the course of official business. Ill-natured gossip and calumny, when they came to his ears, could obtain no hold upon his noble and upright nature, and place hunters whose only source of profit lay in the shamelessness of their flattery had no prospect of success with William I. To backstairs influences and accusations against his servants he was insensible, even if they proceeded from people holding high positions about his person, and if he did take the matter imparted to him into consideration, this was done in open conversation with the person behind whose back it was meant to take effect. If his opinion differed from mine he expressed himself openly as differing from me, discussing the matter with me, and if I did not succeed in winning him over to my views I gave in when it was possible; if it was not possible I postponed the affair or let it drop for good. My independence as a political leader has been honestly overestimated by my friends, and for their own purposes by my adversaries, because I surrendered all hope of fulfilling desires to which the king had as a matter of conviction offered lasting resistance, without continuing to advocate them until they resulted in a dispute. What was attainable I took on account, and on my side it only came to a strike in cases where my personal sense of honor was involved, as in the affair of the *Reichsglocke,* by the Kaiserin, or in the Usedom affair, by Masonic influences; I have never been either a courtier or a Mason.

The kaiser [William II] endeavors, by making concessions to his enemies, to make the support of his friends unnecessary. His grandfather, at the time of his accession to the regency, endeavored to insure the general content of his subjects, without losing their obedience and thereby endangering the security of the state; but after four years' experience he recognized the errors of his advisers and of his wife, who assumed that the opponents of the monarchy would by liberal concessions be transformed into its friends and supporters. In 1862 he was inclined to abdicate rather than surrender further to parliamentary liberalism, and accepted battle, supported by the latent but decisively stronger loyal elements.

The kaiser, with his Christian, but not always (in the worldly sense) successful tendency to conciliation, began with his worst enemy, social democracy. This first mistake, which was embodied in the management of the strike of 1889, led to increased pretensions on the part of the Socialists and fresh ill humor on the part of the monarch, as soon as it became evident that under the new government, just as under the old, the monarch could not, with the best will in the world, change the nature of things and of the human race. The kaiser was without experience in the sphere of human desires and human covetousness; but that he had lost his early confidence in the judgment and experience of others was a result of intrigues by which he was confirmed in his underestimation of the difficulty of governing. . . .

On June 15, 1888, the crown prince became kaiser. Just a week later I heard indirectly of an imperial utterance to the effect that the kaiser was most unpleasantly affected by various articles in the Berlin newspapers, in particular by an article in the *Berliner Tageblatt* evening edition of the 20th of June and another in the *Berliner Zeitung* and the *Berliner Presse* of the 21st of June, which appeared to be written to arouse the belief that there was a dispute between his Majesty and the imperial chancellor in connection with Count Waldersee—that is, that there was already friction in the authoritative governmental circles in connection with recent appointments. They were repeatedly and publicly blamed for the same thing during the reign of Kaiser Frederick; his Majesty was afraid that the foreign press would comment upon these articles, and on this account was anxious that the government press should be correctly informed as to the state of affairs, so that it might assume a defensive position in respect of the press attacks alluded to. The kaiser ended, as he began, with the same point of view as that which he had unfolded in May—that he never allowed Count Waldersee an unjustified influence over foreign policy, in spite of his esteem for him; and that no court camarilla would exist under his government; much more was he convinced that no parties existed among the persons to whom he had given his confidence, and who were serving him, but that all were following him on the path which led to the goal which he recognized as the right one.

From the 19th to the 24th of July the kaiser was on a visit to Peterhof. The impressions which he left behind him there did not fully come to my knowledge until a later period. That he, himself, introduced a discordant note into our policy first became perceptible in two incidents which occurred in the June of the following year, while I was in Varzin.

Count Philip Eulenburg, our diplomatic representative in Oldenburg, was to a notable degree in his Majesty's favor, by reason of his social gifts, and was frequently summoned to court. He confided to my son that the kaiser regarded my policy as pro-Russian, and asked whether my son or I, myself, would not endeavor, by means of interviews and explanatory statements, to alter his Majesty's opinion. My son asked, what was meant by pro-Russian? Political actions which were *too* friendly to the Russians—that is, injurious to our own policy—should be pointed out to him. Our foreign policy is a carefully thought out and carefully manipulated whole, which the amateur and military politicians who whisper in his Majesty's ear do not perceive. If his Majesty has no confidence in us, and allows himself to be deceived by intriguers, then, in God's name, let him allow me and my son to go our ways; he has, with the clearest conscience and to the best of his ability, cooperated in my policy, and sacrificed his health amid the unendurable squabbles of which he was always the central point. If he still wishes to carry out a policy of "harmony," he will succeed more easily today than tomorrow. Count Eulenburg, who may have expected a different answer, broke off here with the urgent request that his remarks should go no farther; he must have expressed himself very awkwardly.

A few days later, while the shah of Persia was visiting Berlin, the kaiser informed my son that the press must write against the new Russian loan; he did not wish still more German gold to go to Russia in return for Russian paper, since the money was used only for military equipment and armaments. One of his generals of high rank—as was ascertained during the day, it was General von Verdy, the minister of war—had just called his attention to this danger. My son replied that the matter was not as stated; it was merely a question of the conversation of an earlier Russian loan, and of the best opportunity which offered itself to the German investors of accepting ready money and getting rid of Russian paper, which in the event of war would perhaps pay no interest to Germany. The Russians also wanted to make a profit, paying a smaller percentage on a given loan in the future; the gold market was favorable, and therefore the matter should not be postponed. The French would take the Russian paper which we returned; the business would be carried out in Paris. His Majesty insisted that articles must appear in the German press attacking this financial operation, and he had arranged for a meeting of the council of the Foreign Office in order to instruct it accordingly. My son said that if he had not succeeded in informing his Majesty of the state of affairs, he would have asked that he might be allowed to make a report from the ministry for finance; for semiofficial articles of this kind could not be written without hearing what the imperial chancellor had to say, since they would influence the general policy of the empire. His Majesty thereupon induced my son to write to me urgently that he wished a press campaign to be undertaken against the Russian loan, and had the representative of the then absent minister for finance informed by the aide-de-camp that the senior board of the stock exchange must be instructed to prohibit the loan.

I, myself, some months later, received a proof of his Majesty's temper in the shape of an incident which could not be passed over, and may be recapitulated here for the sake of coherence. When the tsar's visit to Berlin in October 1881, had come to a close, and I was driving back with the kaiser from the Lehrter railway station, to which we had accompanied the tsar, who was traveling to Ludwigslust, he told me that he had seated himself, at Hubertusstock, on the box of the drag, giving up to his guest the full enjoyment of the hunt, and concluded with the words, "Now I think you will praise me!" After I had satisfied this demand he continued to tell me that he had done more; he had announced that he would pay the Russian emperor a longer visit, part of which he proposed to spend with him at Spala. I ventured to doubt whether this would be welcome to the tsar; he is fond of quiet and seclusion, and his life with his wife and children; Spala is too small a hunting lodge, and not arranged for visits. I reflected that both the royal persons would be unable to avoid the closest intercourse, and in the intimate conversations which would be held during so long a period there might be a danger of touching upon sensitive points.

I took it upon myself to do what I could to prevent this visit. The difference of character and mentality in the two monarchs was perhaps known to no contemporary so well as to myself; and this knowledge made me fear that a longer companionship might lead, without any effective control, to friction, dislike, and ill humor, and that the latter, in the tsar, might already have been aroused by the idea of a more protracted disturbance of his solitude, even though he had naturally accepted his host's announcement of his visit with courtesy. In the interest of the understanding between the two cabinets I thought it a ticklish matter to bring the suspicious defensiveness of the tsar and the aggressive amiability of our sovereign into close and protracted contact without necessity, the more so as the advances were made in an insinuating manner, which was hardly applicable to our Russian policy, and still less to the distrustful self-esteem of the tsar. . . . The secret reports from Petersburg, which, even assuming that they were exaggerated or falsified, must have been written with a knowledge of the situation.

The kaiser was disagreeably affected by my opinion where he had expected approbation, and set me down in front of my dwelling instead of coming in with me for a further chat over official affairs.

The visit which the kaiser paid the tsar from the 17th to the 23d of August in Narva and Peterhof led to the increased personal aversion which I had feared.

Narva was followed by the meeting at Rohnstock and the commercial treaty with Austria. His Majesty's leaning toward England had been furthered on the English side with skillful calculation since the visit to Osborne at the beginning of August 1889, and had led to the treaty relating to Zanzibar and Heligoland. The uniform of the admiral of the fleet may be regarded as the symbol of the end of a chapter of the empire's foreign policy.

95 Angered and Frustrated by Attacks from the Venerable National Hero, William II Tells His Side of the Story

"But my reverence for Bismarck, the great statesman, nevertheless remained unaltered."

Although he professed the greatest admiration for Bismarck, William II regarded him as a representative of an outmoded system of political thought and action. In his Memoirs, *written after his abdication, William II stated his side of the story. The arrogance and impetuousness of his youth are missing from this* apologia.[24]

Prince Bismarck's greatness as a statesman and his imperishable services to Prussia and Germany are historical facts of such tremendous significance that there is doubtless no man in existence, whatever his party predilections, who would dare to question them. For this very reason alone it is stupid to accuse me of not having recognized the greatness of Prince Bismarck. The opposite is the truth. I revered and idolized him. Nor could it be otherwise. It should be borne in mind with what generation I grew up—the generation of the devotees of Bismarck. He was the creator of the German empire, the paladin of my grandfather, and all of us considered him the greatest statesman of his day and were proud that he was a German. Bismarck was the idol in my temple, and I worshipped him.

But monarchs are also human beings of flesh and blood, hence they too are exposed to the influences emanating from the conduct of others. Therefore, looking at the matter from a human point of view, one will understand how, by fighting against me, Bismarck himself destroyed, with heavy blows, the idol which I had set up; but my reverence for Bismarck, the great statesman, nevertheless remained unaltered.

While I was still prince of Prussia, I often thought to myself: "I hope that the great chancellor will live for many years yet, for if I could govern with him I should be safe." My reverence for the great statesman, however, was not such as to make me, when I became emperor, take upon my own shoulders political plans or

24. William II, *My Memoirs, 1878–1918* (London, 1922), pp. 1–3, 36–39.

actions of the prince which I considered to be mistaken. Even the Berlin Congress of 1878 was, to my way of thinking, a mistake, likewise the *Kulturkampf*. Moreover, the constitution of the empire was drawn up so as to fit in with Bismarck's extraordinary preponderance as a statesman; the big cuirassier boots did not fit every man.

Then came the labor protective legislation. I most deeply deplored the dispute which arose out of this, but, at that time, it was necessary for me *to take the road to compromise, a course I have generally followed both in domestic and foreign politics*. For this reason I could not wage the open warfare against the Social Democrats which the prince desired. Nevertheless, this quarrel concerning political measures cannot lessen my admiration for the greatness of Bismarck as a statesman. He remains the creator of the German empire and, surely, no *one* man need have done more for his country than that.

Owing to the fact that the great matter of the unification of the empire was always before me, I did not allow myself to be influenced by the agitations which were the commonplaces of those days. In like manner, the fact that Bismarck was called "the major-domo of the Hohenzollerns" could not shake my trust in the prince, although he, perhaps, had visions of a political tradition for his family. As evidence of this, he was, for instance, unhappy that his son Bill showed no interest in politics and wished to pass on his chance of power to Herbert.

The tragic element for me in the matter of Bismarck lay in the fact that I became the successor of my grandfather—in other words that, to a certain extent, I skipped one generation. That is a serious thing. In such a case one is constantly forced to deal with deserving old men who live more in the past than in the present and cannot look into the future. When the grandson succeeds his grandfather and finds a revered but aged statesman of the caliber of Bismarck, it is not a matter of good luck for him, as one might suppose, and as I, in fact, did suppose. . . .

During the spring and summer a mass of material was collected from the announcements and reports received, which showed clearly that all was not well in industrial circles; that many a demand of the workers was justified and, to say the least, entitled to sympathetic investigation both on the part of the employers and the officials. The realization of this, which was confirmed when I questioned my former tutor, Privy-Councillor Dr. Hintzpeter—a man particularly well informed on social phenomena, especially those in his own province—caused the resolve to ripen in me to summon the State Council, include employers and employees in its deliberations, and to bring about, under my personal direction, a thorough investigation of the labor question. I decided that by this method there would be acquired guiding principles and material which would serve the chancellor and the Prussian government as a basis for working out appropriate projects for new laws.

Inspired by such thoughts I went to his Excellency von Bötticher, who at once prophesied opposition on the part of the chancellor to such action, and advised strongly against it. I stuck to my ideas, adducing, in support of them, the maxim of Frederick the Great: *"Je veux être un roi des gueux."* ["I wish to be a king of the rabble."] I said that it was my duty to take care of those Germans who were exhausted by industry, to protect their strength and better their chances of existence.

The predicted opposition from Prince Bismarck was soon forthcoming. There was much trouble and fighting before I put through what I wanted, owing to the fact that some of the big industrial interests ranged themselves on the side of the chancellor. The state Council met, presided over by me. At the opening session the chancellor unexpectedly appeared. He made a speech in which he ironically criticized and disapproved of the whole undertaking set in motion by me, and refused his cooperation. Thereupon he walked out of the room.

After his departure, the strange scene had its effect on the assembly. The fury and ruthlessness which the great chancellor brought to the support of his own policy and against mine, based upon his absolute belief in the correctness of his own judgment, made a tremendous impression upon me and all those present. Nevertheless, it stood to reason that I was deeply hurt by what had occurred. The assembly proceeded to take up its work again and turned out a wealth of material for the extension of that social legislation called into being by Emperor William the Great, which is the pride of Germany, in that it evinces a protective attitude towards the laboring classes such as is not to be found in any other country on earth.

Thereupon I decided to summon an International Social Congress. Prince Bismarck opposed this also. Switzerland was contemplating something similar and had thought of convening a congress at Berne. Roth, the Swiss ambassador, hearing of my scheme, advised the cancellation of the invitations to Berne and acceptance of an invitation to Berlin. What he wished occurred. Thanks to the generosity of Herr Roth it was possible to convene the congress at Berlin. The material collected as a result of it was worked out and applied in the form of laws—only in Germany, however.

Later on I talked with Bismarck concerning his project of fighting the Socialists with cannon and bayonets in the event of their resort to revolutionary acts. I sought to convince him that it was out of the question for me, almost immediately after William the Great had closed his eyes after a blessed reign, to stain the first years of my government with the blood of my own people. Bismarck was unmoved; he declared that he would assume responsibility for his actions; that all I need do was to leave the matter to him. I answered that I could not square such a course with my conscience and my responsibility before God, particularly as I knew perfectly well that conditions among the laboring classes were bad and must be bettered at all costs.

The conflict between the views of the emperor and the chancellor relative to the social question—*i.e.* the furtherance of the welfare of the laboring classes of the population with participation therein by the state—was the real cause of the break between us, and caused a hostility toward me lasting for years on the part of Bismarck and a large part of the German nation—especially of the official class—that was devoted to him.

This conflict between the chancellor and myself arose because of his belief that the social problem could be solved by severe measures and, if the worst came to the worst, by means of soldiers; not by following principles of general love for mankind or "humanitarian nonsense" which, he believed, he would have to adopt in conforming to my views.

Bismarck was not a foe to the laboring classes—on that I wish to lay stress, in view of what I have previously said. On the contrary! He was far too great a statesman to underrate the importance of the labor question to the state; but he considered the whole matter from the standpoint of pure expediency for the state.

96

Admiral von Tirpitz Recounts how the Last Hohenzollern Makes a Final Visit to Friedrichsruh and Pays Little Attention as the Aged Ex-Chancellor Makes a Prediction, December 15, 1897[25]

Moltke: "This is terrible."

William II was warned by his uncle, Prince Albrecht, that the German people would never forgive him if Bismarck died without a

25. Condensed from A. von Tirpitz, *Erinnerungen* (Leipzig, 1919), pp. 93–94. Translated by the editor.

reconciliation with his monarch. The impulsive emperor decided to make several hasty visits to Friedrichsruh. These were painful occasions for the skeptical old man, who was convinced that these unannounced visitations were made by William only to observe how much closer Bismarck was to the grave. The emperor carefully avoided all political discussions and confined himself to inconsequential matters. The last encounter, on December 15, 1897, was described by Admiral von Tirpitz, later to become grand-admiral of the navy. No longer able to contain himself, Bismarck uttered a solemn prediction. William pretended that he heard nothing, but others present were appalled by the incident.

I visited the old man twice more, the last time together with the emperor, who suddenly decided to go to Friedrichsruh after saying farewell to Prince Heinrich, who was on his way to East Asia. Sitting in a wheel chair, Bismarck received the emperor at the entrance to the manor house. We immediately went inside to dine. I had a place directly opposite the prince, who sat alongside the emperor. At my side was the later General Moltke the Younger. The prince tried to lead the conversation into political channels, such as our relations with France, etc. To my great regret the emperor avoided all such political themes and instead limited himself to court anecdotes and gossip. Whenever Bismarck said anything political, the emperor changed the subject. Moltke whispered to me: "This is terrible." We both sensed a lack of respect for such a man.

Then suddenly Bismarck spoke some words that impressed us as a serious prophecy: "Your Majesty, as long as you have this officer corps, you can, of course, allow yourself to do whatever you wish. But when this is no longer the case, it will be very different." Bismarck said this in an apparently nonchalant tone as if it were an unimportant, passing thought. It was a masterful display.

When we finished, the prince in his wheel chair accompanied the emperor to the door and then we took leave. Bismarck said friendly farewells to von Bülow, von Miquel, and others. Just in front of me was the head of the civil cabinet, von Lucanus, who in 1890 had been the emperor's messenger in Bismarck's forced resignation. He put forward his hand to the prince and attempted to bow. Then came a remarkable scene that made a powerful impression. The prince sat there like a statue, without a muscle moving; he seemed to be staring at a hole in the air, and in front of him Lucanus fumbled. The prince just did nothing—he was an immovable mask. Lucanus finally caught on and moved away. Then I came by, and after me my faithful Captain von Heeringen. The latter was so moved (he was a temperamental fellow) that he bowed low and kissed the hand of the prince. I liked that, and I tried, as much as I could have under the circumstances, to let the prince know of my feelings, but Heeringen was more successful. The prince then took Heeringen's head in his hands and kissed him on the forehead.

That is my last reminiscence of Bismarck.

97 The Bitter Finale: After Increasing Soporific Attacks, Death Comes to the "Faithful Servant of Emperor William the First," July 30, 1898

"His end was as the final flicker of a flame."

Bismarck's physical condition deteriorated rapidly in July 1898. The once powerful body was wracked by facial pains and severe leg cramps. The old man now walked with a cane. He seemed to shrivel as the skin over the great bald pate shone strangely, and his nose became sharp. His eyes remained large in the shrunken face, now scarcely resembling the earlier image of strength and health.

In late July 1898 Bismarck was weakened by an inflammation of the lungs which used up his last strength. He seemed unable to satisfy his thirst. As he became weaker and weaker, Dr. Schweninger gave him large doses of morphine and placed hot sponges on his neck. All of this was to no avail. On July 30, with his family silently gathered around him, the great man lay stricken on his death bed. His heart weakened and his fever rose higher and higher. Then came a rattling noise as his lungs fought for more air. It was all over.

An account of the circumstances of Bismarck's last days was given by Sidney Whitman, the American journalist who had been so well received at Friedrichsruh as early as April 1891.[26]

About a fortnight before Prince Bismarck's death disquieting rumors concerning his health began to appear in the London papers, to be in turn contradicted and reiterated. As this had repeatedly happened of late years, it did not at first cause any particular anxiety among his friends. Only a few weeks previously I had been at Schönhausen and had been assured by Count Herbert

26. Whitman, *Personal Reminiscences of Prince Bismarck*, pp. 256–263.

Bismarck that, although his father's neuralgic pains were more troublesome than ever, yet, according to Doctor Schweninger, there was nothing organically amiss with him. For all that, every recurring alarm could but cause additional concern, if only in view of the prince's great age. However, a few days later the reports became distinctly more reassuring, and a fatal result seemed once more, as so often before, to have been warded off by the prince's skillful physician.

I started for Friedrichsruh early on the 30th of July with the intention of staying in the village until Prince Bismarck should be decidedly better. Loath as I should have been to undertake the journey with the prospect of finding the prince at death's door, I was glad to do so in the hope of seeing him once more on the road to recovery. As it unhappily turned out, Prince Bismarck passed away while I was traveling towards Friedrichsruh. The sea was exceptionally rough for the time of year. A fierce gale raged that very night all along the North Sea coast, and there was quite a raw autumnal chill in the air in the morning. The elements—as at the death of Napoleon the First, when trees were uprooted in the island of St. Helena—seemed to participate in the tragic occurrence.

I arrived at Hamburg early on the morning of the 31st of July, intending to proceed later in the day to Friedrichsruh. However, I had not been half-an-hour in the hotel when, on coming downstairs, I saw an old woman—harbinger of ill luck in German hunting lore—standing at the door of the hotel offering a black-bordered newspaper for sale. "Prince Bismarck died last night at eleven o'clock" was the laconic announcement in big type.

I left Hamburg by the next train for Friedrichsruh. The shops were closed, for it was Sunday; but all flags on public and private buildings, as well as those to be seen flying from ships, were at half-mast. It was the same all along the road to Friedrichsruh.

There was hardly anyone about, either at the Friedrichsruh station or in the village; only a small group of people stood in the road silently peering through the gate of the prince's residence. To anybody arriving at Friedrichsruh under the impression of such a stirring event—one which, at that very moment, was thrilling the telegraph wires from one end of the world to the other—there could but be a sense of disproportion between the stir in the distance and the quietude on the spot. Nobody seemed to have heard or know of anything. At the inn, however, there were already some signs of the unusual. Every bed except the one I was fortunate enough to secure had been engaged by telegraph. Fifteen extra officials had arrived at the post office; four extra telegraph apparatus were already at work, and I was told that sixty soldiers and three officers of the 31st Regiment from Altona—as well as a detachment of Halberstadt Cuirassiers—were expected.

In the afternoon I met Professor Schweninger coming out of the *Schloss*. He was bareheaded, and evidently in a state of nervous depression. He told me that Prince Bismarck had passed away peacefully the previous evening in the presence of his family. The immediate cause of death was congestion of the lungs. His last words were *"Ich danke Dir, mein Kind,"* addressed to his daughter, who had wiped the moisture from her father's forehead. Immediately after his death the windows of the bedroom, which were on the ground floor, were thrown open, and the household gathered in the garden could see their master lying at rest.

Schweninger told me that so little did Bismarck realize the end was near, that as late as the day before his death he gave one of his servants two large meerschaum pipes to color for him, as he had done on previous occasions.

Prince Bismarck had suffered latterly from frequent intermittent soporific attacks, during which he sometimes dropped off into a sound sleep, and at other times suddenly recovered full consciousness. Yesterday afternoon these attacks increased in frequency, and towards the evening took a more serious form until death ensued. But even as late as yesterday morning the prince read the *Hamburger Nachrichten* as usual, and spoke to those around him about politics. His last remarks upon political matters referred to Germany's relations with Russia, at all times a subject of deep concern to him. Schweninger further assured me that Prince Bismarck's death was felt all the more acutely by the family, since they had come to believe in him as a magician, and that the prince would never die as long as he was near. "Years ago I certainly did say that I hoped to bring him to see the age of ninety, but even then I had to reckon with the baneful effects on his health of the worry and excitement connected with his dismissal in 1890. Recently, however, I have been prepared for the worst, and have lived continuously on the move backwards and forwards between Friedrichsruh and elsewhere. Last Thursday I managed to rouse him to come in to dinner. I said to him, 'We must drink a glass of champagne together.' We did, and he was in such good spirits, that incredible as it may seem, he smoked as many as five pipes in succession. I then persuaded him to go to bed before I left for Berlin, which I was obliged to do; although, even then, I feared it might be a case of days only with him.

"Yesterday morning the family telegraphed me to come back at once by special train, but that could not have brought me sooner than I came. His last moments were singularly free from pain. His end was as the final flicker of a flame. This afternoon I shall embalm his body myself—the last service I can render him. He will probably remain for the present in the room in which he died, for he is ultimately to rest in a mausoleum which is to be built on the hill opposite the *Schloss,* on a spot the prince once selected himself. We were out walking together two years ago, when he said, 'I should like to be buried here, just opposite where I have lived the last years of my life.' I told him that in that case it would be best to put it down in writing. He did so, and this morning the document was read aloud in the presence of his family. By his express desire his tomb is to be inscribed with the words:—

'HERE LIES
PRINCE BISMARCK,
A FAITHFUL GERMAN SERVANT
OF THE
EMPEROR WILLIAM THE FIRST.'"

There was a subdued tone in the conversation that evening among the guests in the inn.

Early next morning (Monday) I was awaked by hearing my name called out repeatedly in a loud voice. I opened the window, and looking out saw Schweninger standing below. He asked me to make haste and join him, which I lost no time in doing. He bade me follow him, and silently led the way towards the *Schloss.*

It was between four and five o'clock, and not a soul was about. Everybody was still asleep. Only the birds he loved so well were stirring overhead, chirping merrily in the thickly leaved trees. They could not know that the man who knew no fear, and therefore, according to the German saga, was privileged to understand their language, was lying dead close by and would hearken no more to their lays.

Two cuirassiers in their white uniform stood with drawn swords as sentinels at the door of the house. We glided on tiptoe through the well-known apartments on the ground floor and entered the bedchamber, in which but a few hours before Prince Bismarck had breathed his last. Two of the prince's foresters, clad in a gray-green uniform, stood on guard by the bedside.

Prince Bismarck lay in death in the position habitual to him when asleep, as Schweninger assured me. His head was turned towards the left, and slightly bent down on the chest. His arms were stretched out nearly at full length over the bedclothes. In his left hand was a white rose, placed there by Professor Schweninger, and three dark roses sent by an Austrian lady. His features, rigid in death, still retained their proud repose. Bismarck's whole life had been one continuous battle, and the zest of it—*gaudium certaminis*—had been his throughout. So even in passing into the valley of silence there was a struggle. To look at his ashy, pale face was to feel that a fire had burnt itself out. You could not help saying to yourself, "There must have been a grim battle here before this mighty embodiment of human will had been wrestled with and thrown."

I glanced around the plainly furnished room. On the wall over the head of the bed hung pictures of a favorite horse and dog. To the left portraits of Princess Bismarck, their son William, and one of Schweninger by Lenbach. Near the window stood the little shaving table which Bismarck had used only a few days before. At the foot of the bed I noticed the prince's weighing machine, and a little farther away the sofa on which Schweninger had slept for some months past during his visits.

The next room, which had been the prince's private sitting room, was filled with all sorts of odds and ends, possessing some interesting connection with him who was gone. I noticed a large oil painting—a portrait of the princess encircled with a garland of evergreens—the invalid chair in which, latterly, he used to be wheeled in to dinner, a suit of clothes neatly folded on a chair with a white shirt uppermost ready to be put on in the morning, which, alas! never came for him. Books, papers, letters and telegrams were strewn about. A faded laurel wreath lay side by side with an open leather case containing the insignia of a new Siamese decoration for him who had recked little of such things. Among other items I noticed four pairs of peculiar South American stirrups with leather shafts to protect the leg, lately received as a present, and a birthday gift from the emperor, a beautiful crookstick of the form which Frederick the Great fancied, the crook of solid gold.

A picture of Li Hung Chang rested on the floor, a model globe of the earth, Bismarck's chessboard, his battlefield, with raised mountains and channeled seas, was on the table.

In the hall hung the familiar array of hats and cloaks. The well-known walking sticks were there too, and for the moment they almost seemed to be animate things. Sadly I passed the soldiers at the door, out into the open air of the morning, and strolled far away into the forest along the roads and the bypaths he had loved so well. Suddenly I saw a dark van drawn by two horses standing before me. A flap was wide open and inside a huge coffin was visible. It had come by road from Hamburg during the night, so as to arrive before people were astir in the morning.

98 The New York Times Reports a Final, Half-Hour Visit to Friedrichsruh by His Majesty, Emperor William II of Hohenzollern

"I am surprised that death came so soon."

William II was on his steam yacht cruising along the Norwegian coast when, on July 31, 1898, he received the news that Bismarck was dead. The emperor ordered the ship returned at top speed and landed at Kiel on August 1. The next day the imperial train stopped at Friedrichsruh, where Herbert and Bill Bismarck icily received the imperial guest. Herbert made it clear that the emperor's wish to see his father buried in Berlin Cathedral could not be fulfilled as plans had already been made according to the chancellor's instructions. The enmity between emperor and chancellor thus survived the call of death. The visit, described in this dispatch to The New York Times, *lasted less than half an hour.*[27]

FRIEDRICHSRUH, August 2. The grounds about Prince Bismarck's castle were thronged with people early today, crowds of Hamburgers being attracted there by the prospect of seeing Emperor William pay a tribute of respect to the dead. They wandered about the woods, congregated in the rustic beer gardens, and sent many hundreds of memorial post cards with portraits of the deceased and pictures of the castle. Many of the people were in mourning and hundreds came on bicycles.

Under the trees sixty men of the Thirty-first Infantry from Altona, and the sergeants of Bismarck's regiment, from Magdeburg, had arranged their messes. The sergeants, in their white uniforms with yellow facings and burnished helmets, furnished a guard who were on duty on the terrace facing the garden behind the castle. The latter remains strictly closed. A little gate was opened occasionally to admit messengers with telegrams and wreaths who were constantly arriving. Photographic cameras were planted at a dozen points in front of the gates, their owners hoping to get a snapshot of the emperor as he entered the grounds.

The emperor and empress of Germany arrived here at 6 o'clock this evening, accompanied by Baron von Bülow, the minister for

27. *The New York Times,* August 3, 1898.

foreign affairs, and their suites. His Majesty wore an admiral's uniform and the empress was in mourning.

The members of the late Prince Bismarck's family received the imperial party, and the emperor on alighting kissed Prince Herbert Bismarck on both cheeks and shook hands with Count William Bismarck. The party then entered the castle, passing through detachments of the Thirty-first Regiment of Infantry which were drawn up along the road and up to the castle gate.

The crowds on each side of the road were composed of Hamburgers, who had been arriving by every train; foresters from the Sachsenwald, villagers, bicyclists, children, and travelers from foreign countries. Vendors of cards, photographs, and medals swarmed about the outskirts of the crowds, and waiters from the neighboring beer gardens bearing trays of empty or filled glasses, circulated on all sides, and did a great business among the thirsty. There were only a few gendarmes present but they were perfectly able to maintain order.

When the imperial train arrived here the crowds were so anxious to see the emperor that they swarmed over the fences and upon the platforms. The troops, however, were able to keep a space around the emperor's carriage.

The presentations at the railroad crossing when the Bismarcks received the emperor and empress, consumed ten minutes, the emperor shaking hands with Count von Rantzau, the late prince's son-in-law, and other relatives of the deceased. There was no cheering but an uproar was caused by the excited conversation carried on among the crowds present.

It was a mournful procession that marched into the death chamber, Prince Herbert leading with the empress and the emperor following with Herbert's wife, after whom came the privileged members of the imperial suit, and the wife and daughter of Dr. Schweninger and Baron Merck, in all about thirty personages.

Chairs were placed around the catafalque, and Pastor Westphal stood at the head of the coffin. When their Majesties entered all knelt down around the coffin in silent prayer. Then a hymn was sung, and Pastor Westphal delivered a discourse extolling the deeds of the departed prince. Another hymn and the benediction closed the simple ceremony, which lasted about twenty minutes.

Their Majesties deposited beautiful wreaths on the coffin and under the guidance of Prince Herbert, inspected the numerous floral tributes. The imperial party then left the *Schloss* in the same order as on its arrival, bidding the members of the family a tender farewell. The emperor again kissed Prince Herbert on both cheeks. The public watching the departure preserved a respectful silence, only waving hats and handkerchiefs as the train left for Potsdam. Amateur photographers were all about and displayed the greatest activity.

It is asserted on good authority that on the arrival of the imperial party, and after the meeting, the emperor said to Prince Herbert: "I am surprised that death came so soon." Prince Herbert replied: "We feared the autumn might prove fatal to our father but we never supposed that the end would come now in midsummer. Therefore it was all the more painful to us."

Then, it is said, the emperor again expressed his desire to have a national funeral in the Berlin Cathedral. Prince Herbert, however, still demurred, whereupon his Majesty said: "If this is not acceptable, I should like to place a memorial sarcophagus with a life-size monument in the cathedral." But to this Prince Herbert replied that he would not see how he would be acting in conformity with his father's instructions by accepting it.

Bismarck's body was attired, not as was customary in uniform, but in ordinary grave clothing, with a white neck-cloth adjusted as he used to wear it when not in uniform. Dr. Schweninger himself arranged the body in a sleeping posture, lying on the side. Roses were placed in the hands by Countess Marie von Rantzau, the daughter of Bismarck. . . .

The wreaths are extremely beautiful. That from Count and Countess von Bismarck is inscribed "Bill and Sibylle." That from the Bleichröder bank was so large that it needed a whole carriage in itself."

99 Proclamation of Mourning for the First Chancellor of the German Empire, Prince Otto von Bismarck, Duke of Lauenburg

". . . the man in whom God the Lord created the instrument for realization of the immortal idea of Germany's unity and greatness."

The following proclamation by Emperor William II was addressed to the new chancellor and published in the Imperial Gazette.[28] De mortuis nil nisi bonum!

28. Quoted in G. Barnett Smith, *Heroes of the Nineteenth Century* (London, 1901), pp. 278–279.

With my exalted allies, and with the whole German people, I stand in mourning at the bier of the first chancellor of the German empire, Prince Otto von Bismarck, Duke of Lauenburg. We who were witnesses of his splendid activity, we who looked up to him with admiration as the master of statecraft, as the fearless champion in war as in peace, as the most devoted son of his Fatherland, and as the most faithful servant of his emperor and king, are profoundly moved by the death of the man in whom God the Lord created the instrument for the realization of the immortal idea of Germany's unity and greatness. This is not the time to enumerate all the deeds which he wrought for the emperor and the empire—all the successes which he achieved. They are too mighty and manifold, and history alone can and will engrave them all on her brazen tablets. I, however, am constrained to give expression before the world to the unanimous sorrow and to the grateful admiration with which the whole nation is filled today, and in the name of the nation to register the vow to maintain and complete the edifice which he, the great chancellor, constructed under the Emperor William the Great, and, if need be, to defend it with our life and fortune. So help us God the Lord. I enjoin you to make this my edict public.

WILLIAM, I.R.

Appendix 1: Key Dates in the Life of Otto von Bismarck

1815: April 1 at 1 P.M. Birth of Otto von Bismarck on the estate of Schönhausen in Brandenburg

1816: The Bismarck family moves to Kniephof

1822–1826: Bismarck goes to Plamann's Boarding School

1827: Birth of Malwine von Bismarck, Otto's sister

1827–1830: Bismarck a student in *Tertia* and *Sekunda, Friedrich Wilhelm Gymnasium,* Berlin

1830–1831: Bismarck a student at the *Graue Kloster Gymnasium,* Berlin.

1832–1833: Student at Göttingen

1833–1835: Student at Berlin

1835: Passes final legal examination and becomes *Auskultator*

1836: Raised to rank of *Referendar* at Aix-la-Chapelle

1837: Referendary in Potsdam; Army service in *Jaeger* at Potsdam

1839: Takes possession of estate at Kniephof

1841: Lieutenant in *Landwehr* (National Guard)

1842: Journey to England, Scotland, France, Switzerland

1844: Friendship with Marie von Thadden

1845: Death of father: moves to Schönhausen

1847: Deputy in United *Landtag:* marriage to Johanna von Puttkamer

1848: Birth of Marie von Bismarck

1849: Birth of Herbert von Bismarck

1851–1859: Prussian envoy to the *Bundestag* in Frankfort-on-Main

1852: Birth of Wilhelm (Bill) von Bismarck

1859–1862: Ambassador in St. Petersburg

1862: Envoy in Paris; appointed Prussian minister-president and minister for foreign affairs

1862–1866: Rules without parliament

1864: Danish-Prussian War

1865: Convention of Gastein

1866: Attempt to assassinate Bismarck; Austro-Prussian War; the Prussian Indemnity Bill

1867: Founding of the North German Confederation; Bismarck becomes federal chancellor

1870: Ems Dispatch; Franco-Prussian War

1871: Founding of the German empire; Bismarck becomes imperial chancellor

1872: Beginning of *Kulturkampf;* Three Emperors' League

1873: May Laws against Catholicism

1874: Attempt to assassinate Bismarck at Kissingen

1878: Anti-Socialist Law; Congress of Berlin

1879: Dual Alliance with Austria; from free trade to protection

1880: Bismarck becomes minister of commerce

1881: The Three Emperors' League

1882: Triple Alliance

1884: Bismarck refuses the Lasker Resolution

1885: Seventieth birthday

1887: Reinsurance Treaty

1888: Death of William I; Hundred Days' Reign and death of Frederick III

1890: William II dismisses Bismarck; Bismarck made Duke of Lauenburg

1890–1898: Retirement at Friedrichsruh

1892: Triumphal train trip to Vienna for Herbert's nuptials

1894: Death of Johanna

1895: Celebration of eightieth birthday

1898: Death of Bismarck, July 30

Appendix 2: Otto von Bismarck's Descendants *

Otto von Bismarck in 1847 married Johanna von Puttkamer (1824–1894), daughter of a Pomeranian landed proprietor. There were three children:

—Marie von Bismarck (1848–1926), who became the Countess Rantzau.

—Herbert Prince von Bismarck (1849–1904), who was made secretary for foreign affairs by his father and who resigned at the time of the dismissal of his father in 1890.

—Wilhelm ("Bill") Count von Bismarck-Schönhausen (1852–1901), finally lord lieutenant of East Prussia with office in Königsberg (highest civil position in a Prussian province); married his cousin Sibylle von Arnim (1864–1945), a daughter of Otto von Bismarck's sister, Malwine.

Of the five children of Prince Herbert Bismarck and his Austrian wife Marguerite, born the Countess Hoyos (1871–1945), the eldest son, the sixty-seven-year-old Otto Prince von Bismarck, is currently head of the family and the landed proprietor of Friedrichsruh near Hamburg. The family property also consists of the steam sawmill works at Friedrichsruh and the corn distillery at Schönau, while the rights for the manufacture and sale of "Bismarck Water" from the prince's lands are leased to an enterprise outside the family.

The present Prince Bismarck is a former ambassador and a member of the *Bundestag* representing the Christian Democratic party. With his Swedish wife, Ann Marie, born Tengbom, he has six children and—from the three oldest of his married children—eight grandchildren.

The oldest daughter, Marie Ann, is married to the business man, Dr. Egbert von Oswald. The thirty-four-year-old Hereditary Count Ferdinand is a jurist in Brussels; the thirty-year-old Alexander is a student of law; Maximilian, eighteen, and Guilla, fifteen, are at boarding school; the youngest son, Leopold, is at the Bergdorfer *Gymnasium*.

* *Der Spiegel,* March 31, 1965, p. 62.

Of the descendants of Wilhelm von Bismarck, one grandson—therefore the great-grandson of the founder of the Reich—has become known to the German public. He is Heinrich Count von Einsiedel, forty-three, a son of the still living daughter of Wilhelm, Irene Countess von Einsiedel. A flying officer and holder of the Knight's Cross, he was taken prisoner at Stalingrad, and belongs to the National Committee for a Free Germany. In 1950 he published his reminiscences, *Diary of Temptation.* Einsiedel, divorced from the film actress, Barbara Rüttline, lives as a journalist in Munich.

The manager of the West German Radio, Klaus von Bismarck, fifty-three, is a great-grand-nephew of Otto von Bismarck, a great-grandson of the latter's oldest brother Bernhard (1810–1893).

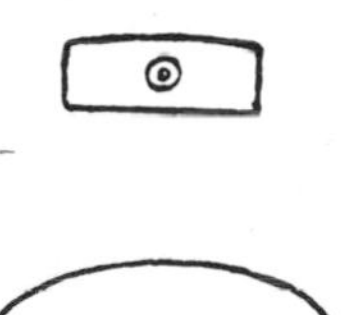

Bismarck in Caricature, 1866-1890

Felix Régamey

Figaro, August 11, 1866

BISMARCK AND KING WILLIAM I OF PRUSSIA
BURY THE GERMAN CONFEDERATION

*"And as they brought it to the grave,
No one wept, but many laughed."*

The French magazine *Figaro* comments on Bismarck's success in bringing an end to the German Confederation. Established in 1815, the German Confederation included both Prussia and Austria, but it was controlled by Austria. The Seven Weeks War between Austria and Prussia ended with Prussia's victory at Königgrätz on August 3, 1866.

New York Public Library Picture Collection

ANTI-PRUSSIAN CARICATURE, AFTER SADOWA, 1866
by Honoré Daumier.

Kikeriki, August 15, 1870

THE BERLINER PEACOCK

"No wonder he is proud!"

All the world was astounded by the quick Prussian victories after the opening of the Franco-Prussian War. The caricature shows Bismarck as a peacock strutting proudly. The main feathers are titled after Prussian victories. The final stunning victory came at Sedan two weeks after the publication of this cartoon.

Figaro, March 5, 1870

BISMARCK CRACKS THE WHIP
IN THE NORTH GERMAN REICHSTAG

GOOD WEATHER CHANGEABLE STORM

"No Minister or Ambassador should be without this guide"

In *Kladderadatsch,* the German satirical magazine, 1881. Bismarck's three hairs became the cartoonists' delight.

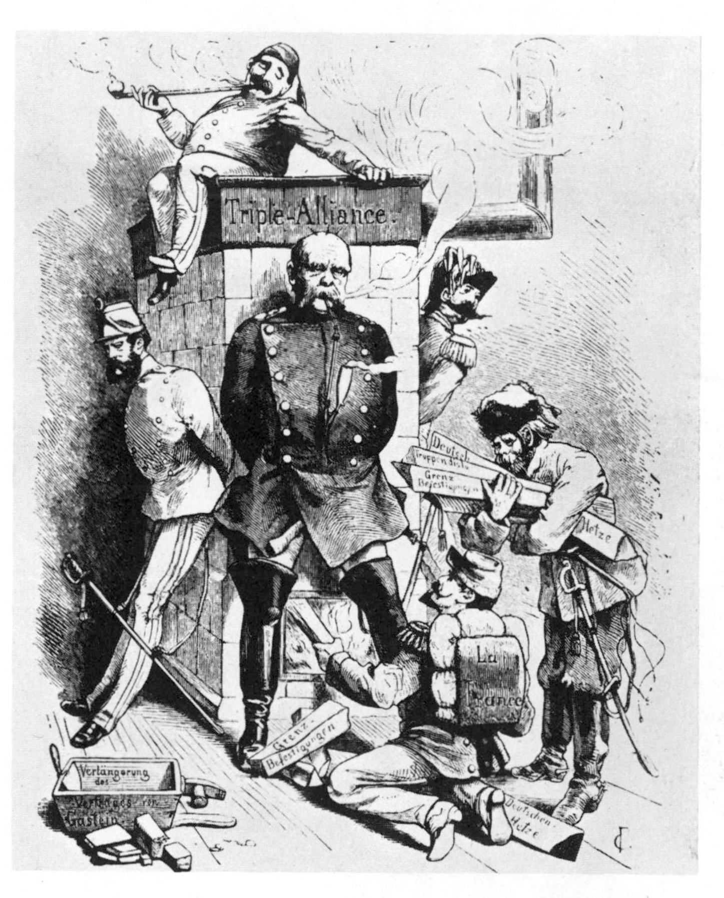

Kladderadatsch, 1883

BISMARCK DEFENDS THE TRIPLE ALLIANCE

In 1882 Bismarck completed the formation of the Triple Alliance, includin Germany, Austria, Hungary, and Italy. The cartoonist shows how the allianc provided "warmth for cold blood."

Kladderadatsch, 1887

BISMARCK AS FAUST

Faust: I greet you, thou only phial
Which I with devotion bring down

Show thy master thy favor!

A Cartoon shows Bismarck as Faust reaching for a *Wahlurne* (ballot box) and asks for it to work its magic for him. This is an election commentary.

Kladderadatsch, 1890

THE RETIRED CHANCELLOR TURNS IN HIS THREE HAIRS, 1890

Throughout Bismarck's career the satirical German magazine, *Kladderadatsch,* had depicted Bismarck again and again with his three hairs. In the issue of March 1890 Bismarck is shown relinquishing his insignia as he departs for Friedrichsruh.

Punch, March 29, 1890

DROPPING THE PILOT

One of the most famous political cartoons of all time shows Bismarck, the pilot, leaving the ship of state. The young Emperor, William II, now in responsible command, leans over to witness the departure.

Index